CYCLING ATLAS NORTH AMERICA

Created by Olo Éditions
www.oloeditions.com
Copyright © 2022 Olo Éditions

ORIGINAL CONCEPT : Nicolas Marçais / Philippe Marchand
EDITORIAL DIRECTION : Nicolas Marçais
ART DIRECTION : Philippe Marchand
TEXTS AND ROUTES DESIGN : Claude Droussent
LAYOUT : Gersende Sabathier
ENGLISH TRANSLATION : Roland Glasser

First published in the United States of America in 2022 by

Universe Publishing
A division of Rizzoli International Publications, Inc.
300 Park Avenue South
New York, NY 10010
www.rizzoliusa.com

For Rizzoli
Publisher: Charles Miers
Editor: Klaus Kirschbaum
Assistant Editor: Meredith Johnson
Managing Editor: Lynn Scrabis

ISBN: 978-0-7893-3776-4
Library of Congress Control Number: 2022933789

2022 2023 2024 2025 / 10 9 8 7 6 5 4 3 2 1

Printed in Bosnia and Herzegovina

Visit us online:
Facebook.com/RizzoliNewYork
Twitter: @Rizzoli_Books
Instagram.com/RizzoliBooks
Pinterest.com/RizzoliBooks
Youtube.com/user/RizzoliNY
Issuu.com/Rizzoli

GREG LEMOND
CLAUDE DROUSSENT

CYCLING ATLAS NORTH AMERICA

THE 350 MOST BEAUTIFUL CYCLING ROUTES IN THE US, CANADA, AND MEXICO

**FEATURING VARIOUS TERRAIN TYPES, INCLUDING
MORE THAN 100 DIRT & GRAVEL ROUTES**

**WITH ROUTES PROVIDED BY
STRAVA**

UNIVERSE

CYCLING MAPS, MY OLD PASSION

It was long before Strava. Perhaps you weren't born yet. Our bikes were fitted with their very first computers: a tiny screen attached to the handlebar and connected to a sensor on the fork by a wire linked to another sensor on the wheel. It gave us our current speed, average speed, and distance traveled, all in real-time. This huge leap forward was developed under the brand name, Avocet, by my first sponsor, Bud Hoffacker, the founder of the bike shop, Palo Alto Bicycles.

There was no internet—GPS was out of the question and screen-based navigation was years away. But I was mad about maps. I remember during my first months in Europe—barely nineteen years old—spending tons of money on road maps. In France, it was the yellow Michelin ones folded like an accordion, at a scale of 1/200,000 (1 cm = 2 km, that is to say, .4 in = 1.25 mi), which I slipped into the back pocket of my jersey. I always wanted to situate myself, know where I was, where I was going, and not miss any amazing experiences in all these new places.

I rediscovered this feeling thanks to Strava, with its rich content and route builder. If I wasn't fully occupied managing and developing my business, LeMond Bikes, I would spend hours on it. I, therefore, took great pleasure in putting together this *Cycling Atlas North America*, which will take you down roads and trails I know well in places such as the California and Nevada of my teenage years, Minnesota (where I discovered gravel over thirty years ago without knowing it!), Wisconsin, New York, and Tennessee where I now live and where, if I was still a racer, I would move to for the variety of rides it offers. There are many other routes too, recommended by enthusiastic local members of the Strava community.

Through this *Cycling Atlas North America*, I wish simply to encourage you, to help you, and to motivate you in your riding. Leap on an e-bike if you wish; the main thing is to keep moving, so pedal off to explore new horizons!

PS: Claude Droussent and I are old teammates. We met in 1981, the day of my first win as a procyclist in Europe! He was a journalist at L'Équipe and covered my whole cycling career. We've kept in touch ever since. In the last few years, he has written the France and Europe Cycling Atlases. I am very happy to have collaborated with him on this Cycling Atlas North America.

HOW TO USE THIS ATLAS

FOR TODAY'S CYCLISTS LOOKING FOR NEW CHALLENGES

Every route listed, analyzed, and enriched in *Cycling Atlas North America* is designed for the avid cyclist, whether or not they are already Strava users. There are three ability levels (Intermediate, Advanced, Expert) which allow riders to choose routes according to their proficiency and hankering for a challenge. The routes have been planned with safety in mind (staying away from motor traffic as much as possible) and with a focus on pleasure, whether from a purely cycling point of view, or in terms of sightseeing and relaxation. *Cycling Atlas North America* is all about the joy of riding and exploring, whether on your own or with friends. A number of the roads are world-famous; most are less well known and full of good surprises. Approximately 30% of the routes are composed largely of dirt/gravel sections. Before setting out, always check the weather forecast, bear in mind the state of the roads and trails you intend to ride, and make sure that that your bike is in good mechanical condition.

 STARTING POINT
Most of our routes start from a well-reputed local bike shop, chosen for its warm welcome, the services it offers, and its interest in creating cycling community.

 ABILITY LEVELS
There are three ability levels specified to make selecting a route easier. The levels are Intermediate: for cyclists having ridden a minimum of 2,000 miles (3,220 km) over the last six months; Advanced for cyclists having ridden a minimum of 4,000 miles (6,440 km); and Expert for cyclists having ridden a minimum of 6,000 miles (9,650 km).

 STRAVA ROUTE LINK
Each route has been created by the Cycling Atlas Strava account. To use it during your ride, download the GPX file and transfer it to your bike's GPS device before you set off.

 GREG'S EYE
Tour de France champion, Greg LeMond, shares insights and anecdotes from his long and rich cycling career and his deep knowledge of North American routes.

 CARTOGRAPHY
Every profile features a map that traces the route, matching the one online on the Cycling Atlas Strava account.

 DIRECTION
The arrow indicates the suggested direction of the route.

 DISTANCE & ELEVATION GAIN (E+)
The total distance in miles and km and the total elevation gain (E+) in feet and meters are those calculated by Strava (and rounded off by us). The elevation gain can sometimes be overestimated, particularly at altitude.

 KEY INFORMATION
This section contains key information on how to get to the route's starting point.

 DIRT/GRAVEL STAMP
This appears on each route where the percentage of unpaved surface is equal to or greater than 35% of the total distance.

 KEY SEGMENTS
For some routes, we suggest two Strava segments that you can add to your favorites for easy identification as you approach them on your ride. You can also compare your times on these segments with your friends and the whole Strava community, including professional riders and top athletes.

 DESCRIPTION
The general context and atmosphere of the route are described, including information regarding its difficulty and appeal, as well as related anecdotes.

 DIFFICULTY AND APPEAL
The physical difficulty and the aesthetic appeal of a route are graded out of five.

 TOP TIPS
Each route features three top tips indicated by icons: the nearest airports to the start point, and the distances by car from the neighboring big cities; a bike shop, which is also usually the route's starting point, or the closest to the route according to the same criteria; the most attractive spots on (or very near) the route that will allow you to bring back the most beautiful photographic memories of your ride.

POINT BLANK
OKAY HOUSTON!

○ Hilly, Intermediate, 75% unpaved

○ Map strava.com/routes/2885604087919016474

○ Test yourself mi 15 (km 24) strava.com/segments/15899450

○ Test yourself mi 37 (km 60) strava.com/segments/5991079

◉ GREG'S EYE

Like all large American cities, Houston enjoys an amazing off-road playground nearby. Fifty mi (80 km) north of Space City, the fast and barely bumpy trails of Sam Houston National Forest span a superb area of pines.

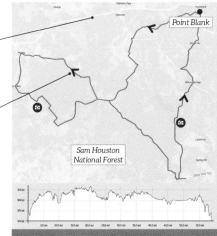

Point Blank

Sam Houston National Forest

Sam Houston National Forest honors the emblematic nineteenth-century Texan after whom America's fourth-largest city (pop. 6.3 million in the metro area) is named. At just a 1h drive from Space City, Houstonians have a prime cycling spot within easy reach. Don't be tempted to swim in Lake Livingston, though—alligators roam there. Better to stay beneath the swamp pines and listen carefully for woodpeckers and frogs as you pedal gravel. There are no major challenges here, just a thick forest (250 sq mi/650 sq km), where you sometimes feel like you're lost. At mi 35 (km 56), you meet the popular Lone Star Hiking Trail, and most likely a bunch of hikers, too. Back in Point Bank, scarf down some shells and cheese at the Bullet Grill House, safe from marauding gators!

 Distance **59 mi** (95 km)

 E+ **2,100 ft** (644 m)

 Difficulty **3/5**

 Appeal **4/5**

Air: George Bush Intercontinental Airport, Houston (1h15 by car). Car: 3h from Dallas, 3h15 from Shreveport, 3h30 from Austin.

Hans Schneider has been building frames for forty years, and his shop, 20 mi (32 km) west of Point Blank, is a veritable treasure chest. Not to be missed.

2930 Old Houston Road Huntsville, TX 77340 hscycles.com

Four Notch Camp and Lone Star Hiking Trail (mi 26/km 42). Rocky Creek (mi 49/km 79). Snow Hill Church and Lake Livingston (mi 58/km 93).

91

CONTENTS

Fifty years after the appearance of its first bike lanes, Central Park remains emblematic of cycling in New York City.

NEW ENGLAND & MID-ATLANTIC

NEW YORK

—

CONNECTICUT

—

RHODE ISLAND

—

MASSACHUSETTS

—

NEW HAMPSHIRE

—

MAINE

—

VERMONT

—

NEW JERSEY

—

PENNSYLVANIA

—

WASHINGTON, D.C.

—

DELAWARE

—

MARYLAND

NEW YORK CITY
PARK TO PARK

⊕ *Fairly flat, Intermediate, 0% unpaved*
⊕ *Map strava.com/routes/2822572229174610666*

⊕ *Test yourself mi 2 (km 3.25) strava.com/segments/7324703*
⊕ *Test yourself mi 24 (km 38) strava.com/segments/613198*

◉ GREG'S EYE

Manhattan and Brooklyn have become bike friendly, and that's partly down to John Lindsay, the mayor who closed Central Park to cars in the 1970s. I recall a race there early in my career: the Apple Lap. We were 500 to start and I finished second.

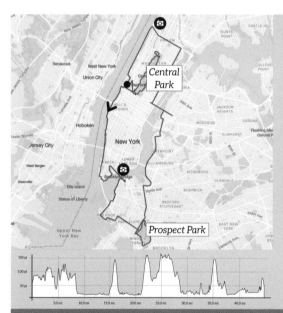

The city that never sleeps has pursued a cycling evolution over the past decade, with funding of 1 billion dollars to improve infrastructure by 2030. You can now cycle safely in New York City, and there's nothing like pedaling to (re)discover the place, so why not explore two of its main outdoor fitness sites in a single ride: Central Park (6.1 mi/9.75 km loop) in Manhattan and Prospect Park (3.3 mi/5.25 km loop) in Brooklyn. Caution: both parks are car-free but full of pedestrians, who have right of way. Most of the route follows cycle paths. Head down the Hudson to Battery Park, with a view across to the Statue of Liberty, then cross the Brooklyn Bridge and ride to Prospect Park, returning through Williamsburg and across the Queensboro Bridge from Long Island City to the Upper East Side and, finally, Harlem. "New York, New York, it's a wonderful town!"

 Distance **45 mi** (72 km)

 E+ **1,250 ft** (382 m)

 Difficulty **2/5**

 Appeal **5/5**

 Air: John F. Kennedy International, Newark Liberty International (outside NYC public transport area), LaGuardia Airport.
Car: 1h45 from Philadelphia, 2h15 from Scranton, 3h30 from Boston, 4h from Washington.

 Toga Bikes, close to Central Park, has been Manhattan's go-to bike shop for more than half a century. Retailer of Specialized, Cannondale, Giant, and Bianchi.

110 West End Avenue New York, NY 10023 togabikes.com

 An embarrassment of choices: at the foot of One World Trade Center; crossing the Brooklyn Bridge with the Manhattan skyline behind you; in front of the General Grant National Memorial when you get back. Everywhere, in fact.

NEW YORK CITY
MAXI GRAN FONDO

- ⊕ Vey hilly, Advanced, 0% unpaved
- ⊕ Map strava.com/routes/2822572366616913642
- ⊕ Test yourself mi 43 (km 69) strava.com/segments/1640683
- ⊕ Test yourself mi 62 (km 100) strava.com/segments/647080

◉ GREG'S EYE

I know this route well; the views over the Hudson toward Nyack are superb. I rode it from Harlem with my New York friend Fred Mengoni, Fred Mengoni, one of my first sponsors. One day, on the way back, we were dehydrated, and a local resident opened a fire hydrant to fill our bottles.

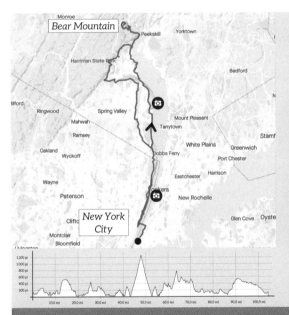

Bear Mountain is the peak of the Hudson Highlands, rising 1,290 ft (325 m) above the Hudson River. From afar, it has a reassuringly rounded shape. Yet the climb is not to be underestimated: 4.5 mi (7.25 km) at an average gradient of nearly 6%, with the second part the hardest. The best thing about Bear Mountain is the long approach up the west bank of the Hudson from Manhattan (our route starts at the General Grant National Memorial): Hudson Park, Palisades, Nyack, Rockland Lake, Stay Point. Bear Mountain and the distance combine to make this the New York cycling challenge, and the course of the Gran Fondo New York (GFNY). Our return route takes in the slopes of Cheesecote Mountain. If that's daunting, there's a fallback: the train to Grand Central from Cortlandt (1h10), on the east bank of the Hudson, 10 mi (16 km) after Bear Mountain Bridge.

Distance	E+	Difficulty	Appeal
105 mi (169 km)	**8,000 ft** (2,445 m)	**4/5**	**4/5**

Air: John F. Kennedy International, Newark Liberty International (outside NY public transport area), LaGuardia Airport. Car: 1h45 from Philadelphia, 2h15 from Scranton, 3h30 from Boston, 4h from Washington.

Strictly Bicycles, on the New Jersey side of the George Washington Bridge, is a natural rallying point for the cycling community beside US 9W. Retailer of Specialized, Cervelo, Pinarello, Cannondale.

2347 Hudson Terrace Fort Lee, NJ 07024 strictlybicycles.com

At the foot of Perkins Memorial Tower, of course, atop Bear Mountain (mi 48/km 77), with a panoramic view over the Hudson. But also Palisades Park, overlooking the river, on both the way out (mi 11/ km 18) and the way back (mi 94/km 151).

NEW YORK CITY
THE NEW BRIDGE

⊕ *Hilly, Advanced, 0% unpaved*　　　　⊕ Map strava.com/routes/2822572490752878736

	Distance		E+		Difficulty		Appeal
⊢–⊣	**78 mi** (125 km)	⬆	**4,350 ft** (1,320 m)	📊	**3/5**	⭐	**4/5**

New Yorkers have a new route up the west bank of the Hudson where, 15 mi (24 km) north of the George Washington Bridge, the dilapidated Tappan Zee Bridge has been replaced by the brand-new Mario M. Cuomo Bridge. Cycle paths along this stretch, which offer splendid views of the river, have been given a makeover. From Manhattan, ride from Innovation Bike shop close to Central Park, via Yonkers and a series of dedicated trails. There are climbs up Toga Hill at mi 27 (km 43), South Mountain at mi 37/km 59 (0.8 mi/1.25 km at 10%), and Closter Dock at mi 63/km 101 (1 mi/1.5 km at 7% in a straight line). Return over the George Washington Bridge.

NEW YORK CITY
BROOKLYN AND QUEENS

⊕ *Fairly flat, Intermediate, 0% unpaved*　　　　⊕ Map strava.com/routes/2822572698794395792

	Distance		E+		Difficulty		Appeal
⊢–⊣	**63 mi** (102 km)	⬆	**1,600 ft** (502 m)	📊	**2/5**	⭐	**4/5**

The densely populated boroughs of Brooklyn and Queens (combined pop. 5 million) might seem unsuited to cycling, but that's not the case, thanks to a network of cycle paths. This route of more than 60 mi (96 km) provides a wonderful escape from the urban crush. The first part is maritime, the second bucolic. We head out from Maglia Rosa bike café in Industry City and past the Verrazzano Narrows Bridge, through Coney Island, Rockaway Beach, and Jamaica Bay, in the shadow of JFK airport, before reaching the virtually flat parks of Queens: Forest, Cunningham, Kissena, Flushing Meadow, and Highland. Cool down with a lap of Prospect Park.

HAMPTON BAYS
GATSBY LOOP

⊕ *Fairly flat, Intermediate, 0% unpaved*   ⊕ Map strava.com/routes/2823203115353244478

 Distance
107 mi
(172 km)

 E+
2,900 ft
(871 m)

 Difficulty
3/5

 Appeal
5/5

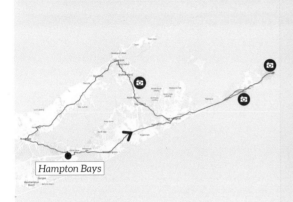

Hampton Bays

Don't be scared by the total distance of this route. Several train stations (the last at Montauk) allow for an early return to Hampton Bays, our starting point, or even Manhattan (2h farther).
But it's unlikely you'll want to give up on this extraordinary ride before the end. The tip of Long Island is a legendary vacation spot for the upper crust, an area full of history that is also commonly used for film shoots, earning it the nickname "Hollywood East." We cycle out along the ocean, past surf spots, for 40 mi (64 km) until chic Montauk. Two ferries fill in the gaps on the return leg via Shelter Island. Most of the ride is on cycle paths.

SUFFERN
BETWEEN TWO STATES

⊕ *Very hilly, Advanced, 7% unpaved*   ⊕ Map strava.com/routes/2822761976117480434

 Distance
68 mi
(109 km)

 E+
5,400 ft
(1,645 m)

 Difficulty
4/5

 Appeal
4/5

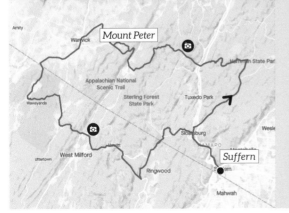

Mount Peter

Suffern

The New York-New Jersey Highlands lie 1h15 northwest of Manhattan by car or train (we start at Suffern station). They're a delight in the fall. But this route is as challenging as it is alluring, with hills (Mount Peter tops out at 1,250 ft/381 m), lakes, the Appalachian Trail, and the crossing of the state line (mi/km 32.25 through New Jersey). In the space of one 10-mi (16-km) section we climb Minturn Bridge Road (1.6 mi/2.5 km at 6%), Mount Peter (1.8 mi/2.75 km at 5%), and Kain Road (0.9 mi/1.5 km at 12%; 16% in places), before Barrett Road (1.6 mi/2.5 km at 9%), which precedes a kinder pedal home via Greenwood Lake and Wanaque Reservoir.

BINGHAMTON
ABOVE THE SUSQUEHANNA

⊕ Very hilly, Advanced, 0% unpaved   ⊕ Map strava.com/routes/2823906288272461388

 Distance
49 mi
(79 km)

 E+
4,500 ft
(1,365 m)

 Difficulty
3/5

 Appeal
3/5

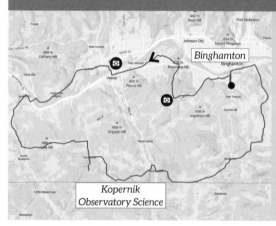

Kopernik Observatory Science

Binghamton (pop. 50,000) seems squeezed by the confluence of the Susquehanna and Chenango rivers and the Pennsylvania state line. But there's great cycling to be had between the longest river on the East Coast, its tributary, and the neighboring state, which we skim on State Line Road—the final bit of relief on this route (mi 35/km 56) past the broadcast towers of Underwood Road, the highest (1,824 ft/556 m) of many hills surrounding Binghamton. There's hard pedaling beforehand, first on Fuller Hollow, then on harsh Collins Road (mi 26/km 42, 0.7 mi/ 1 km at 12%), and Underwood Road. Start at Chenango Point Cycles.

BUFFALO
ARMS OF THE NIAGARA

⊕ Fairly flat, Intermediate, 4% unpaved   ⊕ Map strava.com/routes/2823598881003310544

 Distance
41 mi
(66 km)

 E+
500 ft
(165 m)

 Difficulty
1/5

 Appeal
4/5

Buffalo, the state's second most populous city at the eastern tip of Lake Erie, is many years into a post-industrial revival. Renowned for its architecture, Buffalo has attracted cultural folk, researchers, and students. Cycling-wise, it's wonderful. This route is a house classic of Campus Wheelworks, the shop in Elmwood Village (near Colonial Circus) famous for its Tuesday-night rides. You'll mainly be making a circuit of green and peaceful Grand Island, which lies between two arms of the Niagara River—you don't get quite as far as the falls, which are more tranquilly reached by bike from the Canadian side. Return via superb Delaware Park.

ITHACA
ENJOY YOUR SUNDAE

- ⊕ Very hilly, Advanced, 10% unpaved
- ⊕ Map strava.com/routes/2822869410600105038
- ⊕ Test yourself mi 14 (km 22) strava.com/segments/1194403
- ⊕ Test yourself mi 37 (km 59) strava.com/segments/667096

👁 GREG'S EYE

Undulating relief, multiple lakes and waterfalls, vineyards: the Finger Lakes region reminds me of some parts of Switzerland! A good level of fitness is required, and don't forget to look at the splendid scenery. I've driven some fast cars at the nearby Watkins Glen track.

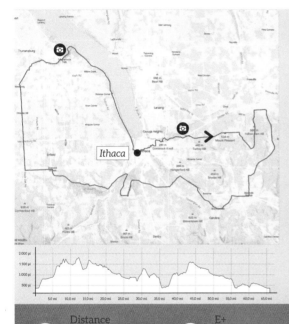

When the sun rises over the shores of Cayuga Lake, the longest of the Finger Lakes, in the center of New York State, Ithaca is lit up like an Italian hill town. From Cornell, the university that's spawned 59 Nobel Prizes and and notable alumni including Christopher Reeve, Hollywood's unforgettable Superman, you might long for some magic powers to tackle this testing ride. The challenge begins almost immediately, on Mount Pleasant (3 mi/4.75 km at 6%, with one long section at 13%), followed by Yellow Barn and Irish Settlement (1 mi/1.5 km at 8%), then on to King Road (mi 29/km 47) and Enfield Falls/Harvey Hill. The last third is much easier, as you pass the sublime Taughannock Falls and the vineyards of pinot noir and gamay on the banks of Cayuga Lake. You'll have earned an ice cream sundae back in Ithaca, where the dessert was invented in 1892.

	Distance		E+		Difficulty		Appeal
⊢⊣	**66 mi** (105 km)	⬆	**5,900 ft** (1,793 m)	📊	**4/5**	⭐	**4/5**

Air: Syracuse Hancock International Airport (1h). Car: 4h from New York City, 4h from Toronto, 5h30 from Pittsburgh.

Cayuga Ski & Cyclery is Ithaca's go-to bike shop. Retailer of Cannondale, Giant, and Surly. Expert advice on both gear and routes.

624 W State Street Ithaca, NY 14850 cayugaskiandcyclery.com

Cascadilla Gorge, Cornell University, Triphammer Falls, peak of Mount Pleasant (mi 1/km 1.5 to mi 8/km 13). Taughannock Falls (mi 55/km 88), of course.

LAKE PLACID
VINTAGE OLYMPICS

 High mountain, Advanced, 0% unpaved   Map strava.com/routes/2822572913427164160

	Distance		E+		Difficulty		Appeal
	59 mi (96 km)	⬆	**6,530 ft** (1,990 m)		**4/5**	★	**4/5**

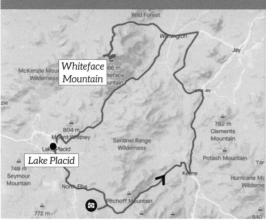

A five-hour drive from New York and two hours from Montréal, Lake Placid is synonymous with the 1980 Winter Olympics, where five gold medals were won by the speed skater Eric Heiden (who rode the Tour de France six years later) and the U.S. ice hockey team beat the USSR in the "Miracle on Ice." This enjoyable 60-mi (96-km) loop runs from the Olympic Center to the summit of Whiteface Mountain, site of the alpine skiing events in 1980. The Whiteface road (4,593 ft/1,400 m at its summit) is a true challenge: 8 mi (13 km) at an average gradient of over 8%, with the final half mile (.75 km) at 16%. Divine panoramas.

TICONDEROGA
ADIRONDACK WATERS

 Very hilly, Intermediate, 0% unpaved   Map strava.com/routes/2823285410650104380

	Distance		E+		Difficulty		Appeal
	59 mi (95 km)	⬆	**4,900 ft** (1,507 m)		**3/5**	★	**4/5**

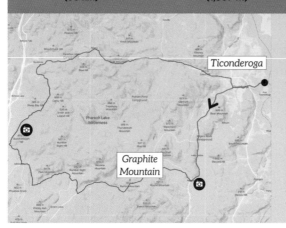

There are thousands of lakes and watercourses in the Adirondacks, but trails and roads are far fewer. To ride a manageable loop a half-day (by train or car) from New York City, stick to the area around two major lakes, Champlain and George. This 59-mi (95-km) route through fabulous scenery southeast of Mount Marcy, the highest point in the Adirondacks, provides a distillation of what the massif offers: a spectacular river (La Chute), sublime lakes (George, Brant, Schroon, Paradox, Eagle), a beautiful climb (Graphite Mountain, 5 mi/8 km at 5%, with fascinating Elephant Rock), then miles of rolling terrain. Start and finish at Ticonderoga railway station.

ALBANY
DUTCH MEMORIES

⊕ Very hilly, Advanced, 0% unpaved

⊕ Map strava.com/routes/2822571916880268432

⊙ Test yourself mi 11 (km 18) strava.com/segments/7303127

⊙ Test yourself mi 21 (km 34) strava.com/segments/17257580

◉ GREG'S EYE

Helderberg Escarpment, to the north of the Catskills, is not the toughest mountain range in the state of New York, but there are a number of respectable climbs to be found here, with some stunning vistas over Vermont. I remember it from a race called the Tour DuPont.

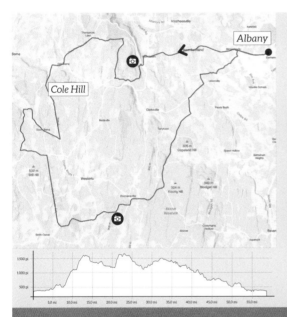

Albany was founded by Dutch settlers in the early seventeenth century and has been New York's state capital since 1797 (the Capitol building is well worth a visit). The city is the last big urban conurbation as you head north along the Hudson River. The slopes of Helderberg Escarpment lie to the west of Albany. From Delmar, the Albany County Helderberg–Hudson Rail Trail provides a safe route up to the wooded plateau overlooking spectacular cliffs, and on toward Thacher State Park. Between New Salem and South Berne, there are several stiff little climbs along Pinnacle Road—a ridge boasting several radio and television transmission towers: 5 mi (8 km) at 5% over Wolf Hill, followed by Cole Hill (1.2 mi/2 km at 8%). The rest of the route, back toward Albany, skirts numerous lakes and rivers, often through forest, and remains challenging.

	Distance		E+		Difficulty		Appeal
⊢─┤	**59 mi** (94 km)	⬆	**4,700 ft** (1,426 m)	�𝗂𝗅	**3/5**	★	**4/5**

Air: Albany International Airport, 6 mi (9.75 km) northwest of downtown. Car: 3h30 from New York City, 3h from Boston, 3h30 from Montréal.

Savile Road, specialists in bespoke bikes, has adopted the slogan "the tailored bicycle." Retailer of Colnago, Cervelo, and Specialized. The ideal stop-off when heading west out of Albany.

257 Delaware Avenue
Delmar, NY 12054
savileroad.com

The panorama from Roemer's High Point (mi 15/km 24); and just after crossing Basic Creek Reservoir (mi 41/km 66).

WOODSTOCK
PEACE AND CLIMBS

- ⊕ Low mountain, Expert, 0% unpaved
- ⊕ Map strava.com/routes/2822572068096358544
- ⊕ Test yourself mi 8 (km 13) strava.com/segments/25547466
- ⊕ Test yourself mi 58 (km 93) strava.com/segments/13395972

◉ GREG'S EYE

Though the famous Woodstock festival actually took place in Bethel, its namesake area in the Catskills is justifiably renowned among cyclists. Friends have told me about Devil's Kitchen: as steep as the famous Huy "wall" in Belgium but twice as long. Wow!

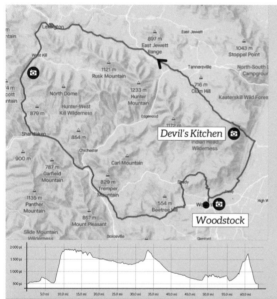

In August 1969, the emblematic gathering of the hippie movement took place not in Woodstock but in Bethel, 60 mi (96 km) to the southwest, after a last-minute change. Half a century on, the small town of Woodstock and its rural surroundings play host to weekending New Yorkers, many of them cyclists drawn to the nearby Catskill Mountains, and some even to Devil's Kitchen (mi 8/km 13), a major challenge that tops out at over 1,900 ft (580 m) in less than 3 miles (4.75 km), with an average double-digit gradient—up to 20% in sections! Farther on, Deep Notch, renowned for frozen waterfalls in winter, climbs at 7% over 1.5 mi (2.5 km). This loop through a splendid landscape ends just after Bearville. But you can also finish with MacDaniel Road (2.4 mi/3.75 km in two very tough ramps) and a view over tranquil Woodstock from the shadow of Overlook Mountain.

	Distance		E+		Difficulty		Appeal
	64 mi (102 km)		**4,750 ft** (1,447 m)		**4/5**		**4/5**

Air: Stewart International Airport, Newburgh (1h by car, I-87 N). Car: 2h from New York City, 3h from Boston, 4h15 from Montréal.

Overlook Bicycles is the meeting place for anyone cycling in the Woodstock area. Open-air café when it's sunny, and luxurious lodgings upstairs—book on Airbnb!

93 Tinker Street Woodstock, NY 12498 overlookbicycles.com

At Platte Clove (mi 10/km 16) for a fine view of Kaaterskill High Peak. And of course, in Woodstock itself, where the wooden houses and a few die-hards ensure that the hippie dream endures.

Fall foliage in the Catskill Mountains, east of the Hudson River, New York.

GLENS FALLS
THE MEANDERING HUDSON

🌐 *Hilly, Intermediate, 7% unpaved*　　🌐 *Map strava.com/routes/2820373721657759856*

	Distance		E+		Difficulty		Appeal
⊢⊣	**42 mi** (68 km)	⬆	**2,550 ft** (773 m)	📊	**3/5**	⭐	**3/5**

Glens Falls

Halfway down its 315-mi (507-km) journey through New York State, the Hudson accelerates in the course of several rapids and rare meanders. The countryside undulates gently between the foothills of the Adirondacks. This 42-mi/67-km route, with several gravel sections, inspired by rides organized by local bike shop Grey Host Bicycles, wends between 2,000-ft (610-m) peaks through an appealing landscape of small lakes and forests of maple and conifer trees. Your calves will get a workout at mi 7 (km 11) on Gurney Lane (1.3 mi/2 km at 6%), mi 17 (km 27) on Howe Road, and mi 32 (km 51) on the packed earth of Bear Town Road (2 mi/3.25 km at 3%).

KINGSTON
TONSHI AND BOWIE

🌐 *Low mountain, Advanced, 25% unpaved*　　🌐 *Map strava.com/routes/2822203931849184256*

	Distance		E+		Difficulty		Appeal
⊢⊣	**63 mi** (101 km)	⬆	**6,100 ft** (1,860 m)	📊	**4/5**	⭐	**4/5**

Tonshi Mountain

Kingston

From Kingston (pop. 24,000), birthplace of IBM and a center for the arts, this route explores a jewel of the Catskill Mountains: Glen Tonche, a stunning property 1,000 ft (305 m) above Ashokan Reservoir, is a recording studio used by the likes of David Bowie and Norah Jones. To reach it, we turn our backs on the Hudson Valley via Woodstock to the west, climbing Meads Mountain Road (1.9 mi/3 km at 11%) on the side of Overlook Mountain. The winding road up Tonshi Mountain is unpaved (2.6 mi/4.25 km at 7%). Return by way of Seven Sisters (0.8 mi/1.25 km at 10%), Bluestone Wild Forest, and the banks of Esopus Creek.

WAWARSING
CATSKILL SPIRIT

- 🌐 Low mountain, Expert 0% unpaved
- 🌐 Map strava.com/routes/2822136904511151104
- ➕ Test yourself mi 15 (km 24) strava.com/segments/866475
- ➕ Test yourself mi 38 (km 61) strava.com/segments/21949577

👁 GREG'S EYE

This route in the southern Catskill Mountains reminds me of a ride through the Belgian Ardennes, in Europe; its very tough challenges evoke those of the monument Liège-Bastogne-Liège. One could surely design an equivalent course to "La Doyenne" east of the Hudson.

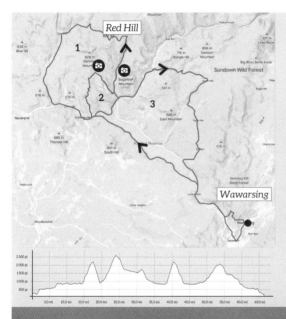

Red Hill

Wawarsing

The Catskill Mountains made their mark on U.S. history as a refuge for the Founding Fathers in the eighteenth century. Cycling them will mark your thighs and calves, particularly in Sullivan County, around Grahamsville and Rondout Reservoir. We're just 12 mi (19 km) from Bethel (to the southwest), where the legendary hippie festival of Woodstock was held in 1969. Our route here is anything but peace and love, though, with 7,600 ft (2,320 m) of elevation gain in 67 mi (107 km), including four famous climbs: Moore Hill Road (3 mi/4.75 km at 8%), Red Hill via Sugarloaf Road (4 mi/6.5 km at 7%), the fearsome Glade Hill Road (2 mi/3.25 km at 12%), and finally Greenville (4 mi/6.5 km at 5%). Between the forests of Sundown and Willowemoc, the scenery is as sumptuous as the riding is rigorous. Back in Wawarsing, enjoy a well-earned beer at New Paltz Brewing.

	Distance		E+		Difficulty		Appeal
	67 mi (107 km)		**7,600 ft** (2,328 m)		**5/5**		**5/5**

Air: Stewart International Airport, Newburgh (1h by car).
Car: 2h from New York City, 3h from Boston, 4h15 from Montréal.

Cinder Track Bicycles in Mountain Dale (10 mi/16 km from Wawarsing on the 209 S) is the pleasantest and most attractive bike shop in Sullivan County.

6 Railroad Avenue Mountain Dale, NY 12763 sullivancatskills.com

Before the summit of Red Hill (mi 21/km 33). If you're prepared to walk 0.5 mi (0.75 km), take Dinch Road to Red Hill Fire Tower for a unique panorama over the lush vastness of the Catskill Mountains. Atop Glade Hill (mi 40/km 64).

POUGHKEEPSIE
THE HEIGHTS OF MINNEWASKA

🌐 *Low mountain, Advanced, 23% unpaved*   🌐 *Map strava.com/routes/2822417122808886272*

 Distance
73 mi
(117 km)

 E+
5,100 ft
(1,554 m)

 Difficulty
3/5

 Appeal
5/5

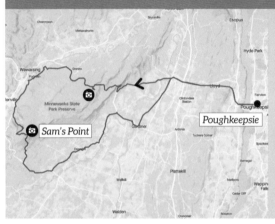

Poughkeepsie (pop. 30,000) lies 70 mi (113 km) north of Manhattan and is the terminus of a Metro-North train line, which means you can ride this route west from one of the loveliest towns in the Hudson Valley on a long day out from NYC. There are three exceptional viewpoints. First, the Walkway Over the Hudson, a cantilever bridge that is the longest in the world closed to motor traffic (1.5 mi/2.5 km). The two others are fascinating promontories of 1,500 ft (460 m) and 2,000 ft (610 m) on the Shawangunk rocky ridge in verdant Minnewaska State Park: Gertrude's Nose (mi 21/km 33) and Sam's Point (mi 38/km 61), at the top of a 4-mi (6.5-km) climb.

COLD SPRING
HIGHLANDS TRAILS

🌐 *Very hilly, Intermediate, 35% unpaved*   🌐 *Map strava.com/routes/2823492162444253804*

 Distance
53 mi
(85 km)

 E+
5,200 ft
(1,585 m)

 Difficulty
3/5

 Appeal
4/5

Barely an hour (by Metro-North train) from Manhattan, the gravel trails of the Hudson Highlands, on the east bank, are a world away. From the station in Cold Spring, quiet roads and paths squiggle from lake to lake: Oscanawa, Bryant Pond, Boyd Corners Reservoir, White Pond. The woody hills make for continuous up and down: total elevation is over 5,000 ft (1525 m), even though we reach the height of 1,000 ft (305 m) only on Barrett Hill (mi 21/km 34). Nature reigns supreme all the way to the Hudson, where, in the lee of Bull Hill (inaccessible by bike), you can enjoy the river view from Foundry Dock Park or Constitution Island.

BROOKFIELD
ROUND CANNONDALE WAY

DIRT & GRAVEL

⊕ *Very hilly, Advanced, 35% unpaved*　　⊕ *Map strava.com/routes/2829364317856878570*

	Distance		E+		Difficulty		Appeal
⊢–⊣	**53 mi** (85 km)	⬆	**6,400 ft** (1,950 m)	📊	**4/5**	★	**3/5**

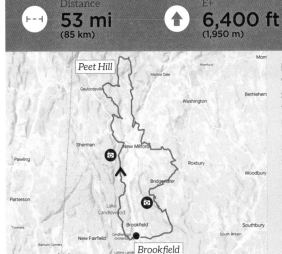

Peet Hill

Brookfield

From New York City (1h30 by car), the pull of the wide-open spaces of western Connecticut is strong. It explains the real estate prices in the vicinity of Candlewood Lake—amid forests and rolling hills that rise to 1,200 ft/365 m. From Bicycle Center in Brookfield, the route is a combination of road and gravel and is stuffed with respectable ramps, never more than 2 mi/3.25 km long, often at 7% to 10%. Surfacing is dodgy in places, such as on Peet Hill (mi 23/km 37) and Mine Hill (mi 35/km 56). The last 10 mi/ 16 km around Rocky Hill, Iron Ore Hill, and Obtuse Hill are tough. Legendary brand Cannondale was founded in nearby Bethel in the 1980s.

HARTFORD
BUCOLIC AND LITERARY

⊕ *Hilly, Intermediate, 0% unpaved*　　⊕ *Map strava.com/routes/2829412591337016954*

	Distance		E+		Difficulty		Appeal
⊢–⊣	**54 mi** (87 km)	⬆	**3,700 ft** (1,125 m)	📊	**3/5**	★	**3/5**

Ratlum Mountain

Hartford

There's more to Connecticut than the 100 mi (161 km) between Boston and New York. Hartford is a gateway to bucolic countryside. Heading west (from Hartford train station), the valley ends at the Farmington River and Burlington Falls in hills surrounding Nepaug Reservoir. We climb above Barkhamsted Reservoir on Ratlum Mountain, reaching close to 1,200 ft (365 m) after Sundown ski resort. The return leg is tranquil, with Penwood Notch providing one last kick. At mile 53 (km 85), you pass the neighboring houses (open to visitors) of Mark Twain and Harriet Beecher Stowe—respective authors of *The Adventures of Tom Sawyer* and *Uncle Tom's Cabin*.

PROVIDENCE
RIVERS RIDE

🌐 *Fairly flat, Intermediate, 0% unpaved*   🌐 *Map strava.com/routes/2833280708003258390*

 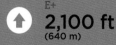

	Distance		E+		Difficulty		Appeal
⊢–⊣	**49 mi** (79 km)	⬆	**2,100 ft** (640 m)	📊	**2/5**	⭐	**3/5**

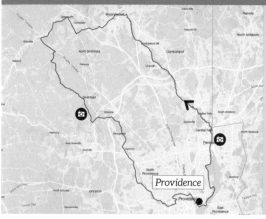

Providence (pop. 178,000) is the capital of Rhode Island, the smallest state in the Union. This friendly yet sophisticated waterside town, home to culinary arts school Johnson & Wales University, is well worth exploring. It's easy to cycle north on the pleasant Blackstone River Bikeway for 19 mi (30 km) to Woonsocket. The homeward leg is more rural, past farms, parks, and small lakes. The final 10 mi (16 km) more or less follow the course of the Woonasquatucket River back to Legend Bicycle in Providence and an espresso in the famous Italian neighborhood of Federal Hill (mi 46/km 74).

NEWPORT
AQUIDNECK HAPPINESS

🌐 *Hilly, Intermediate, 0% unpaved*   🌐 *Map strava.com/routes/2833034480222191272*

	Distance		E+		Difficulty		Appeal
⊢–⊣	**43 mi** (69 km)	⬆	**1,500 ft** (460 m)	📊	**2/5**	⭐	**4/5**

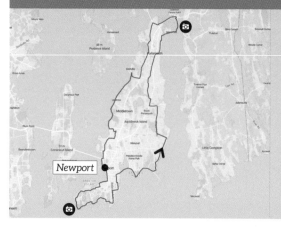

Newport (pop. 25,000, 1h30 south of Boston by car) on the southern tip of Aquidneck Island, played a key role in the Revolutionary War and is now a major pleasure port. Starting from 10 Speed Spokes, we make a circuit of the island on quiet coastal roads. The first 15 miles (24 km) explore Newport, passing the straitlaced New York Yacht Club, close to Fort Adams and Hammersmith Farm, where John F. Kennedy and Jacqueline Bouvier celebrated their wedding in 1953, then beaches and grand residences. The countryside is dotted with farms, vineyards, and golf courses. Return along Narragansett Bay. Rhode Island is rightly called the Ocean State.

WILLIAMSTOWN
MOUNT GREYLOCK TEST

- ⊕ Low mountain, Expert, 0% unpaved
- ⊕ Map strava.com/routes/2833315254689053634

- ⊕ Test yourself mi 7 (km 11) strava.com/segments/5495211
- ⊕ Test yourself mi 37 (km 60) strava.com/segments/632037

👁 GREG'S EYE

Mount Greylock, one of the hardest climbs in the Northeast, draws many cyclists in summer. It's the ideal place to test yourself and find out what condition you're in. Beware though: all the climbs in the Berkshire Mountains are tough. Don't underestimate any of them.

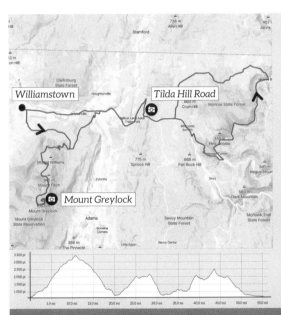

Williamstown

Tilda Hill Road

Mount Greylock

The Berkshire Mountains, on the eastern Appalachian Plateau in Massachusetts, exert the same hold on residents of Boston, Providence, New Haven, and Hartford that the Catskills do on New Yorkers. The area around North Adams and Williamstown makes for attractive cycling. This 55-mi (88-km) route via Mount Greylock (open in June) and three satellite peaks can be ridden over two days. The mountain's north slope is a ride in itself—up to the Veterans War Memorial Tower: 7.7 mi (12.5 km), at an average gradient of 6.8%, with some parts as steep as 13%. The Mohawk Trail (also known as Route 2) is gentler (4.2 mi/6.75 km at 6.6%). Kingsley Hill Road is short but surly: 1.4 mi (2.25 km) at 12.6%, with sections as steep as 24%! It's a demanding ride all the way to Tilda Hill Road: 1.2 mi (2 km) at 10% close to Crum Hill, the "roof" of the Berkshires, at 2,840 ft (865 m).

	Distance		E+		Difficulty		Appeal
⊢─┤	**55 mi** (88 km)	⬆	**7,600 ft** (2,315 m)	📊	**4/5**	★	**4/5**

Air: Albany International Airport (1h10 by car). Car: 2h45 from Boston, 2h30 from New Haven.

The Spoke has been operating from a red-brick building virtually at the foot of Mount Greylock for forty years. Retailer of Felt, Orbea, Bianchi, and Norco.

250 Main Street
Williamstown, MA 01267
spokebicycles.com

At the top of Mount Greylock, in front of the Veterans Tower (mi 11/km 18). On the descent, with a panorama (mi 14/km 22) over Mount Fitch. Top O' The World viewpoint (mi 25/km 40).

GREENFIELD
D2R2 RECONNAISSANCE

DIRT & GRAVEL

- ⊕ Very hilly, Advanced, 60% unpaved
- ⊕ Map strava.com/routes/2833744548706379536
- ⊕ Test yourself mi 13 (km 21) strava.com/segments/1958707
- ⊕ Test yourself mi 54 (km 87) strava.com/segments/736176

◉ GREG'S EYE

The D2R2 has become a landmark summer event in New England, a must-ride for gravel lovers. The rural landscapes of Western Massachusetts are sumptuous, yet we're very near the Berkshire Mountains, so it's pretty steep!

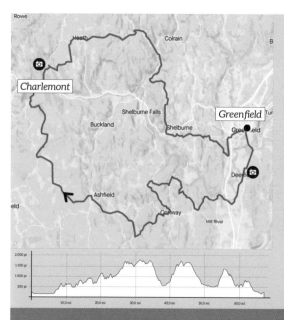

The Connecticut River crosses Massachusetts from north to south, sculpting the landscape on its way. From its west bank, the relief is increasingly accentuated toward the Berkshire Mountains. The hills threaded by the routes of the Deerfield Dirt Road Randonnée—an annual gravel event nicknamed D2R2—rise to 1,800 ft (550 m), and they've got some serious ramps (some as long as 2 mi/3.25 km, with gradients as steep as 20%) on fast trails and paths through lush, wooded scenery. Our itinerary starts from Greenfield and is inspired by various D2R2 routes. The difficulty is real, the feeling of escape extreme. At the finish, head for the beer garden of the Berkshire Brewing Company (South Deerfield), sponsor of the D2R2, to celebrate a beautiful day in the saddle!

 Distance
67 mi
(108 km)

 E+
7,800 ft
(2,380 m)

 Difficulty
4/5

 Appeal
4/5

Air: Bradley International Airport, Hartford (1h by car). Car: 1h35 from New Haven, 1h45 from Boston, 3h from New York City.

Our route starts from *Bicycle World* (close to Greenfield station), an establishment that's been here for thirty years. Retailer of Trek and Kona; rides organized on Facebook.

**104 Federal Street
Greenfield, MA 01301
bicycleworldma.com/about-us/**

Deerfield old town (mi 3/ km 4.75), preserved in its eighteenth-century state. Above Deerfield River and Charlemont (mi 40/km 64). Davenport Brook Reservoir (mi 46/km 74).

WAREHAM
ICE CREAM EXTRAVAGANZA

⊕ *Fairly flat, Intermediate, 0% unpaved*   ⊕ *Map strava.com/routes/2833669476605555398*

 Distance **56 mi** (90 km)   E+ **1,700 ft** (518 m)   Difficulty **3/5**   Appeal **4/5**

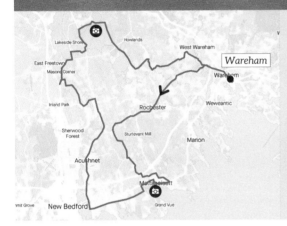

The annual Tour de Crème in southeast Massachusetts inspires our route. The challenge comes not from gradients, but ice cream tastings at local producers in Plymouth County. Heading out from Wareham Village station (2h by train from Boston), stop for sweet refreshment at Captain Bonney's (mi 9/km 14), Oxford Creamery in Mattapoisett (mi 16/km 26)—starting point of the event—Acushnet Creamery (mi 28/km 45), Dorothy Cox Candies (mi 32/km 51), Annie's Ice Cream Shack (mi 36/km 58), and Robin's Nest (mi 51/km 82). You'll have time to think about another tempting trip: a ride around Martha's Vineyard, on the other side of Buzzards Bay.

PROVINCETOWN
CAPE COD EXPLORATION

⊕ *Fairly flat, Advanced, 10% unpaved*   ⊕ *Map strava.com/routes/2829467630864883494*

 Distance **101 mi** (163 km)   E+ **4,000 ft** (1,216 m)   Difficulty **3/5**   Appeal **5/5**

This escapade from Boston explores Cape Cod's horn in one day. Here, on this striking peninsula sticking into the ocean, the Pilgrims made landfall in 1620. Take the ferry (1h30 crossing) from Boston at 8:30 a.m., returning from Provincetown at 7:30 p.m. (approx. $120 with bike), giving you time to ride this century to Chatham and back, through marshes, dunes, and vineyards, and past opulent residences and villages of clapboard houses. In the 1930s, Edward Hopper set up a studio close to Highland Lighthouse (mi 80/ km 129), drawing from beautiful Cape Cod the inspiration that made him the celebrated painter of solitude and melancholy.

BOSTON
MORE THAN TWO MARATHONS

⊕ *Fairly flat, Intermediate, 8% unpaved*   ⊕ *Map strava.com/routes/2833368038869345302*

 Distance
63 mi
(101 km)

 E+
2,200 ft
(670 m)

 Difficulty
3/5

 Appeal
3/5

A cycling homage to the oldest annual marathon. The aim is to reach Hopkinton (our westernmost point)—from the spot where thousands of runners set off on the third Monday in April—following the marathon route as closely as possible. The 11 mi (18 km) of bike paths along the Charles River take us smoothly out of Boston. Don't miss the starting line in Hopkinton, before our return leg past Ashland, Framingham, Natick, Wellesley (half-marathon), Woodland, and Newton. At mi 56 (km 90) we hit Heartbreak Hill, opposite Boston College. We finish close to our starting point, Papa Wheelies, between Fenway Park and Prudential Tower.

LEXINGTON
MINUTEMEN AND KEROUAC

DIRT & GRAVEL

⊕ *Hilly, Intermediate, 40% unpaved*   ⊕ *Map strava.com/routes/2834098044783217992*

 Distance
45 mi
(72 km)

 E+
1,600 ft
(488 m)

 Difficulty
2/5

 Appeal
3/5

Lexington is the town in Massachusetts (30 min by car northwest of Boston) where the first battle of the American Revolution took place on April 17, 1775. At Ride Studio Cafe, you're close to the Lexington Minuteman statue that depicts John Parker, one of the heroes of the colonial militia. From there, cycle back through history on carriageways to Concord, another battle site, with its strategic Old North Bridge (painstakingly rebuilt in 1956) and statue of another Minuteman, Isaac David. Then ride up the Concord River to Lovell, birthplace of Jack Kerouac, who is buried in Edson Cemetery (mi 24/km 39).

KEENE
NEW ENGLAND'S VENTOUX

- ⊕ Low mountain, Advanced, 15% unpaved
- ⊕ Map strava.com/routes/2826778565713172770
- ⊙ Test yourself mi 20 (km 32) strava.com/segments/12538944
- ⊙ Test yourself mi 42 (km 67) strava.com/segments/840132

◉ GREG'S EYE

It is said that Mount Monadnock, which is not too far from Boston, Manchester, or Concord, is the most visited mountain (on foot) in the United States. If you're familiar with Mont Ventoux in France with its stony summit, you can recognize a kindred spirit.

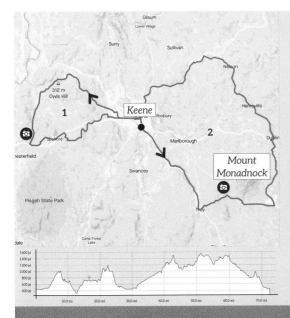

If this *plat de résistance* served by Keene—famed for its October Pumpkin Festival—looks like too big a mouthful, tackle it in two sittings. First, the initial loop west to Spofford and its lake: 30 mi (48 km) through wooded hills overlooking the Connecticut River, to warm up and get a taste of the luxuriant landscapes of New Hampshire. Then, (the next day) the invigorating 42-mi (67-km) tour of Mount Monadnock, which you should absolutely hike up on day three if you can. Its summit (3,170 ft/965 m) has been free of vegetation since fires devastated acres of red spruce two centuries ago, giving it a resemblance to Mont Ventoux in France. East of the mountain, from Troy to Nelson, the relief is undulating—taking you up over 1,500 ft (460 m) on Mountain Road, close to Beech Hill. There are a few gravel sections, so make sure you're suitably equipped.

Distance	E+	Difficulty	Appeal
72 mi (115 km)	**5,200 ft** (1,585 m)	**4/5**	**4/5**

Air: Boston Logan International Airport (2h by car), Manchester-Boston Regional Airport (1h15 by car). Car: 2h from Boston, 3h30 from New York City.

Head out from *Norm's Ski and Bike* in Keene. They'll tell you about the route of Dirty Pizza (a local gravel event) a bit farther north, toward Alstead.

62 Martell Court Keene, NH 03431 normsskibike.com

On the shores of Lake Spofford (mi 16/km 25). Bridge over Perkins Pond (mi 41/km 66), for the most beautiful view of Mount Monadnock. Thorndike Pond (mi 48/km 77).

PLYMOUTH
WHITE MOUNTAINS INTRO

- *Low mountain, Intermediate, 21 % unpaved*
- *Map strava.com/routes/2827144708154841988*
- *Test yourself mi 8 (km 13) strava.com/segments/754497*
- *Test yourself mi 29 (km 47) strava.com/segments/1019649*

👁 GREG'S EYE

New England's White Mountains are majestic, despite not having a single peak over 7,000 ft (2,135 m). Here in New Hampshire, the (not so easy) climbs are 6 to 7 mi (9.7 to 11.25 km) long through a landscape of forest, lakes, waterfalls, and caves that's sublime in fall.

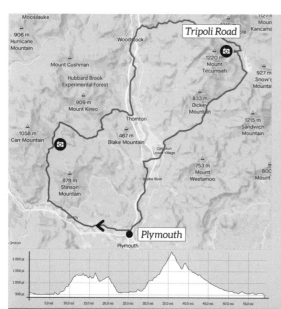

There is no shortage of routes in White Mountain National Forest, a kingdom of maple, spruce, and beech, whether you head out from Gorham, Franconia, Lincoln, or Conway. The riding tends to be sporty. You might as well approach this natural paradise from a little farther south with this initiatory ride from Rhino Bike in Plymouth (pop. 6,000). Discover superb Stinson Lake after the Polar Caves at Rumney (on the 25 W), before the first gravel section that runs to the Pemigewasset River. In Woodstock, you hit the unevenly surfaced Tripoli Road, which climbs beneath the trees for 6 mi (9.75 km) at 4.5% between two peaks (Mount Osceola and Mount Tecumseh) that soar above 4,000 ft (1,220 m), followed by 3 mi (4.75 km) of descent to the pretty ski resort of Waterville Valley. A 20-mi (32-km) stretch with almost no pedaling takes you back to Plymouth.

	Distance		E+		Difficulty		Appeal
	59 mi (95 km)		**4,500 ft** (1,370 m)		**3/5**		**3/5**

Air: Boston Logan International Airport (2h by car), Manchester-Boston Regional Airport (1h15 by car), Portland International Jetport (2h30 by car).
Car: 1h45 from Boston, 2h from Portland, 2h30 from Burlington, 3h30 from Albany.

Founded in 1994, *Rhino Bike* (retailer of Cannondale, Scott, Trek) organizes rides (Rhino Nation on Strava). Another shop is located in Franconia.

**1 Foster Street
Plymouth, NH 03264
rhinobikeworksnh.com**

Stinson Lake (mi 12/km 19). The foot of the Waterville Valley ski runs and Mount Tecumseh (mi 39/km 63).

NORTH CONWAY
NEW HAMPSHIRE PEAKS

⊕ *Low mountain, Advanced, 0% unpaved*   ⊕ *Map strava.com/routes/2828295560569947288*

	Distance		E+		Difficulty		Appeal
⊢–⊣	**54 mi** (87 km)	⬆	**3,600 ft** (1,100 m)	📊	**3/5**	⭐	**4/5**

Mount Washington (the highest point in the Northeast, at 6,288 ft/1,917 m) is one of the hardest road climbs in the world, and highly prized—bikes are banned from the narrow road (no guardrail) except for an official hill climb once a year. It's insane: 7.3 mi/11.75 km (including 1 mi/1.5 km on gravel), at an average gradient of 11.9%, with sections as steep as 22%! Our route takes in Hurricane Mountain (2.2 mi/3.5 km at 10.2%) and Bear Notch (4 mi/6.5 km at 5%). Return to North Conway (and The Bike Shop) via the spectacular Rocky Gorge, or else take the 112 at Passaconaway west to Mount Kancamagus (5 mi/8 km at 5.5%)—an extra 20 mi (32 km) in all.

LACONIA
AROUND WINNIPESAUKEE

⊕ *Very hilly, Intermediate, 3% unpaved*   ⊕ *Map strava.com/routes/2825380113465257822*

	Distance		E+		Difficulty		Appeal
⊢–⊣	**78 mi** (125 km)	⬆	**5,100 ft** (1,555 m)	📊	**3/5**	⭐	**4/5**

Central New Hampshire offers plenty of spicy challenges, such as Mount Kearsarge (2,600 ft/792 m)—3.5 mi (5.75 km) at an average gradient of over 8%. Another delight is Lake Winnipesaukee. It covers 72 sq mi (186 sq km), has 365 islands, and is very popular in summer (Boston is just 1h30 away). An enchanting circuit of the lake covers nearly 80 mi (129 km), past colorful houses and languid ports, with forest all around and a dozen short yet demanding ramps, particularly on the approach to Belknap Mountain at the end. Meredith, Moultonborough, Wolfeboro, and Laconia (starting point: the vibrant Chainline Cycles) are delightful.

Deep in the heart of Franconia Notch State Park in the White Mountains of New Hampshire.

WELLS
LIGHTHOUSES CENTURY

- ⊕ Fairly flat, Advanced, 12% unpaved
- ⊕ Map strava.com/routes/2824925623792789772
- ⊕ Test yourself mi 15 (km 24) strava.com/segments/12945646
- ⊕ Test yourself mi 84 (km 135) strava.com/segments/15376704

👁 GREG'S EYE

Incredible: Maine's Atlantic coast is barely 300 miles (480 km) long as the seagull flies, yet it's so craggy that the actual coastline stretches for 3,478 miles (5,598 km)! Get set for the great adventure of a maritime century ride with a return by train.

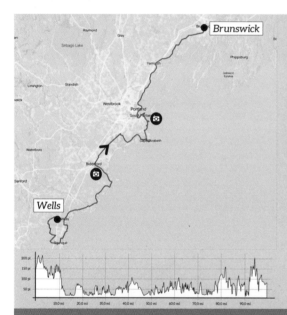

There are two reasons to cycle this route: a century ride in the Northeast and the discovery of Maine's south coast. They combine seamlessly thanks to lack of significant elevation—the distance itself is challenge enough. We head out from Wells station—direction toward Brunswick station at the end of the Downeaster Line. Sandy beaches (the first, Ogunquit, is packed on summer weekends), rocky points, little harbors, historic towns—the setting is magical. Waypoints dot the route in the form of some of the East Coast's most striking lighthouses: Goat Island seen from Cape Porpoise (mi 27/km 43), Wood Island seen from Biddeford Pool (mi 34/km 55), the Two Lights on Cape Elizabeth (mi 38/km 61), Portland Head Light (mi 65/km 104), and Spring Point Ledge (mi 68/km 109) at the end of its 900-ft (275-m) dyke, with its neighbor, Bug Light. A marvelous voyage.

Distance **100 mi** (161 km)		**E+** **3,800 ft** (1,160 m)		Difficulty **3/5**		Appeal **5/5**	

Air: Portland International Jetport.
Car: 1h30 from Boston, 5h from Montréal.

Need assistance? *Gorham Bike and Ski*, close to mi 24 (km 38), also rents road bikes that you can pick up or drop off in Saco, Portland, and Brunswick.

**65 Portland Road
Kennebunk, ME 04403
gorhambike.com**

Every lighthouse is a potential perfect selfie. Don't miss the oldest one of all: Portland Head Light, completed in 1791.

NORWAY
WALLS AND SPRING WATER

- ⊕ Hilly, Intermediate, 0% unpaved
- ⊕ Map strava.com/routes/2824708261419485832
- ⊙ Test yourself mi 14 (km 22) strava.com/segments/7614535
- ⊙ Test yourself mi 42 (km 67) strava.com/segments/4364293

◉ GREG'S EYE

If you get away from the coast in southern Maine, you'll find a tranquil, undulating countryside, its relief unaffected by the nearby White Mountains of New Hampshire. I love this kind of terrain, which always makes you want to extend the distance.

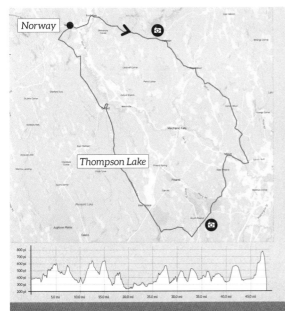

Life is sweet in summertime Norway by the shores of Pennesseewassee Lake, not far from Lewiston—Maine's second city. Separated by stone walls, the agricultural fields of Oxford and Androscoggin counties unfold across gentle slopes that make for an interesting challenge—the roads hit them head-on. These dead straight "walls" are never more than a mile in length, but they sure spice up the route. You'll have to dig deep in the final part of this ride as you tackle Allen Hill and Pike Hill, with sections between 8% and 10%. Before that, Range Pond, Tripp Pond, and Thompson Lake—all prime fishing spots close to the source of Poland Spring Water—announce an already bumpy sector: Carpenter, North Raymond, and Megquier Roads. How about a dip en route?

 Distance
48 mi
(77 km)

 E+
3,800 ft
(1,160 m)

 Difficulty
3/5

 Appeal
3/5

Air: Portland International Jetport (1h by car). Car: 2h30 from Boston, 4h from Montréal.

Angela and John opened *Green Machine* in 2012 in an old Norway house, a superb setting with tip-top service. Retailer of Scott, Felt, Giant. Skiing gear in winter.

**419 Main Street
Norway, ME 04268
greenmachinebikeshop.com**

Beside or above the many lakes that dot this route, in front of Hebron Academy (mi 7/km 11), or at the source of Poland Spring Water (mi 26/km 42).

ROCKLAND
RIDE, FORREST, RIDE!

🌐 *Fairly flat, Intermediate, 3% unpaved* ⊕ Map strava.com/routes/2824636598692702496

 Distance **54 mi** (86 km)

 E+ ⬆ **3,400 ft** (1,038 m)

 Difficulty **2/5**

 Appeal ★ **4/5**

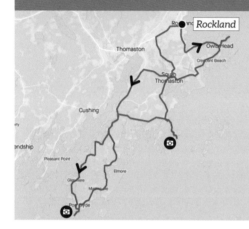

Rockland, 1h30 northeast of Portland, is home to the king of crustaceans. The most succulent lobster in North America are rumored to be found here, thanks to the particular winter temperatures. This route is inspired by a local charity event, the Lobster Ride and Roll, and explores the Knox County peninsula between Saint-George River and the ocean: rocky coast, dairy farms, white clapboard churches and houses, little ports, and eye-catching lighthouses, including Marshall Point (mi 27/km 43), which was featured in *Forrest Gump*. End this salt-spray delight by sampling the lobster rolls at the Lobster Shack, reputedly the best in Rockland.

BANGOR
DON'T BE ANXIOUS

 DIRT & GRAVEL

🌐 *Hilly, Advanced, 40% unpaved* ⊕ Map strava.com/routes/2824692925960788256

 Distance **62 mi** (101 km)

 E+ ⬆ **3,100 ft** (958 m)

 Difficulty **3/5**

 Appeal ★ **3/5**

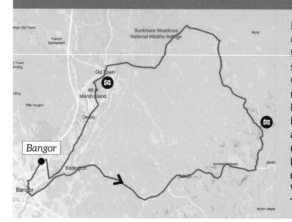

Horror master Stephen King has called Bangor (4h northeast of Boston) home for years. Fans flock to see his Victorian mansion, his rock radio station, 100.3 WKIT, and gloomy Mount Hope Cemetery (mi 60/km 96), which has given him much inspiration. But the banks of the Penobscot River also draw devotees of gravel riding. Numerous trails head east, between forests and lakes. Here, along Indian Camp Brook, 16 mi (25 km) of continuous off-road connect Ducktail Pond Road in the south with County Road in the north. Return via Sunkhaze Meadows National Wildlife Refuge, Old Town, and Marsh Island Park. The route begins at Slipping Gears Cycling.

SOUTHWEST HARBOR
CADILLAC ISLAND

- 🌐 Very hilly, Advanced, 0% unpaved
- 🌐 Map strava.com/routes/2820668982563794800
- ⊕ Test yourself mi 31 (km 50) strava.com/segments/4805779
- ⊕ Test yourself mi 32 (km 51) strava.com/segments/675331

👁 GREG'S EYE

Like many Americans, I have stayed on Mount Desert Island, a delightful corner of Maine and a popular vacation spot. Its varied landscape, featuring hills, lakes, and a rocky coast, is exhilarating—particularly the slopes of the famous Cadillac Mountain.

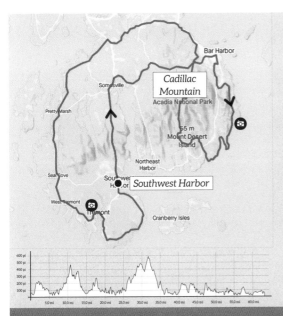

If you don't mind an early wake-up call, on Mount Desert Island you must climb Cadillac Mountain (1,530 ft/465 m) at least once. The first rays of the rising sun hit the summit before any other spot in the United States! Mount Cadillac embodies the sublime seaside of Mid-Coast Maine, with its lakes and rolling hills. This testing climb (3.5 mi/5.5 km at an average gradient of 5%) at mi 32 (km 51) is optional on this route. From Southwest Harbor, we ride first to the east of the island and the 20-mile (32-km) Park Loop Road, exploring beaches, creeks, and cliffs, then to the heart of Acadia National Park and the lower slopes of Cadillac. The return leg around the western part, skirting Mount Desert Narrows —a birdwatcher's paradise—is flatter but offers stunning views, including that of the Bass Harbor Head Lighthouse near Tremont.

Distance **63 mi** (101 km)	E+ **4,500 ft** (1,370 m)	Difficulty **3/5**	Appeal **4/5**

Air: Bangor International Airport (1h by car). Car: 4h30 from Boston, 6h30 from Montréal.

A cyclist at heart, Bob opened *Southwest Cycle* in 1981, and since then he has climbed Cadillac Mountain twice a week! Retailer of Bianchi, Fuji, Surly, and Breezer.

370 Main Street Southwest Harbor, ME 04679 southwestcycle.com

Spoilt for choice: sandy beach at Great Head (mi 20/km 32), Otter Cliffs (mi 22/km 35), Bass Harbor Lighthouse (mi 55/km 88), and, of course, the top of Cadillac Mountain, if you reach it.

PRESQUE ISLE
POTATO VALLEY

- ⊕ *Hilly, Intermediate, 0 % unpaved*
- ⊕ *Map strava.com/routes/2825006319792259302*
- ⊕ *Test yourself mi 6 (km 10) strava.com/segments/16513499*
- ⊕ *Test yourself mi 17 (km 27) strava.com/segments/24922166*

◉ GREG'S EYE

We're right next to the Canadian province of New Brunswick, in the heart of a region known for hot-air ballooning thanks to the quality of the jet stream. The destination feels almost exotic, and if you like the great outdoors, this is a superb area to cycle.

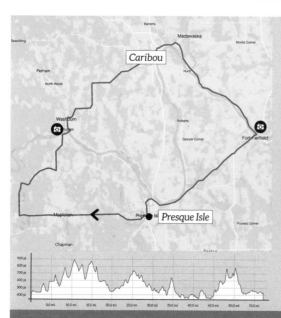

Welcome to the far northeast of Maine, and indeed the United States! Presque Isle (pop. 9,500), on the right bank of the Aroostook, is the starting point for this route that toys with the modest hills lining Aroostook Valley heading west (Sleepy Hollow, Condon Hill, Pyle Mountain, McDonald Mountain), before swinging east for most of the rest of the ride. We encounter the river frequently thanks to its lazy meanders, crossing it no less than four times, at Washburn, Caribou, Fort Fairfield, and, finally, Presque Isle. In summer, the surrounding landscape is lush and green, devoted to livestock farming and fields of broccoli and Russet Burbank and Shepody potatoes. Fort Fairfield (mi 44/km 71) is less than 2 mi (3.25 km) from the Canadian border and a potato capital, proud of its Potato Blossom Festival held every July.

	Distance		E+		Difficulty		Appeal
	57 mi (92 km)		**3,500 ft** (1,065 m)		**3/5**		**3/5**

Air: Presque Isle International Airport, connections to NYC/Newark.
Car: 4h30 from Portland and from Montréal.

Bike Board and Ski right in the center of Presque Isle is a general outdoor store offering quality service. Retailer of Cannondale and Specialized.

**450 Main Street
Presque Isle, ME 04769
bikeboardandski.com**

On the bridges over the Aroostook River at Washburn, Caribou, Fort Fairfield, and Presque Isle. Perhaps you'll see a hot-air balloon, too?

PEACHAM
SO FINE IN FALL

- 🌐 Very hilly, Advanced, 80% unpaved
- 🌐 Map strava.com/routes/2836916082408621788
- ➕ Test yourself mi 23 (km 37) strava.com/segments/5271503
- ➕ Test yourself mi 35 (km 56) strava.com/segments/26365630

👁 GREG'S EYE

I would no doubt have fallen in love with gravel riding, as Ian Boswell did, if that kind of events had existed at the time of my cycling career. The foothills of the Green Mountains in Vermont are the ideal setting for gravel routes. And there's nothing like this area for getting away from cars.

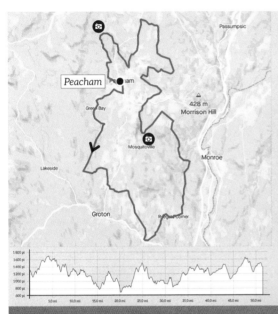

If Vermont seduced Ian Boswell, a strapping Oregon lad who settled here after a wonderful cycling career (finisher of five Grand Tours between 2015 and 2018), it's because it's paradise. Around Peacham, a village with a superb white church east of Montpelier, Boswell was so taken with the infinite variety of trails across Caledonia County that he dreamt up the Peacham Fall Fondo, a gravel event whose seasonality ensures the sublime colors for which autumnal Vermont is renowned. This route is a mixture of Ian Boswell favorites. Twisting between lakes, ponds, rivers, and thickly wooded hills aplenty (up to 2,600 ft/795 m), 80% of it is on trails. There's a bunch of ramps up to 1.5 mi (2.5 km) long at gradients of 7% and 8%, such as Green Bay Loop, Derling Lane, West Barnet Cemetery, Somers Road, and Slack Street.

 Distance **51 mi** (82 km)

 E+ **7,300 ft** (2,225 m)

 Difficulty **3/5**

 Appeal **4/5**

Air: Burlington International Airport (1h30 by car). Car: 3h from Boston, 2h40 from Montréal.

Vermont Bicycle Shop (45 min by car southwest of Peacham). Retailer of Orbea and Norco. Organized rides. Strava Club: VBS Adventure.

105 N Main Street Barre, VT 05641 vermontbicycleshop.com

Peacham, in front of the Northern Skies Observatory and on the streets above the village, with Congregational Church in the background. On Harvey's Lake (mi 28/km 45). Slack Street (mi 47/km 76).

ST. ALBANS
WINDOW ON CANADA

🌐 *Low mountain, Advanced, 57% unpaved*   🌐 *Map strava.com/routes/2836720307647355178*

 Distance
85 mi
(136 km)

 E+
4,300 ft
(1,305 m)

 Difficulty
3/5

 Appeal
4/5

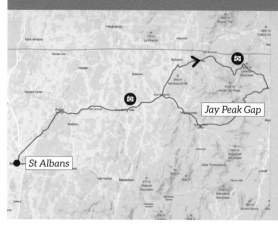

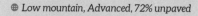 Jay Peak Gap

St Albans

The northern terminus of the Vermonter train (9h from NYC), St. Albans claims to be the Maple Syrup Capital of the World, right under Canada's nose! It's also the starting point of the Missisquoi Valley Rail Trail, which runs along the river to Richford, 27 mi (43 km) northeast. Push along the border and you'll hit two road climbs (up to 2,200 ft/670 m) around Jay Peak, the northernmost summit in the Green Mountains. North Troy is first: 7 mi (11.25 km) at 4%, the last 3 mi (4.75 km) at between 6% and 8%. Jay Peak Gap is second: 4.5 mi (7.25 km) at 5%, the final ramp (0.5 mi/0.75 km) at over 10%. Colors are stunning come fall.

LYNDONVILLE
WARM RASPUTITSA

🌐 *Low mountain, Advanced, 72% unpaved*   🌐 *Map strava.com/routes/2835156304513191756*

 Distance
57 mi
(92 km)

 E+
6,100 ft
(1,860 m)

 Difficulty
4/5

 Appeal
5/5

Toll Road

Lyndonville

Vermont has around sixty peaks higher than Burke Mountain (3,270 ft/995 m). But Toll Road is one nefarious climb, the most brutal in the country for its distance: 2.5 mi (4 km) at 13.4%, with 0.5 mi (0.75 km) at 22% two-thirds up, and sections at 24%. Rasputitsa ("mud season" in Russian) is a classic raced every April, when the combination of snowmelt and freezing rain tests the hardiest cyclists. We advise riding this route (starting at Village Sport in Lyndonville) in summer, when Vermont is at its greenest, the roads dry, and the trails (41 mi/66 km of gravel) less rutted. At mi 45 (km 72.5), you can take a left onto Toll Road for a look-see.

BURLINGTON
FERRIES AND RAIL TRAIL

- ⊕ *Hilly, Advanced, 6% unpaved*
- ⊕ *Map strava.com/routes/2821046249812934048*
- ⊕ *Test yourself mi 17 (km 27) strava.com/segments/626262*
- ⊕ *Test yourself mi 36 (km 58) strava.com/segments/4726753*

👁 GREG'S EYE

Summer's short in Vermont, where winter tramples over spring. But Burlington is a charming town, and the shores and heights of Lake Champlain, including the New York side, offer a unique cycling experience in which the Island Line Rail Trail is the tops.

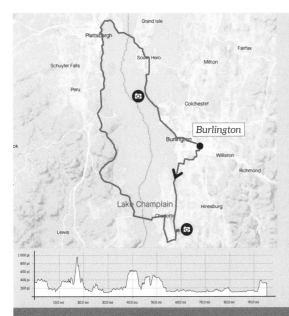

The deepest part of Lake Champlain straddles the border between New York and Vermont. We explore both shores on a grand day out on the bike! From laid-back Burlington, we ride south for a ferry crossing of Champlain (mi 29/km 47) from Charlotte, Vermont to Essex, New York. A second ferry awaits at mi 68 (km 109) to take you from Cumberland Head, New York to Grand Isle, Vermont. The highlight comes next: a 3.5-mi/5.75-km causeway for exclusive use of cyclists and walkers (part of the Island Line Rail Trail) that connects to Champlain's east shore. Mount Philo at mi 16/km 26 (1.25 mi/2 km at close to 10%) provides early spice, with fabulous views from the summit as far as the Adirondacks. For a shorter (50 mi/80 km) version, take a ferry from Burlington across to Port Kent and complete only the northern section, which is pretty much all flat.

| Distance **90 mi** (145 km) | E+ **4,900 ft** (1,495 m) | Difficulty **3/5** | Appeal **4/5** |

Air: Burlington International Airport, South Burlington. Car: 2h from Montréal, 5h30 from New York City.

The vast *Earl's Cyclery* is Vermont's largest bike shop and has been serving Burlington for sixty years and has been named one of the top 100 bike dealers in America.

2069 Williston Road South Burlington, VT 05403 earlsbikes.com

Top of Mount Philo (mi 17/km 27), where the view encompasses all of Lake Champlain. Aboard each of the two ferries (mi 28/km 45 and mi 71/km 114). On the Island Line Rail Trail (mi 83/km 133).

WATERBURY
GREEN AND TOUGH

⊕ *Low mountain, Expert, 17% unpaved*   ⊕ *Map strava.com/routes/2836665486854473002*

 Distance
88 mi
(141 km)

 E+
10,000 ft
(3,050 m)

 Difficulty
5/5

 Appeal
5/5

This challenge in the Green Mountains should be attempted in its entirety by experts only. Starting from Bicycle Express in Waterbury, you can do "just" the southern loop (60 mi/96 km and 8,200 ft/2,500 m E+) over quiet roads around Mount Ellen through beautiful low-mountain scenery with waterfalls galore. Appalachian Gap is first (2.7 mi/4.25 km at more than 9% average gradient), then Lincoln Gap (3.3 mi/5.25 km at 7%, with sections up to 20%, and 3 mi/4.75 km of gravel). Wait a few days before tackling Bolton Mountain (4.2 mi/6.75 km at 8%, with a long section at 16%). Then try some of the climbs in the VT Gran Fondo. Crazy? Just a bit.

KILLINGTON
DOUBLE GRADIENTS

⊕ *Low mountain, Expert, 10% unpaved*   ⊕ *Map strava.com/routes/2835279280819498546*

 Distance
66 mi
(106 km)

 E+
7,500 ft
(2,285 m)

 Difficulty
4/5

 Appeal
4/5

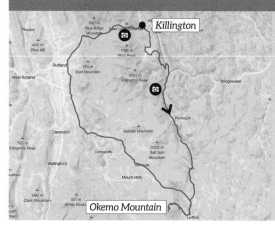

Vermont road climbs are among the steepest in the United States. Mount Equinox (3h northwest of Boston by car) soars 3,840 ft (1170 m) above Manchester and is the most terrifying of these peaks: 5.2 mi (8.4 km) at 11.5% average gradient, with 4.6 mi (7.5 km) at over 10%. It compares to Monte Zoncolan, bogeyman of the Giro d'Italia. But cyclists are only allowed to tackle Mount Equinox once a year, so we head north to Okemo Mountain, star of this testing ride via Killington and Route 100, returning via Sherburne Pass. Above Ludlow, the road to Okemo ski resort climbs for 4 mi (6.5 km) at more than 10%. Nearby Mount Ascutney is of the same caliber.

ANDOVER
ON TOP OF THE GARDEN STATE

- Low mountain, Advanced, 35% unpaved
- Map strava.com/routes/2827850129828594840
- Test yourself mi 23 (km 37) strava.com/segments/4141429
- Test yourself mi 44 (km 71) strava.com/segments/4699603

◉ GREG'S EYE

Climbing to High Point or Sunrise Mountain—the highest points in New Jersey—you always hope to catch sight of Manhattan skyscrapers, 40 mi (65 km) to the southeast. Clear skies or not, I thoroughly recommend this gravel route. You'll be surprised at any rate.

A neighbor of New York State and Pennsylvania, Sussex County stands out from the rest of New Jersey due to the relief of the wild, wooded Kittatinny Mountains. You can't climb higher in the Garden State than High Point (mi 30/km 48) at 1,800 ft (550 m), with its 220-ft (67-m) Veterans Memorial obelisk. The east slope is tough: 3 mi (4.75 km) at 6% (from Colesville), with a long 13.5% section at the start. It's pure joy to reach the summit, before another stretch of gravel—after riding the Sussex Branch Trail from Andover. This time it's a portion of the legendary Appalachian Trail, 4 mi (6.5 km) or 8 mi (13 km), and back on the asphalt at mi 36 (km 58). Next is Sunrise Mountain (1,650 ft/500 m), a heaven of blueberry and pitch pine, and another extraordinary viewpoint. Return via Stokes State Forest, Culver Lake, and the Sussex Branch Trail again.

	Distance		E+		Difficulty		Appeal
	67 mi (108 km)		**5,300 ft** (1,615 m)		**4/5**		**5/5**

Air: Newark International Airport (50 min by car). Car: 1h from New York City, 1h30 from Trenton, 1h20 from Scranton.

Ride Bike Shop is a meeting point for the cyclists of Sussex. They'll be able to recommend the best routes in the area. Retailer of Specialized and Scott.

2 Lenape Road
Andover, NJ 07821
ridebikesnj.com

The top of High Point or beside Lake Marcia (mi 30/ km 48), with the monument in the background. The top of Sunrise Mountain (mi 45/km 72).

PRINCETON
PRESTIGIOUS HILLS

⊕ Very hilly, Advanced, 5% unpaved   ⊕ Map strava.com/routes/2828190577543164056

	Distance		E+		Difficulty		Appeal
	81 mi (130 km)		**5,200 ft** (1,585 m)		**3/5**		**3/5**

Prestigious Princeton University, close to the state capital, Trenton, is the pride of New Jersey. Michelle Obama, Jeff Bezos, and Woodrow Wilson studied here. From Princeton Junction station, you cross the Delaware, the Raritan Canal, and Carnegie Lake to salute this temple of learning (mi 3/km 4.75), before embarking on a long ride through the bucolic and very hilly counties of Mercer, Somerset, and Hunterdon. There are stiff climbs up Sourland Mountain and Stanton Mountain overlooking Round Valley Reservoir, before we take in such renowned vineyards as Mount Salem and Beneduce around Pittstown. A route as invigorating as it is inspiring.

BAYONNE
ISLANDS AND LIBERTY

⊕ Fairly flat, Intermediate, 0% unpaved   ⊕ Map strava.com/routes/2827568229042164440

	Distance		E+		Difficulty		Appeal
	52 mi (84 km)		**1,700 ft** (515 m)		**2/5**		**4/5**

Bayonne feels every inch a part of the Garden State, but New York City exerts an irresistible pull. Liberty State Park, 6 mi (10 km) to the north, offers a stunning panorama of the Manhattan skyline. Head out from RG's Bicycle Shop to take it in, followed by a detour to Ellis Island and the Statue of Liberty. Our second loop (39 mi/63 km) heads out and back to the New York borough of Staten Island. Take in the hills of Moses Mountain and Clove Lakes Park, the view over the Verrazzano-Narrows Bridge, Forts Wadsworth and Tompkins, and Snug Harbor Botanical Garden. At St. George (mi 37/km 60), find the orange ferry for Manhattan, which runs 24/7.

MEDFORD
EXPLORING THE PINES

⊕ *Fairly flat, Intermediate, 38% unpaved* ⊕ Map *strava.com/routes/2828249261964973208*

	Distance		E+		Difficulty		Appeal
⊢-⊣	**55 mi** (88 km)	⬆	**600 ft** (183 m)	⊞	**2/5**	★	**3/5**

The Pinelands is a vast rural area of farmland, wetlands, lakes, and state forest covering nearly one-quarter of New Jersey, from Philadelphia to the Atlantic! It has plenty of trails and paths and is home to beavers, tree frogs, and cranberry plantations. The relief is very flat, making for easy exploration on gravel. Head out from Wheelies Bicycles Sales in Medford, 20 mi (32 km) east of Camden, and you are free to roam throughout the 37,000 acres of Brendan T. Byrne State Forest. Occasionally, you'll meet hikers and cyclists from Toms River on the coast. It's no coincidence that the township at the center of our route is named Woodland.

ATLANTIC CITY
GAMBLING CENTURY

⊕ *Fairly flat, Advanced, 2% unpaved* ⊕ Map *strava.com/routes/2827930188542545454*

	Distance		E+		Difficulty		Appeal
⊢-⊣	**103 mi** (166 km)	⬆	**1,000 ft** (302 m)	⊞	**3/5**	★	**4/5**

Atlantic City's glory days as a gambling mecca are long gone, even though there are still casinos here. But the promise of an oceanic century loop to Cape May, with its lighthouse and beach (a surfing paradise) is a very good reason to visit AC (1h30 by train from Philadelphia or 2h by car from New York City). You'll cycle down a peninsula composed of wetlands and vineyards, with protected areas for birds of prey. The return leg runs along the ocean, past the wild dunes of Wildwood and Avalon, lagoons, and swamps, to Ocean City and its iconic Fishing Pier. Back in AC, take a celebratory selfie in front of the Tropicana or the Hard Rock Hotel.

PHILADELPHIA
GREAT AND GREEN PHILLY

⊕ *Hilly, Intermediate, 10% unpaved*
⊕ *Map strava.com/routes/2830833160709304332*

⊕ *Test yourself mi 15 (km 24) strava.com/segments/21768592*
⊕ *Test yourself mi 36 (km 58) strava.com/segments/612783*

◉ GREG'S EYE

I adore Philadelphia; it's a wonderful city. Yet I only once raced the city's CoreStates Championship (at one time the premier cycling classic in America), owing to my European schedule. I had the eye of the tiger that day on the Manayunk Wall, but I didn't win!

Ah, Philly! The sixth-largest city in the country (pop. 1.6 million) is a major historic, cultural, and artistic center, with plenty to recommend and cycle paths galore. Our route commences on the Delaware River Waterfront, then twirls through Pennypack Park and a pretty northern suburb. It then dives toward the Schuylkill River and the hills of Wissahickon Valley Park before kicking up Manayunk Wall at mi 36/km 58 (0.5 mi at 8.2%) —a key feature of the (sadly discontinued) Philadelphia International Cycling Classic. The final miles are an urban delight. First, Fairmount Park, then Benjamin Franklin Parkway (inspired by Paris's Champs-Élysées) and its key sites (the Museum of Art with its famous Rocky steps, the Barnes Foundation, the Franklin Institute) and back to our starting point and the historic Independence Hall and Liberty Bell.

Distance ⊢–⊣ **46 mi** (74 km)	**E+** ⬆ **2,200 ft** (670 m)	**Difficulty** 📊 **2/5**	**Appeal** ★ **4/5**

Air: Philadelphia International Airport (25 min for 10 mi/16 km by car from downtown). Car: 2h15 from New York City, 2h30 from Washington.

Cadence Cycling (1 mi/1.5 km west of Independence Hall) is a hip local bike shop. Retailer of Specialized, Pinarello, Santa Cruz, Giant, and Liv.

201 South 25th Street
Philadelphia, PA 19103
cadencecycling.com

In front of Independence Hall and the Liberty Bell. The Museum of Art, either at the top of the steps (shouldering your bike), or at the bottom by the statue of Rocky (mi 44/km 70). In front of the LOVE sculpture (mi 45/km 72).

A cobbled street in the historic center of Philadelphia, Pennsylvania

PHILADELPHIA
SEVEN MILES OF HISTORY

⊕ *Hilly, Intermediate, 4% unpaved*　　　⊕ *Map strava.com/routes/2831228683832802384*

 Distance
54 mi
(87 km)

 E+
2,500 ft
(760 m)

 Difficulty
2/5

 Appeal
4/5

Valley Forge (25 mi/40 km northwest of Philadelphia, above a bend in the Schuylkill River) is a major historical site: the encampment where George Washington's troops endured the winter of 1777 to 1778—an ordeal that bonded his army. The 7 mi (11.25 km) through Valley Forge are a journey back in time, passing Washington's Headquarters, Artillery Park, and the National Memorial Arch. We set out from Bicycle Therapy in Philadelphia along the Schuylkill River Trail, returning via the heights of Strafford. At the finish, push on to cobbled Quince Street, then Passyhunk Avenue, 1 mi (1.5 km) south, for an essential Philly cheesesteak at Geno's or Pat's.

LANCASTER
"WILKUM"

⊕ *Hilly, Intermediate, 0% unpaved*　　　⊕ *Map strava.com/routes/2830413547732805326*

 Distance
58 mi
(93 km)

 E+
4,100 ft
(1,250 m)

 Difficulty
2/5

 Appeal
4/5

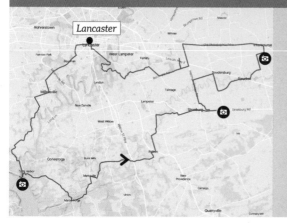

A stay in Philadelphia is a chance to explore Dutch Country (1h30 west by car), so-called because the local Amish speak a German (Deutsch) dialect: Pennsilfaanisch. The terrain is undulating and the cycling tranquil: drivers are used to passing the horse-drawn buggies of the Amish—descendants of Alsatian and Swiss immigrants who live a simple rural life, as if time stopped two centuries ago. It's a real postcard route: covered bridges over the Conestoga River after a stunning view over Lake Clarke (mi 12/km 19); steam train at Strasburg; green-shuttered houses. At Kitchen Kettle Village (mi 40/km 64), the shoofly and schnitz pies are delicious.

NAZARETH
POWERFUL DELAWARE RIVER

- ⊕ Low mountain, Advanced, 7% unpaved
- ⊕ Map strava.com/routes/2832665955663232136
- ✛ Test yourself mi 19 (30 km)strava.com/segments/693110
- ✛ Test yourself mi 45 (km 72) strava.com/segments/688507

👁 GREG'S EYE

As a keen angler, I've often been tempted by a stay near the Delaware Water Gap. And the area around Allentown has always drawn a large cycling community thanks to the very busy Valley Preferred velodrome. What's more, the roads in these parts are superb.

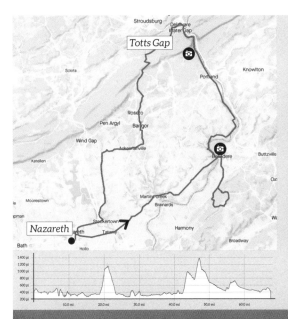

The roiling course of the powerful Delaware River, which forms Pennsylvania's eastern border with New Jersey, flows majestically near Allentown—the state's third-largest urban area. From Nazareth, it's an easy ride to the riverbank, where, at mi 39 (km 63), you can stop to admire one of the loveliest landscapes in the Appalachians: the Delaware Water Gap, an impressive transverse valley cut through a ridge by the eroding forces of water and ice. This section is therefore pretty steep, particularly Totts Gap (1.5 mi/2.5 km at 8.5%) outside Stroudsburg, followed by Bangor Mountain Road (1.3 mi/2 km at 9%). Earlier in the ride, if you're game, you can cross the Delaware at Belvidere for a 15-mi (24-km) loop that includes Fiddlers Elbow Road—1.4 mi (2.25 km) at 10%, with one section at 24%!

	Distance		E+		Difficulty		Appeal
	67 mi (108 km)		**4,900 ft** (1,495 m)		**3/5**		**4/5**

Air: Lehigh Valley International Airport in Allentown (20 min by car).
Car: 1h30 from New York City, 1h30 from Philadelphia.

Curt's Cyclery is an old family business. Retailer of Giant and Liv. Organized rides on Saturday mornings (see Facebook page).

**182 Bath Pike
Nazareth, PA 18064
curtscyclery.com**

Riverton Belvidere Bridge (mi 15/km 24). Mount Minsi and Arrow Island (mi 38/km 61). Point of Gap Overlook (mi 39/km 63).

SCRANTON
"JOE" GRINDER

- Low mountain, Advanced, 35% unpaved
- Map strava.com/routes/2832200484398732288
- Test yourself mi 31 (km 50) strava.com/segments/12404094
- Test yourself mi 65 (km 104) strava.com/segments/1520107

© GREG'S EYE

Scranton is proud to be the birthplace of Joe Biden. For cyclists, it's also the gateway to the wide open spaces of the Moosic Mountains, where the prominent relief makes gravel riding on mixed terrain a joy.

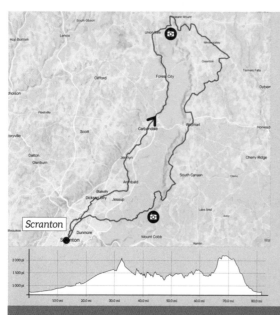

Scranton

With a surface area equivalent to Cuba or Nicaragua, Pennsylvania has plenty of big open spaces to explore once you head out of Philadelphia, Pittsburgh, and other built-up areas. There's some fantastic gravel riding here—a practice that has exploded over the last decade. The Moosic Mountains northeast of Scranton ("Electric City"), birthplace of President Joe Biden and setting of the American TV series *The Office*, is the place to head—a plateau with dour summits and windswept arid moorland, bursting with cranberries, blueberries, rhododendrons, and wind turbines. East of the Lackawanna River, 60% of this challenging route (plan a whole day) is off-road, over tortuous terrain, with nearly 6,000 ft (1,830 m) of elevation. It's a perfect example of the "gravel grinder" concept, spiced up with nice little ramps (never more than 1.5 mi/2.5 km long), sometimes up to 8%.

Distance	E+	Difficulty	Appeal
80 mi (129 km)	**5,800 ft** (1,770 m)	**4/5**	**4/5**

Air: Wilkes-Barre International Airport (15 min from downtown).
Car: 2h15 from New York City, 2h from Philadelphia, 4h30 from Pittsburgh.

Veloce, close to Scranton station. Retailer of Scott, BMC, and Kona. Perfect bike servicing. Organized rides. Café terrace.

120 Franklin Avenue Scranton, PA 18503 velocelogic.com

Summit of East Mountain Road (mi 32/km 51). Eales Preserve (mi 69/km 111). In front of a steam locomotive at Steamtown National Historic Site, at the Trolley Museum, and at Lackawanna County Courthouse (mi 80/km 129).

WARREN
KINZUA CELEBRATION

⊕ Very hilly, Advanced, 14% unpaved   ⊕ Map strava.com/routes/2823517342055733868

	Distance		E+		Difficulty		Appeal
⊢–⊣	**60 mi** (96 km)	⬆	**4,000 ft** (1,220 m)	📊	**3/5**	★	**4/5**

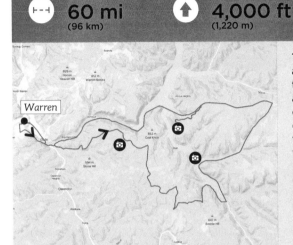

The Allegheny River runs over 300 mi (485 km) across the western slopes of the Appalachians to Pittsburgh. Its striking beauty reaches an apotheosis in the reservoir formed by construction of Kinzua Dam in 1965. Our route departs the Cycle Shop in Warren (pop. 10,000) to tackle the river from the south, commencing with a long gravel portion (including Jake's Rocks Road: 3 mi/4.75 km at 4%), then a second ramp of 5 mi/8 km at 3% on asphalt. At mi 40 (km 64), we leave PA-59 for Rimrock Overlook: superb views of the reservoir, an enchanting vision at sunset. Then it's a gentle downhill to Kinzua Beach, Kinzua Dam, and on back to Warren.

ERIE
GREAT LAKES OPPORTUNITY

⊕ Very hilly, Advanced, 0% unpaved   ⊕ Map strava.com/routes/2831584349298934126

	Distance		E+		Difficulty		Appeal
⊢–⊣	**68 mi** (110 km)	⬆	**3,600 ft** (1,100 m)	📊	**3/5**	★	**4/5**

Northern Pennsylvania has 50 mi (80 km) of coast on Lake Erie, the southernmost of the Great Lakes. The town of Erie (2h north of Pittsburgh by car) boasts a seaside atmosphere, an idyllic peninsula (Presque Isle), and extraordinary sunsets. We set out inland (from John Adams Cycling), heading east to New York State (a 14-mi/22.5-km section, 20% of our route) and ski country (Peek'n Peak resort, mi 27/km 43, altitude 1,750 ft/535 m), and Findley Lake—a fishing paradise. Lakeview, at mi 42 (km 67), is the first of many vineyards, before the homeward leg along the lake. You can add a circuit of Presque Isle for an additional 14 mi (22 km).

PITTSBURGH
POP ART CYCLING

⊕ Very hilly, Advanced, 2% unpaved
⊕ Map strava.com/routes/2829790551306995572

◉ Test yourself mi 20 (km 32) strava.com/segments/686658
◉ Test yourself mi 53 (km 85) strava.com/segments/713710

◉ GREG'S EYE

The Dirty Dozen is legendary, and it was in Pittsburgh that Danny Chew launched the "sportive" concept in the United States. With the exception of San Francisco, Los Angeles, and Flanders, Belgium, I know of no steeper climbable slopes on asphalt.

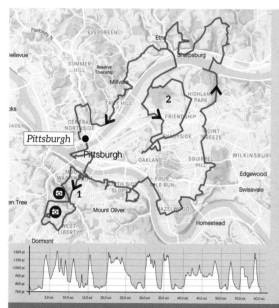

Among the shibboleths shattered by Pop Art was that of an artwork's uniqueness. Cyclists of Pittsburgh (birthplace of Andy Warhol) must have taken inspiration from this. The Dirty Dozen, a fall sportive, serves thirteen of the city's harshest ascents, up hills formed by the erosive gouging of the Allegheny and Monongahela Rivers. Never more than 1 mi (1.5 km) long, there are plenty of sections with gradients of 20%. Canton Street (mi 8/km 12), the American Koppenberg, is the most famous, with its fat cobblestones and a few yards at 39%—a world record! Our route, which starts at the Warhol Museum, is a variant on the Dirty Dozen. Prepare to suffer as you hit Sycamore (mi 3/km 4.75, 12% from the get-go) and on Tesla ramp (mi 20/km 32, 22%), but keep a little in reserve for Logan and Suffolk/Hazelton/Burgess—the final tortures—with gradients of 16% to 20%.

Distance	E+	Difficulty	Appeal
60 mi (96 km)	**6,400 ft** (1,950 m)	**4/5**	**5/5**

Air: Pittsburgh International Airport, 20 min from downtown.
Car: 6h from New York City, 7h from Chicago, 5h from Toronto.

The Dirty Dozen is tough on bikes, so if you suffer a mechanical problem, Thick Bikes (close to mi 14/km 22) could be a useful address. Retailer of Cannondale and Salsa.

**62 S 15th Street
Pittsburgh, PA 15203
thickbikes.com**

Summit of Canton Street of course, because it's so good to make it up there (mi 8/km 12). Above Washington Park (mi 10/km 16), with a panorama over the downtown skyscrapers and the two rivers.

ALTOONA
ALLEGHENY BENDS

- *Low mountain, Expert, 4% unpaved*
- *Map strava.com/routes/2832344221930903730*
- *Test yourself mi 7 (11 km) strava.com/segments/1485477*
- *Test yourself mi 34 (55 km) strava.com/segments/3866076*

GREG'S EYE

There once was a Tour de Toona reserved for women. I don't know if its course took them to the summit of Blue Knob, but even without that climb, I'm sure the routes through the Allegheny Mountains in central Pennsylvania were demanding.

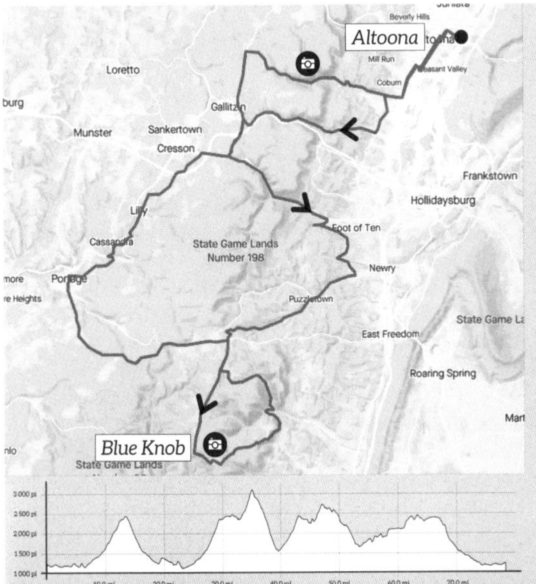

An undulating green horizon, slopes covered in red spruce, golden birch, and maple: the Allegheny Mountains in the heart of Pennsylvania play it modest. But hop on a bike and climb to the gaunt summit of Blue Knob—a ski resort in winter—and you'll soon realize you're in the mountains proper: an initial 4.3 mi (7 km) at 5%, followed by 2 mi (3.25 km) of real harshness, with the gradient rising to 9%. And the descent via Overland Pass shows that there's even tougher riding to be found in the area. Blue Knob is bookended by Sugar Run Road (6 mi/9.75 km at 4%) and Right Hand Gap Road (3 mi/4.75 km at 6%). This long, difficult route (made easier by omitting the 15 mi (24 km) and 1,600 ft (488 m) elevation of the Blue Knob loop) leads to the historic Horseshoe Curve, the most famous railroad bend in the United States (a tight 220 degrees)!

Distance	E+	Difficulty	Appeal
78 mi (125 km)	7,500 ft (2,290 m)	4/5	4/5

Air: BWI Marshall Airport, flights for Altoona-Blair County Airport (30 min by car to the south).
Car: 2h from Pittsburgh, 4h from Philadelphia.

A visit to *Spokes N Skis* bike shop in summer is a must before setting off. Retailer of Specialized and Cannondale.

315 South Logan Boulevard
Altoona, PA 16602
spokesnskis.shopkeystonestate.com

Summit of Blue Knob (mi 35/ km 56). Inside Horseshoe Curve (mi 70/km 113) for the sight of three trains passing simultaneously on the three tracks. Or of Amtrak's daily Pennsylvanian that runs between New York and Pittsburgh.

CHAMBERSBURG
CIVIL WAR MEMORIES

- Very hilly, Advanced, 3% unpaved
- Map strava.com/routes/2832591453123634570
- Test yourself mi 35 (km 56) strava.com/segments/14634056
- Test yourself mi 42 (km 67) strava.com/segments/655717

👁 GREG'S EYE

I've had occasion to ride around Chambersburg, close to the Maryland state line, and the historic Gettysburg site, for a charity event. The scenery is superb, with splendid forests and enticing ramps. And Gettysburg embodies a key moment in the history of the United States.

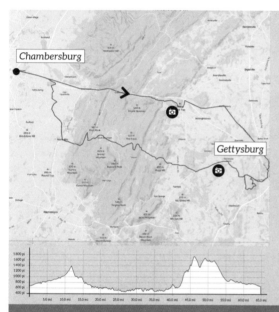

Riding out of Chambersburg, you might be drawn to the ramps of Tuscarora State Forest to the northwest. To the east, the north/south ridge through Michaux State Forest (named after the French botanist who replanted it in the eighteenth century) holds promising challenges, such as Cold Spring Road on the homeward leg of our route (4 mi/6.5 km at 5%). But the relief and landscape of chestnut, scarlet oak, and red maple are not the only points of interest. At mi 25 (km 40) we pass through Gettysburg, scene of the key Civil War battle that took place between July 1 and 3, 1863. Nearly 8,000 men died, and 40,000 were wounded, taken prisoner, or went missing. South of the town, the National Military Park counts some 1,400 monuments, markers, and cannons. Our route passes through it for 8 mi (12.75 km), but there are alternative trails to explore the historic area.

	Distance		E+		Difficulty		Appeal
	65 mi (104 km)		**4,600 ft** (1,400 m)		**3/5**		**4/5**

Air: Gettysburg Regional Airport (40 min by car). Car: 1h40 from Baltimore, 2h30 from Philadelphia, 3h from Pittsburgh.

Quick Release is the ideal meeting point for this route east out of Chambersburg. Retailer of Giant and Liv.

242 Falling Spring Road Chambersburg, PA 17202 qrbicycles.com

Notable monuments in Gettysburg National Military Park, between mi 26 (km 42) and mi 34 (km 55): State of Pennsylvania Memorial, Women's Memorial, Lincoln's Address Memorial. At South Mountain (mi 46/ km 74): panorama over the plain.

WASHINGTON, D.C.
A CAPITAL RIDE

⊕ Hilly, Intermediate, 7% unpaved   ⊕ Map strava.com/routes/2827244405519848090

	Distance		E+		Difficulty		Appeal
⊢–⊣	**49 mi** (79 km)	⬆	**2,300 ft** (700 m)	📊	**2/5**	⭐	**5/5**

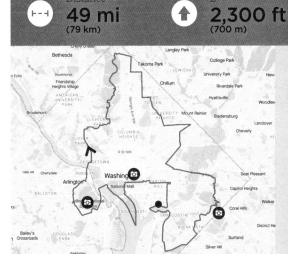

The federal capital is one-quarter the size of New York City and blessed with miles of bike lanes, making it a cyclist's town to explore in a 50-mile (80-km) loop (starting at Conte's Bike Shop in Navy Yard). You hardly notice hills, such as National Cathedral (mi 15/km 24). From the Capitol to the Lincoln Memorial, the 2 mi (3.25 km) of Constitution Avenue are stunning: the Supreme Court, White House, Washington Monument, and Franklin Delano Roosevelt and Martin Luther King, Jr. Memorials. We cross the Potomac, circle Arlington Cemetery (in Virginia), climb through Rock Creek Park, and take in both banks of the Anacostia River. Magnificent.

WASHINGTON, D.C.
POTOMAC AND MANSIONS

⊕ Hilly, Intermediate, 0 % unpaved   ⊕ Map strava.com/routes/2827289904131937156

	Distance		E+		Difficulty		Appeal
⊢–⊣	**56 mi** (90 km)	⬆	**2,500 ft** (765 m)	📊	**3/5**	⭐	**3/5**

Washington, D.C.

The modest size (68 sq mi/176 sq km) of the nation's capital is a strong incentive to skip town. We ride out northwest from Big Wheel Bikes in Georgetown along the beautiful MacArthur Boulevard bike path beside the Potomac. Three-quarters of this route runs through Maryland countryside, where one mansion follows another. After the Glenstone Museum, we pass the Ridge, a historic home in Derwood, and beautiful Lake Needwood, before avoiding built-up Rockville and Bethesda by following the bends of Rock Creek. At mi 44 (km 70), the spires of the Mormon temple soar above the trees, before we reach the District and soon Georgetown.

WILMINGTON
FOLLOWING THE ARC

🌐 Hilly, Intermediate, 14% unpaved   🌐 Map strava.com/routes/2828647333247687832

 Distance **49 mi** (79 km)

 E+ **2,700 ft** (820 m)

 Difficulty **3/5**

 Appeal **3/5**

Delaware is a unique US state: it's the first (having ratified the Constitution in 1787); the second-smallest (after Rhode Island); and the only one whose border (with Pennsylvania, to the north) is not rectilinear, but a 12-mile (19-km) perfect arc. From Wilmington station (20 min to Philadelphia, 50 min to Baltimore), cycle back in time via New Castle and the banks of the Delaware River, then through affluent countryside to the 12-Mile Circle, rolling up and down gentle hills: Drummond, Cameron, and Centreville—the "summit" of this route, at 435 ft (132 m). Glide to Wilmington along Brandywine Creek and through Alapocas Run State Park.

LEWES
ROUTE 1

🌐 Fairly flat, Intermediate, 5% unpaved   🌐 Map strava.com/routes/2828617957712479800

 Distance **64 mi** (103 km)

 E+ **350 ft** (105 m)

 Difficulty **2/5**

 Appeal **4/5**

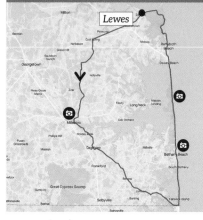

This seashore loop from Lewes starts at the mouth of Delaware Bay. Ride out along the Lewes-Georgetown Trail to Fenwick Island on the Maryland border, through countryside marked by first wetlands, then sand. Hit the ocean at mile 36 (km 58) and follow Route 1 for 28 miles (45 km), passing Bethany and Rehoboth Beaches, the lighthouse of Fenwick Island and Dewey Beach, and the Indian River estuary with its cable-stayed bridge—the Atlantic breeze blowing from the right. Finally, cut across Cape Henlopen (3 mi/4.75 km of gravel) with a view of the Harbor of Refuge Lighthouse at the tip of the impressive Delaware Breakwater.

Bethany Beach, jewel of Route 1, Delaware.

OAKLAND
TRY THE WALL!

⊕ *Low mountain, Expert, 0% unpaved*
⊕ *Map strava.com/routes/2834760884509808050*

⊕ *Test yourself mi 33 (km 53) strava.com/segments/4731398*
⊕ *Test yourself mi 42 (km 68) strava.com/segments/9996946*

◉ GREG'S EYE

I've seen the videos posted by triathletes at SavageMan in Swanton about their experience of Westernport Wall. Wow! Impressive. You can also forfeit the challenge and explore the fabulous far northwest of Maryland, so peaceful this far from the large coastal cities.

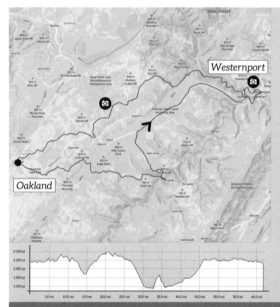

In westernmost Maryland, close to Pennsylvania and West Virginia, the cycling is pleasurable, as we traverse parts of the Allegheny Mountains, the Appalachian Plateau (up to 3,000 ft/915 m), and the valley of the North Branch Potomac River. The profile of this route is choppy: you're always trying to find your rhythm, even on the long climbs of 38 North (mi 15/km 24)—4.6 mi (7.5 km) at 5.1%—and 135 East (mi 40/km 64)—6 mi (10 km) at 6%. But Garrett County is so beautiful you dream of climbing all the way to Friendsville via Swallow Falls and Deep Creek Lake. You'll be itching to tackle the (optional) 5-mi (8-km) loop at the northeast corner of our route, which includes Westernport Wall. This monster climbs for 1.1 mi (1.75 km) at an average gradient of 12%, with one section at 29% where the cobbled section starts! You'd think you were in Pittsburgh. Ready?

 Distance
61 mi
(98 km)

 E+
7,000 ft
(2,135 m)

 Difficulty
4/5

 Appeal
4/5

Air: Pittsburgh International Airport, Greater Cumberland Regional Airport.
Car: 2h from Pittsburgh, 3h from Baltimore.

Leah and A.J. opened the *Tiny Corner Bike Shop* in 2020, and it's worth a visit. Retailer of Jamis Bicycles and a perfect knowledge of the region's cycling spots.

**103 Town Park Line
Oakland, MD 21550
thetinycornerbikeshop.com**

The former Oakland station, now a historic monument. The top of Westernport Wall, on Rock Street S-W (mi 34/km 55). Hazelhurst, on Deep Creek Lake (mi 50).

CUMBERLAND
THE GREAT ESCAPE

◉ *Low mountain, Advanced, 72% unpaved*   ◉ *Map strava.com/routes/2834494105574306580*

	Distance		E+		Difficulty		Appeal
⊢ ⊣	**70 mi** (113 km)	⬆	**5,200 ft** (1,585 m)	📊	**3/5**	⭐	**5/5**

Parallel to the Potomac River, the Chesapeake and Ohio Canal was once a key transportation route. More than 300 mi (480 km) of gravel trail have been laid on the former towpath between Pittsburgh and Washington, D.C. Setting out from bike shop–brewery Cumberland Trail Connection, there is a feeling of escape as you ride the 36-mi (58-km) stretch along the canal, past locks, over aqueducts, and through tunnels. Cycle home through the forested Potomac Highlands—six ramps of around 1 mi (1.5 km) at 7% to 10%, often on gravel. Stop in Paw Paw (mi 28/km 45) for a refuel. There are loads of campsites along the route if you fancy a two-day trip.

CAMBRIDGE
WILD PENINSULA

◉ *Fairly flat, Intermediate, 0% unpaved*   ◉ *Map strava.com/routes/2834424468084882992*

	Distance		E+		Difficulty		Appeal
⊢ ⊣	**74 mi** (119 km)	⬆	**200 ft** (61 m)	📊	**2/5**	⭐	**4/5**

The Delmarva Peninsula—the states of Delaware, Maryland, and Virginia share it—is famous for its vast ocean beaches. Better to opt for the perfect peace of the west side, and a route through woods, fields, ponds, and marshes. Blackwater National Refuge is a haven for migrating ducks, Canada geese, and bald eagles. You can ride for miles without meeting a soul. The immersion becomes magical toward the last of the Hooper Islands, between Chesapeake Bay and the Honga River. Then it's back to Cambridge, a historic town with a picturesque port (1h30 by car from Baltimore and Washington), via Harriet Tubman Underground Railroad State Park (mi 61/km 98).

BUTLER
BALTIMORE FANTASY

- ⊕ *Very hilly, Advanced, 15% unpaved*
- ⊕ *Map strava.com/routes/2834846459830073778*
- ⊕ *Test yourself mi 22 (km 35) strava.com/segments/17274066*
- ⊕ *Test yourself mi 41 (km 66) strava.com/segments/7487580*

👁 GREG'S EYE

I have lovely memories of Annapolis, not far south of Baltimore, where I won the Tour DuPont in 1992. The very hilly Piedmont (up to 800 ft/245 m) north of Baltimore also offers sublime scenery.

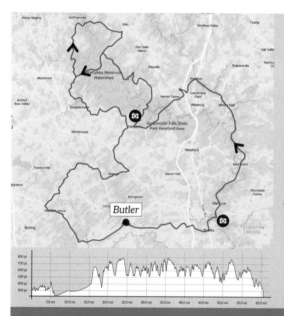

Veloccino Bike and Coffee is the ideal spot to start and finish this purely rural route to the north of Baltimore. Hard to believe that the Maryland city and seaport, with its Washington Monument, Museum of Art, and Fort McHenry, is so close when enjoying the stunning view from the Torrey C. Brown Trail (9 mi/14 km of gravel) alongside the surging Gunpowder Falls River. The asphalt recommences in Parkton, and the gradient soars (1 mi/1.5 km at 8%). A dozen similar ramps dot the route, as your thighs, lower back, and GPS will notice (6,300 ft/1,920 m of elevation). Wend your way for 23 mi (37 km) around serpentine Prettyboy Reservoir, starting at the dam and crossing it twice via Beckeysville Road. Then enjoy an invigorating coffee or refreshing beer back at Veloccino. The annual charity ride Bridges of Hope follows some of these lovely roads.

	Distance		E+		Difficulty		Appeal
⊢─┤	**61 mi** (98 km)	⬆	**6,300 ft** (1,920 m)	📊	**4/5**	★	**4/5**

Air: BWI Marshall Airport (45 min by car, I-695 W). Car: 30 min from Baltimore, 2h from Philadelphia.

In Butler Village's *Veloccino*, Marc has created the perfect bike and coffee concept. Retailer of Specialized, BMC, Wilier, Colnago, and Cinelli. Snacks and changing room.

**15007 Falls Road
Butler, MD 21023
veloccinocoffee.com**

Numerous panoramas over Gunpowder Falls (mi 6/km 10 to mi 15/km 24). Prettyboy Dam (mi 21/km 34) and other views over the lake.

THE SOUTH

VIRGINIA

—

WEST VIRGINIA

—

NORTH CAROLINA

—

SOUTH CAROLINA

—

GEORGIA

—

FLORIDA

—

ALABAMA

—

MISSISSIPPI

—

LOUISIANA

—

TEXAS

—

OKLAHOMA

—

ARKANSAS

CHARLOTTESVILLE
THE DEVIL'S CLIMB

- Low mountain, Expert, 0% unpaved
- Map strava.com/routes/2882207517751534510
- Test yourself mi 17 (km 27) strava.com/segments/9027868
- Test yourself mi 47 (km 76) strava.com/segments/638902

GREG'S EYE

Is it possible to find a challenge in the heavenly setting of the Blue Ridge Mountains? Indeed it is! The climb to Wintergreen Resort is not only the toughest in Virginia, but also one of the most demanding rides in the northeastern United States.

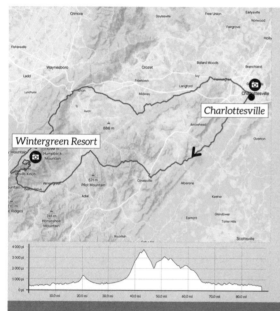

Cyclists who are expert climbers compare these slopes to one of the hardest challenges in the French Alps, the Col de Joux Plane—feared even by Tour de France champions! A 2h drive from Washington, D.C., Wintergreen Resort is Virginia's top ski resort and an ultimate challenge whose renown extends well beyond the Blue Ridge Mountains. From the east, Route 664 kicks up after Beech Grove (mi 35/km 56) into 5 mi (8 km) of hell, with an average gradient of 9% that shoots into double digits as you exit the perfect switchbacks. But the scenery is lush—fir trees line the road—with Devils Knob Loop a reward at the top. Having set off from Charlottesville, it makes for a long, difficult route if, after the summit, instead of turning around and heading back the way you came, you continue on the Blue Ridge Parkway for 14 mi (23 km) to Afton—but the views are sublime.

Distance
88 mi
(141 km)

E+
9,600 ft
(2,919 m)

Difficulty
5/5

Appeal
5/5

Air: Richmond International Airport (1h by car).
Car: 2h from Washington, D.C., 4h from Charlotte, 4h from Charleston.

Blue Wheel Bicycles is situated close to the train station and the University of Virginia. Retailer of Specialized and Jamis. Strava Club.

**941 2nd Street SE
Charlottesville, VA 22902
bluewheel.com**

Founders Vision (mi 42/km 68). Devils Knob (mi 43/km 69). Three Ridges (mi 48/km 77). Ravens Roost and Rock Point (mi 51/km 82). Shenandoah Valley (mi 59/km 95). Rockfish Gap (mi 62/km 100). Monticello Plantation of Thomas Jefferson (near mi 88/km 142).

LEXINGTON
MAGICAL FORESTS OF VIRGINIA

- 🌐 *Low mountain, Advanced, 71% gravel*
- 🌐 *Map strava.com/routes/2882257090551517590*
- ➕ *Test yourself mi 23 (km 37) strava.com/segments/20900578*
- ➕ *Test yourself mi 40 (km 64) strava.com/segments/18685143*

👁 **GREG'S EYE**

You feel like you're far from everything on the trails of George Washington and Jefferson National Forests, a paradise of tranquility. The gravel possibilities are endless. But with over 6,000 ft (1,800 m) of elevation gain in less than 60 mi (95 km), it sure does climb!

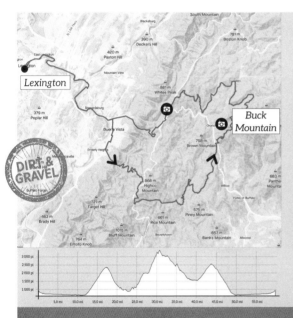

The 7,000 residents of Lexington—birthplace of violinist Hilary Hahn—are lucky to live where Virginia and West Virginia meet. Nearby George Washington and Jefferson National Forests are an environmental paradise in the sublime setting of the Blue Ridge Mountains: modest peaks (up to 5,300 ft/1,615 m), cliffs, waterfalls, and lakes amid 2,800 sq mi (7,250 sq km) of dense, deciduous forest where trails greatly outnumber surfaced roads. This route is just an example of the area's possibilities. Swapping Camp Road (1.6 mi/2.5 km at 8%), Buck Mountain (2.8 mi/4.5 km at over 8%), Jordan Street (4 mi/6.5 km at 5%), Robinson Gap (4.3 mi/7 km at close to 6%), are all mini gravel challenges that together rack up more than 6,000 ft (1,830 m) of elevation gain! The rewards are the superb panoramas from each summit. Bring sufficient supplies—you won't find any on the ride.

	Distance		E+		Difficulty		Appeal
⊢—⊣	**59 mi** (95 km)	⬆	**6,200 ft** (1,876 m)	📊	**4/5**	⭐	**4/5**

Air: Richmond International Airport (2h by car).
Car: 1h from Charlottesville, 3h from Charleston, 3h from Washington, D.C.

"Friendly and fun" is the philosophy of *Red Newt Bikes* in Lexington. Retailer of Surly, Salsa, and Giant.

**314 South Main Street
Lexington, VA 24450
rednewtbikes.com**

Blue Ridge Parkway (mi 17/km 27). Lynchburg Reservoir (mi 21/km 34)). Top of Buck Mountain (mi 30/km 48). Chimney Rock (mi 43/km 69). University Chapel (mi 58/km 93).

LEESBURG
D.C.'S WINE COUNTRY

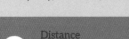

⊕ Very hilly, Advanced, 65% unpaved   ⊕ Map strava.com/routes/2882334500811496178

	Distance		E+		Difficulty		Appeal
⊢⊟⊣	**67 mi** (107 km)	⬆	**5,400 ft** (1,645 m)	▥	**3/5**	★	**5/5**

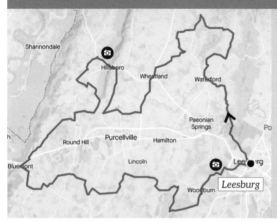

Leesburg (pop. 55,000) is situated just 40 mi (64 km) northwest of Washington, D.C. It's a charming town, surrounded by a magnificent landscape of forest and carefully tended fields. This hilly terrain is one huge playground for gravel lovers. As you ride, two local cultures will surely catch your eye: horse breeding (thousands of magnificent steeds) and winemaking. Having started from Plum Grove Cyclery, indulge in a tasting stop at Sunset Hills (mi 22/km 35), Hillsborough (mi 30/km 48), Bluemont (mi 44/km 71), or Dry Mill (mi 64/km 103), with wonderful vistas over the vineyards. No wonder they call the Leesburg's environs "D.C.'s wine country."

FRONT ROYAL
EXHILARATING SKYLINE DRIVE

⊕ Low mountain, Advanced, 0% unpaved   ⊕ Map strava.com/routes/2881958936946728554

	Distance		E+		Difficulty		Appeal
⊢⊟⊣	**63 mi** (101 km)	⬆	**5,900 ft** (1,793 m)	▥	**3/5**	★	**5/5**

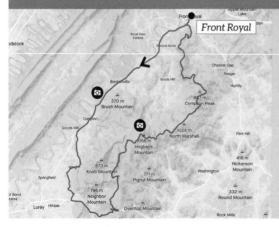

The perfect asphalt of Skyline Drive winds south from Front Royal (1h30 drive from Washington, D.C.) through Shenandoah National Park, jewel of the Blue Ridge Mountains, crossing summits and cols amid stunning scenery. The Skyline runs for 105 mi (169 km) to Waynesboro, with a total elevation gain of 11,000 ft (3,350 m)! This loop from the Virginia Beer Museum in Front Royal heads west along a fork of the Shenandoah River, joining Skyline Drive at mi 30 (km 48), before a stunning 20-mi (32-km) pedal at 2,500 ft to 5,300 ft (760 m to 1,615 m) over Hogback Mountain (3 mi/4.75 km at 6.5%) and Mount Marshall (2 mi/3.25 km at 5%). A taste of Virginia!

The rolling terrain of Skyline Drive in the heart of Shenandoah National Park, Virginia.

RICHMOND
PLAY IT LIKE SAGAN

🌐 Hilly, Intermediate, 0% unpaved   ⊕ Map strava.com/routes/2881982580281131950

	Distance		E+		Difficulty		Appeal
├──┤	**48 mi** (77 km)	⬆	**1,800 ft** (561 m)	📊	**3/5**	⭐	**4/5**

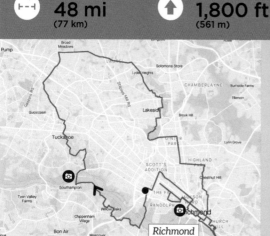

Richmond

Of all the cities to host the Road World Championships, Richmond, capital of Virginia, remains the most popular—not least because of charismatic Peter Sagan, who donned the rainbow jersey in 2015—as well as Zwift, the online cycling program, which features the 15-mi (24-km) Richmond course. If you've pedaled Richmond from your basement on your networked home trainer, come and ride the circuit for real one day! This route reproduces the course (which begins at mi 33/km 53) very closely. Richmond's pretty outskirts include Victorian Maymont, James River, Lewis Ginter Botanical Garden, and Bryan Park.

NORTON
HIGH KNOB, ARE YOU SERIOUS?

🌐 Low mountain, Expert, 0% unpaved   ⊕ Map strava.com/routes/2882331430230868722

	Distance		E+		Difficulty		Appeal
├──┤	**75 mi** (120 km)	⬆	**7,100 ft** (2,167 m)	📊	**4/5**	⭐	**4/5**

Norton

Black Mountain

Norton (pop. 4,000) in the Powell River valley is a few miles north of Tennessee. The western part of our route (starting from Hotel Norton) extends into Kentucky for over 30 mi (48 km). The peaks of the Blue Ridge Mountains (up to nearly 4,000 ft/1,220 m) rise on all sides here in far southwest Virginia. Two of their toughest ascents feature on our route. To complete the loop via the modest Fox and Flat Gaps and panoramic Pine Mountain Road, there's no escaping Black Mountain (5.5 mi/8.75 km at 6%). On the way into Norton, the hellish slopes of partially surfaced High Knob (3 mi/4.75 km at 10%) are optional.

ELKINS
MEMORABLE MONONGAHELA

⊕ *High mountain, Advanced, 78% unpaved*   ⊕ *Map strava.com/routes/2881143837791718258*

	Distance		E+		Difficulty		Appeal
↦	**67 mi** (107 km)	⬆	**8,200 ft** (2,484 m)	📊	**5/5**	⭐	**4/5**

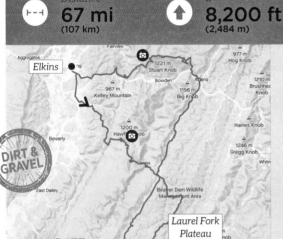

This unforgettable gravel adventure on the trails of the Monongahela National Forest (1,400 sq mi/3,625 sq km) in West Virginia starts from Joey's Bike Shop in Elkins, north of Cheat Mountain. At Glady (mi 18/km 29), you can choose to ignore the southern loop, shaving off 20 mi (32 km). But that would be a shame, because the Laurel Fork plateau is stunning and you'd only miss a few ramps. The day's first two climbs—Ellis Ridge (2.5 mi/4 km at 7%) and Bernis Road (2.2 mi/3.5 km at 9%)—feel mountainous. The views over the stretches of upland pines are divine. Cap it off with the Bickle Knob observation tower at 4,000 ft/1,220 m (mi 56/km 90).

MARLINTON
UP IN THE HIGHLANDS

⊕ *High mountain, Expert, 0% unpaved*   ⊕ *Map strava.com/routes/2880862881267592368*

	Distance		E+		Difficulty		Appeal
↦	**82 mi** (132 km)	⬆	**9,100 ft** (2,776 m)	📊	**5/5**	⭐	**5/5**

You'd never imagine such wild nature barely a 4h drive west of Washington, D.C. The Allegheny Highlands in West Virginia are the most remote massif in the Appalachians. Our route (starting from Dirtbean bike café in Marlinton) includes a 22-mi (35-km) stretch of the Highland Scenic Highway. You'll dig deep on the Black Mountain and Williams River climbs (6 mi/9.75 km and 4 mi/6.5 km, respectively, at close to 6%), and even deeper on the ascent to Thorny Flat (the highest peak in the Highlands, at 4,848 ft/ 1,478 m) and Snowshoe ski resort: 6 mi (9.75 km) at 5%. If your tires are decent, take the Greenbrier River Trail for the final 20 mi (32 km).

HOT SPRINGS
HOT GRAVEL

DIRT & GRAVEL

- Low mountain, Expert, 85% unpaved
- Map strava.com/routes/2883097074890172334
- Test yourself mi 39 (63 km) strava.com/segments/6924559
- Test yourself mi 52 (km 84) strava.com/segments/14149077

GREG'S EYE

There are few mountains in the east that can offer 60 mi (97 km) of pure gravel as demanding as this loop out from the little paradise of Hot Springs. In the second part you can reach the banks of the French Broad River at any moment, which is reassuring.

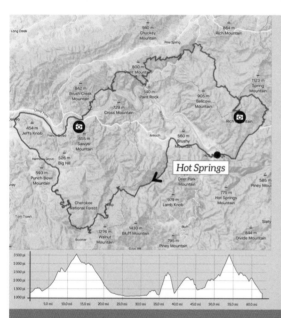

Hot Springs

The village of Hot Springs is a North Carolinian paradise! We're close to Pisgah National Forest, the iconic Appalachian Trail, rivers, and hot springs, all amid the scenery of the Bald Mountains. Looking for a true challenge in North Carolina? Try this off-road route with bulked-up climbs that racks up more than 9,000 ft (2,745 m) of ascent! Barely 12 mi (19 km) from the start, you'll have climbed to 3,600 ft (1,095 m) over Locust and Rattlesnake Gaps. Two-thirds of the route passes through Tennessee. The gradients get crazy on the north bank of the French Broad River: Paint Mountain (2 mi/3.25 km at 12%), Lower Paint Mountain (3 mi/4.75 km at 6%), Hurricane Gap (6 mi/9.75 km at 6.5%, the last one at 12%), Rich Mountain (1.3 mi/2 km at 12%!). Whatever your choice of climbs (all or none), the motivation is a long soak in the natural warm mineral waters.

 Distance
63 mi
(101 km)

 E+
9,300 ft
(2,831 m)

 Difficulty
5/5

 Appeal
5/5

Air: Charlotte Douglas International Airport (3h by car).
Car: 50 min from Asheville, 1h30 from Knoxville, 3h from Chattanooga, 4h30 from Raleigh.

Beer City Bicycles in Woodfin, north of Asheville, can suggest rides throughout the area. Retailer of Cervelo, Orbea, and Felt. Strava Club.

**897 Riverside Drive
Woodfin, NC 28804
beercitybicycles.com**

Wolf Creek Bridge (mi 31/km 50). Atop Rich Mountain Tower (mi 54/km 87). Appalachian Trail sign (mi 55/km 89). French Broad River (mi 62/km 100).

ASHEVILLE
THE SCENIC CENTURY

- 🌐 High mountain, Expert, 0% unpaved
- 🌐 Map strava.com/routes/2883301687241593510

- ➕ Test yourself mi 23 (km 37) strava.com/segments/790025
- ➕ Test yourself mi 72 (km 116) strava.com/segments/6781572

👁 GREG'S EYE

**Charge your smartphone! This will be a long day, and you'll take dozens of photos.
The Blue Ridge Parkway was conceived to be a feast for the eyes. Beware of its difficulty though:
the total elevation gain is the equivalent of a Tour de France mountain stage!**

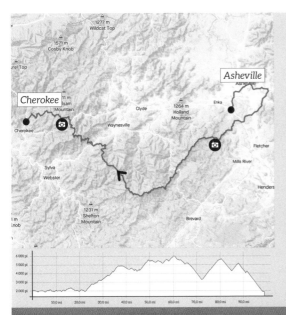

In western North Carolina, 90 mi (145 km) separate Asheville from Cherokee—the final section of the extraordinary 469-mi (755-km) Blue Ridge Parkway. This full day on the bike mixes athletic challenge and contemplative pleasure. At each summit the panoramas surprise and delight, despite the rising fatigue. The 14 mi (23 km) of Buck Spring Gap (average gradient of 4%, with sections at 8%) arrive fast: it's so beautiful that it's a popular site for outdoor weddings! Three more long ascents to come: Lickstone Ridge (3 mi/4.75 km at 6%), Silvermine Bald (4 mi/6.5 km at 6%), and the iconic Waterrock Knob (7.5 mi/12 km at 6%). With stars in your eyes, you'll reminisce about the whole fantastic day on the terrace of Sassy Sunflowers Bakery and Cafe, on the edge of Cherokee. You may have come down from the mountain, but not yet from this wonderful waking dream.

	Distance		E+		Difficulty		Appeal
	**99 mi** (159 km)		**11,900 ft** (3,617 m)		**5/5**		**5/5**

Air: Charlotte Douglas International Airport (2h by car).
Car: 1h from Cherokee, 2h from Knoxville, 3h30 from Atlanta, 7h from Washington, D.C.

Motion Makers in south Asheville, 2 mi (3.25 km) from the Parkway, is a Specialized Elite Store. Retailer of Surly too. Strava Club.

**878 Brevard Road
Asheville, NC 28806
motionmakers.com**

Bad Fork Valley (mi 29/km 47). Mills River Valley (mi 33/km 53). Buck Spring Gap Overlook (mi 37/km 60). Yellowstone Falls (mi 45/km 72). Devil's Courthouse (mi 49/km 79). Smoky Mountains view from Watterrock Knob (mi 80/km 129). Lickstone Ridge Overlook (mi 87/140 km).

ROBBINSVILLE
UNICOI BEAUTY ... AND PAIN

⊕ *High mountain, Advanced, 0% unpaved*   ⊕ *Map strava.com/routes/2883089275154324398*

	Distance		E+		Difficulty		Appeal
⊢━⊣	**62 mi** (100 km)	⬆	**7,700 ft** (2,346 m)	📊	**4/5**	★	**5/5**

A spectacular road snakes through remote Nantahala National Forest in northwest North Carolina to the border with Tennessee. Cherohala Skyway is fascinatingly beautiful, especially in the fall. But owing to its difficulty, this major climb in the Unicoi Mountains easily stands comparison with the principal Alpine cols in Europe. Three ramps soar above Lake Santeetlah, with only short stretches of respite: 2 mi (3.25 km) at 5% to reach the Skyway, 3 mi (4.75 km) at 7% along Cedar Top, and 6.5 mi (10.5 km) at 6% up to Hooper Point (altitude: 5,300 ft/1,615 m). For fun, we roll onto Beech Gap and the State Line, before the run back to Robbinsville (pop. 700).

MARION
TOP OF THE EAST

⊕ *High mountain, Expert, 0% unpaved*   ⊕ *Map strava.com/routes/2882998587459110294*

	Distance		E+		Difficulty		Appeal
⊢━⊣	**65 mi** (104 km)	⬆	**7,600 ft** (2,327 m)	📊	**5/5**	★	**5/5**

Mount Mitchell (6,684 ft/2,037 m at its peak), 100 mi (161 km) northwest of Charlotte, is the champion not just of the Great Smoky Mountains National Park, but all the Appalachians. The ascent (from Marion city hall) of the highest mountain east of the Mississippi is a challenge. It climbs gently for nearly 20 mi (32 km) up to Buck Creek Trout Farm, before 4 mi (6.5 km) at 7%. Curtis Valley (magnificent view) provides a short recovery time before Green Knob (5 mi/8 km at 6%), then Mount Mitchell: an 8-mi (13-km) ramp, the final 2 mi (3.25 km) of which are at 8%. After 0.25 mi (0.5 km) on foot, you'll have the pleasure of a fantastic panorama.

LAKE JAMES
EASTERN GRAND CANYON

⊕ *Low mountain, Advanced, 85% unpaved*   ⊕ *Map strava.com/routes/2883425507112532910*

	Distance		E+		Difficulty		Appeal
	61 mi (99 km)		**7,600 ft** (2,331 m)		**4/5**		**5/5**

In Pisgah National Forest, 80 mi (129 km) northwest of Charlotte, the Linville River has plowed steep-sided Linville Gorge (up to 2,000 ft/610 m), the most spectacular vertical phenomenon east of the Mississippi. Our gravel route (starting from Fonta Flora Brewery) hugs the contours of this mini–Grand Canyon with vertiginous views. There are a half dozen off-road climbs 2 to 4 mi (3.25 to 6.5 km) long, at average gradients of 6–8%. Table Rock (mi 27/km 43), the most hair-raising of promontories, can be reached after 8 mi (13 km) at over 7%! Linville Falls (mi 43/km 69) and Wiseman's View (mi 48/km 77) are more accessible and just as sublime.

CHARLOTTE
QUEEN CITY, NIGHT AND DAY

⊕ *Flat, Intermediate, 5% unpaved*   ⊕ *Map strava.com/routes/2883367824944425638*

	Distance		E+		Difficulty		Appeal
	48 mi (78 km)		**1,400 ft** (432 m)		**2/5**		**3/5**

With its glittering uptown towers, Charlotte (pop. 860,000), the largest city in North Carolina, isn't the bike friendliest of places. But a ride south (starting from the Spoke Easy bike café) is quite pleasant, as we follow the tranquil Little Sugar Creek Greenway along the river through several parks: Freedom Park and Huntingtowne Farms. Next, we cycle past the splendid residences of Weddington, Providence Woods, Olde Heritage, and the historic center of Matthews. Spend the evening amid the lights of uptown, around Spectrum Center (home of the Hornets) and the NASCAR Hall of Fame. Charlotte, the Queen City, is magnificent by night.

GREENVILLE
CLIMB TO PARIS ... MOUNTAIN

- ⊕ Low mountain, Advanced, 0% unpaved
- ⊕ Map strava.com/routes/2881629712950117994
- ◉ Test yourself mi 24 (km 39) strava.com/segments/12302526
- ◉ Test yourself mi 44 (km 71) strava.com/segments/522982

👁 GREG'S EYE

The cyclists of the small city of Greenville are fortunate to have such a fine ascent as Paris Mountain just a few pedal turns away. I love the name, even if it has nothing to do with my wonderful memories of the Champs-Élysées.

Paris Mountain

Greenville

Let's clear up something: Paris Mountain owes its name to Richard Pearis, the first colonist to make a pact with the Cherokees, whose territory contained this 2,000-ft (610-m) high monadnock. A recreational site, it overlooks Greenville (pop. 75,000), offering the cyclists of South Carolina one choice workout: 2.2 mi (3.5 km) at 7%. Perfect asphalt slices through a landscape of Virginia pines, holly, and strawberry trees, with splendid views from the summit. On the way there, we ride the Swamp Rabbit Trail for 10 mi (16 km) toward the Blue Ridge Mountains. Halfway through, on Hightower Mountain (1.2 mi/2 km at 6%), you can feel in your thighs that you're nearly there. Back in Greenville, continue 1 mi (1.5 km) south of Velo Valets for the cascades of Falls Park on the Reedy and a beer at Thomas Creek, the city's oldest brewery.

	Distance		E+		Difficulty		Appeal
	55 mi (89 km)		**4,100 ft** (1,240 m)		**3/5**		**4/5**

Air: Charlotte Douglas International Airport (2h by car), Columbia Metropolitan Airport (2h by car), Hartsfield-Jackson Atlanta International Airport (3h by car). Car: 4h from Charleston, 6h from Nashville.

Velo Valets. Retailer of Moots, Masi, and Fuji.

2901 Old Buncombe Road Greenville, SC 29609 velovalets.com

Swamp Rabbit Trail bridge over the Reedy River (mi 2/ km 3). Furman University Bell Tower, on the lake (mi 6/ km 10). Mountain Park Golf (mi 21/km 34). Summit of Paris Mountain, North Lake, and Fire Tower (mi 46/km 74).

MONCKS CORNER
CHARLESTON SWAMPS

DIRT & GRAVEL

- *Flat, Intermediate, 70% unpaved*
- *Map strava.com/routes/2881553137101465100*
- *Test yourself mi 8 (km 13) strava.com/segments/24963909*
- *Test yourself mi 44 (km 71) strava.com/segments/26062100*

◉ GREG'S EYE

An exploration of Francis Marion National Forest is as exciting by canoe as it is on gravel. For that reason, check for rising waters around Charleston before heading out. It's also a fabulous spot for fishing—my other passion!

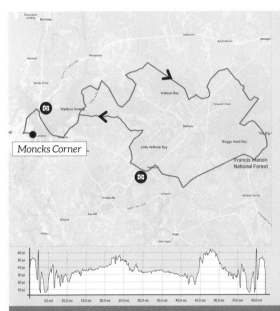

Moncks Corner

Between Cooper River—subject to tides—and the wetlands of Francis Marion National Forest, this adventure near the South Carolina coast requires keeping an eye on the weather. The gravel trails through 400 sq mi (1,035 sq km) of protected conifers are magical—when it's dry. Once you reach Wadboo Swamp (mi 8/km 13), rising waters can catch you off guard. Not for nothing is this a popular area for canoeing. With bald cypresses sticking out of the water, it's like a jungle in places! The Big Opening and Little Hellhole Bay are fickle, too. Alligator Road (mi 46/km 74) suggests the kind of encounters that abound here, as does Mepkin Abbey (Trappist monks). The low country is full of surprises. In Moncks Corner (we start from Old Santee Canal Park, commemorating the first canal to be dug in the United States), visit the historic neighborhood and the Pinopolis district.

	Distance		E+		Difficulty		Appeal
⊢–⊣	**62 mi** (100 km)	⬆	**500 ft** (150 m)	⬛	**2/5**	★	**4/5**

Air: Charleston International Airport (40 min by car). Car: 2h from Columbia, 4h from Charlotte, 5h from Atlanta.

The Bicycle Shoppe (additional outlets in Charleston, Mount Pleasant, and West Ashley), 20 mi (32 km) southwest of Moncks Corner. Retailer of Specialized.

600 Front Street Summerville, SC 29486 thebicycleshoppe.com

Biggin Church (mi 3/km 5 and mi 59/km 95). Mepkin Abbey (mi 4/km 6 and mi 58/km 93). Little Hellhole Bay and Swamp Fox Trail (mi 46/km 74)—"Swamp Fox" was the nickname of Francis Marion, hero of the Revolutionary War, and you can still spot swamp foxes in these parts.

HELEN
GEORGIA IN MY LEGS

- Low mountain, Expert, 0% unpaved
- Map strava.com/routes/2880181844434801760
- Test yourself mi 16 (km 26) strava.com/segments/614827
- Test yourself mi 33 (km 53) strava.com/segments/825969

👁 GREG'S EYE

I discovered Brasstown Bald in the 2000s, during the Tour de Georgia. It's one of the most spectacular and difficult ascents in the eastern United States—each rider's legs still remember it. And the Blue Ridge Mountains are more beautiful in Georgia than anywhere else.

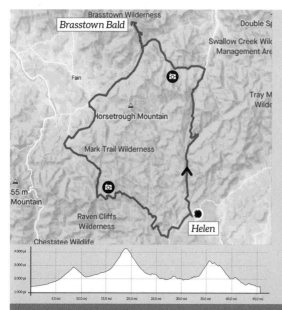

Amid the scenery of the Blue Ridge Mountains, beware the beguiling bright colors of Bavarian-inspired Helen and the splendors of vast Chattahoochee National Forest. By bike, the winding roads are quite a challenge. On this route, Unicoi Gap (7 mi/11.25 km at 4%, with the final 2.6 mi/4.25 km at 6.5%) is a mere warm-up. The ascent of Brasstown Bald—Georgia's highest point—is something else entirely: 2.5 mi (4 km) at an average gradient of close to 11%, with one 200-yard (180-m) passage (The Wall) at 21% halfway up a climb, and the final 0.5 mi (0.75 km) at 14%! On a clear day, you can see four states from the observation deck. On the homeward leg, Hogpen Gap West (2.2 mi/3.5 km at close to 11%) drains any remaining energy. Refuel at Hofer's Bakery and Café in Helen. In springtime, you can enter the TT1 Tour de Georgia Gran Fondo to ride this challenge in a peloton.

Distance **45 mi** (73 km)	E+ **6,600 ft** (2,018 m)	Difficulty **4/5**	Appeal **5/5**

Air: Hartsfield-Jackson Atlanta International Airport (1h30 by car). Car: 1h15 from Athens, 4h from Charlotte, 5h from Nashville.

Woody's Mountain Bikes neither sells nor rents road bikes, but is (by appointment) the only specialized workshop for miles around.

457 Highway 356 Helen, GA 30545 woodysmtb.net

Gurley Creek Falls (mi 13/km 21). Circular road around the Brasstown Bald observation deck (mi 18/km 29 to mi 19/km 31). Summit of Hogpen Gap (mi 35/km 56). Dodd Creek Vista (mi 36/km 58).

DIRT & GRAVEL

BLAIRSVILLE
GIANTS AND GOLD

Low mountain, Expert, 60% unpaved · *Map strava.com/routes/2880433093880345776*

Distance **74 mi** (119 km) · E+ **8,400 ft** (2,556 m) · Difficulty **4/5** · Appeal **5/5**

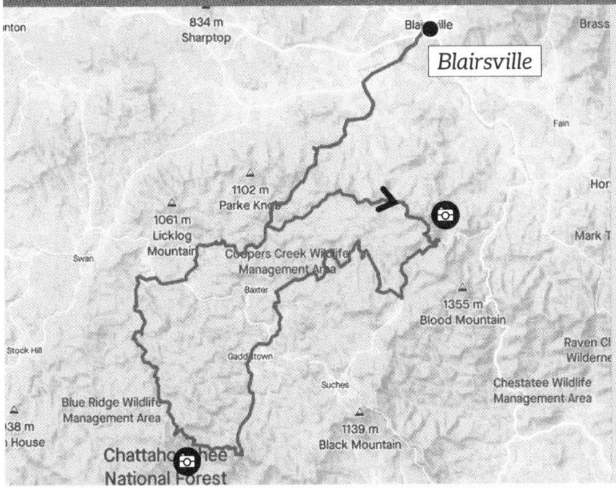

The Valley of the Giants is a gravel event through the lush Chattahoochee National Forest on lesser-known trails. Grinder lovers will be spoiled by this 74-mi (119-km) route (starting from Bikes and Hikes in Blairsville) inspired by the course, with plenty of blissful torment in store (8,400 ft/2,560 m of E+). We climb through the thickly forested valleys of the Blue Ridge Mountains. At Wildcat Gap (3,800 ft/1,160 m), mi 20 (km 32), we're close to the Coosa mines, where the purest gold in the eastern United States was once extracted. At mi 33 (km 53), we emerge into the Valley of the Giants—home to tulip poplars and red oaks 20 ft (6 m) in circumference!

ATHENS
YOU'LL NEVER RIDE ALONE

Hilly, Intermediate, 0% unpaved · *Map strava.com/routes/2880605861815732400*

Distance **62 mi** (99 km) · E+ **3,400 ft** (1,045 m) · Difficulty **3/5** · Appeal **4/5**

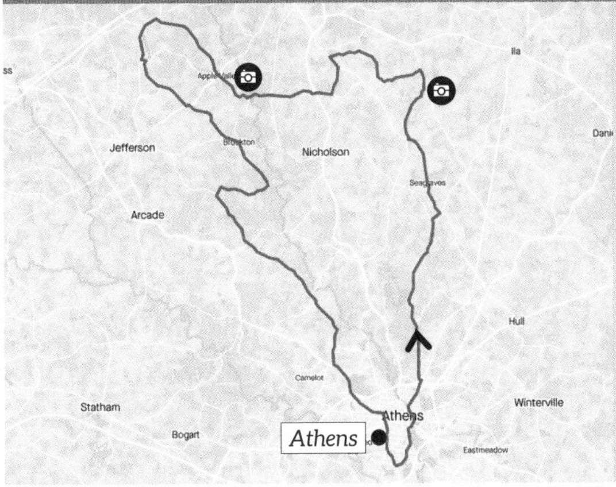

Athens (70 mi/113 km northeast of Atlanta) is home to the University of Georgia and as celebrated for rock bands (R.E.M. and the B-52s) as for cycling. They say it's easy to make friends in Athens, so you'll never ride alone! Starting from Georgia Cycle Sport, we leave the city via Cherokee Forest and then Nowhere Road (to avoid the towns of Commerce, Nicholson, and Jefferson), riding on rolling backroads, with a few aggressive ramps thrown in. Nothing characterizes the rural charm of this route more than the splendid 5-mi (8-km) ascending false flat of Apple Valley Road (mi 30/km 48). Refuel at Heirloom Café in Normaltown.

ATLANTA
FACE-TO-FACE WITH HISTORY

⊕ Hilly, Intermediate, 0% unpaved ⊕ Map strava.com/routes/2880485284986550708

	Distance		E+		Difficulty		Appeal
	48 mi (78 km)		**3,300 ft** (1,011 m)		**3/5**		**4/5**

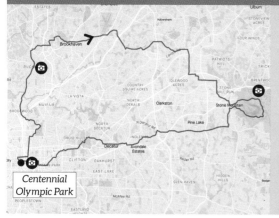

Centennial Olympic Park

Home of Coca-Cola and site of the 1996 Olympics, Atlanta (pop. 6 million across its metro area) is fast becoming very bike friendly. Our route heads east to Stone Mountain, a large dome monadnock with a prominence of 800 ft (245 m), bearing on its north face the largest bas-relief sculpture in the world (200 ft by 100 ft/60 m by 30 m), featuring (controversially) three Confederate leaders. On the way to our 5-mi (8-km) loop around the mountain, we pass Buckhead—scene of the 1996 Olympics road cycling events. The homeward leg takes in Fernbank Forest, Freedom Park Trail, and the birthplace of Martin Luther King, Jr. (mi 47/km 76).

COVINGTON
ATLANTA MONADNOCK

⊕ Very hilly, Advanced, 0% unpaved ⊕ Map strava.com/routes/2880816066399801848

	Distance		E+		Difficulty		Appeal
	62 mi (99 km)		**4,400 ft** (1,326 m)		**3/5**		**4/5**

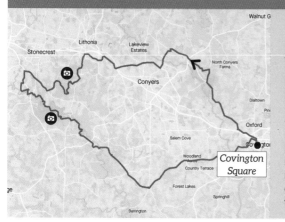

Covington Square

Arabia Mountain and Panola Mountain form a fascinating geological site called a monadnock, just 35 mi (56 km) outside Atlanta. The expanse of denuded granite is tinged pink, with nothing but a few mountain flowers and clusters of berries. Two superb asphalt paths (Arabia Mountain and Rockdale River) cross this vast area of forests, wetlands, and ruins, passing the magnificent Monastery of the Holy Spirit (mi 45/km 72). The road often kicks up, but never for more than 1 mi (1.5 km) or steeper than 3–5%. Our route starts in Covington, dubbed the "Hollywood of the South" for its beautiful period buildings featured in dozens of movies and TV series.

JULIETTE
LIKE A MOVIE

- ⊕ Very hilly, Intermediate, 80% unpaved
- ⊕ Map strava.com/routes/2880519357486459056
- ⊕ Test yourself mi 14 (km 23) strava.com/segments/28646274
- ⊕ Test yourself mi 37 (km 60) strava.com/segments/4882113

👁 GREG'S EYE

Decades after its box-office success, the atmosphere of the movie *Fried Green Tomatoes* can still be found here, in the heart of the Georgian Piedmont, 60 mi (97 km) south of Atlanta: an infinite gravel playground that's simply a joy.

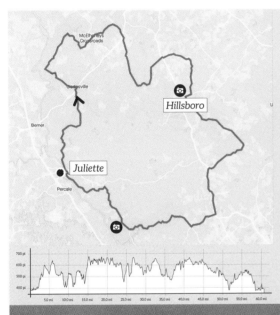

Every February 14, Juliette, Georgia, celebrates Valentine's Day with Romeo, Michigan. They have no shortage of ideas here: after the success of the movie *Fried Green Tomatoes*, a real Whistle Stop Cafe (our starting point) was opened.

East of the river, Otis Redding's ranch and the Jarrell Plantation are still popular with visitors, but there are more and more cyclists sporting fat, knobby tires. The Piedmont National Wildlife Refuge, the heart of central Georgia, is a blessed gravel playground, as bumpy as you could wish, devoid of technical difficulties on its clay soil. You willingly lose yourself in the thick, 35,000-acre forest of loblolly pines and beaver ponds, where you can spy lynxes, silver foxes, and dozens of protected birds. Back in Juliette, sample some fried green tomatoes.

Distance	E+	Difficulty	Appeal
61 mi (98 km)	**4,200 ft** (1,274 m)	**3/5**	**4/5**

Air: Middle Georgia Regional Airport, Macon (40 min by car), Hartsfield-Jackson Atlanta International Airport (1h by car). Car: 3h from Birmingham, 4h from Jacksonville, 4h30 from Charleston.

Bike Tech is the go-to place in Macon, 20 mi (32 km) south of Juliette. Housed in a pretty brick building, it offers impeccable service. Retailer of Specialized, Cannondale, and Jamis.

**909 2nd Street
Macon, GA 31201
biketechmacon.com**

Hillsboro Baptist Church (mi 32/km 51). Otis Redding's Big "O" Ranch (mi 43/km 69), the residence of the rhythm and blues star. Jarrell Plantation State Historic Site (mi 53/km 85). Juliette Park and Juliette Dam on the Ocmulgee River (mi 61/km 98), and the Whistle Stop Cafe.

MIAMI
MIAMI DREAM

- ⊕ Flat, Intermediate, 2% unpaved
- ⊕ Map strava.com/routes/2879105983459426354
- ⊕ Test yourself mi 13 (km 21) strava.com/segments/16700552
- ⊕ Test yourself mi 32 (km 51) strava.com/segments/11763328

◉ GREG'S EYE

Miami is the tourist destination. Exploring it by bike is an amazing experience if you follow this route to the tip of Key Biscayne, then back to the famed beaches of the Atlantic Ocean, and then through the city's most picturesque neighborhoods.

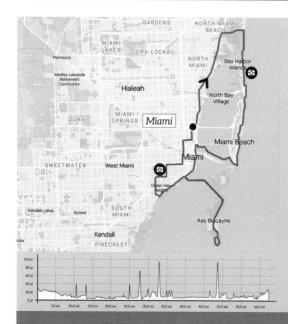

This oceanside route is Miami as you've dreamed it. The miles of bike lanes can be pedaled fast, but with so much to see, what's the point in that? Enjoy it! Why not make two loops of 30 mi (48 km) each? From the Design District and the skyscrapers of Biscayne Bay, we pedal north for 9 mi (14 km), past the Keystone Islands, as far as Oleta River State Park, where we reach the ocean just above Haulover Beach—a nudist hotspot. Bal Harbour and Surfside herald the barrier island of Miami Beach and 10 mi (16 km) of picture postcard: sand, blue horizons, palm trees, and the Art Deco buildings of Ocean Drive. Return to the mainland via MacArthur Causeway, before Rickenbacker Causeway and two more paradise islands: historic Virginia Key, and Key Biscayne. Pass Coconut Grove and Little Havana on the way back. Visit Monty's Raw Bar (mi 52/km 84) for tasty conch fritters.

Distance	E+	Difficulty	Appeal
62 mi (100 km)	**600 ft** (178 m)	**2/5**	**5/5**

 Air: Miami International Airport (20 min by car). Car: 4h from Orlando, 5h30 from Jacksonville, 10h from Atlanta.

 The elegant *Rapha CC* clubhouse is located in the Design District, opposite Miami Beach, and is accessible via the Julia Tuttle Causeway. Events all year round.

3802 North East 1st Avenue Miami, FL 33137 rapha.cc

 Full Moon Beach (mi 15/km 24). FTX Arena (mi 29/km 47) where the Heat basketball team play, and by the giant banyan tree on Bayside Marketplace. Cape Florida Lighthouse (mi 42/km 68). Vizcaya (mi 51/km 82). Calle Ocho, Little Havana (mi 56/km 90).

FERNANDINA BEACH
SALT MARSHES, AND DUNES

⊕ Flat, Intermediate, 0% unpaved   ⊕ Map strava.com/routes/2879777136172197984

	Distance		E+		Difficulty		Appeal
⊢–⊣	**64 mi** (103 km)	⬆	**500 ft** (161 m)	📊	**2/5**	★	**4/5**

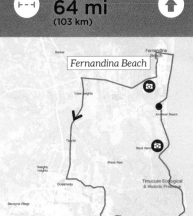

Fernandina Beach

Jacksonville (pop. 1.6 million in the metro area) may be known for economic energy, but the area is not without cycling charms, particularly the First Coast with its islands. Our route from SuperCorsa Cycles in Fernandina Beach runs beside the Atlantic for 21 mi (34 km)—two-thirds of that in the final section following an 11-mi (18-km) stretch along the Saint Johns River. From south to north, it's an enchanting world of salt marshes, dunes, and magnificent beaches. Snap a selfie at the foot of NaNa Dune (mi 63/km 101), the highest on the Florida coast, at 60 ft (20 m). Come here in spring to catch the joyous Isle of Eight Flags Shrimp Festival.

MIAMI
KEYS ADVENTURE

⊕ Flat, Advanced, 0% unpaved   ⊕ Map strava.com/routes/2879418044169767822

	Distance		E+		Difficulty		Appeal
⊢–⊣	**151 mi** (243 km)	⬆	**800 ft** (231 m)	📊	**3/5**	★	**5/5**

Miami

Key West

This 151-mi (243-km) ride (starting from Elite Cycling & Fitness in Miami) is a thrilling adventure: cycling for hours across the Keys in a tropical trance, the ocean to your left and the Gulf of Mexico to your right, not needing to turn on your GPS or constantly change gears. Key Largo (mi 30/km 48) is the first of 34 islands and 42 bridges (including Seven Mile, at mi 103/km 166), with 80 mi (129 km) of bike lanes. Dolphins and turtles frolic in the translucent water. We finish at Key West—Hemingway's stomping grounds—the southernmost point in the United States, 90 mi (145 km) north of Cuba. How about renting a little yacht to sail back to Miami?

The extraordinary Seven Mile Bridge, Florida Keys, Florida.

TAMPA
BRIDGES ON THE BAY

⊕ *Flat, Intermediate, 0% unpaved*
⊕ *Map strava.com/routes/2879036052679980942*

⊙ *Test yourself mi 26 (km 42) strava.com/segments/8805410*
⊙ *Test yourself mi 49 (km 79) strava.com/segments/21101941*

◎ GREG'S EYE

It's as exhilarating to pedal beside the Gulf of Mexico for more than 20 mi (32 km) as it is to cross the two bridges spanning Old Tampa Bay to reach St. Petersburg and Clearwater. A madly maritime adventure in the city where football superstar Tom Brady brought glory.

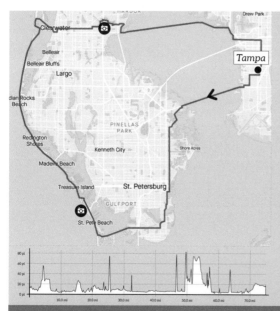

If you're the type to grow bored with the horizon of the Gulf of Mexico, the miles of beaches of St. Petersburg and Clearwater, and finding yourself 50 ft (15 m) above Old Tampa Bay on an 8-mi (13-km) bridge, don't ride this route. But it would be a pity not to if staying in Tampa (pop. 3 million across the metro area). True, 75 mi (121 km) isn't a breeze, but the asphalt is smooth as silk, while the pleasant environment is enhanced by the light from the bay and the open sea. You could count the lagoons, marinas, expanses of white sand, and nature preserves, or else tally the bridges to be sprinted across: fourteen in all. Pride of place goes to Gandy Bridge (3 mi/4.5 km)—crossed first—and Courtney Campbell Causeway (10 mi/16 km), which have separate bike lanes. At mi 25 (km 40), you can detour to the nature preserve of Fort De Soto—10 mi (16 km) there and back.

	Distance		E+		Difficulty		Appeal
⊢━┤	**75 mi** (120 km)	⬆	**700 ft** (213 m)	📊	**2/5**	★	**4/5**

Air: Tampa International Airport (30 min by car), St. Pete-Clearwater International Airport (30 min by car). Car: 3h20 from Jacksonville, 4h from Miami, 6h30 from Atlanta.

Outspokin Bicycles has outlets in Virginia Park (South Tampa) and Clearwater. Retailer of Specialized, Giant, and Liv. Very active Strava Club.

3300 South Dale Mabry Highway Tampa, FL 33629 outspokin.net

Gandy Bridge (mi 6/km 10). St. Pete Pier (mi 16/km 26). Boyd Hill Nature Preserve (mi 20/km 32). On the sand between St. Pete Beach (mi 29/km 47) and Clearwater Beach (mi 48/km 77). Cliff Stephens Park (mi 56/km 90).

DADE CITY
ORLANDO WETLANDS

🌐 *Flat, Intermediate, 90% unpaved*   🌐 *Map strava.com/routes/2879689961579714656*

	Distance		E+		Difficulty		Appeal
⊢–⊣	**64 mi** (102 km)	⬆	**300 ft** (89 m)	📊	**3/5**	⭐	**4/5**

Between Tampa, in the southwest, and the amusement parks of Orlando, Dade City (pop. 6,500) enjoys a prime position on the edge of Green Swamp, a 560,000-acre area of wetlands, cypress ponds, sandhills, pine forests, and oak hammocks that looks like nothing else in southwest Florida. Its endless miles of trails provide a multiplicity of gravel routes. Ours starts from Fat Rick's Bicycle Emporium and heads north, a little off the popular Florida National Scenic Trail, to Withlacoochee State Forest, home to wild boar and Virginia deer. Next comes the Green Swamp, whose ecosystem makes it the largest reserve of fresh water in Florida.

MILTON
PANHANDLE FOREST

🌐 *Hilly, Advanced, 52% unpaved*   🌐 *Map strava.com/routes/2880124389268290656*

	Distance		E+		Difficulty		Appeal
⊢–⊣	**76 mi** (122 km)	⬆	**2,200 ft** (682 m)	📊	**3/5**	⭐	**4/5**

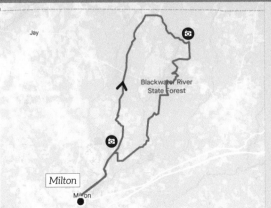

Milton (pop. 10,000), 20 mi (32 km) northeast of Pensacola, turns its back on the sandspits of the nearby Gulf of Mexico to invite you north into the Blackwater River Forest—the gravel spot in the Panhandle. Time has molded the red clay into hills up to 300 ft (90 m) high, an incongruous altitude in Florida. In the damp forest, longleaf pine, white cypress, turkey oak, and magnolia grow, and there are carnivorous plants thriving at either side of the trails on our route after Spring Hill (mi 13/km 21). We start from Truly Spokin and ride the Blackwater Heritage Trail. The relief ramps up between Three Notch Road and Bear Lake Trail.

FAIRHOPE
TURTLES AND CRAB CLAWS

⊕ *Flat, Advanced, 2% unpaved* ⊕ *Map strava.com/routes/2878727439303825116*

 **Distance**
130 mi
(209 km)

 E+
2,400 ft
(722 m)

 Difficulty
3/5

 Appeal
5/5

In Europe, you're considered on another level if you manage 125 miles (200 km) in one day. Here's a similar challenge: a 130-mi (209-km) full tour of Mobile Bay on the Gulf of Mexico. Fear not: the route is virtually flat and the views over the water are fantastic. From Pro Cycle and Tri in Fairhope, we reach the old neighborhoods of Mobile via a causeway. Then it's south to Dauphin Island, crossing by bridge, before the ferry (4 mi/6.5 km) to Fort Morgan—a historic site and gateway to a biosphere that's a protected area for the red-bellied turtle. At mi 102 (km 164), reward yourself at LuLu's with the most succulent fried crab claws on the bay.

OXFORD
SOUTH TO MOUNT CHEAHA

⊕ *Low mountain, Advanced, 0% unpaved* ⊕ *Map strava.com/routes/2878745539532885724*

 Distance
65 mi
(104 km)

 E+
5,300 ft
(1,629 m)

 Difficulty
4/5

 Appeal
4/5

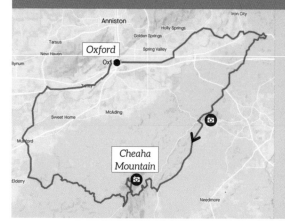

In the south of the Appalachians are the Blue Ridge Mountains. And in the south of those are the Talladega Mountains, which include Mount Cheaha (2,413 ft/735 m). Our route from Fun Wheels in Oxford (pop. 22,000), 60 mi (97 km) east of Birmingham, approaches from the north via two tough ramps: 2 mi (3.25 km) at 6% outside Cleburne, then 0.6 mi (1 km) at 9% at the foot of Horseblock Mountain. The ascent of Mount Cheaha itself is not easy (3 mi/4.75 km at 6%, then 1 mi/1.5 km at 8%). The divine 2-mi (3.25-km) Bunker Loop offers views of forests dotted with gentian flowers. The fauna: black bears, coyotes, and cyclists, of course.

Forest trail around Lake Chinnabee, near Mount Cheaha, Alabama.

TUPELO
RIDE LIKE A KING

⊕ Hilly, Intermediate, 0% unpaved   ⊕ Map strava.com/routes/2881187546304396212

 Distance
78 mi
(126 km)

 E+
2,900 ft
(888 m)

 Difficulty
2/5

 Appeal
4/5

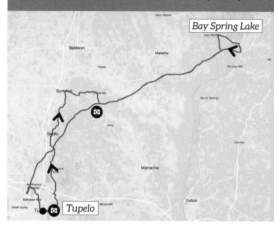

This route, 100 mi (161 km) southeast of Memphis, Tennessee, honors both Elvis Presley and Native Americans. We start in Tupelo (pop. 40,000), outside city hall and the Elvis statue (he was born and grew up here). Our first few miles stick closely to the legend: childhood home, park, Elvis Presley Drive. The following miles explore history. The Natchez Trace Parkway (15 mi/24 km of our outward leg, 31 mi/50 km of our homeward one) follows the original Natchez Trace, cleared 8,000 years ago. The 444-mi (715-km) road is a winding, rolling marvel running across three states through a stunning natural environment. Cycling it, you feel like a king.

VICKSBURG
MISSISSIPPI QUEST

⊕ Hilly, Intermediate, 50% unpaved   ⊕ Map strava.com/routes/2881213731009723316

 Distance
57 mi
(92 km)

 E+
3,200 ft
(963 m)

 Difficulty
3/5

 Appeal
4/5

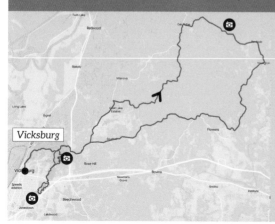

During the Civil War, control of the Mississippi River was crucial. In 1863, the forty-seven-day Siege of Vicksburg, 50 mi (80 km) west of Jackson, helped pave the way for the North's victory. Vicksburg (pop. 22,000) keeps this memory alive at the National Military Park—the Illinois and Iowa Monuments are notable—through which we ride two hilly, perfectly surfaced loops for an exploratory 10 mi (16 km), following two long gravel segments through Bluff Forest (having cycled out from Battlefield Bicycle). After admiring what Lincoln called "the Father of Waters" at Riverfront Park, sample some grilled fish at 10 South Rooftop Bar & Grill.

NEW ORLEANS
HUGE BIG EASY

⊕ *Flat, Advanced, 8% unpaved*
⊕ *Map strava.com/routes/2881664446380776854*

⊕ *Test yourself mi 14 (km 23) strava.com/segments/1804584*
⊕ *Test yourself mi 63 (km 101) strava.com/segments/1114991*

👁 GREG'S EYE

If, like me, you've soaked up some European culture, how could you fail to be drawn to the charms of New Orleans? This long urban route can also be ridden over two days—northern loop and southern loop—for twice the pleasure.

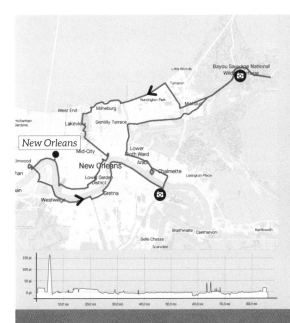

Big Easy. The nickname for New Orleans fits this XXL route (starting from Jefferson) like a glove. You'll ride the energy of the largest conurbation in Louisiana (pop. 1.3 million) and its extraordinary natural environment. So what's there to discover here, with no bumps at all on the horizon? First, the bends of the Mississippi, with its paddle steamers like something from a movie. Next, Bayou Sauvage as far as the Chef Menteur bridge: 35 sq mi (91 sq km) of swampland, lagoons, and canals, home to waterfowl and white and brown pelicans. Then, the shores of Lake Pontchartrain and, finally New Orleans itself, with its colorful houses and its unique friendly atmosphere: City Park, Frenchmen Street, French Quarter, the Cabildo, and the superb colonial houses of the Garden District. Refuel with coffee and beignets at Café du Monde in the French Market (mi 77/ km 124).

	Distance		E+		Difficulty		Appeal
↦	**86 mi** (138 km)	⬆	**500 ft** (165 m)	📊	**3/5**	★	**5/5**

Air: Louis Armstrong New Orleans International Airport (20 min by car). Car: 2h from Mobile, 3h from Jackson, 5h from Houston.

Bicycle World of Louisiana. Retailer of Giant, Liv, and Fuji. Supporter of the NOLA Social Ride, a cycling institution in New Orleans.

701 Jefferson Highway Jefferson, LA 70121 bicycleworldla.com

Lower Algiers–Chalmette ferry (mi 22/km 35). Chalmette Battlefield (mi 25/km 40). Bayou Sauvage (mi 51/km 82). Frenchmen Street (mi 75/km 121). St. Charles Avenue (mi 77/km 124)—don't miss the green streetcar named Desire. Garden District houses (mi 79/km 127).

ST. FRANCISVILLE
AMAZING ROUGE ROUBAIX

- ⊕ Hilly, Advanced, 50% unpaved
- ⊕ Map strava.com/routes/2881914871460567446
- ⊕ Test yourself mi 47 (km 76) strava.com/segments/6355045
- ⊕ Test yourself mi 63 (km 101) strava.com/segments/2664529

◉ GREG'S EYE

Gravel was not yet wildly popular when the Rouge Roubaix (which runs near the Louisiana-Mississippi state line) was created in 1999. Encouraging amateur cyclists to push their limits over hostile terrain, in an echo of "The Hell of the North," was ahead of its time.

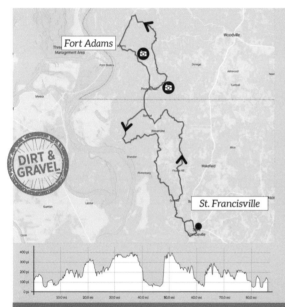

Gravel event Rouge Roubaix takes place 30 mi (48 km) north of Baton Rouge, on the backroads of West Feliciana Parish (Louisiana) and Wilkinson County (Mississippi). The course is a series of sections of rough and unmaintained asphalt, sandy gravel, and bedrock through rolling countryside: a world of former plantations and short slopes with gradients that sometimes hit double figures! The Rouge Roubaix, open to all, takes place in springtime to avoid the worst of Louisiana's high humidity. Starting from Rosedown Plantation Historic Site in St. Francisville, our route runs close to the Mississippi River, of which you'll get more than a glimpse come fall. At mi 62 (km 100), you'll pass close by Louisiana State Penitentiary, the largest maximum-security prison in the United States. Refuel with a po' boy at the Francis as you digest this exciting ride!

Distance **86 mi** (139 km)	E+ **3,800 ft** (1,165 m)	Difficulty **4/5**	Appeal **5/5**

Air: Baton Rouge Metropolitan Airport (30 min by car), Louis Armstrong New Orleans International Airport (2h by car). Car: 2h30 from Jackson, 4h from Mobile, 4h30 from Houston.

The Bicycle Shop in Baton Rouge is a linchpin of the local cycling community. Retailer of Specialized. They know the Rouge Roubaix trails by heart. Strava Club.

**3315 Highland Road
Baton Rouge, LA 70802**
bicycleshop.com

Rosedown Plantation and Afton Villa Garden (mi 0/km 0). White Oak Estate (mi 31/km 50). Top of Blockhouse Hill (mi 48/km 77), Mississippi River view. Clark Creek Hiking Trail (mi 50/km 80). Tunica Hills (mi 66/km 106).

POINT BLANK
OKAY HOUSTON!

- ⊕ *Hilly, Intermediate, 75% unpaved*
- ⊕ *Map strava.com/routes/2885604087919016474*
- ⊕ *Test yourself mi 15 (km 24) strava.com/segments/15899450*
- ⊕ *Test yourself mi 37 (km 60) strava.com/segments/5991079*

👁 GREG'S EYE

Like all large American cities, Houston enjoys an amazing off-road playground nearby. Fifty mi (80 km) north of Space City, the fast and barely bumpy trails of Sam Houston National Forest span a superb area of pines.

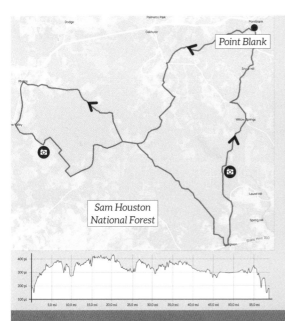

Point Blank

Sam Houston National Forest

Sam Houston National Forest honors the emblematic nineteenth-century Texan after whom America's fourth-largest city (pop. 6.3 million in the metro area) is named. At just a 1h drive from Space City, Houstonians have a prime cycling spot within easy reach. Don't be tempted to swim in Lake Livingston, though—alligators roam there. Better to stay beneath the swamp pines and listen carefully for woodpeckers and frogs as you pedal gravel. There are no major challenges here, just a thick forest (250 sq mi/650 sq km), where you sometimes feel like you're lost. At mi 35 (km 56), you meet the popular Lone Star Hiking Trail, and most likely a bunch of hikers, too. Back in Point Bank, scarf down some shells and cheese at the Bullet Grill House, safe from marauding gators!

Distance	E+	Difficulty	Appeal

Distance
59 mi
(95 km)

E+
2,100 ft
(644 m)

Difficulty
3/5

Appeal
4/5

Air: George Bush Intercontinental Airport, Houston (1h15 by car). Car: 3h from Dallas, 3h15 from Shreveport, 3h30 from Austin.

Hans Schneider has been building frames for forty years, and his shop, 20 mi (32 km) west of Point Blank, is a veritable treasure chest. Not to be missed.

**2930 Old Houston Road
Huntsville, TX 77340
hscycles.com**

Four Notch Camp and Lone Star Hiking Trail (mi 26/ km 42). Rocky Creek (mi 49/ km 79). Snow Hill Church and Lake Livingston (mi 58/km 93).

AUSTIN
TEXAN RODEO

- ⊕ Very hilly, Expert, 0% unpaved
- ⊕ Map strava.com/routes/2885853877121973764
- ⊕ Test yourself mi 32 (km 51) strava.com/segments/880587
- ⊕ Test yourself mi 49 (km 79) strava.com/segments/884837

◉ GREG'S EYE

Seventy-six mi (122 km) is long, and with more than 5,000 ft (1,525 m) of climbing, it's hard, too! Of the large cities in Texas, Austin has the steepest cycling terrain. It feels like the Belgian Ardennes, except we're above the Colorado River and Lake Travis.

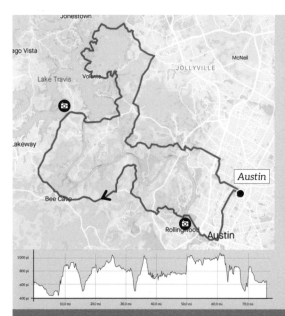

Austin (pop. +2 million in the metro area and expanding rapidly) buzzes with energy, with its billion-dollar Apple campus, 50,000 students at the University of Texas, and the South by Southwest festival. You'll be energized, too, as you cycle this tough "Gran Fondo" across the hills northwest of the state capital. The slopes of Red Bud Trail, Austin Lake Hills, and Maul Hill, beyond Bee Cave, set the tone on the south bank of the Colorado River. The climb from the Mansfield Dam to the Comanche Trail (mi 36/km 58) isn't easy. Chez Soleil Hill (0.6 mi/1 km at close to 9%) will cool your jets after 12 mi (19 km) above the shores of Lake Travis, while the 1 mi (1.5 km) at 8% of Far West Boulevard (mi 70/km 113) will drain you. The greater Austin area offers terrain reminiscent of classic European cycling sites such as the Belgian Ardennes and the Dutch Limburg.

Distance	E+	Difficulty	Appeal
76 mi (122 km)	**5,300 ft** (1,622 m)	**4/5**	**4/5**

Air: Austin-Bergstrom International Airport (20 min by car). Car: 1h30 from San Antonio, 2h30 from Houston, 3h from Dallas.

The Peddler Bicycle Shop in the Hyde Park neighborhood, north of downtown Austin. Retailer of Cannondale, Scott, and Giant. Strava Club.

5015 Duval Street Austin, TX 78751 peddlerbike.com

Texas Capitol (mi 4/km 6). Red Bud Isle (mi 8/km 13). Bee Cave Central Park (mi 24/km 39). Lake Travis (mi 31/km 50 and mi 37/km 60). Volente Beach and Marina (mi 43/km 69). Above River Place (mi 63/km 101).

FREDERICKSBURG
PINK AND BLUE

- ⊕ Very hilly, Intermediate, 0% unpaved
- ⊕ Map strava.com/routes/2884105928680811438
- ⊕ Test yourself mi 8 (km 13) strava.com/segments/10152151
- ⊕ Test yourself mi 42 (km 68) strava.com/segments/8837139

Come in April if you can! The temperature is ideal in Fredericksburg and on the Willow City Loop, the bluebonnets are in bloom, and the riding is simply sublime. These tranquil, rolling roads, distant from Austin and San Antonio, are a cycling haven.

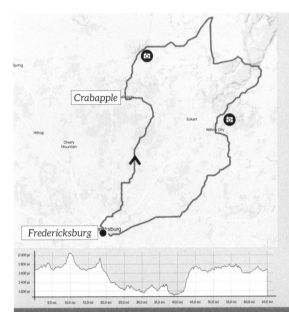

The German immigrants of the past have left their traces in Fredericksburg (named in honor of their Prussian emperor), 70 mi (113 km) north of San Antonio and 80 mi (129 km) west of Austin. Their typical "Sunday houses" give the historic town center a unique feel, while their Texas German dialect is still spoken. You can understand how tempting it was to settle in Gillespie County.

As a cyclist, you can enjoy all the benefits, too: the hills of Cross Mountain and Cedar Mountain, north of the town; the "Col de Crabapple" (name of a Strava segment) a little higher; and then the huge Enchanted Rock—a single chunk of pink granite soaring 425 ft (130 m). There are peach orchards and, in early spring, the flowering of the magnificent bluebonnets. If there is a Texan heaven, it must surely be in the environs of Fredericksburg.

	Distance	E+	Difficulty	Appeal
	65 mi (105 km)	**3,800 ft** (1,159 m)	**3/5**	**4/5**

Air: San Antonio International Airport (1h10 by car), Austin-Bergstrom International Airport (1h40 by car). Car: 4h from Houston, 4h30 from Dallas.

Jack and Adam's Bicycles organizes rides and has a six-person guesthouse for rent on Airbnb. Retailer of Scott, Felt, and Giant.

206 S. Lincoln Street Fredericksburg, TX 78624 jackandadamsfredericksburg.com

Cross Mountain (mi 2/ km 3). Lower Crabapple Road (mi 9/km 15). Enchanted Rock (mi 21/km 34). Willow City Loop (mi 44/km 71). Fredericksburg Historic Center (mi 65/km 105).

BIG BEND NATIONAL PARK
THE GREAT ADVENTURE

- High mountain, Advanced, 38% unpaved
- Map strava.com/routes/2884502577407849264

- Test yourself mi 18 (km 29) strava.com/segments/14169093
- Test yourself mi 89 (km 143) strava.com/segments/1914613

◉ GREG'S EYE

Bike-packing required! It would be a shame to cram an exploration of Big Bend National Park, in western Texas, into a single day. Head there in spring or fall (avoiding the high heat) for one of the finest cycling adventures in North America.

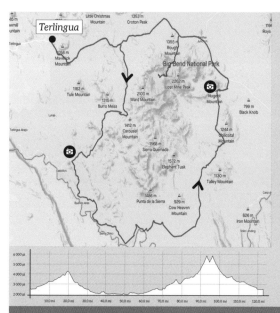

It's a half-day drive from the nearest bike shop, in Odessa, to the ghost town of Terlingua (and our starting point of Big Bend Resort and Adventures) before you can knock on the door of the most remote national park in the United States.

You're likely to meet more collared peccaries and roadrunners than tourists! Our route includes a 20-mi (32-km) stretch of the Rio Grande (on the Mexican border), following the iconic River Road. At mi 32 (km 51) you can extend west (more than 40 mi/64 km and 3,000 ft/915 m of elevation gain) to the extraordinary Santa Elena Canyon. Situated in the northern Chihuahuan desert, the park covers 1,250 sq mi (3,240 sq km) of steep cliffs, fissures, crevasses, sand, and cacti stretching as far as the eye can see. This massive adventure reaches a zenith below Emory Peak (summit at 7,825 ft/2,385 m) in the Chisos Mountains.

Distance	E+	Difficulty	Appeal
123 mi (197 km)	**7,825 ft** (2,385 m)	**4/5**	**5/5**

Air: El Paso International Airport (4h30 by car), San Antonio International Airport (6h30 by car). Car: 3h30 from Odessa, 10h from Monterrey.

Peyton's Bikes, in Odessa, 225 mi (362 km) north of Terlingua, and another outlet in San Angelo, 130 mi (209 km) east of the first. Retailer of Giant, Liv, and Specialized. Strava Club.

**3600 Billy Hext Road
Odessa, TX 79765
peytonsbikes.com**

Sotol Vista (mi 20/km 32). Tuff Canyon (mi 31/km 50). Rio Grande (mi 36/km 58 to mi 53/km 85). Nugent Mountain (mi 77/km 124). Panther Path (mi 85/km 137). Lost Mine Trail (mi 93/km 150). Window Trail (mi 95/km 153).

A section of paved road at the foot of the Chisos Mountains, Big Bend National Park, Texas.

SAN ANTONIO
GREENWAYS TO THE ALAMO

🌐 *Flat, Advanced, 0% unpaved*　　　🌐 *Map strava.com/routes/2885938985737956134*

 Distance
69 mi
(111 km)

 E+
1,900 ft
(574 m)

 Difficulty
3/5

 Appeal
4/5

If you're heading to San Antonio, jump in a taxi at the airport and head to Britton's Bicycle Shop in Hollywood Park (15 min). America's seventh city is big—1.5 million residents—and our circumnavigation of it will cover 69 mi (111 km), though largely on a series of easy greenways: Salado Creek Trail (16 mi/26 km) to the east, Apache Creek Trail to the west, then Leon Creek Greenway (15 mi/24 km) on the last leg north. Between these country passageways in the city, we visit downtown, of course, viewing both skyscrapers and the Alamo, part of the legend of Davy Crockett (mi 33/km 53). That's followed by 5 mi (8 km) along the River Walk.

EL PASO
ALONG THE BORDER

🌐 *Low mountain, Advanced, 0% unpaved*　　　🌐 *Map strava.com/routes/2884128798307340694*

 Distance
46 mi
(75 km)

 E+
4,300 ft
(1,310 m)

 Difficulty
3/5

 Appeal
4/5

The Franklin Mountains embedded in the border city of El Paso–Ciudad Juárez hold the twin draw of bracing slopes and breathtaking views. Southward, you glimpse the meager strip of the Rio Grande in an industrialized setting between two towns, with Mexico just beyond. Starting from Border Sports, we're soon climbing Scenic Drive (mi 3/km 5), then Smugglers Pass, a four-lane highway (beware of traffic): 5 mi (8 km) at 4.5%, with sections at 9%. McKelligon Canyon Road (2.6 mi/4.25 km at 5%) expands the register, with rocky, arid scenery at the summit, and a surprise: an amphitheater in the canyon, enjoyed by the citizens of El Paso in the evening.

HICO
CHASING BILLY THE KID

⊕ *Hilly, Advanced, 70% unpaved* ⊕ *Map strava.com/routes/2885529771049207726*

	Distance		E+		Difficulty		Appeal
⊢–⊣	**56 mi** (90 km)	⬆	**2,600 ft** (777 m)	☰	**3/5**	★	**4/5**

Famous outlaw Billy the Kid was shot down in Fort Sumner, New Mexico, in 1881. He was just twenty-one, and claimed to have killed twenty-one people as well. In Hico (100 mi/161 km southwest of Dallas), where the Kid spent time, a different legend persists. A plaque commemorates Brushy Bill Roberts, supposedly the real Billy the Kid. Muse upon the conflicting tales as you ride a local gravel course (starting at the Billy the Kid Museum) between Hico and Hamilton, the Kid's base camp, and the North Bosque and Leon Rivers. Neither the trails and backroads nor Hico's historic shopfronts seem to have changed since the Kid's days.

TYLER
ROSES AND THE BEAST

⊕ *Hilly, Intermediate, 0% unpaved* ⊕ *Map strava.com/routes/2884406202269187888*

	Distance		E+		Difficulty		Appeal
⊢–⊣	**54 mi** (87 km)	⬆	**3,500 ft** (1,000 m)	☰	**2/5**	★	**4/5**

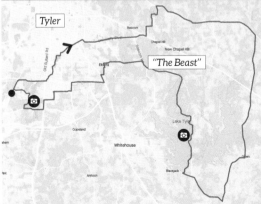

Tyler (pop. 100,000), 100 mi (161 km) southeast of Dallas, is the "Rose Capital of America," and springtime here is a wonder—the Azalea and Spring Flower Trail transforms the place into an extraordinary garden. The surrounding countryside is no wallflower, though, with lovely pine forests and tranquil Lake Tyler, explored on a 20-mi (32-km) stretch of this route starting from Elite Bicycles. At mi 40 (km 64), Old Omen Road serves up "The Beast," a ramp with short stretches where the gradient hits double digits. This route through East Texas partly follows the course of the local annual Beauty and the Beast Bicycle Tour. The name says it all.

DALLAS
GO, BIG D, GO!

⊕ *Flat, Intermediate, 25% unpaved*
⊕ *Map strava.com/routes/2885203091298027926*

⊕ *Test yourself mi 3 (km 4.75) strava.com/segments/4111198*
⊕ *Test yourself mi 33 (km 53) strava.com/segments/10721253*

👁 GREG'S EYE

Dallas has twice been nominated "Worst City for Cycling" by *Bicycling* **magazine (in 2008 and 2012). But if you hop on your bike in the Big D, you'll soon realize that this is no longer the case. Go for it! Let's encourage Dallas to do even better!**

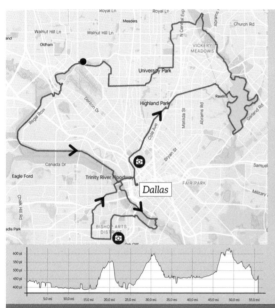

This 56-mi (90-km) route jumps from trail to trail (Trinity Levee, Katy Greenbelt, Ridgewood, White Rock Lake, White Rock Creek) away from traffic, with some unpaved sections. After Bachman Lake, we ride along the capricious Trinity River and through its park, with an unbeatable view of the skyline. Then we take a tour through the picturesque Bishop Arts District, stopping to refuel at Emporium Pies. The Ronald Kirk pedestrian bridge, with its 400-ft (120-m) white arch, takes us back to downtown. We can't ignore John F. Kennedy Memorial Plaza, nor Dealey Plaza, where the thirty-fifth president was assassinated on November 22, 1963. Farther on, we roll for 5 mi (8 km) beside bucolic White Rock Lake, then Fair Oaks and Harry S. Moss Parks, before the upscale homes of University Boulevard announce the end of this pleasant jaunt.

	Distance		E+		Difficulty		Appeal
	56 mi (90 km)		**1,100 ft** (349 m)		**2/5**		**3/5**

Air: Love Field Airport, Dallas (10 min by car), Dallas–Fort Worth International Airport (30 min by car).
Car: 40 min from Fort Worth, 3h from Austin, 3h15 from Oklahoma City, 3h45 from Houston.

Preston Hollow Bicycles, close to Love Field Airport, is a beautiful space devoted to all forms of cycling. Retailer of Giant, Liv, and Orbea. Strava Club.

3850 W. Northwest Highway Dallas, TX 75220
phbicycles.business.site

Trinity Overlook (mi 13/km 21). Street art in Bishop Arts District (mi 19/km 31). Ronald Kirk Bridge (mi 23/km 37). John F. Kennedy Memorial (mi 25/km 40). American Airlines Center (mi 26/km 42), where the Mavericks play.

MUENSTER
METROPLEX GRINDER

- 🌐 *Very hilly, Advanced, 80% unpaved*
- 🌐 *Map strava.com/routes/2885807776213888658*
- ⊕ *Test yourself mi 29 (km 47) strava.com/segments/11135252*
- ⊕ *Test yourself mi 40 (km 64) strava.com/segments/22419150*

👁 GREG'S EYE

Metroplex gravel lovers sure are spoiled. A 1h drive from Dallas–Fort Worth, close to the Oklahoma state line, the hills of northern Texas rear up, while the many trails require real commitment. A delight.

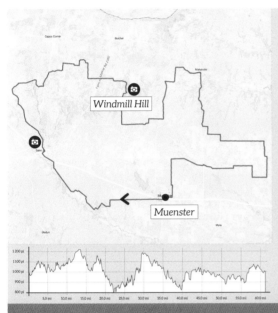

Windmill Hill

Muenster

Three hundred mi (483 km) separate Muenster—situated between the Metroplex and the Red River (which forms the state line with Oklahoma)—from Fredericksburg, farther south in Texas. Curiously, nineteenth-century German immigrants left their architectural traces in these two distant towns. In Muenster (pop. 1,600), the half-timbered houses are beautiful, while Fischer's Meat Market (the start of this route inspired by the Red River Riot gravel race) hasn't changed a bit. Write your own history with a bike on the trails of the Red River Valley, between and on the wooded slopes. Windmill Hill (mi 28/km 45) is the most spectacular—finishing with a section at 12%. 4R Ranch Vineyards and Winery provides a welcome break. This challenging pedal across Cooke and Montague counties can be ridden in any weather. It's the perfect gravel grinder!

Distance	E+	Difficulty	Appeal
61 mi (99 km)	**3,900 ft** (1,186 m)	**3/5**	**4/5**

Air: Dallas-Fort Worth International Airport (1h by car).
Car: 2h30 from Oklahoma City, 4h from Austin, 5h from Houston.

Bullseye Bicycle Shop on the edge of the Dallas–Fort Worth Metroplex, 45 mi (72 km) southeast of Muenster, is an old-school joint. Retailer of Bianchi and Jamis.

**700 W. Hickory Street
Denton, TX 76201
dentonbikeshop.com**

The Stonewall Saloon Museum, Saint Jo (mi 12/km 19). Windmill Hill and 4R Ranch (mi 28/km 45). Muenster Historic Center (mi 61/km 98).

OKLAHOMA CITY

RIVER, LAKES, AND MEMORIAL

⊕ *Flat, Intermediate, 0% unpaved*　　　⊕ *Map strava.com/routes/2882593415880582550*

Distance	E+	Difficulty	Appeal
⊢⊣ **65 mi** (105 km)	⬆ **1,300 ft** (399 m)	📊 **2/5**	★ **4/5**

This route round "OKC" offers escape without leaving the urban area of 1.4 million residents. There's room to breathe: 15 mi (24 km) beside the Oklahoma River, two stretches of 5 mi (8 km) and 6 mi (9.75 km) along the shores of Lakes Overholser and Hefner, 5 mi (8 km) next to North Lake Hefner Canal, and 5 mi (8 km) on Katy Trail. That's a full circuit of the Oklahoma state capital in a little over 40 mi (64 km). We also take in the Oklahoma Contemporary Arts Center, Paycom Center (home of the OKC Thunder), and the National Memorial (mi 55/km 89) to the 168 victims of the 1995 terrorist attack. Start and end at bike café the Boxcar in Moore.

TULSA

EVEN FOR FREE!

⊕ *Hilly, Advanced, 0% unpaved*　　　⊕ *Map strava.com/routes/2882624917272558998*

Distance	E+	Difficulty	Appeal
⊢⊣ **69 mi** (112 km)	⬆ **2,800 ft** (854 m)	📊 **2/5**	★ **4/5**

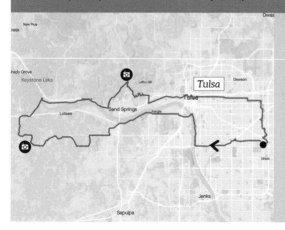

Have you heard of Tulsa Remote, an organization offering 10,000 dollars to anyone willing to work in Oklahoma's second city? Sadly, the initiative does not extend to those who wish simply to cycle here. Fortunately, there's more than cash to lure you to Tulsa, what with the wide Arkansas River, and the ramps of Coyote Trail (mi 23/km 37) and Casino Hill (mi 44/km 71). Our route starts from Bicycles of Tulsa, in Alsuma, and also visits the city's downtown, passing the superb Art Deco buildings and the intriguing Center of the Universe (a selfie is a must) before finishing on the very pleasant Mingo Trail. Give Tulsa a try, even for free.

FAYETTEVILLE
CX CAPITAL

DIRT & GRAVEL

- Hilly, Intermediate, 50% unpaved
- Map strava.com/routes/2882744826955288982

- Test yourself mi 29 (km 47) strava.com/segments/7737062
- Test yourself mi 53 (km 85) strava.com/segments/24463346

GREG'S EYE

Cyclocross fans all know where to find Fayetteville, Arkansas on the map. The awarding of the 2022 UCI Cyclo-cross World Championships to the city confirmed its place as a stronghold of cycling in North America. And from CX to gravel, it's just a few pedal strokes.

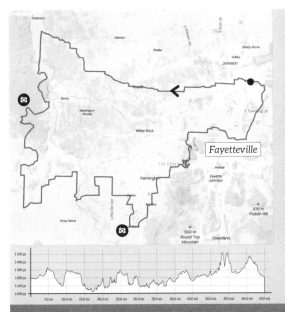

It's too tempting. Riding back into Fayetteville—Arkansas's second-biggest urban area (pop. 400,000)—who could resist traversing Centennial Park and tackling the short and nasty slope of Millsap Mountain (in emulation of the 2022 UCI Cyclo-cross World Championships)? The event has made Fayetteville the North American CX capital! Your bike should be able to manage a little cyclocross fun, given that our well-balanced route is gravel-oriented: ten perfect off-road sectors 2 to 6 mi (3.25 to 9.75 km) in length, with never more than 4 mi (6.5 km) of asphalt (or dodgier surface) in between, except in the city at the start and finish. We venture as far as Lake Wedington, in the hills and woods of northwest Arkansas, between Hamestring Creek and the quarries of Farmington. Above all, keep something in reserve for the Idiot—the essential Strava segment in Centennial Park!

	Distance	E+	Difficulty	Appeal
	65 mi (104 km)	**3,500 ft** (1,057 m)	**3/5**	**4/5**

Air: Tulsa International Airport (2h by car), Clinton National Airport (3h by car), Northwest Arkansas National Airport, Highfill (40 min by car). Car: 3h30 from Kansas City, 4h30 from Memphis.

The Bike Route, very near the Mud Creek Trail corridor, is one of Fayetteville's most respected bike shops. Retailer of Specialized and All City.

3660 N. Front Street Fayetteville, AR 72703 thebikeroutenwa.com

Illinois River Bridge (mi 17/km 27). Lake Wedington (mi 22/km 35). The Chapel at Walnut Grove Church (mi 45/km 72). 2022 UCI Cyclo-cross World Championships sign, Centennial Park (mi 52/km 84). University of Arkansas (mi 59/km 95).

LAKE FORT SMITH
OZARK FOREST WANDER

- ⊕ Low mountain, Advanced, 90% unpaved
- ⊕ Map strava.com/routes/2882660265269051798
- ⊕ Test yourself mi 23 (km 37) strava.com/segments/969150
- ⊕ Test yourself mi 40 (km 64) strava.com/segments/1591132

◎ GREG'S EYE

Do you feel you have wings, like the bald eagles you can see soar above you, here in the Ozark National Forest, the jewel of Arkansas? Don't get carried away—these trails are infinite.

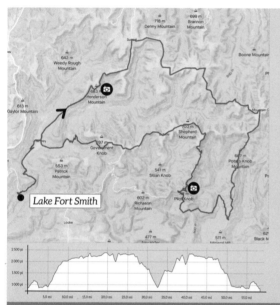

Lake Fort Smith

There's no way you can explore it in one day. Ozark National Forest in northwest Arkansas is a vast, 1,900 sq mi (4,920 sq km) stretch of oak, ponderosa pine, walnut, and much more: around five hundred tree types, planted over a century ago. It surprises and delights with its hills, its cliffs, the waterfalls that seem to spring out of nowhere, and the possibilities it offers gravel lovers. Autonomy is essential, since towns are far apart and farms few. Our route starts from Lake Fort Smith, in the far west of the forest, where you can fuel up at Black Bear Dining Hall for the day ahead, which involves 6,600 ft (2,010 m) of climbing. First, we have to climb to the plateau (at over 2,000 ft/610 m) via Henderson Mountain, then climb the equivalent again halfway through the ride, from Salt Fork Creek Valley. All of this on trails, far from anywhere. An utter treat.

Distance **59 mi** (95 km)	E+ **6,600 ft** (2,010 m)	Difficulty **4/5**	Appeal **5/5**

Air: Clinton National Airport, Little Rock (2h by car). Car: 40 min from Fayetteville, 2h from Tulsa, 3h from Oklahoma City, 4h from Memphis.

Spokes Giant in Little Rock, close to the Arkansas River Trail System, is the state capital's leading bike shop. Retailer of Giant and Liv.

11525 Cantrell Road Little Rock, AR 72212 spokesgiant.com

Henderson Mountain (mi 10/ km 16). Potato Knob (mi 27/ km 43). Pilot Knob (mi 38/ km 61). Mount Shepherd (mi 43/km 69). Government Knob (mi 48/km 77). Lake Fort Smith (mi 57/km 92).

MIDWEST & GREAT PLAINS

TENNESSEE

KENTUCKY

INDIANA

OHIO

MICHIGAN

WISCONSIN

ILLINOIS

IOWA

MISSOURI

KANSAS

NEBRASKA

MINNESOTA

SOUTH DAKOTA

NORTH DAKOTA

MEMPHIS
BLUES WITHOUT THE BLUES

⊕ *Fairly flat, Intermediate, 0% unpaved*   ⊕ *Map strava.com/routes/2921177736792439278*

Distance	E+	Difficulty	Appeal
65 mi (105 km)	**1,700 ft** (520 m)	**2/5**	**4/5**

Cordova

This route travels 65 mi (105 km) through Memphis, from Shelby Farms Park to the banks of the Mississippi and back, offering a tour of the dense web of bike lanes across Bluff City (pop. 1.3 million in the urban area). Heading out from Latting Speed Shop in Cordova, we explore the heart of Memphis, where the blues still rules: detour via legendary Beale Street (mi 40/km 64) and the statue of Elvis Presley a little farther on. We're never far from water and there's no significant climbing. You might be tempted to turn off near the airport (mi 27/km 43) and go visit Graceland, but we'd advise against it because of the traffic.

NASHVILLE
RHYTHMIC TRACE

⊕ *Very hilly, Advanced, 0% unpaved*   ⊕ *Map strava.com/routes/2920763867810822452*

Distance	E+	Difficulty	Appeal
73 mi (117 km)	**5,300 ft** (1,615 m)	**3/5**	**4/5**

Bellevue

Kinderhook

Nashville, Tennessee (pop. 1.6 million in the urban area), known as Music City, is a cycling destination, with numerous trails along the Cumberland River. It is also the terminus of the Natchez Trace Parkway—450 mi (724 km) of blessed asphalt starting in the eponymous Mississippi town. Riding on this end (this route commencing at Trace Bikes) is equally pleasurable—we take the Parkway for 29 mi (47 km)—with a thrill as you cross the elegant bridge at mi 6 (km 10). The homeward leg only confirms the initial impression: a longish ride through the bucolic scenery of the Harpeth Hills southwest of Nashville is physically demanding.

SPARTA
FALLS AND MUSIC

- ⊕ Low mountain, Advanced, 0% unpaved
- ⊕ Map strava.com/routes/2923937436072589130
- ⊕ Test yourself mi 12 (km 19) strava.com/segments/2626952
- ⊕ Test yourself mi 23 (km 37) strava.com/segments/6776250

👁 GREG'S EYE

The Eastern Highland Rim in central Tennessee is an area of low mountains, winding rivers, deep gorges, and many waterfalls and caves. The roads are in keeping with the scenery. This surprising route leads to the spectacular Great Falls and Twin Falls.

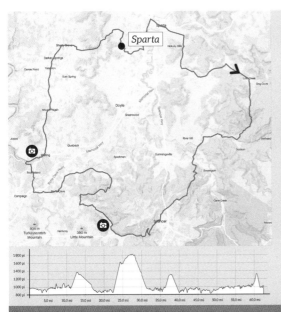

The small town of Sparta (pop. 5,000), halfway between Nashville and Knoxville, is crossed by US-70, nicknamed the Broadway of America; we ride it for less than 1 mi (1.5 km). Instead, we head south to Caney Fork, where the Collins and Rocky Rivers meet at Rock Island State Park. There are so many waterfalls in this area (horseshoe-shaped Great Falls and Twin Falls are the best known) that it has been dubbed the Land of Falling Water. There are low mountains, too, and our route climbs four punchy ramps 1 mi to 1.8 mi (1.5 km to 2.9 km) long: Lost Creek Road (6.7%), Lemont Yates Road up to 1,800 ft/ 550 m (8%), Bone Cave Mountain Road (5%), and Gum Springs Mountain Road (5%). Finish off this Tennessee must-ride at bluegrass music spot the Coffee Collective, in Sparta.

	Distance		E+		Difficulty		Appeal
⊢—⊣	**63 mi** (101 km)	⬆	**5,900 ft** (1,800 m)	📊	**4/5**	★	**5/5**

Air: Nashville International Airport (1h30 by car), McGhee Tyson Airport, Alcoa (1h45 by car). Car: 1h30 from Chattanooga, 3h30 from Atlanta, 3h30 from Louisville, 4h30 from Memphis.

Town Hill Bicycle Shop has operated on the edge of Sparta since 2014. Strava Club. Retailer of Specialized and many secondhand bikes.

**1066 Parker Road
Sparta, TN 38583**
townhillbikeshop.com

Lost Creek Falls area (mi 16/km 26). Keener Mountain (mi 33/km 53). Tandy Knob (mi 37/km 60). Caney Fork Dam, Great Falls, and Twin Falls (mi 48/km 77). Caney Fork River (mi 49/km 79).

CHATTANOOGA
CYCLING CHOO CHOO

⊕ Low mountain, Advanced, 1% unpaved ⊕ Map strava.com/routes/2924359722616013606

	Distance		E+		Difficulty		Appeal
⊢⊣	**68 mi** (109 km)	⬆	**5,700 ft** (1,740 m)	▊	**4/5**	★	**4/5**

Suck Creek Road

Chattanooga

Chattanooga (pop. 180,000), made famous by bandleader Glenn Miller and the song "Chattanooga Choo Choo," sits on the Tennessee River, just a few pedal strokes from the Georgia state line. The area has become popular due to its quality of life and beautiful natural surroundings. We ride out from Suck Creek Cycle and over Walnut Street Bridge, a local landmark, before following the lazy riverbends round Lookout Mountain and Raccoon Mountain. The homeward leg sees us tackle the tough slopes of Walden's Ridge (up to 2,000 ft/ 610 m) on Suck Creek Road (4 mi/km 7 at 5.9%) then Signal Mountain (4 mi/ km 6.7 at 5.4%). Phenomenal views!

TELLICO PLAINS
THE CHEROHALA SNAKE

⊕ High mountain, Advanced, 0% unpaved ⊕ Map strava.com/routes/2916374737557504524

	Distance		E+		Difficulty		Appeal
⊢⊣	**62 mi** (100 km)	⬆	**7,000 ft** (2,135 m)	▊	**4/5**	★	**5/5**

Tellico Plains

Beech Gap

Cherokee National Forest

Cherohala Skyway, named for the Cherokee and Nantahala National Forests it crosses, is a jewel of the Smokies. Climb, then descend its western slope on this route starting from Tellico Grains Bakery in Tellico Plains. The trail gets steeper as it goes: 9 mi (14 km) of gentle gradient, then 5 mi (8 km) at 7%, and two ramps of 0.7 mi (1.1 km) and 2 mi (3.25 km) at 8% to finish, interspersed by short breathers. Continue downhill after Beech Gap (the highest point, at 4,500 ft/1,370 m) into North Carolina as far as Robbinsville, then return to Tellico Plains, and you'll rack up another 4,900 ft (1,494 m) of elevation and make it a century. Watch out for motorcyclists.

TOWNSEND
SMOKY WONDERS

- Low mountain, Advanced, 0% unpaved
- Map strava.com/routes/2924050798339783498

- Test yourself mi 10 (km 16) strava.com/segments/6509565
- Test yourself mi 26 (km 42) strava.com/segments/2775587

👁 GREG'S EYE

Foothills Parkway, Little River Gorge, Cades Cove: this 64-mi (103-km) route starting from Townsend takes three of the most emblematic roads in the Great Smoky Mountains. It's a wonderful ride, to be consumed without moderation if you're staying in eastern Tennessee.

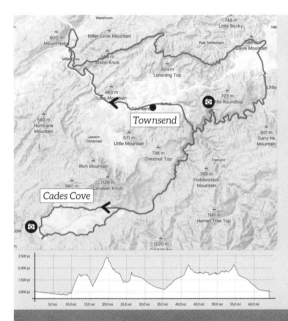

This double loop in the heart of the Tennessee Smokies, close to the North Carolina state line, presents a certain relative difficulty. The first challenge is the 2.2-mi (3.5-km) climb of Webb Knob at 7%. Next comes the 3.8-mi (6-km) ascent to Caylor Gap at an average gradient of 5.7% with sections at 10%. The Line Springs wall (0.7 mi/1 km at 8%) and the final ramp (1.5 mi/2.5 km at 6%) that bookend Cades Cove are no picnic. But they won't stop you from enjoying to the max the wonders served up by the fantastic asphalt ribbon of Foothills Parkway (14 mi/23 km), sublime Little River Gorge (8 mi/13 km), and the fascinating isolated valley of Cades Cove—its 11-mi (18-km) loop is reserved for cyclists on summer Wednesday mornings. Best ridden before or after the influx of tourists drawn by the historic places and the most spectacular views over the Tennessee Valley.

 Distance
64 mi
(103 km)

 E+
4,900 ft
(1,495 m)

 Difficulty
3/5

 Appeal
5/5

Air: McGhee Tyson Airport, Alcoa (30 min by car), Charlotte Douglas International Airport (4h by car).
Car: 2h15 from Chattanooga, 3h15 from Nashville, 4h from Atlanta.

Bike Zoo has been doing business in Knoxville, 45 min northwest of Townsend, for thirty years. Strava Club. Retailer of Specialized and Salsa.

5020 Whittaker Drive Knoxville, TN 37919 bikezoo.com

Foothills Parkway View (mi 14/km 23). The Sinks (mi 29/km 47). Meigs Falls (mi 31/km 50). Cane Creek Twin Falls (mi 33/km 53). Cades Cove Scenic View (mi 43/km 69). Methodist Churches (mi 46/km 74). Valley View (mi 51/km 82).

HARTFORD
UNSUSPECTED!

- Low mountain, Expert, 90% unpaved
- Map strava.com/routes/2924005914475292878
- Test yourself mi 24 (km 39) strava.com/segments/5099665
- Test yourself mi 37 (km 60) strava.com/segments/2405127

◎ GREG'S EYE

The wooded trails of the Blue Ridge Mountains are a must for (experienced) gravel lovers. We join the famous Appalachian Trail on the ridgeline separating Tennessee and North Carolina (30% of this route runs through the latter).

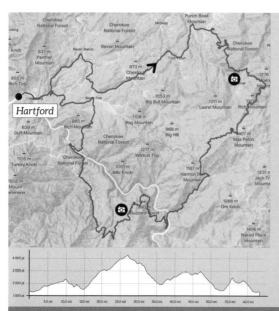

There's no point searching, you won't find more than 4 mi (6.5 km) of asphalt on this thoroughly gravel route (starting from Tennessee Welcome Center in Hartford) that's as demanding as it is stunning. We climb through Cherokee National Forest and the Great Smoky Mountains National Park on forest trails, reaching 4,300 ft (1,300 m) beneath the bald summit of Max Patch Mountain (mi 27/km 43). It's a real tough ride to get there: 9 mi (14 km) at 3% on Big Creek Road, then 11 mi (18 km) at 4.5% on Round Mountain Road and the Appalachian Trail! More is in store on Forest Service Road 288 above Pigeon River (five ramps of around 1 mi (1.5 km) in length, each at 6%) and Green Corner Road (2.5 mi/4 km) at close to 8%). These are authentic little cols of dirt and pebbles, but they lead to a spectacular landscape you might not have imagined existed before setting foot in eastern Tennessee.

Distance	**E+**	**Difficulty**	**Appeal**
64 mi (102 km)	**8,200 ft** (2,489 m)	**5/5**	**5/5**

Air: McGhee-Tyson Airport, Alcoa (1h by car), Charlotte Douglas International Airport (3h by car).
Car: 3h from Chattanooga, 3h30 from Nashville, 4h from Atlanta.

Harpers, 60 mi (97 km) west of Hartford, is one of the top bike shops in Knoxville. Strava Club. Retailer of Giant, Liv, Salsa, and Surly.

118 S. Northshore Drive
Knoxville, TN 37919
harpersbikeshop.com

Chestnut Mountain (mi 10/km 16). Tom Town (mi 13/km 21). Round Mountain (mi 21/km 34). Rich Mountain (mi 25/km 40). Max Patch Mountain (mi 27/km 43). Brown Gap and Hawk's Roost (mi 31/km 50). Pigeon River (mi 36/km 58). Longarm Mountain (mi 43/km 69).

TOWNSEND
IMPRESSIVE PARKWAY

◉ *Low mountain, Advanced, 0% unpaved*   ◉ *Map strava.com/routes/2921143740524912110*

	Distance		E+		Difficulty		Appeal
⊢–⊣	**74 mi** (119 km)	⬆	**7,600 ft** (2,315 m)	📊	**4/5**	★	**5/5**

This triple-loop route starts from the Visitors Center in Townsend, one of the gateways to the Great Smoky Mountains. We explore the amazing (yet little ridden) Foothills Parkway in its entirety, winding spectacularly across the mountainside. First (mi 9/km 14 to mi 26/km 42) we ride south to the Little Tennessee River, then east (mi 52/km 84 to mi 66/km 106) to Wear Valley. The climbing comes in 2-mi to 4-mi (3.25–km to 6.4–km) ramps, at gradients of 5% to 9%, all the way up to Look Rock (mi 18/km 29) and then Caylor Gap (mi 62/km 100). Such is the price of accessing some truly exceptional views. Back in Townsend, pop into the Artistic Bean for a coffee.

OAK RIDGE
THE WILD BREAKAWAY

◉ *Low mountain, Advanced, 0% unpaved*   ◉ *Map strava.com/routes/2924631826640320294*

	Distance		E+		Difficulty		Appeal
⊢–⊣	**61 mi** (98 km)	⬆	**6,000 ft** (1,821 m)	📊	**4/5**	★	**5/5**

This route turns its back on the Smokies, but is full of character. It starts from Bicycle Center in Oak Ridge (pop. 30,000), founded in 1942 as part of the Manhattan Project, a research effort that produced the first nuclear weapons. We brush the edge of Frozen Head State Park, site of the Barkley, the most extreme ultramarathon in the world, inspired by a failed prison escape. We tackle four aggressive ramps (Walden Ridge, Mount Larry, Fork Mountain, and Bald Mountain Road) 1.5 mi (2.5 km) to 3 mi (4.75 km) in length, at gradients of 6% to 8%—descents to be ridden with care.

RICHMOND
SURPRISING PALISADES

⊕ *Very hilly, Advanced, 0% unpaved*
⊕ *Map strava.com/routes/2883629241300839342*

⊕ *Test yourself mi 13 (km 21) strava.com/segments/999381*
⊕ *Test yourself mi 48 (km 77) strava.com/segments/3770698*

◉ GREG'S EYE

When I hear "Kentucky," I think of the Kentucky Derby, the queen of flat races for three-year-old horses. But here, 80 mi (129 km) southeast of the Churchill Downs track, it's the Kentucky River Palisades and their unexpected cycling terrain that count.

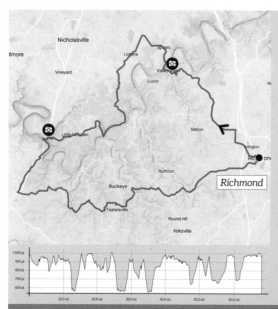

The steep gorges and rocky outcroppings of the Kentucky River Palisades are a surprise in the rural heart of the Bluegrass State. They frame the river's bends and have sculpted the surrounding prominent hills, which the steep roads hit straight on. On this route that starts at Mike's Hike and Bike in Richmond, you'll be out of the saddle on a dozen of them. Valley View (mi 14/km 23), Mount Beulah (mi 23/km 37), Sulphur Well (mi 28/km 45) north of the river, Old Lexington (mi 36/km 58), Jack Turner Branch (mi 48/km 77), and Barnes Mill (mi 61/km 98) in the south are the most striking: 1 mi/1.5 km to 2 mi/3.25 km at 4% to 5%. The picturesque is never far, whether on the ferry at Valley View that takes you across the Kentucky River, or through the rolling green hills on the way back. Make a stop at Chenault Vineyards (mi 60/km 97) to taste a perfect cabernet franc.

Distance **68 mi** (110 km)	**E+** **5,300 ft** (1,606 m)	**Difficulty** **3/5**	**Appeal** **4/5**

Air: Blue Grass Airport, Lexington (50 min by car), Louisville Muhammad Ali International Airport (1h30 by car).
Car: 2h from Cincinnati, 2h15 from Knoxville, 3h30 from Nashville.

"Bikes, beer, community" is an apt slogan for *Bicycle Face* in Lexington, 25 mi (40 km) north of Richmond. Retailer of Specialized and All City. Strava Club.

**331 E. Short Street
Lexington, KY 40507
bicyclefacelex.com**

Valley View ferry (mi 13/km 21). River Road (mi 27/km 43). Old Lexington Road (mi 37/km 60). Camp Nelson footbridge (mi 35/km 56). Chenault Vineyards (mi 60/km 97).

GRAND RIVERS
BETWEEN THE LAKES

- Very hilly, Advanced, 85% unpaved
- Map strava.com/routes/2883627248535452606
- Test yourself mi 30 (km 48) strava.com/segments/5837082
- Test yourself mi 61 (km 98) strava.com/segments/6781800

◉ GREG'S EYE

Land Between the Lakes in western Kentucky is a unique place: 270 sq mi (700 sq km) of forest and prairie surrounded by water, with endless deserted lakeshore. There are 500 mi (805 km) of trails crisscrossing a hilly relief. Gravel heaven.

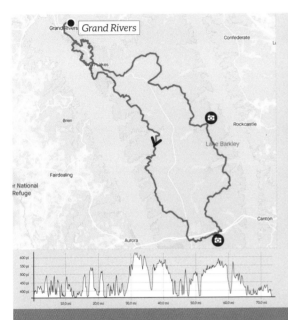

The 5 mi (8 km) of the Central Hardwoods Trail—a sinuous, singletrack forest trail in the southern portion of this route—are worth the trip to Land Between the Lakes National Recreation Area in the far southwest of the Bluegrass State. They are a distillation of the joy one feels riding a gravel bike in these parts. The final 2 mi (3.25 km), downhill, have been dubbed "the Fun Zone" on Strava, but this entire route (starting from Dockers on the Bay restaurant in Grand Rivers, northern gateway to the area) is a delight: an endless up and down, first along the length of Kentucky Lake to the west, then back up Lake Barkley to the east. Just before the Central Hardwoods Trail (mi 31/km 50) lies Elk and Bison Prairie, whose 3.5-mi (5.5-km) circumference is off-limits to cyclists. But all 73 mi (117 km) are packed with wonderful panoramas.

	Distance	E+	Difficulty	Appeal
	73 mi (117 km)	**6,000 ft** (1,830 m)	**3/5**	**5/5**

Air: Nashville International Airport (2h by car). Louisville Muhammad Ali International Airport (3h by car).
Car: 3h from St. Louis, 3h30 from Memphis.

Bikes and Moore in Hopkinsville, 50 mi (80 km) east of Grand Rivers, enjoys a fine reputation. Retailer of Specialized and Trek. Route suggestions on their website. Strava Club.

**200 Sivley Road
Hopkinsville, KY 42240
bikesandmoore.com**

Moss Creek (mi 9/km 14). Pisgah Bay (mi 12/km 19). Duncan Bay (mi 22/km 35). Golden Pond Overlook (mi 35/km 56). Energy Lake Bridge (mi 44/km 71). Honker and Hematite Lakes (mi 48/km 77). Cumberland River (mi 68/km 109).

BLOOMINGTON
ESCAPE FROM INDYCAR

- *Very hilly, Advanced, 60% gravel*
- *Map strava.com/routes/2877992657718529578*
- *Test yourself mi 35 (km 56) strava.com/segments/13814090*
- *Test yourself mi 48 (km 77) strava.com/segments/4934301*

👁 GREG'S EYE

Bloomington lies barely 50 mi (80 km) south of the legendary Indianapolis Motor Speedway, but you won't be bothered by the throbbing engines. What you will get are luscious views of Monroe Lake and Brown County State Park.

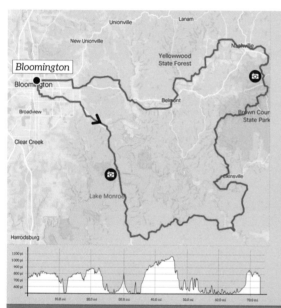

Bloomington (pop. 85,000)—centered around Indiana University—is often described as a city in the countryside. And the countryside truly is right there, particularly near Monroe Lake and Brown County State Park, which offer breathtaking views over the kind of forested expanses you might not expect in Indiana. A gravel bike is the proper option for this tranquil place—at least once you've crossed the lake. Tower Ridge Road (mi 16/km 26) marks the start of a long series of trails (nearly 30 mi/48 km) that are sometimes little more than narrow paths over the hills of Brown County State Park—blazing with color come fall. When the accumulated climbing begins to take its toll, worry not: there's a beautiful 13-mi (21-km) section of pleasurable off-road riding after Nashville, along the edge of Yellowwood State Forest. You won't find better in all of Indiana.

	Distance		E+		Difficulty		Appeal
	72 mi (116 km)		**4,900 ft** (1,490 m)		**3/5**		**4/5**

Air: Indianapolis International Airport (1h15 by car). Car: 2h from Louisville, 2h30 from Cincinnati, 3h45 from Louisville, 4h from Chicago.

Revolution Bike and Bean, close to the Sample Gates, serves delicious coffee roasted locally in town. Retailer of Specialized, Scott, and BMC. Strava Club.

**401 E. 10th Street
Bloomington, IN 47408
revolutionbikeandbean.com**

On the bridge carrying IN-446 (mi 11/km 18). Top of Hickory Ridge Lookout Tower (mi 22/km 35). On the Old Bridge (mi 32/km 51). North Lookout (mi 46/km 74).

MICHIGAN CITY
DUNES ON THE LAKE

- Hilly, Intermediate, 10% unpaved
- Map strava.com/routes/2877929178789170028
- Test yourself mi 15 (km 24) strava.com/segments/2110851
- Test yourself mi 44 (km 71) strava.com/segments/11559823

👁 GREG'S EYE

Lake Michigan can feel like an ocean. Indiana Dunes National Park is a place apart, a tranquil stretch of sand and water nestled between Michigan City and Gary, the birthplace of Michael Jackson.

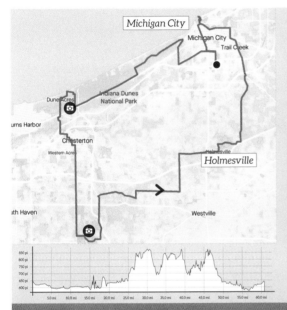

We're not in Illinois anymore, but Indiana Dunes National Park, just east of Gary (Indiana)— part of greater Chicago—and home to the Jackson family. Upon entering the park, the scenery changes and the Michigan lakeshore becomes beach and dune belt, the flora a mix of boreal and desert plants. You'll even pass a trio of little "summits"—Mounts Tom (192 ft/58.5 m high), Holden, and . . . Jackson—above Porter Beach, not to mention Mount Baldy on the way out of Michigan City. The first 15 mi (24 km) or so are an exploration of this dunescape (including a 5-mi/8-km segment of sandy Calumet Trail). As you exit the park, you'll see the hulking U.S. Steel facilities that are the jewel of the area's industrial heritage. The homeward leg is just a few miles inland. It snakes between sand hills, pine forests, and pretty lakes—an unusual landscape in Indiana.

	Distance		E+		Difficulty		Appeal
	61 mi (98 km)		**1,939 ft** (591 m)		**2/5**		**3/5**

Air: Chicago O'Hare International Airport (1h30 by car), Chicago Midway International Airport (1h15 by car).
Car: 3h from Indianapolis, 3h30 from Detroit.

Bike Stop Cycling, on US-20, is the go-to bike shop in the Michigan City area. Retailer of Giant, BMC, and Trek. Strava Club.

609 East, US-20 Michigan City, IN 46360 bikestopcycling.com

Car park of Mount Baldy (mi 5/km 8). Duneland Drive, on Mount Tom (mi 15/km 24). On Greenbelt Trail, Cowles Bog (mi 18/km 29). Grandview Avenue, on Loomis Lake (mi 28/km 45). Michigan City East Pierhead Lighthouse (mi 57/km 92).

CINCINNATI
WESTERN HILLS RODEO

⊕ Very hilly, Advanced, 0% unpaved   ⊕ Map strava.com/routes/2876588287926657164

Distance
65 mi
(105 km)

E+
3,900 ft
(1,185 m)

Difficulty
3/5

Appeal
4/5

Cincinnati

Cincinnati (metro pop. 2 million), birthplace of Steven Spielberg and home to the Art Deco marvel Carew Tower, sits on Ohio's border with Kentucky. Our route explores the state lines—west of the Great Miami River and along the Ohio River—after having tackled the heights of Eagle Creek Road and Miami Whitewater Forest. The final section through the Western Hills comprises three punchy climbs (1 to 1.5 mi/1.5 to 2.5 km in length at 8% to 10% average gradient) in less than 20 mi (32 km), before depositing us back at Montgomery Cyclery Western Hills, which is aptly named and also the perfect starting and ending spot in this impressive city.

COLUMBUS
SMALL YET BIG

⊕ Hilly, Intermediate, 0% unpaved   ⊕ Map strava.com/routes/2877233086315828408

Distance
56 mi
(91 km)

E+
1,200 ft
(351 m)

Difficulty
2/5

Appeal
4/5

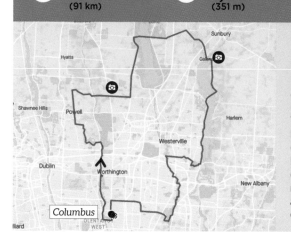

Columbus

Life is peaceful and friendly in Columbus (pop. 950,000), the capital of Ohio. Not for nothing is it called the "Biggest Small Town in America." It's easy and safe to cycle here, and the bike lanes are well used. We ride north on Olentangy Trail (from Johnny Velo Bikes) and take Alum Creek Trail back: green scenery all the way. There's hardly any climbing once you're over the 0.5-mi (0.75-km) ramps at 6% to 8% on Clubview Boulevard (mi 8/km 13) and Orange West Road (mi 16/km 26). Parks and golf courses line the route (this is Jack Nicklaus's hometown), but we also cross Alum Creek Lake and Hoover Reservoir. Columbus deserves its reputation.

Bike path close to downtown Columbus with its emblematic LeVeque Tower, Ohio.

MASSILLON
TOWPATH TRAIL AND MORE

- Hilly, Intermediate, 85% unpaved
- Map strava.com/routes/2877196673866153196
- Test yourself mi 30 (km 48) strava.com/segments/4627818
- Test yourself mi 46 (km 74) strava.com/segments/10414633

👁 GREG'S EYE

Ohio is a superb place for gravel riding, with trails that are wide and smooth once you leave the urban areas behind. One of them is the superb Towpath Trail, which follows the Ohio River to Lake Erie. It's a must-cycle of the Midwest.

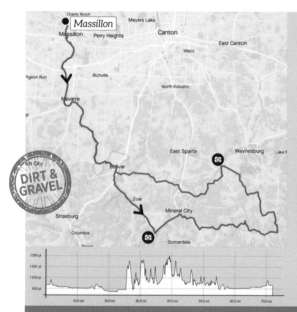

There are two fantastic experiences on this route, where wide, knobby tires are a must. Massillon (pop. 32,000) and the neighboring town of Canton, in northeast Ohio, feel very far from big cities. The first part of our route takes a section of the popular Towpath Trail, which offers a very tranquil cycling experience from way back in Cleveland and through the Cuyahoga Valley. These pancake-flat 17 mi (27 km) follow the Tuscarawas River to Bolivar and beyond, before the second part of our ride commences in Mineral City, where we start climbing, through striking terrain, over a dozen short ramps (off-road, of course) at gradients of 5% to 7%. North of Atwood Lake, we toy with the foothills of the Allegheny Mountains. Then we return to Bolivar and another 17 mi (27 km) back on the Towpath Trail. We might as well make the most of it.

	Distance		E+		Difficulty		Appeal
	72 mi (116 km)		**3,652 ft** (1,113 m)		**3/5**		**4/5**

Air: Cleveland Hopkins International Airport (1h15 by car), John Glenn International Airport, Columbus (2h by car). Car: 35 min from Akron, 2h from Pittsburgh.

Ernie's organizes several rides a week, starting from its shops in Massillon, North Canton, and New Philadelphia. Retailer of Giant, Surly, and Trek.

135 Lake Avenue NW Massillon, OH 44647 erniesbikeshop.com

The first 17 mi (27 km) on the Towpath Trail, notably at the Bolivar Aqueduct (mi 15/km 24). Zoarville Station Bridge (mi 23/km 37). Magnolia Flouring Mills (mi 44/km 71).

CLEVELAND
BIKES, BEER, ROCK "N" ROLL!

🌐 Hilly, Intermediate, 0% unpaved   🌐 Map strava.com/routes/2876517116887416644

	Distance		E+		Difficulty		Appeal
⊢–⊣	**62 mi** (99 km)	⬆	**2,500 ft** (751 m)	📊	**2/5**	⭐	**3/5**

Cleveland (metro pop. 2 million) has a reputation for beer, sports, and rock "n" roll. But let's go cycling first, east of the city (bike lanes in town and beside Lake Erie). The first 20 mi (32 km) run along the lakefront, the rest through the hills of Cleveland Metroparks—evoking C-Town's erstwhile nickname, "Forest City." Don't miss the Rock and Roll Hall of Fame (mi 1/km 1.5), and pause in Wildwood Park (mi 11/km 18) for a view over the lake. At the Chagrin River, the first hill takes you 600 ft (185 m) above the water. Holden Arboretum after Kirtland Hills (mi 31/km 50) is a pleasant spot for a break, before more climbs. You'll earn that beer.

LOUDONVILLE
MOHICAN TRACKS

DIRT & GRAVEL

🌐 Very hilly, Advanced, 89% unpaved   🌐 Map strava.com/routes/2876543146034563212

	Distance		E+		Difficulty		Appeal
⊢–⊣	**48 mi** (77 km)	⬆	**5,900 ft** (1,807 m)	📊	**4/5**	⭐	**4/5**

Loudonville (pop. less than 3,000) sits halfway between Columbus and Akron (1h by car from each), next to Mohican State Park: a forest of beech and oak on hills sculpted during the ice age. Our route starts from Bills Bike Shop. A few single-track sections might prove tricky for a gravel bike, so portage may be necessary. It's worth it, though. Mohican Covered Bridge (mi 11/km 17) and the Gorge Overlook (mi 16/km 26) are sublime. At mi 17 (km 27), we leave the park and continue off-road along the Mohican River to Greer. The incessant up and down is demanding—just look at that 0.5-mi (0.75-km) ramp at 15% on Big Hill (mi 27/km 43)!

PENINSULA
CUYAHOGA DIRTY DOZEN

⊕ Very hilly, Expert, 0% unpaved
⊕ Map strava.com/routes/2876479099353325708

⊕ Test yourself mi 26 (km 42) strava.com/segments/2220649
⊕ Test yourself mi 74 (km 119) strava.com/segments/752785

👁 GREG'S EYE

Cuyahoga Valley National Park is only a two-hour drive from Pittsburgh. So it's not surprising that some enthusiasts dreamed up an extreme challenge to be ridden over its maple- and oak-covered hills, one that is comparable to Steel City's famous Dirty Dozen.

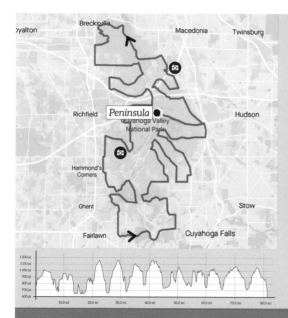

A full 95 percent of Ohio's 11.5 million citizens live in urban areas, which explains the popularity of Cuyahoga Valley National Park (the only one in the Buckeye State). It covers 50 sq mi (130 sq km) between Cleveland and Akron and is covered in thick forests, ravines, waterfalls, and wetlands; you can even spot white-tailed deer and coyotes! The Cuyahoga River is enclosed by hills rising to 1,200 ft (365 m) and crisscrossed by backroads. The staff of Century Cycles have conceived an Extreme Hill Climb Challenge (83 mi/133 km on our route, adaptable to taste) with an elevation of more than 6,000 ft (1830 m) if you ride the whole course, which starts in the village of Peninsula. It is reminiscent of the Pittsburgh Dirty Dozen by virtue of the number of climbs involved. The key differences are that the gradient is never more than 8% and the setting is in no way urban.

	Distance		E+		Difficulty		Appeal
	81 mi (131 km)		**6,200 ft** (1,889 m)		**4/5**		**5/5**

Air: Cleveland Hopkins International Airport (30 min by car), John Glenn International Airport, Columbus (2h by car). Car: 20 min from Akron, 2h from Pittsburgh, 3h from Detroit.

Century Cycles is a famed establishment located close to the Towpath Trail—another local option that's an easy-peasy ride. Retailer of Giant, Liv, and Salsa.

**1621 Main Street
Peninsula, OH 44264
centurycycles.com**

Brandywine Falls (mi 11/km 18). Deer Lick Cave (mi 20/km 32). Blue Hen Falls (mi 31/km 50). Everett Covered Bridge (mi 38/km 61). And in front of the many historic buildings (forge, taverns, mill) you pass in the course of the ride.

HASTINGS
BARRY-ROUBAIX FOREVER

🌐 *Very hilly, Expert, 85% unpaved*
🌐 *Map strava.com/routes/2878238640288662236*

⊕ *Test yourself mi 35 (km 56) strava.com/segments/10167019*
⊕ *Test yourself mi 68 (km 109) strava.com/segments/1131343*

👁 **GREG'S EYE**

Having always venerated Paris-Roubaix, I have followed Barry-Roubaix since its first edition, long before the gravel movement really took off. This Michigan meet added a century to its program in 2021. Ready, set, go!

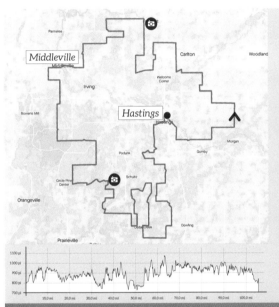

Let's give a standing ovation to the pioneers in Barry County, 130 mi (210 km) west of Detroit, who in 2008 had the genius idea of calling their gravel event Barry-Roubaix. This homage to the legendary Paris-Roubaix race reflected its popular imagery (champion cyclists covered in mud and dust) more than its terrain—the cobbles of northern France. Barry-Roubaix and its dozens of miles of trails even added a 100-miler (160-km)—the Panaracer Psycho Killer—in 2021. It's this century route that we ride here (shorter options and other variants exist, of course), never more than 6 mi (10 km) from Hastings. The hills Oof western Michigan are wearing, the climbs short and intense. A typical example is "the Wall" (mi 68/km 109): 0.3 mi/0.5 km at an average gradient of close to 12%. Yet nothing can spoil the euphoria of exploring the Barry-Roubaix trails!

	Distance		E+		Difficulty		Appeal
⊢⊣	**106 mi** (170 km)	⬆	**7,600 ft** (2,308 m)	📊	**4/5**	★	**5/5**

Air: Gerald R. Ford International Airport, Grand Rapids (30 min by car), Coleman A. Young International Airport, Detroit (2h15 by car). Car: 3h30 from Chicago, 4h15 from Cleveland.

Alger Bikes, which opened in Grand Rapids more than sixty years ago, is the closest recommended bike shop to Hastings. Retailer of Cannondale and Orbea.

120 28th Street SW Grand Rapids, MI 49548 algerbikes.com

McKeown Bridge (0.5 mi/ 0.75 km from mi 4/km 6.5). Maher Sanctuary (mi 32/ km 51). Top of "the Wall" above Head Lake (mi 68/ km 109). Long Lake (mi 72/ km 116). In front of any of the permanent green Barry-Roubaix signs along the route.

DETROIT
DO YOU KNOW MOTOWN?

⊕ *Flat, Intermediate, 0% unpaved*　　⊕ *Map strava.com/routes/2878355706388720348*

	Distance		E+		Difficulty		Appeal
⊢⊣	**55 mi** (88 km)	⬆	**351 ft** (107 m)	📊	**2/5**	★	**4/5**

Leave all preconceived ideas of difficult urban riding behind when you come to "Motown." Contemporary Detroit (metro pop. 4 million) is resolutely bike friendly. This safe 55-mi (88-km) route (starting from Bikes and Coffee in Woodbridge) is a tour of the city's renewal, an impressive comeback since its 2013 bankruptcy. After a circuit of popular Belle Isle Park at the mouth of Lake St. Clair, ride along the riverfront, taking in the architectural wonders of downtown and Ambassador Bridge. Farther on, Rouge and Palmer Parks are green beacons to the suburbs. Don't finish without a little detour via the Lexus Velodrome (mi 52/km 84).

ANN ARBOR
ENLIGHTENED HURON RIVER

⊕ *Flat, Intermediate, 10% unpaved*　　⊕ *Map strava.com/routes/2878614270247014108*

	Distance		E+		Difficulty		Appeal
⊢⊣	**66 mi** (105 km)	⬆	**1,040 ft** (317 m)	📊	**2/5**	★	**4/5**

In beautiful Ann Arbor—40 mi (64 km) west of Detroit—you can't escape the University of Michigan. A third of the city's 120,000 residents study here, while another third work here. Our route from Sic Transit Cycles leaves campus to head down the Huron River for 30 mi (48 km) via Ford and Belleville Lakes and Lower Huron and Willow Metroparks—plus another 16 mi (26 km) on the way back, meaning you can cut short the ride at mi 20, 23, 25, or 28 (km 32, 37, 40, or 45). Back in Ann Arbor, check out vast Michigan Stadium, home to the Wolverines, and Zingerman's Deli (mi 65/km 104) for the best Reuben sandwich in the state.

TRAVERSE CITY
SLEEPING BEAR TRAVERSE

- Hilly, Intermediate, 0% unpaved
- Map strava.com/routes/2878267103026485802
- Test yourself mi 15 (km 24) strava.com/segments/763471
- Test yourself mi 98 (km 158) strava.com/segments/4043922

GREG'S EYE

Don't worry! These 115 mi (185 km) can be ridden as two separate routes. Starting from Traverse City, one leads to the impressive Sleeping Bear Dunes, the other up Old Mission Peninsula, with its vineyards. A perfect two days in the saddle.

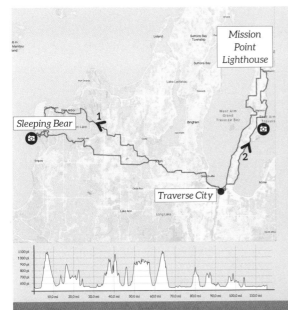

Mission Point Lighthouse

Sleeping Bear

Traverse City

Either 70 mi (113 km) west or 45 mi (72 km) north, here are two pleasure rides starting from the exquisite resort of Traverse City (pop. 15,000) on the shores of Lake Michigan, 250 mi (400 km) northwest of Detroit. Two routes, two vibes. The first, bumpier route takes in open spaces via Maple City, Big Glen Lake, and Sleeping Bear Dunes—like a chunk of desert stuck 600 ft (185 m) above the lake. At mi 35 (km 56), you must tackle the 7 mi (11 km) of Pierce Stocking Scenic Drive, where the views are outstanding. The second loop is a circuit of Old Mission Peninsula: panoramic roads looking over Grand Traverse Bay, affluent homes, nine wine-growing estates, and the picturesque Mission Point Lighthouse at the tip. It's not beyond the realm of possibility to attempt all 115 mi (185 km) in one day—if you're fit enough. But isn't it worth taking your time?

| Distance **115 mi** (185 km) | E+ **5,600 ft** (1,700 m) | Difficulty **3/5** | Appeal **5/5** |

Air: Gerald R. Ford International Airport, Grand Rapids (2h30 by car), Coleman A. Young International Airport, Detroit (4h by car). Car: 5h from Chicago, 7h from Toronto.

City Bike Shop, run by a young team, has been a mainstay of Traverse City for over half a century. Retailer of Giant, Liv, and Scott.

747 East Eighth Street Traverse City, MI 49686 citybikeshop.com

Grand Traverse Bay from East Hoxie Road (mi 6/km 10). At mi 40 (km 64), walk 600 ft (185 m) for a view of Sleeping Bear and Lake Michigan. Center Road Scenic Overlook, just before Chateau Grand Traverse winery (mi 80/ km 129). Anywhere on Old Mission Peninsula.

Lake Michigan viewed from the top of Sleeping Bear Dunes, Michigan.

MACKINAW CITY
BIG MAC GATEWAY

🌐 *Flat, Advanced, 85% unpaved* 🌐 Map strava.com/routes/2878587027810453206

	Distance		E+		Difficulty		Appeal
⊢–⊣	**79 mi** (127 km)	⬆	**1,500 ft** (467 m)	�📊	**2/5**	★	**4/5**

No Big Mac with your bike. Big Mac isn't a burger, but the 5-mi (8-km) Mackinac Bridge that has linked Michigan's two peninsulas since the 1950s and is closed to bicycles. Shuttle and ferry are the only options to make the crossing. Here's a long, green, gravel route heading south from Straits States Harbor for 23 mi (37 km) on the North Western State Trail to the vineyards of Alanson, then on the North Central State Trail for 23 mi (37 km) to Cheboygan, followed by 12 mi (19 km) home. Wildwood Hills will loosen up your legs halfway through, before an enchanting stretch along Mullett Lake, taking in Bois Blanc Island and Big Mac on the final segment by Lake Huron.

MARQUETTE
SUPERIOR ADVENTURE

🌐 *Hilly, Intermediate, 89% unpaved* 🌐 Map strava.com/routes/2878561742056789718

	Distance		E+		Difficulty		Appeal
⊢–⊣	**68 mi** (109 km)	⬆	**3,500 ft** (1,077 m)	📊	**3/5**	★	**5/5**

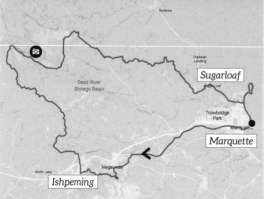

Marquette (pop. 21,000), 400 mi (645 km) north of Chicago, enjoys a blissful setting amidst luxuriant nature and the vastness of Lake Superior, the largest expanse of fresh water in the world—comparable in area to Panama! But we venture inland, initially on the Iron Ore Heritage Trail, a vestige of Upper Michigan's mining past (they've counted 300 mines here, mainly iron or copper). After circumnavigating Dead River Storage Basin, the homeward section takes in Sugarloaf ski resort, the Black Rocks of Presque Isle, and the imposing wooden Superior Dome. This superb gravel ride ends near Marquette Harbor Lighthouse, at Lakeshore Bike.

LA CROSSE
DRIFTLESS TREASURES

⊕ *Very hilly, Advanced, 0% unpaved*
⊕ *Map strava.com/routes/2920097221768804794*

⊕ *Test yourself mi 19 (km 31) strava.com/segments/1249030*
⊕ *Test yourself mi 50 (km 80) strava.com/segments/1625421*

👁 GREG'S EYE

No hills in Wisconsin? The surprising contours of the Driftless Area say otherwise. This is one of my favorite routes in the US, by the Mississippi River and the Minnesota state line. Kathy, my wife, is from La Crosse, and I trained often on these roads, which I adore.

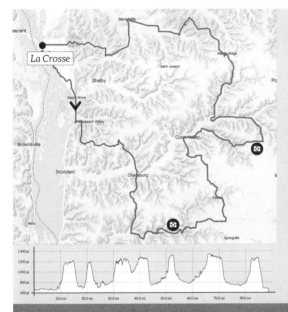

The Driftless Area in southwest Wisconsin is an enchanting landscape of steep hills, forested ridges, and deep valleys laced with famed trout streams. The roads climb sharply and road traffic is minimal, which only adds to the intense pleasure. Our route heads out from the pretty town of La Crosse (pop. 51,000) on the banks of the Mississippi River, to explore this area and relief on seven brisk climbs, none longer than 2 mi (3.25 km) but at average gradients of 6% to 9%. There are surprises too, such as at mi 81 (130 km), before we drop back down to La Crosse, where the final quarter mile of County Road FO climbs at 14 %! You'll surely welcome a refuel at the Fjord Bar (mi 44/km 71). In La Crosse, toast the treasures of the Driftless Area on the deck of the Waterfront Restaurant and Tavern, our starting point—you might even see a boat pass.

	Distance		E+		Difficulty		Appeal
	88 mi (142 km)		**5,900 ft** (1,800 m)		**4/5**		**5/5**

Air: Minneapolis–St. Paul International Airport (2h), Milwaukee General Mitchell International Airport (3h), Chicago O'Hare International Airport (4h).
Car: 3h30 from Green Bay, 4h from Des Moines.

Coulee Bicycle Co., close to the start of the Great River Trail, 5 mi (8 km) south of La Crosse, is well worth a visit. Retailer of Specialized.

213 Main Street
Onalaska, WI 54650
couleebike.com

Chaseburg Valley (mi 18/km 29). Duck Egg County Forest (mi 29/km 47). Spring Coulee Road (mi 49/km 79). Lovas Hill Road (mi 52/km 84). Coulee Experimental State Forest (mi 69/km 111).

DURAND
WESTERN TEMPTATIONS

⊕ Very hilly, Advanced, 10% unpaved   ⊕ Map strava.com/routes/2920865086725636808

 Distance
55 mi
(88 km)

 E+
5,500 ft
(1,680 m)

 Difficulty
3/5

 Appeal
5/5

Durand · Lima

Western Wisconsin attracts enthusiastic cyclists from the nearby Twin Cities of Minneapolis and St. Paul. Here they find quiet roads, farmland, and an aggressive relief unknown in Minnesota. This route, starting from Memorial Park in Durand (pop. 2,000) beside the Chippewa River, is a fine example: 5,500 ft (1,680 m) of elevation in 55 mi (88 km), seven ramps 0.8 mi to 1.5 mi (1.3 km to 2.4 km) long, with gradients of 6% to 9%! One of them, Weichman Road (mi 33/km 53), is gravel. Two addresses of note: the Stone Barn (mi 14/km 23) for a delicious slice of wood-fired pizza, and SHIFT Cyclery & Coffee Bar in Eau Claire (30 mi/km 43 northeast of Durand).

SPARTA
THE ICONIC RAIL TRAIL

 DIRT & GRAVEL

⊕ Hilly, Intermediate, 50% unpaved   ⊕ Map strava.com/routes/2921095597415383534

 Distance
86 mi
(138 km)

 E+
3,500 ft
(1,065 m)

 Difficulty
3/5

Appeal
5/5

Sparta

A nineteenth-century dandy astride a penny farthing welcomes you to Sparta (pop. 10,000), 30 mi (48 km) northeast of La Crosse. Cycling has been important to the town ever since the 1967 opening of the Elroy-Sparta State Trail, the first recreational rail trail in the United States. This loop (starting from Speed's Bicycle Shop) heads out to Elroy on paved road via the hills of the Driftless Area, before mi 32.5 (km 52.5) on the limestone of the iconic trail. You can also do a Sparta-Elroy-Sparta ride exclusively on the rail trail: 65 mi (105 km) of pure gravel and a double dose of the three tunnels (mi 64/km 103, mi 73/km 117, and mi 80/km 129 on our route).

PRAIRIE DU CHIEN
DAIRY BLISS

DIRT & GRAVEL

- Very hilly, Advanced, 70% unpaved
- Map strava.com/routes/2920480131528066976
- Test yourself mi 13 (km 21) strava.com/segments/3884627
- Test yourself mi 59 (km 95) strava.com/segments/3882806

👁 GREG'S EYE

When I was eighteen, it was Paris-Roubaix that fascinated me (through the pictures in *Miroir du Cyclisme* magazine), not the Tour de France (yet). That is why I have a soft spot for Dairy Roubaix, Wisconsin's leading gravel event. It's one beautiful course!

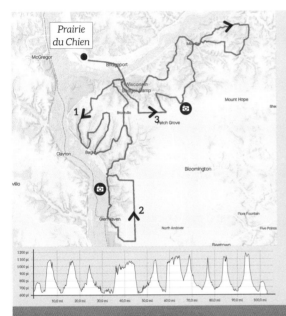

Dairy Roubaix is an evocative name for this gravel event west of Madison (the state capital) in southwest Wisconsin. It draws parallels between this cheese-producing area—nicknamed Dairyland—and the tortuous terrain of the Paris-Roubaix, the queen of European classics, called the "Hell of the North." This route starting from the Walmart Supercenter in Prairie du Chien (pop. 6,000), at the confluence of the Mississippi and Wisconsin Rivers, is inspired by the courses the Dairy Roubaix has served up since 2011. Once over Bridgeport Bridge (mi 3/km 4.75), it's a festival of backroads and dirt trails that wend their way from one dairy farm to the next. You'll see more cows in their pastures than you will pickups. Warning: if you're attempting this century (there are several options to shorten it), you'll feel the burn from the accumulation of short, merciless, often straight ramps.

Distance **103 mi** (166 km)	E+ **7,600 ft** (2,315 m)	Difficulty **4/5**	Appeal **5/5**

Air: Minneapolis–Saint-Paul International Airport (3h), Milwaukee General Mitchell International Airport (3h), Chicago O'Hare International Airport (3h30).
Car: 3h30 from Des Moines, 4h from Green Bay.

Main Street Hobby, in Richland Center, is the expert bike shop closest to Prairie du Chien (1h to the northeast). Retailer of Marin.

165 N. Main Street Richland Center, WI 53581
mainstreethobbyandbikes.com

Mississippi River (mi 14/km 23 and mi 23/km 37). Upper Mississippi River National Wildlife Refuge (mi 32/km 51). Wisconsin River (mi 55/km 88). Military Road (mi 69/km 111). Campbell Ridge (mi 95/km 153).

MILWAUKEE
LAKE BEAUTIES

🌐 *Fairly flat, Intermediate, 0% unpaved*　　　🌐 Map strava.com/routes/2919355808008643810

	Distance		E+		Difficulty		Appeal
⊢–⊣	**71 mi** (114 km)	⬆	**1,500 ft** (455 m)	📊	**2/5**	★	**4/5**

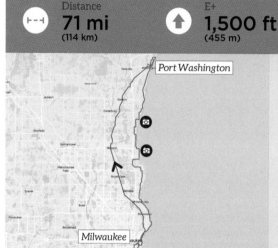

Port Washington

Milwaukee

Milwaukee (pop. 1.6 million in its urban area), with more than 100 mi (161 km) of bike lanes, fully deserves its reputation as the Midwest's "coolest" city. Our route (starting from Ben's Cycle) heads due north on the popular Oak Leaf, Brown Deer, and Ozaukee Interurban Trails all the way to Port Washington and its famous Breakwater Light. From there, the return leg virtually traces the shoreline of vast Lake Michigan, which is sometimes subject to surprisingly heavy swells. Along the way lie some real natural treasures: Cedar Gorge, Lion's Den Gorge, Virmond Park. At finish, celebrate with a beer in honor of Milwaukee's Germanic roots.

FOND DU LAC
KETTLE MORAINE ARC

🌐 *Fairly flat, Intermediaite, 25% unpaved*　　　🌐 Map strava.com/routes/2916394437571202556

	Distance		E+		Difficulty		Appeal
⊢–⊣	**59 mi** (95 km)	⬆	**2,000 ft** (610 m)	📊	**2/5**	★	**4/5**

Fond du Lac

Kewascum

Lake Winnebago, the largest in Wisconsin, is a 1h drive northwest of Milwaukee, is a popular fishing and boating spot. Its 80-mi (129-km circumference provides the course of the annual cycling event Race the Lake. Our route starts from Cyclery & Fitness in Fond du Lac (pop. 42,000), at the lake's southern tip, where Mercury outboard motors are manufactured. We're heading to Kettle Moraine State Forest: 90 sq mi (233 sq km) of thickly wooded hills, bowl-shaped depressions, and mounds from the glacial era. The roads are quiet, and we return via the perfect 15-mi (24-km) Eisenbahn Trail, before a selfie in front of Fond du Lac Lighthouse.

HOFFMAN ESTATES
GREEN SUBURBS

- ⊕ *Hilly, Intermediate, 0% unpaved*
- ⊕ *Map strava.com/routes/2873307705020372044*
- ⊕ *Test yourself mi 34 (km 55) strava.com/segments/8381046*
- ⊕ *Test yourself mi 48 (km 77) strava.com/segments/24854900*

◉ GREG'S EYE

"Chicagoland," between O'Hare International Airport and the Fox River, has a surprising multitude of extensive green spaces where cycling is welcome. This 64-mi (103-km) route never leaves the urban area, yet you hardly ever feel as if you're riding through a city.

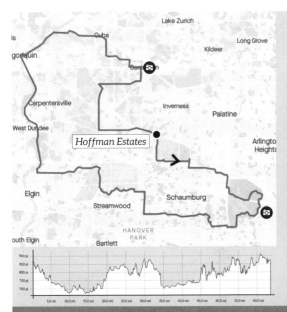

Chicago's inner suburbs are not hostile to cyclists. Toward the northwest, between O'Hare International Airport and the Fox River, there's a shift from an "edge city"—giant shopping malls and company headquarters—to something else: an urban area where the "urban" is barely perceptible, despite Hoffman Estates, Schaumburg, Elgin, Carpentersville, and Algonquin. There are loads of cycle paths here, a few quiet backroads, and an environment that's green, very green. It's noticeable as you enter Paul Douglas Preserve, followed by 8 mi (13 km) through Busse Woods, 6 mi (10 km) through Shoe Factory Road Prairie Nature Preserve, and 10 mi (16 km) across Barrington Hills with its grazing fields—a quite unexpected rural environment that is only enhanced by the 11-mi (18-km) stretch along the Fox River.

	Distance		E+		Difficulty		Appeal
	64 mi (103 km)		**1,800 ft** (557 m)		**3/5**		**4/5**

Air: Chicago O'Hare International Airport (20 min by car), Chicago Midway International Airport (1h by car).
Car: 30 min from Chicago downtown, 40 min from Aurora, 1h20 from Milwaukee.

Crank Revolution is the hub of a very active cycling community: open-space workshop, café corner, podcasts, Strava Club. Retailer of Specialized.

1636 W. Algonquin Road Hoffman Estates, IL 60192 crankrevolution.com

On Busse Lake (mi 13/km 21). On Bode Lake (mi 25/km 40). On the Algonquin footbridge over the Fox River (mi 41/km 66). In the meadows on the heights of Barrington Hills (mi 53/km 85).

CHICAGO
WISCONSIN CENTURY

⊕ Flat, Intermediate, 0% unpaved
⊕ Map strava.com/routes/2873316828118095530

⊕ Test yourself mi 69 (km 111) strava.com/segments/15283961
⊕ Test yourself mi 87 (km 140) strava.com/segments/853374

◎ GREG'S EYE

This century ride to the Illinois/Wisconsin state line and back is one of the most popular cycling challenges in Chicago. With no real climbing to speak of, it's a very pleasant route, as long as there's not too much wind coming off Lake Michigan.

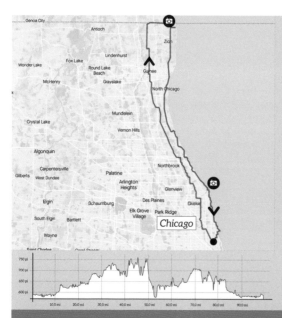

Here's a 100-mi (161-km) loop as flat as a Dutch polder, heading north up Lake Michigan. This challenging Wisconsin century (plan a refuel) is well regarded in Chicago and, given the distance, serves as a benchmark for a certain level of cycling. The route itself is something of a surprise. Starting from Heritage Bikes and Coffee in Lakeview, you ride up the Chicago River and through tunnels of greenery (Skokie Lagoons, Botanic Garden, County Forest, Waukegan Forest) to the state line. The return leg is a thrill, via Winthrop Harbor, North Dunes, and Waukegan before hitting the Lake Michigan shoreline at Fort Sheridan (mi 73/km 117). The run-in to Chicago passes beaches (Rosewood, Glencoe, Lighthouse, Loyola, Foster, Montrose), the skyline sprouting taller as you go, to finish several blocks past Wrigley Field, lair of the Cubs. A magnificent day out.

Distance **100 mi** (161 km)	E+ **1,200 ft** (380 m)	Difficulty **3/5**	Appeal **4/5**

Air: Chicago O'Hare International Airport (40 min by car), Chicago Midway International Airport (30 min by car).
Car: 1h30 from Milwaukee, 3h from Indianapolis, 6h from Minneapolis.

Heritage Bikes and Coffee is the most perfect iteration of the bike café, and the friendliest, too. An absolute must.

2959 N Lincoln Avenue Chicago, IL 60657 heritagebikesandcoffee.com

Ed Rudolph Velodrome in Meadowhill Park, 1 mi (1.5 km) off the route (mi 18/ km 29). The Welcome to Wisconsin Sign (mi 51/km 82). Homeward, on a Lake Michigan beach. In front of the Bahá'í House of Worship (mi 87/km 140). Heritage Bikes and Coffee!

The waterfront skyline of Chicago, Illinois, as you arrive from the north.

CHICAGO
LAKE, SKYLINE, AND MORE

🌐 *Flat, Intermediate, 0% unpaved*   🌐 *Map strava.com/routes/2873569410346855082*

	Distance		E+		Difficulty		Appeal
⊢⊣	**46 mi** (74 km)	⬆	**350 ft** (107 m)	📊	**2/5**	⭐	**5/5**

This 46-mi (74-km) ride (half a day if you take your time) includes everything that Chicago and its 600 mi (965 km) of cycle paths have to offer. Start rolling south (from the Rapha CC Clubhouse in Wicker Park) to the state line between Illinois and Indiana, past Douglass Park, Guaranteed Rate Field (the White Sox stadium), the University of Chicago, and Calumet Park. Head downtown on the Lakefront Trail to Soldier Field (home of the Bears), and the best views of the Loop skyline: Shedd Aquarium (mi 37/km 60 km) and Navy Pier. You even pass by the foot of the Willis (formerly Sears) Tower—once the world's tallest skyscraper (1,450 ft/442 m).

ORLAND PARK
THE THREE FORESTS

DIRT & GRAVEL

🌐 *Hilly, Intermediate, 65% unpaved*   🌐 *Map strava.com/routes/2873593646590623402*

	Distance		E+		Difficulty		Appeal
⊢⊣	**58 mi** (94 km)	⬆	**2,700 ft** (828 m)	📊	**3/5**	⭐	**4/5**

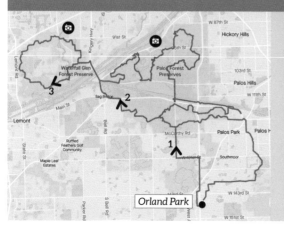

Chicagoans have a secret garden less than an hour's drive southwest from Willis Tower: Palos Forest Preserve in Cook County. This 25-sq-mi (65-sq-km) wooded area of oak, walnut, elm, and maple is a web of watercourses (Des Plaines River, Chicago Sanitary and Ship Canal, Calumet Sag Channel), small towns (Palos Heights, Lemont, Orland Park—we start from Orland Park Cyclery), and modest hills and is a renowned gravel spot. Two-thirds of our route is off-road, on four rolling sections of trail through Palos Forest, Cap Sauers Holding Preserve, and Waterfall Glen Forest. You'll be over the moon when you return to Chicago come evening.

AURORA
FAREWELL CHICAGOLAND!

- ⊕ Flat, Intermediate, 55% unpaved
- ⊕ Map strava.com/routes/2873994395435838644
- ⊙ Test yourself mi 14 (km 22) strava.com/segments/4693775
- ⊙ Test yourself mi 33 (km 53) strava.com/segments/23764689

◉ GREG'S EYE

Aurora, "The City of Lights," is a beacon to cyclists of the Chicago metro area, indicating the way to escape the urban sprawl! This gravel-tinged recreational route loops west through tranquil countryside.

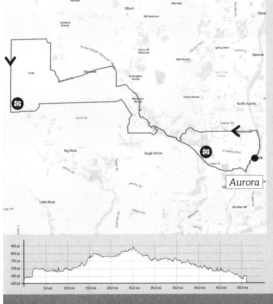

Aurora

To get fresh air in Chicago, you can either make for the beaches and paths by Lake Michigan or head 35 mi (56 km) the other way to the edge of the arc delimiting the urban area known as "Chicagoland." Aurora, the second-largest city in Illinois (pop. 200,000) and one of the first in the United States to install street lighting in the late nineteenth century, seems to straddle the Fox River like a lighthouse pointing west. Here, it's gravel time! Our route skips from parks to islands of greenery (Aurora West Forest, Bliss Woods, Hannaford Woods), crosses just one village (Kaneville), rolls merrily down some long off-road segments (Pritchard Road, Lasher Road), and comes back into town via the Virgil Gilman Trail. This 51-mi (82-km) ride without the slightest hill will whet your appetite to venture even farther afield, around

	Distance		E+		Difficulty		Appeal
⊢-⊣	**51 mi** (82 km)	⬆	**900 ft** (268 m)	📊	**2/5**	★	**3/5**

Air: Chicago O'Hare International Airport (45 min by car), Chicago Midway International Airport (1h15 by car).
Car: 1h15 from Chicago downtown, 2h from Milwaukee, 4h from Minneapolis.

Start from *All Spoked Up*, on Stolp Island, which has been operating here for a quarter of a century. Retailer of Cannondale, GT, Orbea, and Kona.

**14 W. Downer Place
Aurora, IL 60506
allspokedup.com**

On Orchard Lake (mi 5/km 8). Beside Blackberry Creek (mi 10/km 16). At the end of long, straight Pritchard Road (mi 29/km 47). On Aurora Chain of Lakes (mi 46/km 74). On the bridge to Stolp Island (mi 50/km 80).

CARBONDALE
LITTLE EGYPT

- ⊕ Hilly, Advanced, 0% unpaved
- ⊕ Map strava.com/routes/2873628276000166872
- ⊕ Test yourself mi 27 (km 43) strava.com/segments/679595
- ⊕ Test yourself mi 40 (km 64) strava.com/segments/1409304

◉ GREG'S EYE

Hilly southern Illinois, "Little Egypt," is a lovely cycling surprise, as we explore the superb slopes of Shawnee Forest, which nestles between the Ohio and Mississippi Rivers. A perfect getaway.

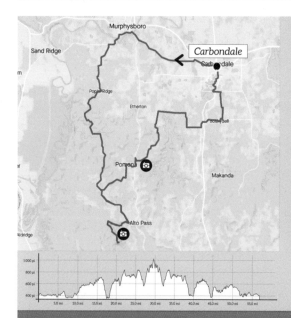

We're closer to St. Louis and Indianapolis than Chicago, between the majestic Mississippi and Ohio Rivers. "Little Egypt," as the southern tip of the state is known, is a topographic exception in Illinois. From the highest point on our route (1,000 ft/305 m), at the foot of the Bald Knob Cross of Peace, there's an incredible feeling as you look out over hilly Shawnee National Forest stretching to the horizon. Before that, on the first climbs, you'll pass close to Little Grand Canyon—carved out by the Big Muddy River—and reach the westernmost vineyards of Little Egypt, Pomona, and Hickory Ridge. The 2.6-mi (4.25-km) climb to Bald Knob might surprise you (sections between 10% and 14%). At the summit stands the imposing 111-ft (33.75-m) white cross, a monument from the 1960s. The second part of the ride, via Pomona and Cedar Lake, is just as bumpy and exciting.

	Distance		E+		Difficulty		Appeal
	57 mi (92 km)		**4,700 ft** (1,440 m)		**3/5**		**4/5**

Air: St. Louis Lambert International Airport, Missouri (2h30 by car).
Car: 3h from Nashville, 4h from Indianapolis, 5h from Chicago.

Carbondale Cycle Shop, the ideal starting point, is the go-to place in this pleasant town that's home to Southern Illinois University (pop. 25,000). Retailer of Trek.

303 South Illinois Avenue Carbondale, IL 62901 carbondale-cycle-shop.business. site

Car park of Little Grand Canyon (mi 15/km 24)—a 1-mi (1.5-km) walk to the viewpoint. Vineyards of Pomona Winery (mi 20/km 32). At the foot of Bald Knob Cross of Peace (mi 29/km 47). Atop Dutch Ridge (mi 42/km 67) for the view over Cedar Lake.

PEORIA
CAN YOU GRAVEL HERE?

🌐 *Hilly, Intermediate, 60% unpaved*　　🌐 *Map strava.com/routes/2873887473499684398*

	Distance		E+		Difficulty		Appeal
⊢–⊣	**55 mi** (89 km)	⬆	**2,400 ft** (745 m)	📊	**2/5**	★	**3/5**

Peoria (pop. 115,000), situated halfway between Chicago and St. Louis, is not only the largest city on the Illinois River and the oldest (est. 1691) in the state, but also the embodiment of the average American: the question "Will it play in Peoria?" is often asked when a new idea or product is floated. So, can you ride gravel in Peoria? Definitely! Peoria's bucolic surroundings, dotted with low hills (both wooded and cultivated), have just the right trails for some great off-road cycling, amply illustrated by this route (starting from Bike Peoria Co-op) via Bartonville, Glasford, Smithville, Hanna City, Edwards, and Pottstown.

ELIZABETH
APPLE RIVER CALLING

🌐 *Very hilly, Advanced, 70% unpaved*　　🌐 *Map strava.com/routes/2873928033735062708*

	Distance		E+		Difficulty		Appeal
⊢–⊣	**68 mi** (109 km)	⬆	**6,000 ft** (1,830 m)	📊	**4/5**	★	**4/5**

Far northwest Illinois—between the majestic Mississippi River (Iowa on the other side) and the Wisconsin state line—rears up and down. Charles Mound, the state's highest point (1,235 ft/376 m), is not far off our 68-mi (109-km) route comprising 6,000 ft (1,830 m) of elevation and a dozen ramps of 1 to 2 mi (1.5 to 3.25 km) with average gradients of 6% to 7%. This is a scenic gravel ride on a succession of trails. From the village of Elizabeth, we cycle up the Apple River to its canyon (near mi 15/km 24). The return leg delights: Valley of Eden Bird Sanctuary, Schurmeier Teaching Forest, vineyards, shores of the Mississippi (mi 50/km 80).

DUBUQUE
ABOVE THE MISSISSIPPI

DIRT & GRAVEL

- ⊕ Very hilly, Advanced, 50% unpaved
- ⊕ Map strava.com/routes/2875079277057390770
- ⊕ Test yourself mi 37 (km 59) strava.com/segments/12496916
- ⊕ Test yourself mi 53 (km 85) strava.com/segments/8082149

◉ GREG'S EYE

From the roads and trails of this loop along the fringes of the states of Iowa, Illinois, and Wisconsin, we embrace the majestic course of the Mississippi (sometimes from above). Before coming to Dubuque, we'd never have imagined exploring this major river this way.

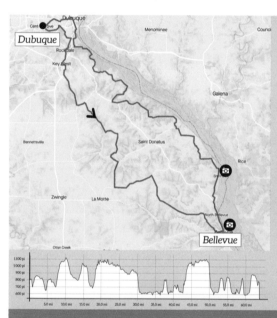

Dubuque (pop. 60,000), on the west bank of the Mississippi, bears the name of its eighteenth-century founder, the Canadian Julien Dubuque, as does the iconic arch bridge linking Iowa to neighboring Illinois and Wisconsin.

The picturesque landscape is one of hills and wooded cliffs overlooking the river (sometimes from as high as 500 ft/150 m as you head south toward aptly named Bellevue). The first half of our very up-and-down route on road and gravel heads through the hinterland before following the Mississippi back from Bellevue. It is there, first on Saint Catherine Road, and then on Mines of Spain Road and Horseshoe Bluff, that you get such surprisingly high panoramas over the river. Indeed, local cyclists have dubbed the last ramp on the way back to Dubuque "Grandview Pass."

	Distance		E+		Difficulty		Appeal
	64 mi (103 km)		**5,100 ft** (1,560 m)		**4/5**		**5/5**

Air: Milwaukee General Mitchell International Airport (2h30 by car), Chicago O'Hare International Airport (3h by car), Dubuque Regional Airport.
Car: 3h from Des Moines, 4h30 from Minneapolis.

The Bike Shack, right by the university, has been operating in Dubuque for forty years. Experienced staff. Retailer of Giant and Specialized.

3250 Dodge Street Dubuque, IA 52003
thebikeshack.com

Grandview Avenue (mi 2/km 3.25 and mi 61/km 98). The off-route climb up to Bellevue State Park (mi 31/km 50)—1 mi/1.5 km at 5%. Spruce Creek Harbor (mi 36/km 58). The off-route climb up to the Julien Dubuque Monument (mi 58/km 93).

CEDAR RAPIDS
THE FIFTH SEASON

🌐 *Hilly, Intermediate, 60% unpaved*　　　　🌐 *Map strava.com/routes/2875465743860209892*

	Distance		E+		Difficulty		Appeal
⊢–⊣	**65 mi** (105 km)	⬆	**2,100 ft** (639 m)	📊	**2/5**	⭐	**4/5**

Center Point

Cedar Rapids

Known as the "City of Five Seasons," because you need an extra one to enjoy the other four at leisure, Cedar Rapids (pop. 130,000) is another Midwest destination for gravel fans. Starting from Goldfinch Cyclery, enjoy the banks of Cedar River from Ellis Trail, riding west, then north onto the 100% gravel Young Road (mi 9/km 14), for over 30 mi (48 km) of crunching tires and dust. We cross just one village, Center Point, and glimpse a few farms, large houses, and pretty churches. We return to Cedar Rapids, rolling through its suburbs and hitting the river—which we never really left—by other trails: first Indian Creek, then Sac and Fox Trail.

OSKALOOSA
TRANS IOWA REMINDER

🌐 *Hilly, Intermediate, 80% unpaved*　　　　🌐 *Map strava.com/routes/2875049771466883250*

	Distance		E+		Difficulty		Appeal
⊢–⊣	**66 mi** (106 km)	⬆	**2,300 ft** (702 m)	📊	**3/5**	⭐	**3/5**

Oskaloosa

Grinnell, 60 mi (96 km) east of Des Moines, was (until 2018) the epicenter of the Trans Iowa, a pioneering 330-mi (531-km) gravel challenge over the rollercoaster trails of the Great Plains ridden in under thirty-four hours! Our route captures its spirit, but over a more manageable distance, starting from Bobzilla's Bicycle Werks in the neighboring town of Oskaloosa (pop. 11,000). Here, between the Des Moines and South Skunk Rivers, we pass farms and the occasional village. Avoid early spring (when the Trans Iowa was run): rain turns some trails into skating rinks and the ascending false flats into long drags of claggy mud.

DES MOINES
GREEN SURPRISE

- ⊕ Hilly, Intermediate, 15% unpaved
- ⊕ Map strava.com/routes/2875356209513796836
- ⊕ Test yourself mi 21 (km 34) strava.com/segments/9403270
- ⊕ Test yourself mi 31 (km 50) strava.com/segments/14171806

👁 GREG'S EYE

With its hot, humid summers and long, harsh winters, one doesn't always feel like straying far from Des Moines, Iowa. Which is fine, because this pleasant city is as bike friendly as you could wish. Let's go!

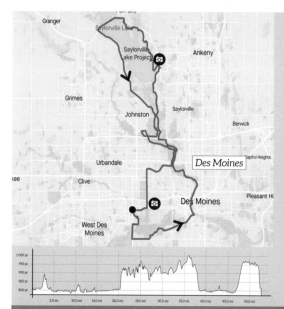

Iowa's capital, Des Moines (metro pop. 500,000 in its metro area), is a very pleasant place to live. Parks, rivers, and lakes jostle with unexpected contemporary museums and a capitol with a gilded dome. There's no lack of space. Our semi-urban route, which commences in West Des Moines, beside Walnut Creek, is all about nature. We ride along dedicated trails (Bill Riley, John Pat Dorrian, and Neal Smith for over 25 mi/40 km on the outward leg) lined with trees and never far from water: Water Works Park, Raccoon River, Des Moines River, Botanical Garden, Birdland Park, Saylorville Lake. We cross the latter at mi 30 (km 48) before a swift cycle home via Beaver Drive and another greenway, Sycamore Trail (mi 38/km 61), that—unbelievably—is already within the city bounds. A sincere thank-you, Des Moines!

Distance	E+	Difficulty	Appeal
52 mi (85 km)	**1,500 ft** (448 m)	**2/5**	**4/5**

Air: Des Moines International Airport (20 min by car to downtown).
Car: 3h from Kansas City, 3h30 from Minneapolis, 5h from Chicago.

Erik's (very close to Water Works Park) is a community hub through its Rasmussen Strava Club. Retailer of Specialized, Cervélo, and Raleigh.

**950 First Street
West Des Moines, IA 50265
eriksbikeshop.com**

On Walnut Street Bridge (mi 9/km 14). Above Saylorville Lake (mi 23/km 37).
On Saylorville Lake Marina (mi 27/km 43). In front of an artwork in the Pappajohn Sculpture Park (nr mi 51/km 82).

BLUE SPRINGS
KANSAS CITY ESCAPADE

⊕ *Very hilly, Advanced, 55% unpaved*   ⊕ Map *strava.com/routes/2874622481042506354*

	Distance		E+		Difficulty		Appeal
⊢–⊣	**66 mi** (106 km)	⬆	**3,800 ft** (1,144 m)	▋	**3/5**	★	**4/5**

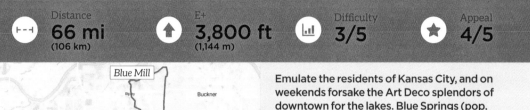

Emulate the residents of Kansas City, and on weekends forsake the Art Deco splendors of downtown for the lakes. Blue Springs (pop. 53,000), just 30 mi (48 km) from the Liberty Memorial, is the ideal starting point for a mixed asphalt/off-road route (leaving from Bike Stop). Ride north to the popular Little Blue River Trail (1 mi/1.5 km from the Missouri River), which follows the eponymous tributary for 15 mi (24 km) through a pastoral setting, before turning off to Lake Jacomo and Blue Springs Lake. The Fleming Park, Lake Vista, and North Shore trails are bumpy (ramps up to 6%), but even modest Lake Tapawingo is enchanting.

JEFFERSON CITY
KATY TRAIL AND OTHERS

⊕ *Hilly, Advanced, 78% unpaved*   ⊕ Map *strava.com/routes/2874379356938582194*

	Distance		E+		Difficulty		Appeal
⊢–⊣	**82 mi** (132 km)	⬆	**2,600 ft** (801 m)	▋	**3/5**	★	**4/5**

The picturesque Katy Trail—the longest recreational rail trail in the United States (237 mi/381 km)—crosses Missouri on an east-west axis, from Machens, a suburb of St. Louis, to Clinton, close to the Lake of the Ozarks. It follows the Missouri River on the first 29 mi (47 km) of this route from Red Wheel Bike Shop in Jefferson City, the state capital. The next part brushes Columbia's southern edge via the MKT Trail (5 mi/8 km), the Hinkson Creek Trail (4 mi/6.5 km), and the Grindstone Trail (3 mi/4.75 km), beneath trees and beside lovely streams. There's more gravel farther on, toward Ginlet, Englewood, and Folsom, before returning to Jefferson City.

EMPORIA
A BIT OF THE UNBOUND!

- Hilly, Intermediate, 85% unpaved
- Map strava.com/routes/2874675829832500638
- Test yourself mi 21 (km 34) strava.com/segments/4543610
- Test yourself mi 37 (km 60) strava.com/segments/11715720

◉ GREG'S EYE

It is now the dream of thousands of American cyclists to take part at least once in Unbound Gravel, an event that has become legendary in just a decade and a half. The rest of the year, you can enjoy the rocky trails of the Flint Hills around Emporia all to yourself.

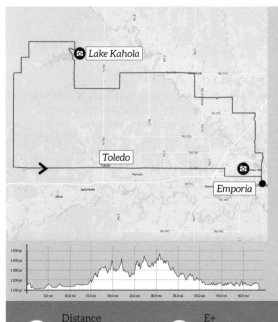

The "Mecca of Gravel" is what they now call Emporia, halfway between Kansas City and Wichita. This little town in east Kansas (pop. 25,000) has transformed itself into a permanent home for fans of the discipline. Even if you aim to participate one day in the dusty high mass that is Unbound (challenges from 25 mi/40 km to 350 mi/565 km), you can come to the Flint Hills around Emporia at other times of the year than late spring, and so avoid the intense heat. The extraordinary trails are, of course, open 24/7. Gravel City Adventure suggests several routes inspired by various Unbound courses. This one heads to privately-owned Lake Kahola, an iconic landmark for cyclists in the middle of the prairies, with tall grass stretching to the horizon and perfect soil of crushed flint—take extra-special care when choosing your tires. The best gravel adventures start here.

	Distance		E+		Difficulty		Appeal
⊢–⊣	**54 mi** (87 km)	⬆	**2,300 ft** (712 m)	📊	**2/5**	⭐	**5/5**

Air: Eisenhower International Airport, Wichita (1h30 by car), Kansas City International Airport, Missouri (1h45 by car). Car: 3h30 from Oklahoma City, 5h from St. Louis.

The Unbound is a daily preoccupation at *Gravel City Adventure*, in Emporia, a gravel-oriented establishment that offers year-round challenges on the legendary course.

716 Commercial Street Emporia, KS 66801 gravelcityadventure.com

Lake Kahola (mi 23/km 37). To the south of the route, on the long straight road (13 mi/21 km) back to Emporia, with an endless horizon. In Emporia (mi 54/km 87), in front of the Unbound course, while looking forward to being a finisher someday.

MANHATTAN
BIG BLUE AND LITTLE APPLE

- ⊕ Hilly, Intermediate, 40% unpaved
- ⊕ Map strava.com/routes/2874718333667916190

- ⊕ Test yourself mi 30 (km 48) strava.com/segments/6048137
- ⊕ Test yourself mi 47 (km 76) strava.com/segments/3445155

◉ GREG'S EYE

Manhattan, nestled between the Kansas and Big Blue Rivers and Tuttle Creek Lake, is without a doubt the town that offers the best outdoor life in the Flint Hills. And it has some surprising backroads. This mixed asphalt/gravel route is accessible to all.

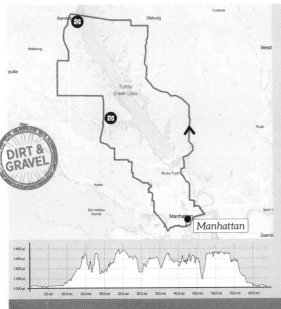

The nickname of Manhattan, Kansas (pop. 55,000) is "Little Apple," a reference to the other Manhattan in New York City, that perfectly conveys the good living in this charming spot in the Flint Hills. The damming of the Big Blue River half a century ago to create the 15-mi- (24-km-) long Tuttle Creek Lake embellished it further. This circuit of the reservoir on backroads—some made of dirt or gravel—is a delight. We leave the town center on the Linear Trail, along the Kansas River and then the Big Blue River before riding up onto the hills east of the lake on steep Carnahan Road. At mi 30 (km 48), you cross the Randolph Bridge, also known as Mile-Long Bridge, the longest in the state of Kansas, before a pedal home down the west side, made breathtaking by the panoramas and the variety of the terrain. This corner of the Flint Hills is a fine place to ride.

	Distance	E+	Difficulty	Appeal
	64 mi (103 km)	**3,200 ft** (961 m)	**3/5**	**4/5**

Air: Eisenhower International Airport, Wichita (2h by car), Kansas City International Airport, Missouri (2h by car). Car: 3h from Omaha, 4h30 from Oklahoma City.

The Pathfinder (near Manhattan Town Center) is a highly competent general outdoors store with a great cycling department. Retailer of Specialized.

**304 Poyntz Avenue
Manhattan, Kansas 66502
thepathfinder.net**

Just after Mile-Long Bridge (mi 31/km 50). Left on Secrest Road (mi 33/km 53), for a superb view of the lake. Left on Stockdale Park Road (mi 46/km 74) for same. On Linear Trail (mi 63/km 101), by the Kansas River.

LINCOLN
GRAVEL WORLDS

⊕ Very hilly, Advanced, 80% unpaved　　　⊕ Map strava.com/routes/2874981813974668466

 Distance
85 mi
(135 km)

 E+
5,300 ft
(1,612 m)

 Difficulty
4/5

 Appeal
5/5

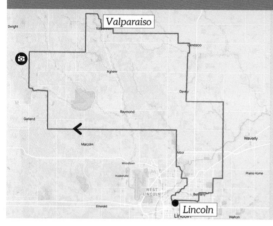

Long before gravel caught the attention of the Union Cycliste Internationale (UCI), a handful of enthusiasts decided to call the Lincoln event they'd dreamed up—now a major summer rendezvous—"Gravel Worlds." This 85-mi (135-km) route (starting from Cycle Works) is inspired by several Gravel Worlds courses. The Nebraska hills make this loop north of Lincoln a constant up and down on straight, wide trails, with the rural, agricultural landscape stretching as far as the eye can see. The ground is smooth—making for very fast riding—and less rough than Emporia's Unbound, for example, 200 mi (320 km) to the south in neighboring Kansas.

OMAHA
GATEWAY TO THE EAST

⊕ Hilly, Intermediate, 10% unpaved　　　⊕ Map strava.com/routes/2874999769910105266

 Distance
65 mi
(105 km)

 E+
2,400 ft
(720 m)

 Difficulty
3/5

 Appeal
4/5

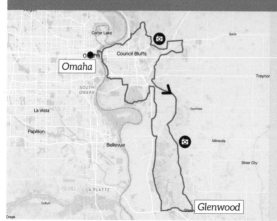

Omaha, the largest city in Nebraska, was dubbed "Gateway to the West" owing to its position on the west bank of the Missouri, across the water from Council Bluffs, Iowa. The two cities have become a single urban area of 1 million inhabitants. Cyclists like to transit from one side to the other on "Bob," the superb Bob Kerrey Pedestrian Bridge (a selfie from the middle is a must). But Omaha also offers fine opportunities for escapades east, in Iowa. Our route skirts Council Bluffs to the north, before pivoting due south over the Loess Hills. There's a gravel segment at mi 47 (km 76). The ride can easily be divided into two or three shorter loops.

MINNETONKA
PERFECT TRAIL

- *Fairly flat, Intermediate, 65% unpaved*
- *Map strava.com/routes/2920866277786358068*
- *Test yourself mi 7 (km 11) strava.com/segments/15665724*
- *Test yourself mi 60 (km 97) strava.com/segments/28384210*

◉ GREG'S EYE

When I moved to Minnesota in the late 1980s, nobody spoke of "gravel" yet, but I recall fitting fat tires to go ride the trails west of the city. Among them, a jewel: the Luce Line State Trail.

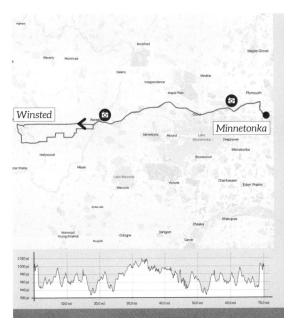

Nature seekers from the Twin Cities of Minneapolis and St. Paul tend to head for neighboring hilly Wisconsin or else west, to a world of lakes, rivers, woods, and farms. Greg lived near Lake Minnetonka and recalls this classic "recovery" ride he often did. Two-thirds of the route are off-road, on the pleasant crushed limestone of the Luce Line State Trail, which we take for 28 mi (45 km) on the way out and 20 mi (32 km) on the way back. The railway line was initiated by Colonel William L. Luce in 1908, but closed in 1970; it traces a path trod by Indigenous bison-hunters and later by nineteenth-century fur trappers. We head out from north of Lake Minnetonka—an area of luxury homes—to Winsted, the site of a famous country music festival, then back again. With no hills to speak of from beginning to end, the Luce Line State Trail offers a relaxing day out.

Distance **70 mi** (113 km)	E+ **1,100 ft** (335 m)	Difficulty **2/5**	Appeal **4/5**

Air: Minneapolis–St. Paul International Airport (30 min by car).
Car: 2h30 from Duluth, 4h from Des Moines, 5h from Milwaukee, 6h from Bismarck, 6h30 from Chicago.

Erik's is a well-reputed multisport store west of Minneapolis. Recognized cycling competence. Strava Club. Retailer of Specialized and Cervelo.

12500 W. Wayzata Boulevard Minnetonka, MN 55305 eriksbikeshop.com

Wayzata Country Club (mi 6/ km 10). Watertown (mi 22.5/ km 36,2 and 47/km 76). Winsted Lake (mi 32/km 51). South Lake (mi 34/km 55). Gleason Lake (mi 65/km 105).

MINNEAPOLIS
TWIN PARTY

⊕ *Fairly flat, Intermediate, 0% unpaved*　　　⊕ *Map strava.com/routes/2923639927365126320*

	Distance		E+		Difficulty		Appeal
	51 mi (81 km)		**1,300 ft** (405 m)		**2/5**		**4/5**

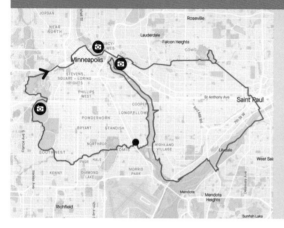

The Twin Cities of Minneapolis (pop. 430,000) and St. Paul (pop. 311,000), 400 mi (645 km) northwest of Chicago, ideally blend urban refinement and outdoors culture. Minneapolis has two hundred parks, and St. Paul, capital of Minnesota, now has a cycling infrastructure to rival that of its neighbor. This delightful 51-mi (82-km) route (starting from One on One Bicycle Studio) runs from Minnehaha Creek and the Chain of Lakes in the west over to Como Lake in the northeast, then down the Mississippi for 21 mi (34 km). There is a magical moment at mi 17 (km 27) as you cross the Stone Arch Bridge, built in 1883, above the frothing St. Anthony Falls.

SPRING VALLEY
ALMANZO MEMORY

⊕ *Hilly, Advanced, 70% unpaved*　　　⊕ *Map strava.com/routes/2913140540015811650*

	Distance		E+		Difficulty		Appeal
	94 mi (151 km)		**6,500 ft** (1,980 m)		**3/5**		**4/5**

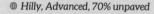

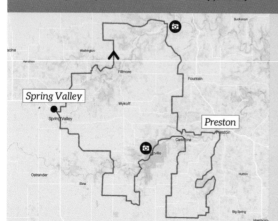

Minnesota has an infinite wealth of trails. One of the emblematic gravel events of the 2010s evolved here. It was dubbed Almanzo in homage to local figure Almanzo Wilder, the husband of Laura Ingalls Wilder, author of *Little House on the Prairie*. This route (starting from Rack's Bar & Grill) is inspired by a new, similar race, Spring Valley 100 Gravel. You have to stay constantly focused on this course composed mostly of straight dirt and limestone trails across low hills near the Iowa state line. You feel really privileged here in the charming countryside of southeast Minnesota, where the early gravel pioneers once cycled.

RED WING
DRIFTLESS ALTERNATIVE

⊕ *Hilly, Intermediate, 50% unpaved*
⊕ *Map strava.com/routes/2923691376319539548*

⊕ *Test yourself mi 27 (km 43) strava.com/segments/5858397*
⊕ *Test yourself mi 35 (km 56) strava.com/segments/20527945*

◉ GREG'S EYE

As in Wisconsin, on the other side of the river, the Driftless Area proffers seductively hilly terrain on the banks of the Mississippi. Two differences: there are many gravel trails—we're in Minnesota, after all—and there's much more forest than farmland.

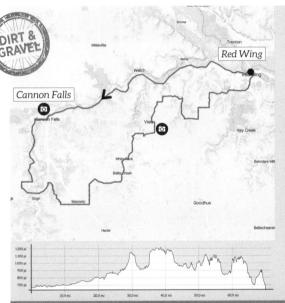

Red Wing (pop. 16,000), on the shores of the Mississippi River, 55 mi (89 km) southeast of Minneapolis, is surrounded by cliffs and wooded hills. The Driftless Area, formed by the lack of glacial deposits during the last ice age, extends to this part of Minnesota. After riding the impeccable Cannon Valley Trail (20 mi/km 32 of asphalt), the second part of this route transitions to something more vigorous, with ramps up to 2 mi (3.25 km) long and sections at gradients of 8% to 12%, such as on Shady Lane Trail (mi 35/km 56). All have a perfect gravel surface as well as earthier sections. They run through the Richard J. Dorer Memorial Hardwood State Forest, which covers 1,600 sq mi (4,145 sq km) and is named after the man behind the replanting of the valleys and of southeastern Minnesota in the early twentieth century. Toast your day in the saddle at Bev's Café back in Red Wing.

	Distance		E+		Difficulty		Appeal
	70 mi (113 km)		**3,200 ft** (975 m)		**3/5**		**4/5**

Air: Minneapolis–St. Paul International Airport (1h by car).
Car: 4h from Des Moines, 4h30 from Chicago, 4h30 from Sioux Falls, 6h from Chicago.

Red Wing Bicycle Company, close to Eisenhower Bridge, is the go-to bike shop in southeastern Minnesota. Retailer of Trek and Salsa.

319 Main Street
Red Wing, MN 55066
redwingbikes.com

Welch Village Ski Area (mi 11/km 18). Cannon River Winery (mi 22/km 35). Little Cannon River (mi 29/km 47). Shady Lane Trail (mi 35/km 56). Vasa Overlook (mi 52/km 84). Hoffman Spring Brook Valley (mi 60/km 96). Barn Bluff (mi 70/km 113).

DULUTH
SUPERIOR POWER

🌐 *Hilly, Intermediate, 70% unpaved*   🌐 Map strava.com/routes/2921256785872388590

	Distance		E+		Difficulty		Appeal
⊢–⊣	**73 mi** (117 km)	⬆	**4,200 ft** (1,280 m)	📊	**3/5**	★	**4/5**

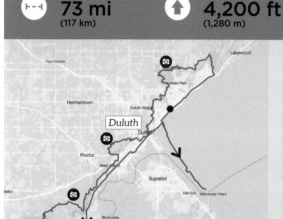

Duluth (pop. 90,000), on the edge of Lake Superior, is no longer the destination for wealthy folk that it was in the early twentieth century, though it has retained some Victorian architecture and shares the bustling Twin Ports with neighboring Superior, Wisconsin. Our route (starting from Continental Ski & Bike) commences with a 14-mi (23-km) pedal to the tip of the breakwater and back, allowing you to appreciate the vastness of Lake Superior. Trails then climb into the heights around Ely's Peak, followed by Piedmont Heights, Observation Hill, Hunters Park, and Hawk Ridge, all with panoramas over the largest expanse of fresh water in the world.

BEMIDJI
MISSISSIPPI SOURCE

🌐 *Fairly flat, Advanced, 5% unpaved*   🌐 Map strava.com/routes/2921877466886325180

	Distance		E+		Difficulty		Appeal
⊢–⊣	**79 mi** (127 km)	⬆	**2,200 ft** (670 m)	📊	**3/5**	★	**4/5**

The Mississippi River rises from Lake Itasca, in northwest Minnesota, before its majestic 2,552-mi (4,107-km) journey south to the Gulf of Mexico. But first it curves northeast toward Bemidji (pop. 15,000), a town famous for the giant statues of Midwest folk icons Paul Bunyan and Babe the Blue Ox, and a place where boats begin to appear on the river at dawn. The first 20 mi (32 km) of our route, which starts at Northern Cycle, follow a superb trail named after the illustrious lumberjack. We glide through wooded Itasca State Park to the Mississippi Headwaters over relatively flat terrain, past an abundance of lakes and ponds.

SIOUX FALLS
PINK GRAVEL

- Hilly, Intermediate, 65% unpaved
- Map strava.com/routes/2875787265025160420

- Test yourself mi 12 (km 19) strava.com/segments/4975040
- Test yourself mi 60 (km 96) strava.com/segments/20442434

👁 GREG'S EYE

The renown of the Midwestern town of Sioux Falls rests on its wide cascades and the particular pink hue of their rocks. Once you ride out of the city, it's gravel a-go-go—we are in the Great Plains, after all!

Sioux Falls

Nature is at the heart of Sioux Falls, an urban area of 280,000 people in southeast South Dakota. Falls Park is one of the finest natural sites within city limits in the country. The wide falls of the Big Sioux River impress with their pink quartzite rocks. The facades of some of the surrounding public buildings are of the same hue! We reach Falls Park at mi 3 (km 4.75), after exploring the SculptureWalk—an amazing open-air museum. Outside of town, it's countryside all the way, with a total 45 mi (72 km) of trails—the section as far as Dell Rapids, in the north, has just a few sparse stretches of poorly surfaced road. Near Garretson (mi 40/km 64), we are barely 3 mi (4.75 km) from the Minnesota state line. Riding back into Sioux Falls, often ranked as the best small city in America, we experience Falls Park again, from the reverse perspective.

	Distance	E+	Difficulty	Appeal
	62 mi (100 km)	**2,000 ft** (621 m)	**3/5**	**4/5**

Air: Minneapolis–St. Paul International Airport, Minneapolis (4h by car), Sioux Falls Regional Airport (20 min to downtown). Car: 2h45 from Omaha, 3h from Pierre, 4h from Des Moines.

Sioux Falls Bicycle Company, upstream of Falls Park, is a major rendezvous point for the local cycling community.

1740 South Cliff Avenue Sioux Falls, SD 57105
siouxfallsbicyclecompany.com

Arc of Dreams (mi 2/km 3.25). Falls Park (mi 3/km 4.75 and mi 59/km 95). On the Garfield Avenue bridge above the Big Sioux River in Dell Rapids (mi 25/km 40).

RAPID CITY
CRAZY HORSE & 4 X POTUS

- ⊕ Low mountain, Advanced, 25% unpaved
- ⊕ Map strava.com/routes/2875997368504062614
- ⊕ Test yourself mi 9 (km 14) strava.com/segments/779115
- ⊕ Test yourself mi 34 (km 55) strava.com/segments/952274

👁 GREG'S EYE

Here's a long and very hard day out on the bike through the Black Hills mountain range. This exceptional 83-mi (133-km) route starting in Rapid City takes in two symbolic American monuments: Mount Rushmore and the Crazy Horse Memorial.

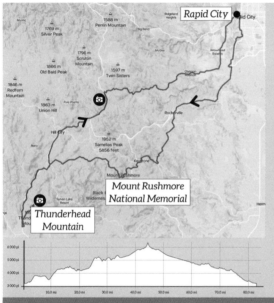

Rapid City

Mount Rushmore National Memorial

Thunderhead Mountain

The Black Hills in southwest South Dakota are tough terrain. The roads, which usually have cycle paths running alongside, ascend in interminable false flats with bracing ramps, such as Sitting Bull Road (mi 9/km 14). This route requires a robust level of fitness. At mi 25 (km 40) is Mount Rushmore, the monumental sculpture (completed in 1941) of the faces (60 ft/18 m high) of four U.S. presidents: George Washington, Thomas Jefferson, Theodore Roosevelt, and Abraham Lincoln. Proceed 20 mi (32 km) and we encounter another monumental work (begun in 1948 and far from complete): the Crazy Horse Memorial on Thunderhead Mountain, an homage to one of the greatest Sioux chiefs of the nineteenth century. You can shave 20 mi/32 km (of gravel) and 1,100 ft (335 m) of climbing off the ride if you choose not to visit the Crazy Horse Memorial. But who would want to do that?!

Distance **83 mi** (133 km)	E+ **6,800 ft** (2,078 m)	Difficulty **4/5**	Appeal **5/5**

Air: Rapid City Regional Airport (20 min by car to downtown), Denver International Airport, Colorado (6h by car). Car: 5h from Sioux Falls, 5h from Bismarck, 8h from Minneapolis.

Black Hills Bicycles is the most authentic and lively bike shop in Rapid City (pop. 70,000). Retailer of Norco and Specialized.

**1401 West Omaha Street
Rapid City, SD 57701**
blackhillsbicycles.com

In front of the 1880s steam train (mi 22/km 35). At the foot of Mount Rushmore (between mi 25 (km 40) and mi 26 (km 42). At the foot of the Crazy Horse Memorial (between mi 43/km 69 and mi 45/km 72). On Sheridan Lake (mi 63/km 101).

SPEARFISH
BLACK HILLS CANYON

⊕ *Low mountain, Intermediate, 36% unpaved*   ⊕ *Map strava.com/routes/2876003604580539400*

	Distance		E+		Difficulty		Appeal
⊢–⊣	**50 mi** (81 km)	⬆	**3,600 ft** (1,109 m)	📊	**3/5**	⭐	**4/5**

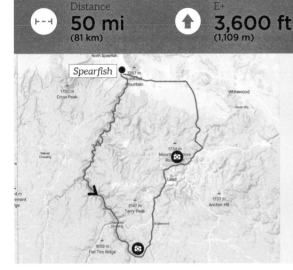

The beating heart of the Black Hills lies 60 mi (96 km) north of Mount Rushmore, around Spearfish (pop. 10,000). Heading south from Rushmore Bicycles on an unevenly surfaced backroad, through scenery that blazes with color in fall, we follow Spearfish Creek for 20 mi (32 km), at gradients of 2% to 3%, passing cliffs and waterfalls, such as Bridal Veil Falls (mi 7/km 11) and Roughlock Falls (mi 14/km 22). The canyon reaches an altitude of 6,000 ft (1,830 m) on Hanna Road. Two sites of note: Broken Boot Gold Mine (mi 34/km 55), a relic of the 1870s gold rush, and Tatanka (mi 38/km 61), a center devoted to the American bison.

SISSETON
COTEAU DES PRAIRIES 100

⊕ *Hilly, Advanced, 3% unpaved*   ⊕ *Map strava.com/routes/2876030280408081046*

	Distance		E+		Difficulty		Appeal
⊢–⊣	**100 mi** (161 km)	⬆	**2,900 ft** (875 m)	📊	**3/5**	⭐	**5/5**

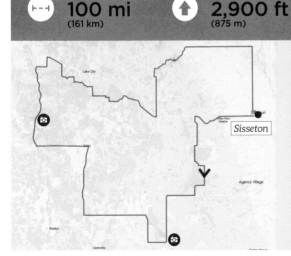

Coteau des Prairies is a plateau (200 mi/320 km by 100 mi/160 km) in northeast South Dakota at an altitude of 2,000 ft (610 m), covered with small glacial lakes. This is an unforgettable century across a green landscape with water glinting all around. We start from Stavig House Museum in Sisseton—200 mi (320 km) west of Minneapolis. Pedaling between Drywood, Pickerel, Roy, and Clear Lakes, we pass Fort Sisseton (a relic of the Civil War) and Sica Hollow State Park—a moorland where Native American legends mingle with supernatural tales. With only two villages (Eden and Lake City) in 100 mi (160 km), make sure you take plenty of supplies!

BISMARCK
ALKEMIST QUEST

◉ Hilly, Intermediate, 78% unpaved

◉ Map strava.com/routes/2875727447742671790

	Distance		E+		Difficulty		Appeal
⊢–⊣	**65 mi** (105 km)	⬆	**3,100 ft** (931 m)	☷	**3/5**	★	**4/5**

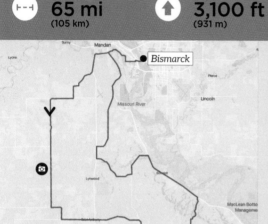

In North Dakota, as elsewhere, we have witnessed the emergence of the gravel movement and its machines that are better suited than mountain bikes for covering miles of fast trails, of which there are many in the Midwest. Bismarck, the state capital (pop. 61,000) holds an annual event each fall: the AlKemist Gravel Fest, our inspiration for this route (starting from 701 Cycle and Sport). Heading south through Mandan—Bismarck's twin city on the west bank of the Missouri—the long, straight trails of Drift Prairie climb progressively up to 600 ft (183 m) through the Huff Hills. The local ski lifts indicate the return route. Gravel all the way.

MEDORA
ICONIC ROOSEVELT PARK

◉ Very hilly, Intermediate, 0% unpaved.

◉ Map strava.com/routes/2875674620024357612

	Distance		E+		Difficulty		Appeal
⊢–⊣	**37 mi** (59 km)	⬆	**2,800 ft** (845 m)	☷	**3/5**	★	**5/5**

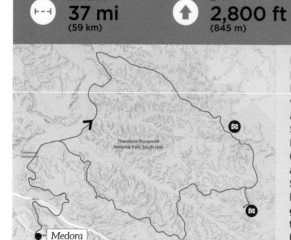

Badlands is an apt name for this part of southwest North Dakota, with one exception: Theodore Roosevelt National Park, 110 sq mi (285 sq km) of wild beauty, huge hills of clay and red sandstone, and lush meadows dotted with juniper bushes. Starting from Dakota Cyclery, in the town of Medora, this short road route (under 40 mi/ 64 km) packs in a plethora of fantastic viewpoints atop short but challenging ramps (up to 8%): Skyline Vista, Big Plateau, Wind Canyon, Boicourt, Buck Hill, Coal Vein, Paddock Creek. You'll get glimpses of bison, mustangs, bighorn sheep, and the occasional rattlesnake at the side of the road! Bad? Not by bike.

CANADA & ALASKA

ONTARIO

—

NEW BRUNSWICK

—

NOVA SCOTIA

—

PRINCE EDWARD ISLAND

—

QUÉBEC

—

MANITOBA

—

SASKATCHEWAN

—

ALBERTA

—

BRITISH COLUMBIA

—

ALASKA

TORONTO
A PERFECT DAY IN TOWN

- ⊕ Hilly, Intermediate, 1% unpaved
- ⊕ Map strava.com/routes/2892459863625716308
- ⊕ Test yourself mi 13 (km 21) strava.com/segments/1255700
- ⊕ Test yourself mi 19 (km 31) strava.com/segments/9126505

◉ GREG'S EYE

You need a whole day to enjoy this more than 80-mi (129-km) grand tour of Toronto. You'll view the CN Tower from all sides, both close up and from afar, and soak up the vibe of this magnificent, cosmopolitan, exciting city. Break it down into sections if you wish.

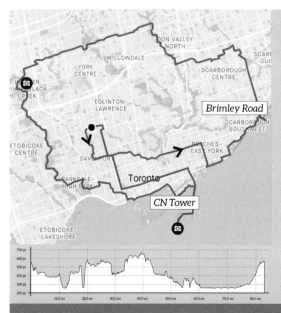

Toronto, North America's fourth-largest city, does everything big: 2.9 million inhabitants (7 million across the urban area), 28 mi (45 km) of shoreline on Lake Ontario—and this XXL route. We start in the southeast district of York for the pleasure of climbing the most popular local ramp, Brimley Road (1 mi/1.5 km at 6%). The long loop north is a breeze: together Birkdale, Betty Sutherland, East Don Parkland, Finch Hydro, and Humber River recreational trails add up to close to 40 mi (64 km). At Fort York (mi 61/km 98), Martin Goodman Trail leads to the foot of the CN Tower (1,750 ft/533 m high), then onto the intriguing peninsula of Leslie Street Spit. Then it's back to the high-rises of the Financial District and Little Italy. For the perfect day, make a refuel stop at Fix Coffee + Bikes (mi 59/km 95) on the edge of Little Portugal and Little Tibet.

	Distance		E+		Difficulty		Appeal
	83 mi (134 km)		**2,700 ft** (815 m)		**3/5**		**4/5**

Air: Toronto Pearson International Airport (30min by car).
Car: 2h from Buffalo, 4h from Detroit, 4h30 from Ottawa, 5h30 from Montréal.

La Bicicletta is a taste of Italy in the Toronto heights, serving a perfect espresso. Retailer of Pinarello, De Rosa, Colnago, Bianchi, and Basso. Strava Club.

La Bicicletta
1180 Castlefield Avenue
Toronto, ON M6B 1G1
labicicletta.com

Prince Edward Viaduct (mi 7/km 11). Kew Beach (mi 12/km 19). Bluffers Park (mi 18/km 29). Birkdale Ravine (mi 23/km 37). Humber River Park (mi 45/km 72). High Park (mi 56/km 90). CN Tower (mi 62/km 100). Harbor Lighthouse (mi 69/km 111). Downtown (mi 71/km 114).

COLLINGWOOD
BLUE MOUNTAIN TEST

- ⊕ Very hilly, Advanced, 5% unpaved
- ⊕ Map strava.com/routes/2892072604429631060
- ⊕ Test yourself mi 22 (km 35) strava.com/segments/21532256
- ⊕ Test yourself mi 47 (km 76) strava.com/segments/693667

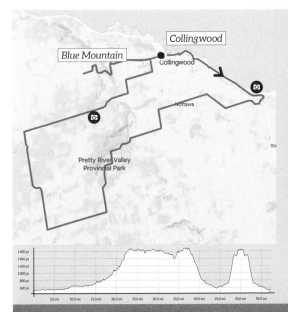

⊙ GREG'S EYE

Ontario's hills are nothing to compare with the Canadian Rockies to the west, nor parts of Québec. So there's no excuse to miss out on the short but vigorous ascent of Blue Mountain above Lake Huron.

Collingwood (pop. 25,000), 90 mi (145 km) northwest of Toronto, enjoys a fine reputation in the cycling community. This small resort on Georgian Bay, the northeastern arm of Lake Huron, is known as the step stool to the toughest hill in all Ontario: Scenic Caves Road. Facing west, the climb skirts the ski lifts of the popular Blue Mountain resort via two wide switchbacks. It's a short but challenging climb: 1.5 mi (2.5 km) at an average gradient of 9%, with a short segment at 15% halfway up. It concludes this route, which tackles the long climb of Pretty River Valley Park (final mile at 6%)—after a lakeside warm-up—before a 15-mi (24-km) ride along the rolling ridge of the Duncan Escarpment, itself part of the Niagara Escarpment, responsible for those stunning cliffs above Lake Huron.

Distance	E+	Difficulty	Appeal
57 mi (92 km)	**3,400 ft** (1,041 m)	**3/5**	**4/5**

Air: Toronto Pearson International Airport (2h by car). Car: 50 min from Barrie, 4h40 from Detroit, 5h30 from Ottawa, 9h from Chicago.

Little Ed's, close to the small marina, is Collingwood's go-to outdoors shop. Retailer of Scott and Marin.

15 Balsam St Collingwood, ON L9Y 4H6 littleeds.com

Collingwood Inukshuk (mi 2/km 3). Brocks Beach (mi 7/km 11). Pretty River Valley from Castle Glen Estates (mi 38/km 61). Bruce Trail Lookout and Scenic Caves (mi 51/km 82). Blue Mountain (mi 53/km 85).

ST. CATHARINES
CHEERS, NIAGARA FALLS !

◉ *Fairly flat, Intermediate, 0% unpaved* ◉ *Map strava.com/routes/2891689451746289536*

	Distance		E+		Difficulty		Appeal
⊢–⊣	**80 mi** (129 km)	⬆	**1,100 ft** (332 m)	📊	**2/5**	⭐	**5/5**

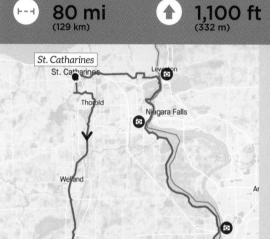

Niagara Falls are best viewed from the Canadian side. There, you are directly opposite the stunning spectacle of the Horseshoe Falls, a wonder of nature where the Niagara River makes a leap of nearly 200 ft (60 m) over a curved drop 0.5-mi (0.75-km) wide. You could stay watching the powerful waters for hours, having ridden from the bike shop Liberty! in St. Catharines along the Welland Canal, the Welland River, and Lake Erie, before Niagara Parkway opposite New York State. You get closest to the falls in Queen Victoria Park (mi 61/km 98). Celebrate with an Ontario merlot or pinot noir in the Niagara vineyards on the way back.

HAMILTON
ABOVE THE HAMMER

DIRT & GRAVEL

◉ *Hilly, Advanced, 45% unpaved* ◉ *Map strava.com/routes/2891642336960099154*

	Distance		E+		Difficulty		Appeal
⊢–⊣	**71 mi** (114 km)	⬆	**2,600 ft** (794 m)	📊	**3/5**	⭐	**4/5**

Hamilton (pop. 550,000), at the western end of Lake Ontario, is the epicenter of this bucolic, mixed-surface route (starting from Bicycle Works in Waterdown). We take the charming Hamilton Brantford Rail Trail for 12 mi (19 km), followed by other gravel byways on both sides of the Grand River, before the Chippewa Trail and Red Hill Valley Parkway on the way back to "The Hammer." Try to make time to ride the (surfaced) Waterfront Trail on Hamilton Harbour for a maritime vision of Lake Ontario—which we salute from on high on Waterdown Road, before pretty Smokey Hollow Waterfall. Take care on Argyle Street Bridge (mi 40/km 64)—it's narrow and busy.

DIRT & GRAVEL

THUNDER BAY
THE NIAGARA OF THE NORTH

- ⊕ Hilly, Advanced, 55% unpaved
- ⊕ Map strava.com/routes/2891764360163494572
- ⊕ Test yourself mi 20 (km 32) strava.com/segments/3959794
- ⊕ Test yourself mi 48 (km 77) strava.com/segments/21435152

◉ GREG'S EYE

The farmland surrounding Thunder Bay resembles that of neighboring Minnesota, where I lived for many years. I love this half-asphalt/half-gravel ride, the goal of which is the spectacle of the Kakabeka Falls—dubbed "Niagara of the North"—in wide-open Ontario.

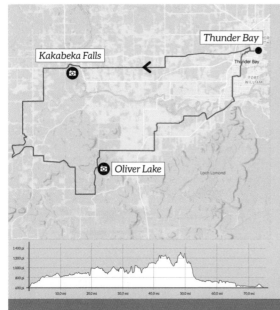

The largest expanse of fresh water in the world—its area exceeds that of Panama—Lake Superior and its surroundings have hidden treasures. At mi 19 (km 31) on our route, at the end of the long (8-mi/13-km) gravel Pole Line Road, you approach Kakabeka Falls and can hear the roar of the waters of the Kaministiquia River. In a few moments you're looking down at the 120-foot (37-m) drop from the footbridge. The sight of the "Niagara of the North" is well worth this long ride from Thunder Bay (pop. 110,000)—a proud Canadian lakehead. The route is more playful farther south, particularly around Oliver Lake, with a few short off-road ramps as steep as 8%. For a refuel, you can't do much better than the deli sandwiches at AJ's Trading Post (mi 55/km 89). Option: cut the distance to around 55 mi (89 km) by taking gravel Harstone Road (mi 25/km 40), then Highways 11 and 17.

 Distance **75 mi** (120 km)

 E+ **3,100 ft** (945 m)

 Difficulty **3/5**

 Appeal **4/5**

Air: Thunder Bay International Airport (20 min by car). Car: 6h from Minneapolis, 7h30 from Winnipeg, 10h from Chicago, 14h from Toronto.

Rollin' Thunder has been Thunder Bay's go-to outdoors emporium for twenty years, catering to summer cyclists and winter skiers. Retailer of Scott, Argon 18, Orbea, and Devinci.

485 Memorial Ave Thunder Bay, ON P7B 3Y6 rollinthunder.ca

Pole Line Road (mi 16/km 26). Kakabeka Falls (mi 19/km 31). Oliver Lake (mi 49/km 79). Mount McKay and Fort William Historical Park (mi 67/km 108). Current River Park, Centennial Park, Boulevard Lake, and Terry Fox Statue (near mi 75/km 121).

NORTH BAY
GATEWAY TO PEACE

⊕ *Hilly, Intermediate, 10% unpaved*　　　⊕ *Map strava.com/routes/2892381347225778772*

	Distance		E+		Difficulty		Appeal
⊢--⊣	**61 mi** (99 km)	⬆	**2,700 ft** (833 m)	📊	**3/5**	⭐	**4/5**

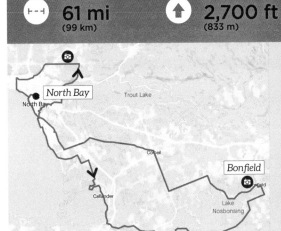

A good 3h drive north of Toronto and west of Ottawa, North Bay (pop. 50,000) has dubbed itself "Gateway to the North." Known to cyclists in Ontario, this section of the popular Voyageur Cycling Route is also the pretext for hilly rides (our own route starts at Wheelhouse bike shop) through the nature surrounding Nipissing and Nosbonsing Lakes, via the tranquil little towns of Callander, Bonfield, and Corbeil. Spice up the experience at the end of the ride by climbing Lees Road and Tower Drive, between Laurentian Ski Hill and Jack Garland Airport: 1.6 mi (2.5 km) at an average gradient of 6%. North Bay is indeed a gateway, to peace.

KENORA
AROUND THE LAKES

⊕ *Very hilly, Advanced, 0% unpaved*　　　⊕ *Map strava.com/routes/2892441386166603832*

	Distance		E+		Difficulty		Appeal
⊢--⊣	**68 mi** (111 km)	⬆	**3,700 ft** (1,124 m)	📊	**3/5**	⭐	**5/5**

You can barely go any farther west in Ontario. Kenora (pop. 15,000) is 1,000 mi (1,610 km) from Toronto as the crow flies, yet just 130 mi (209 km) from Winnipeg, Manitoba. Sitting on the Lake of the Woods, the town's marina is one of the busiest in North America. A race around the lakes is the preferred challenge of any local cyclist. Our own version starts from the Hardwear Company store and takes in Longbow, Island, Black Sturgeon, Sandy, Lulu, and Louise Lakes for a day of blue horizons and bumpy terrain. When you get back to Lake of the Woods, don't forget to snap a selfie in front of the famous outdoor sculpture Husky the Muskie.

OTTAWA
PARLEZ-VOUS FRANÇAIS ?

- ⊕ Very hilly, Intermediate, 55% unpaved
- ⊕ Map strava.com/routes/2891734573814521682
- ⊕ Test yourself mi 22 (km 35) strava.com/segments/21415279
- ⊕ Test yourself mi 35 (km 56) strava.com/segments/25740741

👁 GREG'S EYE

You can go trail riding all around Ottawa, the federal capital. The most tempting plan is to ride north to seek 40 mi (64 km) of pure delight in Gatineau Park. You'll hear French all around—that's normal, we're in Québec!

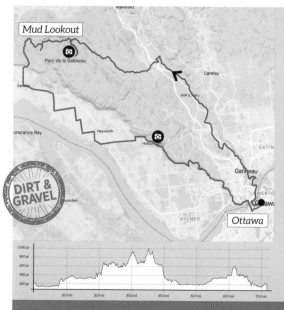

Mud Lookout

Ottawa

One mi (1.5 km) on the way out and 2 mi (3.25 km) on the way back is all you'll get of Ontario (and Ottawa) on this route that's 95% Québécois. Canada's federal capital is a border city; you only have to cross the Ottawa River to hear French and enjoy the paths and trails of Gatineau Park, the most visited in Québec—which makes sense, given that Ottawa has close to a million residents and nearly as many fans of the outdoors. We reach it after nearly 20 mi (32 km) on the (surfaced) Chelsea Trail along the Gatineau River. The park consists of 80% deciduous forest, with many lakes and streams. It is home to white-tailed deer and beavers. Two tough ramps lead to wonderful viewpoints: the first, the cabin above Lusk Lake (mi 30/km 48); the second, Mud Lake Lookout over Lac de la Vase (mi 35/km 56). Return via the Ottawa River and Pink Lake, another superb panorama.

	Distance		E+		Difficulty		Appeal
	72 mi (115 km)	⬆	**3,900 ft** (1,193 m)	📊	**3/5**	⭐	**4/5**

Air: Ottawa International Airport (30 min by car). Car: 2h15 from Montréal, 4h30 from Toronto, 5h from Albany.

Ottawa Bike Cafe, close to Place de la Confédération, is a model of its kind, with plenty of space, excellent coffee, beer, and snacks, hand-built bikes, and live music.

**79b Sparks St
Ottawa, ON K1P 5A5
bikecafe.ca**

The Ottawa River from Jacques-Cartier Park (mi 30/km 48). Lusk Lake (mi 30/km 48). Mud Lake Lookout (mi 35/km 56). Lac Mountains (mi 57/km 92). Pink Lake (mi 62/km 100). Chaudière Falls (mi 69/km 111). Historic buildings of Parliament Hill (mi 71/km 114).

FREDERICTON
START EARLY !

🌐 *Hilly, Advanced, 75% unpaved*   🌐 *Map strava.com/routes/2891250636222636716*

	Distance		E+		Difficulty		Appeal
⊢⊣	**88 mi** (142 km)	⬆	**3,300 ft** (1,004 m)	📊	**3/5**	⭐	**4/5**

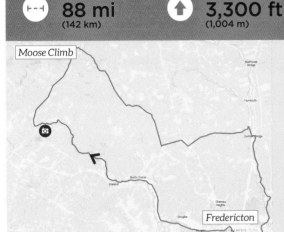

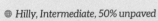

Fredericton (pop. 60,000), which declares itself "Atlantic Canada's Riverfront Capital," is the gateway to an array of sublime gravel routes through a vast landscape of spruce and pine. This loop north of the Saint John River through the hills of Crabbe Mountain ski resort (starting from Savage's Bicycle Center) can take up a whole summer day. The terrain is somewhat surly in places, such as on Moose Climb (mi 44/km 71): 1 mi (1.5 km) at 7%. Leave early to be back in Fredericton in time to catch the picturesque changing of the guard on Officers' Square at 4 p.m., before a well-earned ice cream at the foot of the Lighthouse On the Green.

HALIFAX
A TASTE OF SALT WATER

🌐 *Hilly, Intermediate, 50% unpaved*   🌐 *Map strava.com/routes/2891296890445916292*

	Distance		E+		Difficulty		Appeal
⊢⊣	**58 mi** (94 km)	⬆	**2,400 ft** (726 m)	📊	**3/5**	⭐	**4/5**

Before the great adventure of the Cabot Trail on Cape Breton Island, in far northeast Nova Scotia, how about a warm-up on mixed terrain, starting from Giant Bicycle in Halifax (pop. 400,000)? Heading east, we leave the fishing port behind on perfect trails, including the popular Salt Marsh Trail—a former railway line that crosses the Cole Harbour–Lawrencetown Coastal Heritage Park at water level, then Porters Lake. The latter, open to the Atlantic Ocean, holds both fresh and salt water. Atlantic View Trail carries you to the edge of the waves, before returning over several tough little ramps to Halifax and its emblematic clock tower.

CHARLOTTETOWN
RED SANDS

⊕ *Hilly, Intermediate, 0% unpaved*   ⊕ Map *strava.com/routes/2891383731048959872*

Distance
65 mi
(104 km)

E+
3,700 ft
(1,132 m)

Difficulty
3/5

Appeal
5/5

Prince Edward Island is Canada's smallest province: a marvelous place where you're never more than 10 mi (16 km) from the coast. It is also renowned for its red sandy beaches, caused by a high iron-oxide content, particularly in the soil of the southwest. You can see this on our route on Kingston Road as we traverse the fields.
At Victoria (mi 24/km 39), Northumberland Strait provides the startling sight of a rusty red coast where you won't know which way to look, so surprising is each mile, from DeSable to Canoe Cove, Argyle Shore Park to Cumberland.
Begin your ride at MacQueen's Bike Shop in Charlottetown.

CHARLOTTETOWN
CONFEDERATION RIDE

⊕ *Hilly, Intermediate, 80% unpaved*   ⊕ Map *strava.com/routes/2891338290446636928*

Distance
67 mi
(108 km)

E+
1,600 ft
(499 m)

Difficulty
3/5

Appeal
4/5

There's more to Prince Edward Island than coast. Its backcountry of villages, farms, and hills is full of charm when the wind isn't blowing too hard. We celebrate all that with a gravel ride (starting from Receiver Coffee—the Brass Shop in Charlottetown) via the winding, bumpy Confederation Trail, which our route hops onto in the center of the island (mi 5/km 8 to mi 27/km 43, then mi 36/km 58 to mi 63/km 101).
Its moniker commemorates the Charlottetown Conference of 1864, which was the decisive step toward the union of the Canadian provinces. Make a halt on Mount Stewart bridge (mi 42/km 68) for the ballet of belugas on the Hillsborough River.

BAIE-SAINT-PAUL
CHARLEVOIX CLIFFS

- Very hilly, Expert, 0% unpaved
- Map strava.com/routes/2888823279393997050
- Test yourself mi 12 (km 19) strava.com/segments/14276191
- Test yourself mi 37 (km 60) strava.com/segments/9368147

👁 GREG'S EYE

"La Misère" is the name given by local Strava cyclists to the segment of terrifying ramp that takes us back to Baie-Saint-Paul on this route, and which overlooks the Saint Lawrence River. The Charlevoix cliffs are a tough test. But so beautiful.

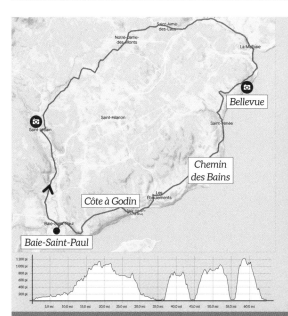

Bellevue

Chemin des Bains

Côte à Godin

Baie-Saint-Paul

A succession of stunning vistas, Charlevoix owes its particular relief to the impact of a giant meteorite that fell 400 million years ago! Starting from the Musée d'Art Contemporain in Baie-Saint-Paul (pop. 7,000), we cross a plateau of forests and fields, pretty villages, and solitary farms to Saint-Aimé-des-Lacs. La Malbaie (mi 34/km 55) marks the beginning of a sporty adventure with panoramic views along the Saint Lawrence River. Three epic climbs are the order of the day: first Bellevue (1.5 mi/2.5 km at an average gradient of 7.5%), then Chemin des Bains after Saint-Irénée (2.6 mi/4.25 km at 6%), and finally the formidable "La Misère" (officially called the Côte à Godin) after Saint-Joseph-de-la-Rive (1.4 mi/2.25 km at more than 13%, with the first third at 16% followed by a section at 19%). But once you've cleared this obstacle, the view is amazing.

 Distance
65 mi
(104 km)

 E+
5,900 ft
(1,796 m)

 Difficulty
4/5

 Appeal
5/5

Air: Jean Lesage International Airport, Québec City (1h20 by car), Pierre Elliott Trudeau International Airport, Montréal (4h by car).
Car: 3h30 from Sherbrooke, 5h30 from Ottawa.

A suitable establishment is expected to open in Baie-Saint-Paul in the near future. Until then, *Velo Cartel* in Québec City is your nearest best choice. Retailer of BMC. Training center, Strava Club.

**367 Rue Soumande
Québec City, QC G1M 1A5
velocartel.cc**

Rivière du Gouffre (mi 10/km 16). Lac Nairne (mi 24/km 39). Observatoire de l'Astroblème (mi 38/km 61). Bellevue, in front of the airport runway (mi 42/km 68). Jetée des Capelans (mi 44/km 71). The river and Isle-aux-Coudres (mi 52/km 84 and mi 58/km 93).

The impressive cliffs in Charlevoix, overlooking the Saint Lawrence River, Québec.

SHAWINIGAN
MAURICIE THE BEAUTIFUL

⊕ Very hilly, Advanced, 0% unpaved
⊕ Map strava.com/routes/2888829018782594910

⊕ Test yourself mi 23 (km 37) strava.com/segments/4364142
⊕ Test yourself mi 38 (km 61) strava.com/segments/18138096

◉ GREG'S EYE

The road through the Parc National de la Mauricie, halfway between Montréal and Québec City, seems conceived for a perfect ride with friends, being neither too long nor too hard, with an extraordinary landscape of forests and lakes. Put it at the top of your list.

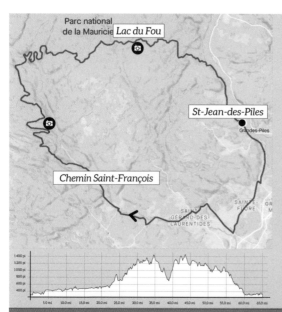

Parc national de la Mauricie
Lac du Fou
St-Jean-des-Piles
Grandes-Piles
Chemin Saint-François
SAINT-GÉRARD-DES-LAURENTIDES
SAINTE-FLORE

A full 200 sq mi (520 sq km) of dense forest (deciduous, with many pines) and an abundance of lakes (around 150) distinguish the Parc National de la Mauricie, north of the Saint Lawrence River. The road that circles it is about 60 mi (97 km) of winding asphalt that's up and down all the way. You won't get bored. Our route starts 12 mi (19 km) from the center of Shawinigan, in Saint-Jean-des-Piles, close to one of the two park gates. Riding clockwise, we meet our first proper ramp just after the other gate: 1 mi (1.5 km) at 6% from the get-go, on Chemin Saint-François. Only the ramp at mi 39 (63 km), just after crossing Lac Wapizagonke, is harder (2 mi/3.25 km at 6%). Just beyond that is the outlook, with views north and south. You won't pass a single village or see any sign of life until you return to Saint-Jean. "The Beauty Next Door"—Mauricie merits its nickname.

	Distance		E+		Difficulty		Appeal
⊢⊣	**65 mi** (105 km)	⬆	**5,000 ft** (1,539 m)	▥	**4/5**	★	**5/5**

Air: Jean Lesage International Airport, Québec City (1h30 by car), Pierre Elliott Trudeau International Airport, Montréal (2h by car).
Car: 30 min from Trois-Rivières, 2h from Sherbrooke, 3h30 from Ottawa.

Le Yéti, a store catering to all outdoor disciplines, has branches in Trois-Rivières and Shawinigan. Perfect road-bike servicing. Retailer of Specialized, Devinci, and Argon 18.

**363 5ᵉ rue de la Pointe
Shawinigan, QC G9N 1E4
leyeti.quebec**

Lac Modène (mi 28/km 45). Belvédère de l'Île-aux-Pins (mi 30/km 48). Belvédère du Passage (mi 40/km 64). Lac Écarté (mi 46/km 74). Lac du Fou (mi 53/km 85). Rivière Saint-Maurice (mi 59/km 95). Church of Saint-Jean-des-Piles (mi 65/km 105).

SAINTE-ROSE-DU-NORD
RIDE AROUND THE FJORD

⊕ *Very hilly, Advanced, 13% unpaved*   ⊕ *Map strava.com/routes/2890670176293089246*

	Distance		E+		Difficulty		Appeal
⊢–⊣	**157 mi** (254 km)	⬆	**10,500 ft** (3,191 m)	📊	**3/5**	⭐	**5/5**

At Tadoussac, the oldest surviving French settlement in the Americas, 130 mi (209 km) northeast of Québec City, the Saint Lawrence River is so wide that it feels like an ocean. A tributary, the Saguenay River, flows into it through a intracontinental fjord, to be explored over two to three days. There are villages, grandiose panoramas, vertiginous cliffs, sublime bays, and whale shows. We start from Sainte-Rose-du-Nord on a sweeping ride to L'Anse-Saint-Jean, from which we return via shuttle boat. The crossing from Tadoussac to Baie-Sainte-Catherine (mi 81/ km 130) takes a mere 10 min. An extraordinary adventure beside and above the fjord.

MONT-LOUIS
CHIC-CHOCS IN GASPÉSIE

DIRT & GRAVEL

⊕ *Low mountain, Advanced, 65% unpaved*   ⊕ *Map strava.com/routes/2890569400946492868*

	Distance		E+		Difficulty		Appeal
⊢–⊣	**116 mi** (187 km)	⬆	**8,500 ft** (2,594 m)	📊	**4/5**	⭐	**5/5**

The Gaspé Peninsula is far-flung territory, so bike-packing is the proper way to explore it. Avoid Route 132 as much as possible. This 500-mi (805-km) long highway, 80% of which hugs the coast, has heavy traffic. With few other surfaced roads, a gravel bike is a must. Starting from Auberge l'Amarré in Mont-Louis, on the Saint Lawrence River, we explore the Chic-Chocs Wildlife Reserve over two days. Riding through a landscape of conifers, birch, and (above 2,000 ft/610 m) tundra, keep your eyes peeled for moose, which are native to the area. Man has left few traces, except around the former copper mines of Murdochville (mi 91/km 146).

BROMONT
GREEN TRAILS

- 🌐 Low mountain, Expert, 70% unpaved
- 🌐 Map strava.com/routes/2888813813681815390
- ◉ Test yourself mi 57 (km 92) strava.com/segments/5200539
- ◉ Test yourself mi 64 (m 103) strava.com/segments/2785641

👁 GREG'S EYE

You won't meet a Québécois cyclist who'll fail to vaunt the virtues of Bromont and its environs: quiet roads; dozens of miles of cycle paths; great MTB single tracks; even a velodrome! And if they mention fabulous gravel routes, you'd best listen closely.

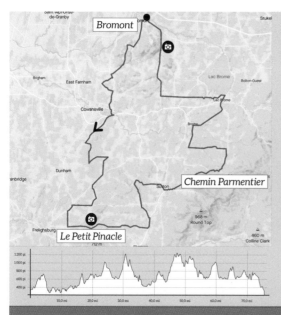

Situated between Montréal and Sherbrooke, Bromont (pop. 10,000) is a cycling hub, even housing a national cycling center where you can experience the thrill of riding a velodrome—the only one in Québec. All disciplines are catered to, including gravel, of which there's plenty on this route south of Bromont via Cowansville, Sutton, and Brome Lake. It explores the trails of the Green Mountains, which present some challenging relief, an endless rodeo that's particularly aggressive on the Chemin du Pinacle close to the border with Vermont; Chemin Parmentier near the Sommet des Hollandais; and Sugar Hill toward the end of the ride. It's a difficult loop, but the landscapes are staggeringly beautiful—the Green Mountains wear their name well. Another must is Lac Memphrémagog, a little farther east, circled by a surfaced road that crosses into the United States.

Distance	E+	Difficulty	Appeal
76 mi (122 km)	**6,800 ft** (2,067 m)	**4/5**	**4/5**

Air: Pierre Elliott Trudeau International Airport, Montréal (1h15 by car). Car: 1h from Sherbrooke, 3h from Quebec, 3h from Ottawa, 4h from Albany, 4h30 from Boston.

Pittstop Vélo-Café is a young establishment that has quickly made a name for itself in Bromont. Very good coffee and excellent food. Retailer of BMC, Kona, and Argon 18.

**80 Bromont Blvd
Bromont, QC J2L 2K3
pittstopvc.com**

Mont Gale (mi 4/km 6). Lac Davignon (mi 11/km 18). Sommet du Mont Pinnacle (mi 31/km 50). Sommet des Hollandais (mi 47/km 76). Mont Brome—foot of the ski runs (mi 72/km 116). Velodrome of the Centre National de Cyclisme (mi 76/km 122).

LAC MÉGANTIC
BIG BORDER RAMPS

⊕ *Low mountain, Advanced, 0% unpaved*   ⊕ *Map strava.com/routes/2888802749162081530*

	Distance		E+		Difficulty		Appeal
⊢–⊣	**68 mi** (110 km)	⬆	**7,500 ft** (2,284 m)	📊	**4/5**	★	**5/5**

Lac Mégantic
Lac Mégantic
Mont-Mégantic
Mont Scotch

In the most remote part of the Cantons-de-l'Est, nestled against Maine, stands iconic Mont Mégantic, a highlight of the annual Tour de Beauce. The climb to its observatory is a fearsome one: 3 mi (4.75 km) at 10%, the preceding 3 mi (4.75 km) at 5%, and sections at 12% to 14%. At the summit (close to 3,600 ft/1,095 m), the vistas are simply breathtaking. The view over Lac Mégantic from neighboring Mont Saint-Joseph is even more stunning, but it comes at a cost of 1 mi (1.5 km) of pedaling at 13.5%. Indeed, the relief is pretty bold throughout this route, which starts at the town of Lac Mégantic in the heart of the Québécois Appalachians.

MONTRÉAL
TO ONTARIO CENTURY

⊕ *Fairly flat, Advanced, 0% unpaved*   ⊕ *Map strava.com/routes/2890180949541298846*

	Distance		E+		Difficulty		Appeal
⊢–⊣	**107 mi** (173 km)	⬆	**2,600 ft** (781 m)	📊	**3/5**	★	**4/5**

Mont Royal

This XXL escapade west (from Ma Bicyclette bike café) is an ambitious quest out of Canada's second-largest urban area (pop. 4.1 million) to the border between Québec and Ontario, with the common thread of water. That includes Lachine Canal, Lacs Saint-Louis and Deux Montagnes, a 5-min ferry crossing of the Ottawa River, and bridges over the Rivières des Milles Îles et des Prairies, interspersed with charming spots linked by bike paths. Montréal awaits at the end of this century. Will you have the strength to climb Mont Royal via the Camillien Houde segment (1.2 mi/2 km at 8%), and then the Belvédère de Westmount (0.5 mi/0.75 km at 7%)?

MONT-TREMBLANT
LAURENTIDES EXPRESS

- Low mountain, Advanced, 0% unpaved
- Map strava.com/routes/2890143082679613314
- Test yourself mi 15 (km 24) strava.com/segments/21036207
- Test yourself mi 22 (km 35) strava.com/segments/10245634

◉ GREG'S EYE

Skiing, fishing, mountain biking: there is much to compose a contented life around Mont-Tremblant, in the Laurentides massif. No long climbs, but routes that test your mettle, on an impeccable network of backroads, between peaks over 2,000 ft (610 m) and countless lakes.

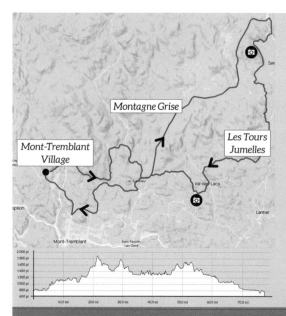

Montagne Grise

Les Tours Jumelles

Mont-Tremblant Village

Have you heard of the P'tit Train du Nord? It's one of the most popular recreational rail trails in Québec, climbing gently for 145 mi (233 km) on a mixture of asphalt and gravel through the Laurentides, from Saint-Jérôme to Mont-Laurier. On the way, it passes through touristy Mont-Tremblant (pop. 10,000). Our route is a more bracing ride, taking the network of backroads to Lac Archambault and back again in a winding loop over the rough and wearing terrain of the Laurentides. The harder slopes are short: 1 mi (1.5 km) at 8% to ascend Montagne Grise (mi 21/km 34) up to 1,900 ft (580 m), and the same again near Mont Coutu (mi 29/km 47) and Les Tours Jumelles (mi 48/km 77). The scenery is rich, with many lakes, and the emblematic summit of Mont Tremblant (3,175 ft/970 m).

	Distance		E+		Difficulty		Appeal
	78 mi (125 km)		**6,100 ft** (1,846 m)		**4/5**		**5/5**

Air: Pierre Elliott Trudeau International Airport, Montréal (1h15 by car). Car: 1h45 from Ottawa, 3h30 from Québec City, 6h from Toronto.

Cybercycle, on the shores of Lac Mercier, is a cozy bike café with a pretty terrace and an expert team. Retailer of Specialized and Argon 18.

1908 Chemin du Village Mont-Tremblant, QC J8E 1K4
cybercycletremblant.com

Mont Tremblant (mi 3/km 5). Rivière du Diable (mi 8/km 13). Lac Supérieur (mi 12/km 19). Montagne Blanche (mi 21/km 34). Cap de la Fée (mi 38/km 61). Lac Archambault (mi 42/km 68). Lac Bœuf (mi 49/km 79). Lac Quenouille (mi 57/km 92).

WINNIPEG
COLD, REALLY?

- ⊕ *Flat, Intermediate, 25% unpaved*
- ⊕ *Map strava.com/routes/2887358656800071856*

- ⊕ *Tes yourself mi 16 (km 26) strava.com/segments/20378873*
- ⊕ *Test yourself mi 54 (km 87) strava.com/segments/20553766*

◉ GREG'S EYE

Winnipeg, reputed to be the city with the coldest winters in the world, is often neglected by visitors to Canada, but the capital of Manitoba has much to offer. If the vast surrounding plains don't attract you, the town will—especially in fall, its pleasantest season.

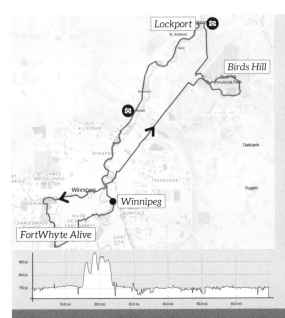

Given that Neil Young grew up and learned the guitar here, might we suggest cycling around Winnipeg under a harvest moon? Or perhaps on a beautiful autumn day? Late fall is showy in the capital of Manitoba (pop. 750,000). This route explores its urban heart, from the Saint Boniface French district in the east to the Forks (its historic center)—there's also the option of quickly crossing between the two in a few pedal strokes via the elegant Esplanade Riel footbridge (mi 1.5/km 2.5 and mi 50/km 80). We're never far from abundant nature, be it the imposing Red and Assiniboine Rivers that meet at the Forks, Birds Hill Provincial Park (Winnipeg's only hill) to the north (a 7-mi/11.25-km loop starting at mi 14/km 23), or Assiniboine Forest to the south (mi 57/km 92), which leads to FortWhyte Alive and its bison enclosure.

	Distance		E+		Difficulty		Appeal
⊢─┤	**70 mi** (112 km)	⬆	**700 ft** (207 m)	📊	**2/5**	★	**3/5**

Air: James Armstrong Richardson International Airport, Winnipeg (30 min by car).
Car: 6h from Regina, 7h from Minneapolis, 7h30 from Thunder Bay, 13h from Calgary.

Yellow Derny Cafe is the perfect place for an espresso or more at *Woodcock Cycle Works*, close to the Saint Boniface French district.

433 St Mary's Rd
Winnipeg, MB R2M 3K7
woodcockcycle.com

Saint Boniface Cathedral, Esplanade Riel, and downtown (mi 1.5/km 2). Lockport Lock and Dam (mi 30/km 48). Kildonan Park (mi 44/km 71). Forks Historic Port and Forks Market (mi 50/km 80). The bison of FortWhyte Alive (mi 60/km 97).

ONANOLE
ABOVE THE GREAT PLAINS

- Low mountain, Advanced, 76% unpaved
- Map strava.com/routes/2887792407956269186
- Test yourself mi 40 (km 64) strava.com/segments/2493019
- Test yourself mi 57 (km 92) strava.com/segments/5277862

◉ GREG'S EYE

On the map of Canada, Riding Mountain National Park appears remote, with a modest surface area compared with the neighboring Lakes Manitoba and Winnipeg. Yet it offers immense gravel pleasures, from around Clear Lake to the spectacular Manitoba Escarpment.

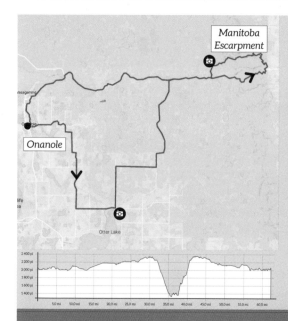

Manitoba Escarpment

Onanole

There is much pleasure to be had on the bumpy trails of Riding Mountain National Park, with the crystal waters of Clear Lake (170 mi/274 km northeast of Winnipeg) as a reference point. With a wild plateau, boreal forest, the Lake Audy Bison Enclosure, and little lakes and glacial meltwater channels all around, Riding Mountain National Park (1,150 sq mi/2,980 sq km) is a distillation of the Canadian North, West, and East. It offers a feeling of freedom, particularly on the eastern portion of this route (starting from Poor Michael's Emporium bookstore and café in Onanole) on the crests of the Manitoba Escarpment, a geological feature from the last ice age. On top, you overlook forest and the great plains from nearly 1,500 ft (455 m). It's a slog to get there (narrow 5-mi/8-km trail, with two 1-mi/1.5-km segments at between 6 and 8%), but the views wipe it all away.

Distance	E+	Difficulty	Appeal
62 mi (100 km)	**3,300 ft** (1,004 m)	**3/5**	**4/5**

Air: James Armstrong Richardson International Airport, Winnipeg (3h by car). Car: 4h from Regina, 9h30 from Minneapolis, 10h from Thunder Bay, 11h from Calgary.

A&L Cycle in Brandon, 100 mi (161 km) south of Onanole, is the nearest specialist to the route. Retailer of Cervelo and Trek. Strava Club.

201 Rosser Avenue Brandon, MB R7A 0J8 alcycle.ca

Otter Lake (mi 13/km 21). Gate to the park (mi 35/km 56). Crest of the Manitoba Escarpment (mi 42/km 68). Clear Lake (mi 57/km 92). Wasagaming Visitors Center (mi 59/km 95).

REGINA
HEART OF THE PRAIRIES

⊕ *Fairly flat, Intermediate, 20% unpaved*   ⊕ *Map strava.com/routes/2888071847096252546*

	Distance		E+		Difficulty		Appeal
	**50 mi** (80 km)	⬆	**600 ft** (179 m)	📊	**2/5**	⭐	**3/5**

White Butte
Regina
Regina
Coppersands
EMERALD PARK
Emerald Park
POPLAR

Regina (pop. 200,000), 160 mi (257 km) southeast of Saskatoon, is the capital of Saskatchewan. Although little of the city's architectural heritage has survived its turbulent past, you'll appreciate the Royal Saskatchewan Museum (mi 1/km 2), the MacKenzie Art Gallery (near mi 2.5/km 4), and above all the bucolic Wascana Lake once you cross Albert Memorial Bridge. This route (starting from Dutch Cycle) then leads east via other green vistas (University, Wascana View) to two popular recreational spots in "Prairie City," Emerald Park and White Butte: cross-country skiing in winter, 5 mi (8 km) of trails in summer.

SASKATOON
URBAN AND RURAL AT ONCE

⊕ *Fairly flat, Intermediate, 15% unpaved*   ⊕ *Map strava.com/routes/2888030345194631368*

	Distance		E+		Difficulty		Appeal
	51 mi (81 km)	⬆	**700 ft** (207 m)	📊	**2/5**	⭐	**4/5**

LAWSON
BLAIRMORE
Saskatoon
Saskatoon
MWOOD
NUTANA LAKEWOOD
Hillcrest Gardens

For half this route (starting from Bruce's Cycle Works), we stick to the banks of the South Saskatchewan River, which is so important to Saskatoon (pop. 250,000), the city nicknamed "Paris of the Prairies." A total of nine bridges span the river. At mi 10 (km 16), we head south to try a famous Saskatoon pie at the Berry Barn. Before and after, you'll sample river views and green vistas, pedaling down the Meewasin Trail and through Kiwanis, Victoria, and Holiday Parks on the west bank, then Hyde Park, Forestry Farm Park, and many others. A city of bridges and biking, nearly 400 mi (645 km) east of Calgary.

CALGARY
OLYMPIC BREAKAWAY

- ⊕ *Very hilly, Intermediate, 10% unpaved*
- ⊕ *Map strava.com/routes/2888415637378462558*
- ⊕ *Test yourself mi 11 (km 18) strava.com/segments/21139573*
- ⊕ *Test yourself mi 43 (km 69) strava.com/segments/15732901*

👁 GREG'S EYE

When you think of Calgary, you think of the 1988 Winter Olympics, of course, where the United States won fewer medals than Finland and the Netherlands! Calgary is also a beautiful destination for fly fishing and, above all, for cycling.

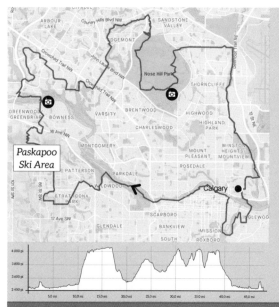

Paskapoo
Ski Area

Calgary is Canada's fourth-largest urban area (pop. 1.6 million). The city revolves around ecotourism and the Rocky Mountains, and is very pleasant to cycle around. There is no shortage of bike lanes along the Bow River or through the many parks. The memory of the 1988 Winter Games endures. We encounter the Olympics at mi 4 (km 6.5) in front of the elegant Saddledome, where Katarina Witt and Brian Boitano set the ice ablaze (now home to the Flames), and again at mi 17 (km 27) on the descending switchbacks by the Paskapoo ski jumps. Before that, you'll have hauled yourself up the challenging Coach Hill (2 mi/3.25 km at 6%), while farther on, there await the hills of Scenic Acres, Edgemont Ravine, and Nose Hill Park: 4.5 mi (7.25 km) of up-and-down gravel through a steppe-like landscape. Olympic champion Calgary is now bike friendly indeed.

Distance **48 mi** (77 km)	**E+** **2,900 ft** (891 m)	**Difficulty** **3/5**	**Appeal** **4/5**

Air: Calgary International Airport (20 min by car). Car: 3h from Edmonton, 7h from Regina, 11h30 from Vancouver, 12h from Seattle.

Bike and Brew, on First Avenue, north of the Bow River, is the go-to bike café in Calgary. Retailer of Kona, Marin, Masi, and Cinelli.

921 First Avenue NE Calgary, AB T2E 2L3 gobikeandbrew.ca

Downtown from Scotsman's Hill (mi 3/km 5). Prince's Island Park (mi 6/km 10). Top of Coach Hill Road (mi 12/km 19). Paskapoo Ski Area (mi 18/km 29). Baker Park (mi 20/km 32). View over the city from Nose Hill Park (mi 37/km 60).

CANMORE
WARM-UP IN BOW VALLEY

- High mountain, Advanced, 1% unpaved
- Map strava.com/routes/2888376725132697438
- Test yourself mi 13 (km 21) strava.com/segments/1435800
- Test yourself mi 25 (km 40) strava.com/segments/20649815

Canmore owes much to the 1988 Winter Olympics. The little town 60 mi (97 km) west of Calgary hosted cross-country skiing and acquired a reputation that still attracts cyclists in summer. This is a gorgeous route on the edge of Banff National Park, the most beautiful in Canada!

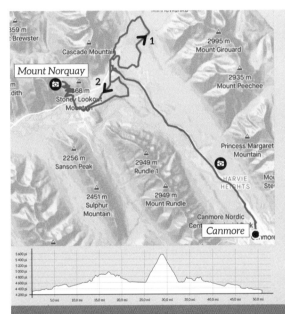

Bow Valley, west of Calgary, is the way to the finest ascents in the Canadian Rockies. Farther north from Canmore (pop. 15,000), where our route starts, Lake Louise ski resort (in the sublime and popular Banff National Park) has two fine climbs for cyclists: Moraine Lake (5.4 mi/8.75 km at 4%) and Montée du Château (2 mi/3.25 km at 6%). Farther south, you can climb the long Highwood Pass (8.5 mi/13.75 km at 4%) in the shadow of Mount Assiniboine (11,870 ft/3,620 m). The route suggested here is a perfect warm-up before those more ambitious challenges. The loop of Lake Minnewanka Scenic Drive, Tunnel Mountain Drive above Banff, and above all the final switchback (mi 28/km 45) before the summit of Mount Norquay (3.5 mi/5.75 km at 5.5%) also has formidable promontories. The splendors of mountainous Alberta unfold before your eyes!

Distance	E+	Difficulty	Appeal
51 mi (82 km)	**2,700 ft** (824 m)	**3/5**	**5/5**

 Air: Calgary International Airport (1h15 by car). Car: 4h from Edmonton, 8h from Regina, 10h from Vancouver, 11h from Seattle.

 Bicycle Cafe is the headquarters of the Bow Valley cycling community. Retailer of Kona, Specialized, Giant, and Liv. Strava Club.

630 Main Street
Canmore, AB T1W 2B5
bicyclecafe.com

 Cascade Ponds (mi 12/km 19). Lake Minnewanka (mi 18/km 29). Mount Norquay Lookout (mi 28/km 45). Hoodoos Viewpoint (mi 35/km 56). Bow River (mi 46/km 74).

Panorama over the Bow Range from Bow Valley Parkway in the heart of Banff National Park, Alberta.

WATER VALLEY
GRAVEL GHOST HUNT

DIRT & GRAVEL

- ⊕ *Low mountain, Advanced, 75% unpaved*
- ⊕ *Map strava.com/routes/2889913131347829284*

- ⊕ *Test yourself mi 26 (km 42) strava.com/segments/9520278*
- ⊕ *Test yourself mi 76 (km 122) strava.com/segments/14957403*

👁 GREG'S EYE

The legendary Forestry Trunk Road in Alberta runs along the eastern slopes of the Rocky Mountains between 4,000 ft (1,220 m) and 5,500 ft (1,675 m). It is mostly gravel surfaced. We make use of it on this route inspired by the popular annual off-road event Ghost of the Gravel.

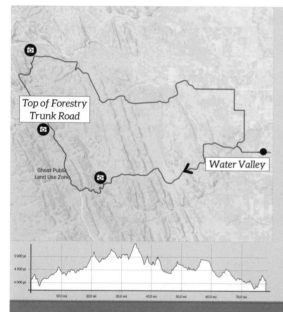

Top of Forestry Trunk Road

Ghost Public Land Use Zone

Water Valley

Even though we don't properly attack the slopes of the Rocky Mountains, this route racks up quite an elevation gain! The trails of the Alberta hills, 50 mi (80 km) northwest of Calgary, don't lead to superb panoramas by chance. First, you have to steer your bike up and down, to reach an altitude of 5,400 ft (1,645 m). Our ride extends no farther west than the 14-mi (23-km) stretch (mi 25/km 40 to mi 39/km 63) of the legendary Forestry Trunk Road, a wide gravel track that follows the Rocky Mountains for over 600 mi (965 km). The scenery is magnificent wild forest (no villages in sight) explored by the Ghost of the Gravel founders between the Ghost River in the south and the Red Deer River in the north. At mi 70 (km 113), quaff a refreshing glass of mead at Fallentimber Meadery, before refueling with a buffalo burger at the picturesque Water Valley Saloon upon your return.

	Distance		E+		Difficulty		Appeal
🚩	**78 mi** (125 km)	⬆	**7,100 ft** (2,151 m)	📊	**4/5**	⭐	**5/5**

Air: Calgary International Airport (1h by car). Car: 3h from Edmonton, 8h from Regina, 12h from Vancouver.

Bow Cycle, in northwest Calgary, is a major sponsor of Ghost of the Gravel. Retailer of Kona, Norco, Specialized, and Salsa. Strava Club.

6501 Bowness Rd NW Calgary, AB T3B 0E8 bowcycle.com

Range Road 54 (mi 2/km 3). Little Red Deer River (mi 21/km 34). Hunter Valley (mi 28/km 45). Top of the route (mi 34/km 55). Burnt Timber Canyon (mi 42/km 68). Water Valley Saloon (mi 78/km 126).

JASPER
SKYTRAM AND GLACIER

⊕ *High mountain, Expert, 1% unpaved*
⊕ *Map strava.com/routes/2888385173656706910*

⊕ *Test yourself mi 10 (km 16) strava.com/segments/724238*
⊕ *Test yourself mi 33 (km 53) strava.com/segments/9939316*

◉ GREG'S EYE

North of Banff National Park lies Jasper National Park, another paradise in the Albertan Rocky Mountains. The long ascent of Cavell Road, with its extraordinary scenery, reminds me of the great Alpine passes of Switzerland, France, and Italy.

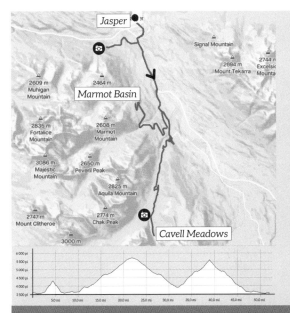

Jasper National Park, west of Edmonton, boasts the Columbia Icefield, hot springs, black bears, grizzlies, and caribou. And there is plenty of climbing to be done above the waters of the Athabasca River. Our route covers two superb climbs south of Jasper (pop. 4,000). Cavell Road resembles some of the great European cols: 11 mi (18 km) long, an average gradient of 4%, with some slopes as steep as 8%, and a 19% section at the start! The views of the sheer sides of Mount Edith Cavell and its impressive Angel Glacier are breathtaking. On the way back, you can add the climb up to Marmot Basin ski resort (7 mi/11.25 km at 5%). Of course, SkyTram Road near the beginning of the route is a worthy initial challenge (2 mi/3.25 km at more than 8%), although from the top you can take the aerial tramway to the Whistlers for an emotional ride of quite another sort.

	Distance		E+		Difficulty		Appeal
⊢–⊣	**52 mi** (84 km)	⬆	**5,500 ft** (1,691 m)	📊	**4/5**	★	**5/5**

Air: Edmonton International Airport (4h by car), Calgary International Airport (4h30 by car).
Car: 8h30 from Vancouver, 8h30 from Saskatoon, 9h30 from Seattle.

The Bench Bike Shop, founded in 2018 and surrounded by cafés and restaurants, is the perfect Jasper base camp. Retailer of Salsa and Kona. Rentals.

**606 Patricia St
Jasper, AB T0E 1E0
thebenchbikeshop.com**

SkyTram Platform (mi 4.5/km 7). Athabasca River (mi 14/km 23). Cavell Lake (mi 21/km 34). Cavell Meadows (mi 22/km 35). Marmot Basin (mi 39/63 km). Colorful houses in Jasper (mi 52/km 84).

VERNON
SILVERSTAR AND RED APPLES

⊕ *High mountain, Advanced, 0% unpaved*
⊕ *Map strava.com/routes/2893209205031024856*

⊕ *Test yourself mi 10 (km 16) strava.com/segments/24843964*
⊕ *Test yourself mi 32 (km 51) strava.com/segments/12630923*

◉ GREG'S EYE

I'm more familiar with Whistler Mountain, where I trained as a young freestyle skier, but the road to SilverStar (up to 5,400 ft/1,645 m) is also one of the hardest ascents in British Columbia. On the way back, enjoy the pleasant Okanagan Valley.

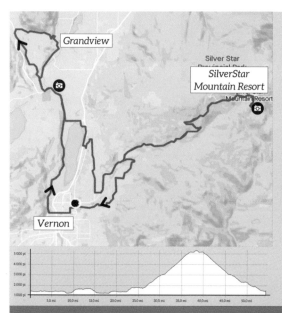

In southern British Columbia, the western slopes of the Rocky Mountains are pitted with deep north-south valleys at the foot of the western Shuswap Highland. There are narrow lakes and wide rivers. There are a few towns, too, such as Vernon (pop. 40,000)—at the northern ends of Okanagan Lake and the smaller Kalamalka Lake. We climb 3,700 ft (1,130 m) through this mountainous landscape to the SilverStar ski resort, built in the 1960s. This 11-mi (18-km) climb is quite a regular pedal, at an average gradient of around 6%, rising to over 8% halfway up, between the two wide switchbacks. Our route commences with a warm-up of around 25 mi (40 km) through the hills of the Okanagan Valley. When you get back, go taste the apples at Davison Orchards (near mi 2/km 3.25), reputed to be the most scrumptious in all of Canada.

	Distance		E+		Difficulty		Appeal
	**54 mi** (87 km)		**5,900 ft** (1,791 m)		**4/5**		**4/5**

Air: Vancouver International Airport (5h by car), Calgary International Airport (6h by car).
Car: 1h30 from Kamloops, 1h30 from Penticton, 6h30 from Seattle.

Skyride is MTB oriented, as are the other bike shops of the Okanagan Valley, but they do have some road expertise, and a very good café. Retailer of Kona and Devinci.

**4815 Silver Star Road
Vernon, BC V1B 3K3
skyride.ca**

Historic O'Keefe Ranch (mi 8/km 13). Swan Lake (mi 21/km 34). Second Silver Star Road hairpin (mi 33/km 53). Top of Silver Star Road (mi 38/km 61). BX Falls (mi 50/km 80). Murals of Vernon legends (mi 54/km 87).

VANCOUVER
THE TRIPLE CROWN

⊕ *Low mountain, Expert, 0% unpaved*
⊕ *Map strava.com/routes/2893168717996136028*

⊕ *Test yourself mi 13 (km 21) strava.com/segments/18307924*
⊕ *Test yourself mi 50 (km 80) strava.com/segments/626705*

◉ GREG'S EYE

A green city, virtually at the ocean's edge, and at the foot of the mountains: Vancouver is a dream, and a beacon for cyclists. The Triple Crown is a coveted local challenge involving the ascents of Cypress Mountain, Grouse Mountain, and Mount Seymour in the same day.

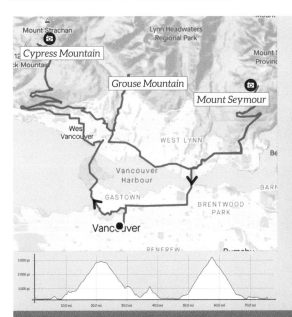

Passing through Vancouver? If you feel you have the legs, this adventure (starting from La Bicicletta, in the Mount Pleasant neighborhood) will make you a local legend! The Triple Crown is the diploma of the elite cyclist in these parts. It involves climbing the roads leading to the three ski resorts of the neighboring North Shore Mountains in the same day. From west to east: Cypress Mountain (6.5 mi/10.5 km at 6.3%), Grouse Mountain (2.4 mi/3.9 km at 5%, with sections at between 10 and 12%), and Mount Seymour (7.7 mi/12.4 km at 7.5%, with long sections at between 8 and 11%—a test in itself). The scenery is one of noble trees and luxuriant vegetation, with sumptuous panoramas as you ascend, stretching well beyond Vancouver and the Lions Gate Bridge. Celebrate your successful completion of the challenge at Forêt Noire Patisserie opposite La Bicicletta.

	Distance	E+	Difficulty	Appeal
	75 mi (121 km)	**8,700 ft** (2,666 m)	**5/5**	**5/5**

Air: Vancouver International Airport (20 min by car). Car: 3h from Seattle, 5h30 from Portland, 10h from Calgary, 12h from Edmonton.

La Bicicletta, in the Mount Pleasant neighborhood, is Vancouver's (vast) go-to bike shop. Retailer of BMC, Cannondale, and Cervelo. Strava Club.

**233 W. Broadway
Vancouver, BC V5Y 1P5
bicicletta.cc**

Lions Gate Bridge from Ambleside Park (mi 8/km 13). Cypress Mountain switchbacks (mi 15/km 24, mi 17/km 27, and mi 18/km 29) and top (mi 21/km 34). Capilano Lake (mi 37/km 60). Indian Arm (mi 52/km 84). Top of Mount Seymour (mi 57/km 92).

VANCOUVER
CITY OF GLASS

⊕ Hilly, Intermediate, 10% unpaved   ⊕ Map strava.com/routes/2892711996779107476

Distance	E+	Difficulty	Appeal
55 mi (89 km)	**2,800 ft** (855 m)	**3/5**	**4/5**

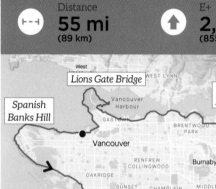

There's no doubt that the host city of the 2010 Winter Games is bike friendly, as illustrated by our grand tour of Vancouver (starting from Enroute Coffee). We pass Burrard Inlet, haul up Spanish Banks Hill (1 mi/1.5 km at 4%), gaze at the Strait of Georgia, and coast along the Fraser River, returning via Vancouver Harbour, downtown (selfie in front of the Gastown Steam Clock), and Stanley Park, at the foot of Lions Gate Bridge. On the way, we climb Burnaby Mountain (nearly 3 mi/4.75 km at 6%), enjoying the fine panorama of the skyline of the "City of Glass"—those glinting facades give Vancouver residents much appreciated luminosity in winter.

PENTINGTON
FANTASTIC KVR

DIRT & GRAVEL

⊕ Low mountain, Expert, 65% unpaved   ⊕ Map strava.com/routes/2892803048664069066

Distance	E+	Difficulty	Appeal
107 mi (172 km)	**6,300 ft** (1,929 m)	**4/5**	**5/5**

You're unlikely to cycle in British Columbia for any length of time without hearing about the Kettle Valley Rail Trail (KVR), a former railway line situated nearly 5h by car east of Vancouver. It's a perfect gravel adventure (380 mi/612 km in total), and the second part of this century (starting from the Bike Barn in Penticton) offers a veritable best of: 44 mi (71 km) of riding over the vertiginous trestle bridges of Myra Canyon (5 mi/8 km at 8% to get there) past sumptuous views, such as those around the surprising Little Tunnel. Another joy, on the way back: we pass some of British Columbia's best vineyards in the final 10 mi (16 km).

VICTORIA
GARDENS AND VIEWS

⊕ *Very hilly, Advanced, 0% unpaved*
⊕ *Map strava.com/routes/2893257605404655832*

⊕ *Test yourself mi 22 (km 35) strava.com/segments/6425304*
⊕ *Test yourself mi 34 (km 55) strava.com/segments/16317507*

👁 GREG'S EYE

Vancouver Island (which doesn't include the eponymous city) is the largest island off the west coast of North America, and a cycling paradise for all types of riders. This 53-mi (85-km) route, which never really leaves Victoria (capital of British Columbia), gives a taste.

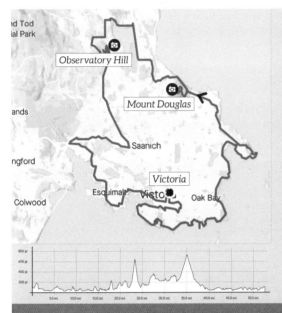

Facing the San Juan Islands of Washington State, southwest Vancouver Island boasts the mildest climate in Canada. And its coasts and hills exert a siren call to cyclists. From Victoria, for example, the West Coast Road, Munn Road, and the Highlands are terrifically tempting road routes. But why not start by sticking to the magnificent capital of British Columbia (pop. 90,000), with its flower-filled parks and gardens and hills offering views as far as the Rocky Mountains? The architecture (Craigdarroch, Parliament House, the huts of Fisherman's Wharf) is worth it, too, and a certain British air still lingers here (oh, those double-decker buses). The route does include a couple of challenges, though: Mount Douglas (1 mi/1.5 km at an average gradient of 11%) and Observatory Hill (1.5 mi/2.5 km at 6%). In short, a perfect day out on the bike.

	Distance		E+		Difficulty		Appeal
├─┤	**53 mi** (85 km)	⬆	**3,700 ft** (1,136 m)	📊	**3/5**	⭐	**4/5**

Air: Victoria International Airport (30 min by car) Car: 4h from Vancouver (including a 45-min ferry from Tsawwassen to Swartz Bay), 4h30 from Seattle (including a 2h ferry from Port Angeles to Victoria).

North Park, east of downtown Victoria, offers a very warm welcome in its location since 2018. Retailer of Marin, Cannondale, Surly, and Salsa.

**1833 Cook Street
Victoria, BC V8T 3P5
northparkbikeshop.com**

The breakwater and its lighthouse (mi 4/km 6). Mile Zero Monument (mi 5/km 8). Harling Point (mi 9/km 14). Phyllis Park (mi 18/km 29). Mount Douglas (mi 23/km 37). Observatory Hill (mi 35/km 56). Johnson Street Bridge (mi 51/km 82).

GIBSONS
SUNSHINE COAST CENTURY

- ⊕ Very hilly, Expert, 0% unpaved
- ⊕ Map strava.com/routes/2886522236113277572
- ⊙ Test yourself mi 51 (km 82) strava.com/segments/2082021
- ⊙ Test yourself mi 78 (km 126) strava.com/segments/2198489

◉ GREG'S EYE

Gibsons, on the Sunshine Coast, is only 15 mi (24 km) from Vancouver as the seagull flies, yet it's a whole other world. The experience is well worth this century to spectacular Jervis Inlet and back, along a very jagged and undulating coast.

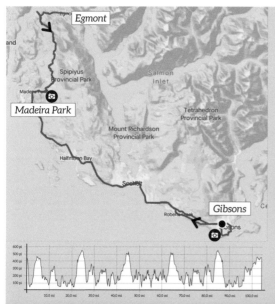

In 2009, Gibsons—with its art galleries and wooden houses—was named the most livable community in the world with a population under 20,000. From Vancouver, there are just two ways to reach it: swim or take the ferry. We advise the latter for this century through an astounding natural environment to Earls Cove and Egmont, on Jervis Inlet. Majestic bays, sounds, and salmon rivers, little cliffs, pebble beaches, superb fishing villages, forests of pine, spruce, and strawberry tree, and panoramas of snowy mountains: such is the idyllic scenery, which you'll generally have all to yourself. The climate of the Sunshine Coast is often mild. For a refuel halfway, try Cove Restaurant and Lodge (mi 51/km 82) or Skookumchuck Bakery in Egmont, on a track down to the spectacular Narrows (mi 55/km 89).

Distance **104 mi** (168 km)	E+ **9,100 ft** (2,768 m)	Difficulty **4/5**	Appeal **5/5**

Air: Vancouver International Airport (2h by car, including 40 min by ferry from Horseshoe Bay to Langdale). Car: 4h from Seattle, 5h from Kamloops, 12h from Calgary.

Elphi Cycles is the go-to bike shop in Gibsons. Retailer of Cervelo, Cube, Santa Cruz, and Rocky Mountain. Rentals.

**1058 Gibsons Way
Gibsons, BC V0N 1V7
elphicycles.com**

Secret Beach (mi 3/km 5). Roberts Creek (mi 10/km 16). Wakefield Beach (mi 18/km 29). Sakinaw Lake (mi 45/km 72). Earls Cove (mi 51/km 82). Egmont Narrows (mi 55/km 89). Ruby Lake (mi 61/km 98). Pender Harbour (mi 70/km 113).

REVELSTOKE
CANADIAN ALPE D'HUEZ

⊕ *High mountain, Expert, 1% unpaved*　　　　⊕ *Map strava.com/routes/2892675455950451658*

	Distance		E+		Difficulty		Appeal
⊢–⊣	**59 mi** (95 km)	⬆	**6,100 ft** (1,857 m)	⃞	**4/5**	★	**5/5**

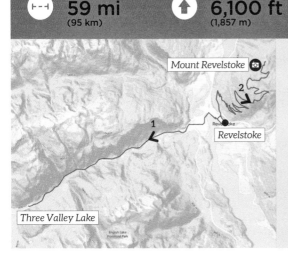

Mount Revelstoke

2

1

Revelstoke

Three Valley Lake

English Lake
Provincial Park

What's the hardest climb in Canada? Some say McBride Peak, 300 mi (483 km) north (6.5 mi/ 10.5 km at 10%), others Mount Revelstoke (16.2 mi/26 km at close to 6%), which we climb here. Halfway between Calgary and Vancouver (a 6h drive), it has several things going for it: length; elevation gain (nearly 4,800 ft/1,465 m); sixteen switchbacks evoking that Tour de France legend Alpe d'Huez; and forest. After a 26-mi (42-km) ride to Three Valley Lake as a warm-up, we attack the monster (from Skookum bike shop). In the course of the ascent, the views over the Monashee and Selkirk ranges prefigure the glory of the summit and its historic fire lookout.

SMITHERS
TOUCHING THE ICE

DIRT & GRAVEL

⊕ *High mountain, Advanced, 80% gravel*　　　　⊕ *Map strava.com/routes/2893827031619076786*

	Distance		E+		Difficulty		Appeal
⊢–⊣	**74 mi** (119 km)	⬆	**6,700 ft** (2,044 m)	⃞	**4/5**	★	**5/5**

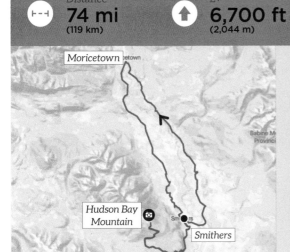

Moricetown

Babine M
Provinci

Hudson Bay
Mountain

Smithers

Here we are on the road to the great north, far from anywhere. Smithers, a little town evocative of the Tyrol, is a 12h drive from Vancouver and Edmonton, and nearer to Juneau, Alaska, than the first two! At the foot of impressive Hudson Bay Mountain (8,494 ft/2,589 m at its summit), whose superb glacier seems to surge from the plains, the trails stretch forever. The high point of this route is the exclusively gravel ascent to Hudson Bay Mountain Resort: 3 mi (4.75 km) at 6% followed by 4.5 mi (7.25 km) at more than 10%, through thick forest above the pretty Bulkley River. You won't regret having traveled so far.

ANCHORAGE
FROM SUNRISE TO SUNSET

🌐 *Low mountain, Advanced, 15% unpaved*　　🌐 *Map strava.com/routes/2885990529918271122*

	Distance		E+		Difficulty		Appeal
⊢–⊣	**124 mi** (200 km)	⬆	**5,000 ft** (1,544 m)	📊	**3/5**	★	**5/5**

A long ride through the largest state in the Union. This daylong adventure down to Seward—southern terminus of the Alaska Railroad—is one of the most accessible in the Last Frontier. Do it in late June, of course, when the days are long enough, taking the 6 p.m. train back from Seward and admiring the sunset west of Anchorage airport. Leave at dawn (4:30 a.m.) from Boom! Coffee (open 24/7) and cycle up Turnagain Arm, spotting beluga whales, before exploring the pleasures of the Kenai Peninsula: blue-tinged glaciers, fjords, lakes, vestiges of a mining past, gentle slopes (up to 1,500 ft/455 m on Summit Lake), eagles, and caribou. Simply amazing.

PAXSON
INTO THE WILD

DIRT & GRAVEL

🌐 *Low mountain, Advanced, 50% unpaved*　　🌐 *Map strava.com/routes/2886196055717583080*

	Distance		E+		Difficulty		Appeal
⊢–⊣	**163 mi** (262 km)	⬆	**9,700 ft** (2,948 m)	📊	**4/5**	★	**5/5**

Another extraordinary Alaskan adventure, less than 200 mi (320 km) from the Arctic Circle, to be ridden over at least three days (bike-packing). The logistical challenge is reaching Paxson (5h from Anchorage) for 135 mi (217 km) of up and down on crushed-gravel tracks. The Alaska Range and Denali (the highest peak in North America, at 20,310 ft/6,190 m) lie straight ahead, providing stunning panoramas over the wild landscape. At the end of the wide Denali Highway is Cantwell, where Sean Penn shot Into the Wild (2007). Then it's 30 mi (48 km) of easy riding on Parks Highway to finally reach the Denali Park Depot for the 7h train journey to Anchorage.

ROCKY MOUNTAINS

MONTANA
—
IDAHO
—
WYOMING
—
COLORADO
—
UTAH
—
NEVADA
—
ARIZONA
—
NEW MEXICO

WEST GLACIER
RIDE TO PARADISE

⊕ *High mountain, Expert, 15% gravel*
⊕ *Map strava.com/routes/2894602257532758706*

⊕ *Test yourself mi 21 (km 34) strava.com/segments/4578499*
⊕ *Test yourself mi 62 (km 100) strava.com/segments/17842026*

◎ GREG'S EYE

Glacier National Park is a wonder of Montana and one of the most amazing splendors of the Rocky Mountains. On Going-to-the-Sun Road, forget your quest for King of the Mountains status and fully enjoy these unique moments amid a stunning high-mountain landscape.

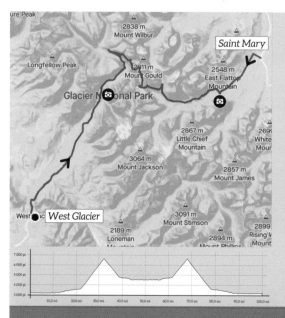

If you decide to ride Going-to-the-Sun Road, plan to do it in May or June, when cars are banned from this fantastic road through Glacier National Park. That time of year the scenery takes on a particularly extraordinary aspect, as melting snow and ice trickle down the rockfaces. From the Amtrak station in West Glacier, the initial 12 mi (19 km) along Lake McDonald are a delight, as Mount Jackson—one of six peaks in the park over 10,000 ft (3,050 m)—rises before you. The views on the 10-mi (16-km) regular ascent (at 5% to 6%) of Logan Pass (up to 6,646 ft/2,025 m) are simply stunning. So much so that you won't be able to resist descending as far as Saint Mary, then turning around and climbing Logan Pass East (6.6 mi/ 10.5 km at 5%) to make it a century, drinking your fill of visual splendor with each bend.

Distance	E+	Difficulty	Appeal
100 mi (161 km)	**7,100 ft** (2,167 m)	**4/5**	**5/5**

Air: Glacier Park International Airport, Kalispell (1h by car), Calgary International Airport (4h30 by car).
Car: 4h from Helena, 4h30 from Calgary, 8h30 from Seattle, 11h from Vancouver.

Glacier Cyclery, in Whitefish (30 mi/48 km southwest of our starting point), is the place to go. Retailer of Kona, Giant, Liv, and Surly.

326 E. Second Street Whitefish, MT 59937 glaciercyclery.com

Lake McDonald (mi 6/km 9.8). Heaven's Peak from the Loop (mi 24/km 39). Triple Arches Bridge (mi 30/km 48). Bird Woman Falls (mi 31/km 50). Saint Mary Lake (mi 51/km 82). Wild Goose Island Lookout (mi 57/km 92). Trail of the Cedars (mi 83/km 134). Logan Pass (mi 68/km 109).

HELENA
TOUR DIVIDE PREVIEW

◉ *High mountain, Advanced, 90% unpaved*   ◉ *Map strava.com/routes/2894660593805184084*

	Distance		E+		Difficulty		Appeal
⊢⊣	**61 mi** (98 km)	⬆	**5,900 ft** (1,811 m)	⊪	**4/5**	★	**5/5**

Helena

Chessman Reservoir

The Great Divide Mountain Bike Route (GDMBR) for the Tour Divide ultra-cycling race starts in Banff in Alberta, Canada, and finishes 2,700 mi (4,345 km) south in Antelope Wells, New Mexico. It crosses Montana, passing by Helena, the charming state capital (pop. 35,000), and nearby Gates of the Mountains canyon. Our almost exclusively gravel route (starting from Great Divide Cyclery) includes two sections of the GDMBR: 12 mi (19 km) via Mullan Pass (4.3 mi/ 6.9 km at 5%) and Priest Pass (2 mi/3.25 km at 5.6%), then 20 mi (32 km) via Chessman Reservoir (altitude 6,200 ft/1,890 m) to Grizzly Gulch Drive. Speaking of grizzlies, pack a can of bear spray!

RED LODGE
SWITCHBACK GIANT

◉ *High mountain, Expert, 1% unpaved*   ◉ *Map strava.com/routes/2894664737678779826*

	Distance		E+		Difficulty		Appeal
⊢⊣	**77 mi** (124 km)	⬆	**7,900 ft** (2,412 m)	⊪	**5/5**	★	**5/5**

Red Lodge

Island Lake

A gentle 30-mi (48-km) ascent to nearly 11,000 ft (3,355 m) on a paved road is unusual, but remote Beartooth Pass, 60 mi (97 km) south of Billings, gives us the opportunity. Starting from the Spoke Wrench bike shop in Red Lodge, we climb most of the north slope in Montana, but enter Wyoming 6 mi (10 km) from the top, after a series of exquisite switchbacks providing vistas over the surrounding Beartooth Mountains—a landscape of pasture, rock, and snowy peaks. At the summit, we descend to beautiful Island Lake, then turn around to pedal the 6 mi (10 km) back up the south slope at a gradient (4% to 6%) as reasonable as that of the first climb.

MISSOULA
RATTLESNAKE BITES

- High mountain, Expert, 80% unpaved
- Map strava.com/routes/2894890165693022642
- Test yourself mi 12 (km 19) strava.com/segments/15871653
- Test yourself mi 39 (km 63) strava.com/segments/12647383

👁 GREG'S EYE

Director David Lynch was born in Missoula, at the foot of the Rattlesnake Mountains —a recreational area for Missoulians and a harsh gravel playground between lakes and summits over 7,000 ft (2,135 m). Riding here can feel as surreal as a classic Lynch film.

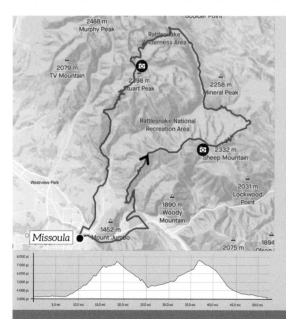

Missoula (pop. 75,000), Montana's "Garden City," is a green place with a rich heritage and a plethora of bike paths. Overlooking the city to the north are the forbidding Rattlesnake Mountains. Their rocky landscape—bare, save for the odd patch of vegetation—seems hostile at first glance: the territory of elk, Rocky Mountain goats, and even mountain lions! The trail descending from Stuart Peak on our route features on a list of dangerous roads. This is indeed one brutal gravel adventure: 2 mi (3.25 km) of hell at 15% conclude the ascent of Sheep Mountain (mi 18/km 29), with another 2.4 mi (3.9 km) rising at 14% from Carter Lake (mi 35/km 56). You'll be tempted to step off and push your bike the rest of the way. Surely this place fed David Lynch's dark imagination, spurring creation of *Blue Velvet* and *Twin Peaks*.

Distance	E+	Difficulty	Appeal
52 mi (83 km)	**8,800 ft** (2,685 m)	**5/5**	**4/5**

Air: Missoula Montana Airport (20 min by car), Helena Regional Airport (2h by car), Bozeman Yellowstone International Airport, Belgrade (3h by car).
Car: 7h from Seattle, 7h from Calgary, 8h30 from Portland.

Missoula Bicycle Works, based in a beautiful, renovated building on the edge of Clark Fork and the University District, is a well-reputed establishment in Missoula. Retailer of Cannondale.

708 S. Higgins Avenue Missoula, MT 59801
missoulabicycleworks.com

Canyon River Golf Club (mi 5/km 8). Mount Jumbo from Middle Trail (mi 9/km 14). Blue Point (mi 16/km 26). Sheep Mountain (mi 18/km 29). Mineral Peak (mi 24/km 39). Carter Lake (mi 35/km 56). Stuart Peak (mi 37/km 60).

DIRT & GRAVEL

SANDPOINT
PANHANDLE PARTY

- ⊕ Low mountain, Advanced, 60% unpaved
- ⊕ Map strava.com/routes/2896133460352626400

- ⊕ Test yourself mi 15 (km 24) strava.com/segments/11965481
- ⊕ Test yourself mi 63 (km 101) strava.com/segments/2404741

◎ GREG'S EYE

Sandpoint is the ideal destination in the Idaho Panhandle, with the Selkirk Mountains and Lake Pend Oreille nearby. This gravel-toned route includes the paved ascent of Schweitzer Mountain, a local ski resort (remember to adjust your tire pressure at the bottom).

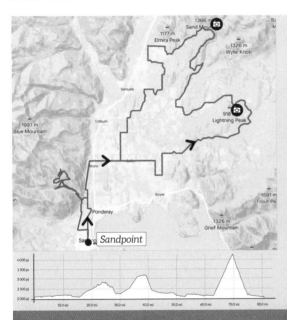

Sandpoint

On the map, the Idaho Panhandle seems squashed between the Canadian border (50 mi/80 km north of our route) and the neighboring states of Montana and Washington. Yet it's a territory of vast open spaces. A famous panoramic route runs through the Selkirk Mountains outside of Sandpoint (pop. 9,000). For our route, we'll follow the backroads, dirt tracks, and unevenly surfaced trails north of Lake Pend Oreille recommended by the Syringa Cyclery crew. Until mi 40 (km 64), the foothills of the Selkirk Mountains look like a magnificent landscape picture. You can content yourself with a 65-mi (105-km) ride before enjoying Sandpoint City Beach and its (modest) replica of the Statue of Liberty. Or opt for the challenging (paved) switchbacks of Schweitzer Mountain Road (6.5 mi/10.5 km at 6%) before a quite technical off-road descent.

Distance **81 mi** (130 km)	E+ ⬆ **5,000 ft** (1,522 m)	Difficulty **3/5**	Appeal ★ **4/5**

Air: Spokane International Airport (1h30 by car). Car: 3h30 from Missoula, 5h30 from Seattle, 6h30 from Calgary, 8h from Boise, 8h from Vancouver.

Syringa Cyclery, in its pretty red house, is also the cozy rendezvous point for Sandpoint cycling enthusiasts. Retailer of Bianchi and Moots.

**518 Oak Street
Sandpoint, ID 83864**
syringacyclery.com

Lightning Peak (mi 24/km 39). Grouse Mountain and Bald Eagle Mountain (mi 39/km 63). Schweitzer Mountain (mi 69/ km 111). Lower Basin (mi 71/ km 114). Liberty Pier (mi 79/ km 127).

KETCHUM
HEMINGWAY MEMORY

- High mountain, Intermediate, 90% unpaved
- Map strava.com/routes/2895993213434431476
- Test yourself mi 8 (km 13) strava.com/segments/1468360
- Test yourself mi 44 (km 71) strava.com/segments/4092531

◉ GREG'S EYE

Every year, ultra-endurance athlete Rebecca Rusch invites gravel lovers to come ride the trails around Ketchum, in the Pioneer Mountains, where she lives. The route of Rebecca's Private Idaho also offers an opportunity to pay homage to the great Ernest Hemingway.

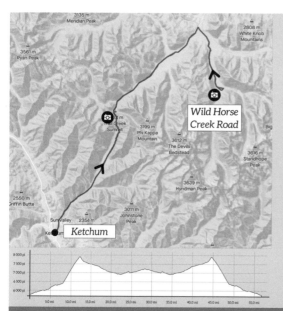

Wild Horse Creek Road

Ketchum

Literary legend Ernest Hemingway left his mark on Ketchum (pop. 3,000), gateway to the ski resort of Sun Valley. Here he completed *For Whom the Bell Tolls* in 1939 and died from suicide in 1961. We pass a bronze memorial to him beside Trail Creek, a favorite fishing spot of his, at mi 3 (km 4.75) of this totally gravel route. Then we climb to nearly 8,000 ft/2,440 m (4-mi/6.5-km ramp at 6.5%) through the stunning Pioneer Mountains (one of the wildest areas in Idaho), in the shadow of their highest point: Hyndman Peak. The turnaround at the foot of other peaks rising to close to 12,000 ft (3,660 m) provides an array of sublime views. This route is inspired by the medium version of Rebecca's Private Idaho, dubbed French Fry. You can also make an attempt on Baked Potato, which extends the adventure east: 103 mi (166 km) with an elevation gain of 6,300 ft (1,920 m).

	Distance		E+		Difficulty		Appeal
├┤	**57 mi** (92 km)	⬆	**3,800 ft** (1,152 m)	▥	**3/5**	★	**5/5**

Air: Friedman Memorial Airport, Hailey (30 min by car), Salt Lake City International Airport (4h30 by car). Car: 2h30 from Boise, 4h15 from West Yellowstone, 6h from Helena, 9h from Portland.

PK's Bike Shop is the place to go in Ketchum for an adjustment or repair. Wooden interior. Friendly welcome. Attentive service. Rentals. Retailer of Marin.

320 N. Leadville Avenue Ketchum, ID 83340 pksbike.com

Sun Valley homes and Dollar Mountain (mi 1/km 1.5). Hemingway Memorial (mi 3/km 4.75). Trail Creek Summit (mi 12/km 19 and mi 44/km 71). Wild Horse Creek Ranch (mi 22/km 35). Big Black Dome and the Devil's Bedstead (mi 28/km 45).

BOISE
TESTING BOGUS BASIN

- ⊕ *High mountain, Intermediate, 0% unpaved*
- ⊕ *Map strava.com/routes/2896055044657134580*
- ⊕ *Test yourself mi 18 (km 29) strava.com/segments/1283987*
- ⊕ *Test yourself mi 22 (km 35) strava.com/segments/13514939*

◎ GREG'S EYE

After Alaska, Idaho is the state with the vastest expanse of remote and mountainous nature in the United States. So it's not surprising that you face an imposing mountain as soon as you leave Boise, the state capital. The Bogus Basin climb is a must.

If you head east toward Arrowrock Reservoir or into the Sawtooth Range—up to Aldape Summit, for example—take a gravel bike, since those routes will mostly be on trails. For this ride from Boise (pop. 230,000), it's asphalt all the way as we climb North Bogus Basin Road up to the eponymous ski resort, after an urban warm-up through southeast Boise, then the Boise River Greenbelt. This is a favorite ride of local cyclists keen to test themselves. The climb is long (14.3 mi/23 km), amazingly winding with contorted switchbacks that make it interesting, and of irregular but reasonable gradient: an average of 4.3%, although some sections hit 8%. At around 5,000 ft (1,525 m), you enter thick forest of spruce and pine. Such an effort deserves a reward, and the place for that is Bittercreek Alehouse (mi 50/km 80), a temple to beer and hearty dishes in downtown Boise.

	Distance	E+	Difficulty	Appeal
⊢–⊣	**54 mi** (86 km)	⬆ **4,200 ft** (1,294 m)	📊 **3/5**	⭐ **4/5**

Air: Boise Air Terminal (20 min by car). Car: 2h from Twin Falls, 5h from Salt Lake City, 5h30 from West Yellowstone, 6h30 from Portland.

Bikes & Beans, a wonderful place south of the Boise River, has a slogan that says it all: "A place to repair bicycles and drink exceptional coffee."

**1350 S. Vista Avenue
Boise, ID 83705**
bikesandbeansboise.com

Boise River (mi 11/km 18). Warm Springs Park (mi 12/km 19). Camel's Back Park (mi 16/km 26). Miller Gulch Trailhead (mi 19/km 31). Upper Dry Creek Switchback (mi 28/km 45). Idaho State Capitol (mi 50/km 80).

KETCHUM
SUMMIT OF BEAUTY

🌐 *High mountain, Advanced, 1% unpaved*   🌐 *Map strava.com/routes/2896117086153861108*

	Distance		E+		Difficulty		Appeal
⊢⊣	**62 mi** (99 km)	⬆	**3,300 ft** (1,013 m)	⊞	**3/5**	★	**5/5**

Highway 75 in central Idaho is a must-ride, particularly the 30-mi (48-km) stretch from Ketchum (where we start from PK's Bike Shop) and Galena Summit Pass. There are few cars and the panoramas over the Boulder Mountains and the Sawtooth Range are simply magical. At the col's summit (8,701 ft/2,652 m), after a winding 5-mi (8-km) ascent at 5%, you coast downhill for 1 mi (1.5 km) before climbing the same to the amazing Galena Summit Overlook. From there, the Stanley Basin unfolds before you. Galena Summit is one of the highest paved roads in Idaho and, for many, the most beautiful. Stop at Galena Lodge (mi 38/km 61) on the way back to refuel.

BURLEY
EXCEPTIONAL MOUNT HARRISON

🌐 *High mountain, Expert, 0% unpaved*   🌐 *Map strava.com/routes/2896165855162903540*

	Distance		E+		Difficulty		Appeal
⊢⊣	**70 mi** (113 km)	⬆	**5,600 ft** (1,704 m)	⊞	**4/5**	★	**4/5**

Mount Harrison (9,265 ft/2,824 m) in the south of Idaho is not the highest peak in the Albion Mountains, but it boasts the rarity of a road all the way up to its summit. This means more than 4,000 ft (1,220 m) of elevation gain in barely 13 mi/21 km (at an average gradient of 5.6%, the last 2 mi/3.25 km at 8%), giving it the air of a major European col. The road is impeccably paved all the way up, as it climbs through steppe, deciduous forest, then conifers, and, finally, rocks. Mount Harrison is the hardest ascent in Idaho. Epic Ride in Burley is the ideal starting point to avoid cycling the 40 mi (64 km) from larger Twin Falls to the west.

Highway 75 offers sublime panoramas over the Sawtooth Range to the north of Ketchum, Idaho.

POCATELLO
SMILE, STEEP GRADIENT!

- *Low mountain, Advanced, 2% unpaved*
- *Map strava.com/routes/2895765093164774112*
- *Test yourself mi 16 (km 26) strava.com/segments/24745003*
- *Test yourself mi 45 (km 72) strava.com/segments/12558678*

◉ GREG'S EYE

Need to wash your bike? Then Pocatello, and its Museum of Clean, is the place for you! I joke, but the "Smile Capital" welcomes you with open arms for a superb low-mountain route and one very difficult climb.

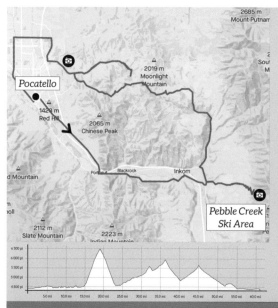

Pocatello

Pebble Creek Ski Area

Before you get carried away by the gentle euphoria of Pocatello (pop. 55,000), one-third of whose residents are students at Idaho State University, study the profile of what awaits you at the foot of the North and South Putnam Mountains, sentinels of the southeast Gem State. The ascent to Pebble Creek Ski Area (6,500 ft/1,980 m) on East Green Canyon Road is nicknamed "Pebble Everest" by local cyclists, and considered the most brutal climb in Idaho at 4.5 mi (7.25 km) long with a bracing 9% average gradient (the first half hits double digits) and seven tight switchbacks to finish. But it would be a shame to redescend this cul-de-sac and not explore the neighboring heights via Buckskin Road, then West Moonlight Mine Road. As you ride around Camelback Mountain, the scent of sage and juniper will make you forget the aggressive slopes.

Distance	E+	Difficulty	Appeal
61 mi (99 km)	**5,200 ft** (1,588 m)	**4/5**	**4/5**

Air: Pocatello Regional Airport (20 min by car), Salt Lake City International Airport (2h30 by car).
Car: 2h30 from West Yellowstone, 3h30 Boise, 4h from Bozeman.

Oregon Trail Bikes, situated in the charming Old Town District, is happy to suggest other rides around Pocatello. Retailer of Orbea, Marin, and Salsa.

**216 N. 2nd Avenue
Pocatello, ID 83201
oregontrailbikes.com**

Red Hill (mi 1/km 1.5). Pebble Creek Ski Area (mi 19/km 31). Pocatello from West Buckskin Road (mi 38/km 61). West Moonlight Mine Road (mi 45/km 72). Sister City Park (mi 51/km 82).

CANYON VILLAGE
GEYSER PARADISE

- High mountain, Advanced, 0% unpaved
- Map strava.com/routes/2895008694003462834

- Test yourself mi 40 (km 64) strava.com/segments/2097091
- Test yourself mi 77 (km 124) strava.com/segments/28061283

◉ GREG'S EYE

You'll have to deal with tourist traffic from July to September and roadside snowdrifts in spring. But if you're cycling in Wyoming, how can you resist the call of Yellowstone National Park and its geysers?

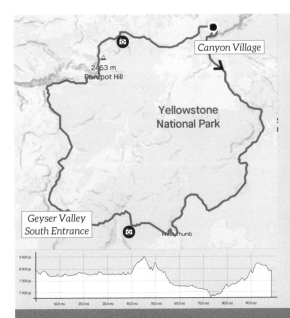

Canyon Village

2453 m
Painpot Hill

Yellowstone
National Park

Geyser Valley
South Entrance

West Thumb

Let's clear something up: Grand Loop Road, the legendary asphalt ribbon that explores the wonders of Yellowstone National Park, continues farther north, beyond this high-altitude route, as far as Mammoth Hot Springs, for a total length of 140 mi (225 km). Our own ride passes some magnificent sites, including Hayden Valley, LeHardy's Rapids, Yellowstone Lake, and Fountain Freight Road. Geyser Valley, which we ride from mi 57 (km 92), after Yellowstone Caldera, as far as Steamboat Geyser (the world's most powerful active geyser), is truly magical. Having set out from Canyon Visitor Education Center, we turn onto Norris Canyon Road at mi 87 (km 140) to head back to the start and complete a century (or very nearly). How about getting back on the bike the next day to ride the rest of Grand Loop Road (68 mi/109 km and 5,500 ft/1,675 m of E+)? You'll be sorely tempted.

Distance	E+	Difficulty	Appeal
99 mi (159 km)	**5,200 ft** (1,591 m)	**3/5**	**5/5**

 Air: Yellowstone Airport, West Yellowstone (1h by car), Billings Logan International Airport (3h30 by car). Car: 5h from Cody, 6h from Salt Lake City, 12h from Seattle.

 Freeheel and Wheel in West Yellowstone (1h by car) is the closest bike shop to Canyon Village. Excellent café. Rentals. Retailer of Specialized and Trek.

**33 Yellowstone Avenue
West Yellowstone, MT 59758
freeheelandwheel.com**

 Yellowstone Canyon (mi 2/km 3.5). Shoshone Lake (mi 46/km 74 and mi 50/km 80). Old Faithful and Grand Geyser (mi 58/km 93). Grand Prismatic Spring (mi 62/km 100). Firehole Spring (mi 63/km 101). Gibbon Falls (mi 78/km 126). Steamboat Geyser (mi 86/km 138).

CODY
TRIBUTE TO BUFFALO BILL

⊕ *High mountain, Advanced, 1% unpaved* ⊕ *Map strava.com/routes/2895022630476131762*

 Distance **100 mi** (162 km)   **E+** **7,907 ft** (2,410 m)   **Difficulty** **4/5**   **Appeal** **4/5**

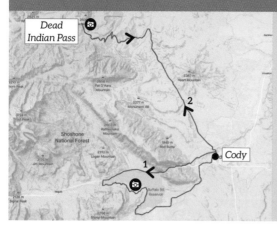

In Cody, Wyoming (pop. 10,000), they still raise their Stetsons to salute the town's founder, William Frederick Cody, better known as Buffalo Bill. This long route (starting from Joyvagen Bicycle Shop), to split over two days if you have the time, is a tribute to this legend of the Far West. The first 40 mi (64 km) along the Shoshone River and around lush Buffalo Bill Reservoir are pleasantly undulating. Heading north, we tackle Heart Mountain (and again on the way back), followed by formidable Dead Indian Pass East, which snakes up for 13.3 mi (21 km), although the average gradient is a reasonable 4.2% and the views superb.

SHELL
GREAT MEDICINE

⊕ *High mountain, Expert, 60% gravel* ⊕ *Map strava.com/routes/2895031346099915186*

 Distance **90 mi** (144 km)   **E+** **10,600 ft** (3,221 m)   **Difficulty** **5/5**   **Appeal** **5/5**

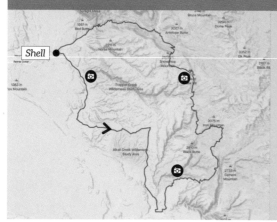

Shell is a mere dot on the map of central northern Wyoming. Raise a glass at the Fossil Rock Tavern (our start and finish) to toast this amazing mixed-surface route inspired by the Bad Medicine Ride. We climb high and long: up to 9,500 ft (2,895 m) on Crooked Creek Hill (mi 65/km 105), 10 mi (16 km) at 4% on a trail, and then 15 mi (24 km) at 6% on a patchy surface. You'll spot iconic backcountry Wyoming sights: the ochre cliffs of Devils Leap; Red Basin; Medicine Lodge Archaeological Site; Snowshoe Mountain; Shell Canyon and Falls; and Chimney Rock. The adventure can be cut to 56 mi/90 km (6,700 ft/ 2,040 m of E+) via Alkali Road (mi 20/km 32).

JACKSON
TETON AND CANYON

- ⊕ High mountain, Advanced, 1% unpaved
- ⊕ Map strava.com/routes/2895007009380343218
- ⊕ Test yourself mi 8 (km 13) strava.com/segments/25198950
- ⊕ Test yourself mi 55 (km 89) strava.com/segments/903285

👁 GREG'S EYE

Did you know that téton means "nipple" in French? It's a nod to the shape of the mountain, Grand Teton, and an indication of the language spoken by some European explorers. The slopes of Teton Pass are brutal, but compensated by stunning Snake River Canyon.

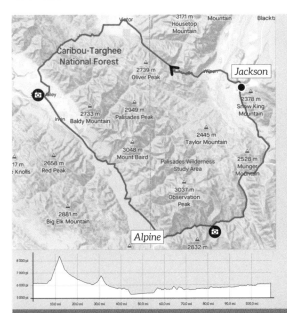

It's tempting to rack up miles in Wyoming to avoid the frustration of turning around at the top of a col. From Jackson, in the western part of the Equality State, we descend into neighboring Idaho from the western slope of Teton Pass for a long and pleasurable high-altitude route. The main challenge comes early on, in the form of Teton Pass: 5.5 mi (8.75 km) on Old Pass Road (avoiding the traffic on the WY-22) at an average gradient of 8%, with sections up to 12%. The topography is unusual for the Rocky Mountains. We soon arrive in Idaho (50% of our route) and the gentler Pine Creek Pass (2.6 mi/4.25 km at 4%) and Snake Valley, then down to Palisades Reservoir, a beautiful expanse of blue set against the Teton Range. Alpine sees us back in Wyoming, with over 70 mi (113 km) in the legs and a joy to come: the ride up beautiful Snake River Canyon.

	Distance		E+		Difficulty		Appeal
	109 mi (175 km)	⬆	**6,400 ft** (1,946 m)	📊	**4/5**	⭐	**5/5**

Air: Idaho Falls Regional Airport (2h by car), Salt Lake City International Airport (4h30 by car).
Car: 2h30 from West Yellowstone, 6h from Boise, 7h from Cheyenne.

Fitzgerald's Bicycles has outlets south of Jackson, in Victor (mi 26/km 42) and Idaho Falls. Rentals. Retailer of Salsa, Moots, and Trek.

**500 US-89
Jackson, WY 83001
fitzgeraldsbicycles.com**

Welcome to Idaho sign (mi 19/km 31). Mikesell Canyon (mi 20/km 32). Pine Creek Pass (mi 31/km 50). Fall Creek Falls (nr mi 45/km 72). Palisades Dam (mi 56/km 90). Palisades Reservoir (mi 60/km 97). Snake River Canyon (mi 81/km 130).

BOULDER
CYCLIST CITY

- ⊕ High mountain, Advanced, 5% unpaved
- ⊕ Map strava.com/routes/2914986305162165328
- ⊕ Test yourself mi 27 (km 43) strava.com/segments/638399
- ⊕ Test yourself mi 39 (km 63) strava.com/segments/617452

👁 GREG'S EYE

Boulder was already the epicenter of American cycling in the 1980s, when many pro cyclists lived or trained here. That culture and a policy of sustainable development have been maintained. The scenery is stunning, with the mountains of the Front Range just outside town.

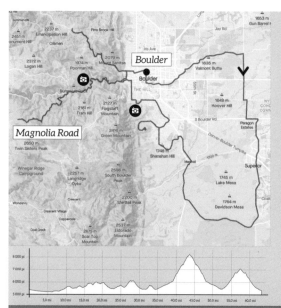

This energetic route starting in bike-friendly Boulder combines the very pleasant setting of Boulder (altitude: 5,300 ft/1,615 m) with a string of challenges in the surrounding area. The first two-thirds explore the Boulder Creek Path and other protected trails (of which there are a total of 300 mi/485 km in the urban area!) heading east, then south. The NCAR ramp (mi 28/km 45), below the striking Flatirons, is a perfect warm-up (1.2 mi/2 km at 6.6%). At mi 38 (km 61), we hit Magnolia Road: 4.5 mi (7.25 km) of very irregular gradient until the asphalt runs out, at an average of 9.1%, with sections at 17%! Turn around and head back down to the start of Sunshine Drive (mi 52/km 84): 5 mi (8 km) at an average gradient of 6.4%, with 2 mi (3.25 km) of very tough climbing at 9% in the middle. You can see why so many champions call Boulder home.

	Distance		E+		Difficulty		Appeal
⊢⊣	**63 mi** (102 km)	⬆	**7,500 ft** (2,278 m)	📊	**4/5**	⭐	**4/5**

Air: Denver International Airport (40 min by car). Car: 1h from Fort Collins, 1h30 from Colorado Springs, 1h30 from Cheyenne, 4h from Grand Junction.

Boulder is the smallest American town with a *Rapha Club House*. Really beautiful space, ideally situated on Pearl Street.

**1815 Pearl Street
Boulder, CO 80302
rapha.cc**

Davidson Mesa Viewpoint (mi 18/km 29). National Center for Atmospheric Research and Flatirons (mi 28/km 45). Chautauqua Park (mi 33/km 53). Twin Sisters Peak (mi 44/km 71). Boulder Canyon (mi 50/km 80). Bald Mountain (mi 57/km 92).

BOULDER
CANYON TO CANYON

🌐 *High mountain, Intermediate, 0% unpaved*   🌐 *Map strava.com/routes/2915580850884232610*

	Distance		E+		Difficulty		Appeal
⊢⊣	**47 mi** (76 km)	⬆	**5,200 ft** (1,600 m)	📊	**3/5**	⭐	**5/5**

It's hard to leave pleasant Boulder (pop. 115,000) and its vibrant college-town atmosphere, except to explore the wonderful canyons west of the city. This route (starting from University Bicycles) is a Boulder weekend classic, though one to be tackled with care. Lee Hill Drive rears up from the start: 3 mi (4.75 km) at 6%, then 1 mi (1.5 km) at 8.5%. Next comes Lefthand Canyon: 10 mi (16 km) at 4.5% average gradient, the last 2 mi (3.25 km) at 9%. By the halfway point, the hardest part is behind you. After the hippie villages of Ward and Nederland comes Boulder Canyon (mi 33/km 53): 15 mi (24 km) of delicious winding descent.

DENVER
HIGHER THAN A MILE

🌐 *High mountain, Advanced, 0% unpaved*   🌐 *Map strava.com/routes/2915614263979575010*

	Distance		E+		Difficulty		Appeal
⊢⊣	**75 mi** (120 km)	⬆	**5,700 ft** (1,732 m)	📊	**4/5**	⭐	**4/5**

This popular escapade for Denver cyclists heads southwest on Platte River Trail. Our version starts at SloHi bike café, close to Empower Field, home of the Broncos. Destination: the enchanted though challenging loop of Deer Creek Canyon, the most amazing route in South Park Hills. It starts with a 10-mi (16-km) climb, at an average of 4.5%, with sections at 9%, before offering, at close to 8,500 ft (2,590 m), a panorama over Crystal View and City View Drives. Then there's a gentle descent via West Ranch Trail (with a short ramp of 0.6 mi/1 km at 6%), Mount Carbon, and Lakewood. It's great to look down on the Mile High City.

COLORADO SPRINGS
THE RIDE TO THE CLOUDS

- ⊕ High mountain, Expert, 0% unpaved
- ⊕ Map strava.com/routes/2914111230571503736
- ⊙ Test yourself mi 14 (km 23) strava.com/segments/14085850
- ⊙ Test yourself mi 24 (km 39) strava.com/segments/21469807

👁 GREG'S EYE

The legendary Pikes Peak International Hill Climb (over a century old) sees cars roaring up this mountain above Colorado Springs. I tackled it by bike at age eighteen with the national juniors team, when the final section was still gravel. Not everyone reached the top.

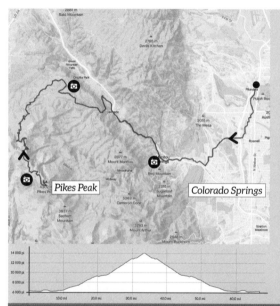

Make no mistake, climbing Pikes Peak demands both superlative fitness and honed skills. In addition to the gradient, the altitude and thin air are redoubtable foes. Indeed, the car race that takes place on the last Sunday in June is nicknamed the Race to the Clouds. At Crystal Creek Reservoir (mi 20/km 32), we are already over 9,000 ft (2,745 m)—as high as the legendary Stelvio Pass in Italy. Pikes Peak is in sight, but there are 13 mi (21 km) to climb. You'll have to spin your legs without excessive effort as far as Cascade, keep your cool on an average gradient of 6.7% (for a total 19 mi/31 km), negotiate 156 bends and 20 switchbacks, as well as terrifying drops with few guardrails, and conquer the 3 mi (4.75 km) following Glen Cove Lodge at gradients of 8% to 11%. In 2021, bicycle access to Pikes Peak Toll Road (mi 15/km 24) cost 15 dollars.

	Distance		E+		Difficulty		Appeal
	67 mi (108 km)		**9,400 ft** (2,876 m)		**5/5**		**5/5**

Air: Colorado Springs Airport (30 min by car), Denver International Airport (1h by car). Car: 2h from Fort Collins, 5h from Grand Junction, 5h from Albuquerque, 8h from Kansas City, 9h from Salt Lake City.

Criterium Bicycles in Colorado Springs is fifty years old. It boasts a lovely little terrace outside the Crit Cafe. Strava Club. Retailer of Cannondale and Specialized.

**6150 Corporate Drive
Colorado Springs, CO 80919
criterium.com**

Crystal Creek Reservoir (mi 20/km 32). Glen Cove (mi 27/km 43). Devil's Playground (mi 30/km 48). Mountain views (mi 31 to 33/km 50 to 53). Pikes Peak Summit (mi 33.5/km 54). Historic Manitou Springs (mi 57/km 92).

COLORADO SPRINGS
THERE'S ROOM FOR YOU!

⊕ *High mountain, Intermediate, 18% unpaved*   ⊕ *Map strava.com/routes/2915550764727907042*

	Distance		E+		Difficulty		Appeal
⊢⊣	**59 mi** (95 km)	⬆	**3,800 ft** (1,169 m)	📊	**2/5**	⭐	**4/5**

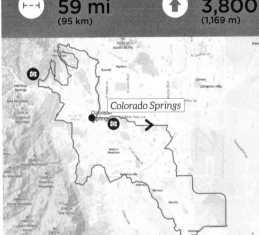

Colorado Springs

The slogan of Colorado Springs (pop. 480,000), 70 mi (113 km) south of Denver, is "There's room for you here!" Our route (starting from CS Bike Shop) combines pleasant bike paths protected from the surrounding city (Sand Creek, Fountain Creek, Palmer Mesa, Sinton Trail, Pikes Peak Greenway) with the splendid foothills of the Rockies: first around Cheyenne and Red Rock Canyons, then in the fantastic Garden of the Gods (snap a selfie at Balanced Rock, mi 39/km 63). Colorado Springs is also the epicenter of the American Olympic movement, so make a stop at the 7-Eleven Velodrome (mi 2/km 3.25) with its spectacular movable roof.

STEAMBOAT SPRINGS
HOT GRAVEL

DIRT & GRAVEL

⊕ *High mountain, Intermediate, 75% unpaved*   ⊕ *Map strava.com/routes/2915685855148665250*

	Distance		E+		Difficulty		Appeal
⊢⊣	**68 mi** (110 km)	⬆	**5,300 ft** (1,630 m)	📊	**3/5**	⭐	**4/5**

Steamboat Springs

Steamboat Springs (pop. 14,000), 150 mi (240 km) northwest of Denver, is best known for its hot springs and its neighboring ski resorts. The increasingly popular annual event SBT GRVL has put the town on the map as a prime gravel destination in Colorado. Our route (starting from Orange Peel Bicycle) is inspired by the race's various courses on perfect, rolling trails north of the Yampa River and more aggressive terrain south of it, as you draw closer to Quarry Mountain (mi 55/km 89)—the highest point on this escapade through North Central Colorado, on the edge of Medicine Bow-Routt National Forest.

EVERGREEN
AN OLD FRIEND

⊕ *High mountain, Expert, 0% unpaved*
⊕ *Map strava.com/routes/2913899821213545574*

⊕ *Test yourself mi 23 (km 37) strava.com/segments/18281340*
⊕ *Test yourself mi 39 (km 63) strava.com/segments/1754765*

👁 GREG'S EYE

Ever since the entirety of Pikes Peak was paved, Mount Evans—a hitherto sacred ascent in Colorado—seems rather passé. Nevertheless, it remains an outsized challenge, in the top five most difficult climbs in the United States. Conquering it is always an accomplishment.

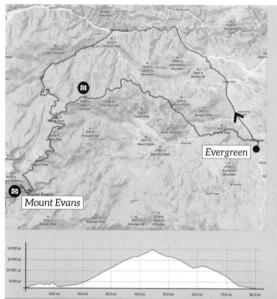

Mount Evans and Pikes Peak lie 100 mi (161 km) apart on a north/south axis, right in the center of Colorado. The very similar altitudes of their road summits (over 14,000 ft/4,270 m) and the endless climbing (27.8 mi/44.75 km for the former, 19 mi/31 km for the latter) give them much in common. The profile of Mount Evans might look gentler, but it demands the same humility as its impetuous challenger, even if the segment from Squaw Pass West to the 1-mi (1.5-km) flat part by Summit Lake has an average gradient of just 5%, and the final 5 mi/8 km (through twelve switchbacks) have a few sections at 7%, no more. Otherwise, we find the typical challenges related to altitude and a sense of solitude amid a desolate landscape once you're out of the forest (above 11,000 ft/3,350 m), a little as if you were riding on the moon.

Distance **80 mi** (129 km)	**E+** **9,700 ft** (2,949 m)	**Difficulty** **5/5**	**Appeal** **5/5**

Air: Denver International Airport (1h by car). Car: 1h30 from Colorado Springs, 1h30 from Fort Collins, 2h from Cheyenne, 4h from Grand Junction.

Evergreen Bike Shop, at the foot of Juniper Pass, is the place to pick up some last tips before your Mount Evans adventure. Retailer of Specialized, Scott, Surly, and Salsa.

**28677 Buffalo Park Road
Evergreen, CO 80439
evergreenbikeshop.com**

Argo Gold Mill (mi 17/km 27). Echo Lake (mi 30/km 48). Mount Goliath (mi 33/km 53). Summit Lake (mi 39/km 63). Mount Evans Summit and Switchbacks (mi 44/km 71). Juniper Pass (mi 61/km 98). Warrior Mountain (mi 62/km 100). Evergreen Lake (mi 80/km 129).

The legendary asphalt ribbon of Mount Evans, Colorado, which climbs to over 14,000 ft (4,265 m).

ESTES PARK
THE HIGHEST ROUTE

⊕ *High mountain, Advanced, 0% unpaved*   ⊕ *Map strava.com/routes/2914218442853583898*

	Distance		E+		Difficulty		Appeal
⊢−⊣	**65 mi** (105 km)	⬆	**7,400 ft** (2,264 m)	▬	**4/5**	★	**5/5**

Milner Pass

Estes Park

Trail Ridge Road, 65 mi (105 km) northwest of Denver, is the spectacular gateway to the neighboring Rocky Mountain National Park. Our route starts at the Mountain Shop (opposite the sublime Stanley Hotel) in Estes Park. At the highest point (12,183 ft/3,715 m), you are blessed with panoramas over lava cliffs and tundra. Trail Ridge Road is an 18-mi (29-km) ascent at an average gradient of 4.8%, never exceeding 7%. Carry on to Milner Pass, then turn around for a 5-mi (8-km) climb back at 5%. You will have cycled 32 mi (51 km) in succession above 10,000 ft (3,050 m), an experience offered by no other paved route in the United States.

ASPEN
BILLIONAIRE'S FEAST

⊕ *High Mountain, Expert, 0% unpaved*   ⊕ *Map strava.com/routes/2914103688367661764*

	Distance		E+		Difficulty		Appeal
⊢−⊣	**88 mi** (142 km)	⬆	**8,800 ft** (2,673 m)	▬	**5/5**	★	**5/5**

Aspen

Castle Creek Road

Aspen, known as "Billionaire Mountain," is the poshest ski resort in the world. This outsized route (starting from Aspen Bicycles) may be better ridden over two days. Either way, it reveals Aspen's prime assets. Castle Creek Road (13 mi/ 21 km and an E+ of 2,000 ft/610 m) climbs in stages into the Elk Mountain Range, which witnessed the silver rush of the late nineteenth century. Narrow, winding Independence Pass (15.9 mi/25.6 km at 4.7%) blazes with color in fall. Maroon Creek Road (8 mi/13 km and an E+ of 1,500 ft/455 m), which has restricted traffic, leads to the Maroon Bells, the most photographed mountains in North America.

VAIL
FESTIVE ROCKIES

- ⊕ High mountain, Advanced, 0% unpaved
- ⊕ Map strava.com/routes/2914549712861696708
- ⊕ Test yourself mi 10 (km 16) strava.com/segments/624334
- ⊕ Test yourself mi 50 (km 80) strava.com/segments/10016028

👁 GREG'S EYE

In the 1980s, the Coors Classic stopped off in Vail. I remember the majestic scenery and climbs that had to be tackled with prudence in summer, owing to the altitude and the traffic. This triptych via Copper Mountain and Leadville is nevertheless a Colorado classic.

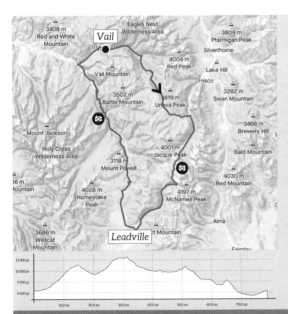

Here is a long day out on the bike, at high altitude with enchanting scenery. Our route (used by the annual Copper Triangle Gran Fondo) passes over three cols above 10,000 ft (3,050 m), framed by summits that are among the most delightful in the Rockies. We make a circuit of the Gore Range and its twenty-five peaks over 11,000 ft (3,355 m). The beauties of the Mosquito Range accompany the ascents of Vail Pass (10 mi/16 km at 4%) and Fremont Pass (10 mi/16 km at 2.7%, with 2 mi/3.25 km at 6% in the middle) on your left. We finish with Tennessee Pass (3 mi/4.75 km at 3%) and Battle Mountain (1.5 mi/2.5 km at 6%), with the wonderful Sawatch Range ahead. You'll see that Vail and Copper Mountain (mi 20/km 32) are dream destinations in summer, too. We start from Vail Brewery Company, whose terrace is the ideal spot to celebrate and unwind.

	Distance		E+		Difficulty		Appeal
⊢-⊣	**79 mi** (127 km)	⬆	**6,200 ft** (1,879 m)	📊	**4/5**	⭐	**5/5**

Air: Eagle County Regional Airport (30 min by car), Denver International Airport (3h by car).
Car: 2h from Grand Junction, 3h from Colorado Springs, 6h30 from Salt Lake City.

High Gear Cyclery, in Avon, is 10 mi (16 km) from Vail, but worth the trip for last-minute service. Retailer of Allied, Open, and BH.

82 E. Beaver Creek Boulevard Avon, CO 81620
highgearavon.com

Black Lake (mi 14/km 23). Vail Pass (mi 15/km 24). Kokomo Landmark (mi 29/km 47). Fremont Pass (mi 31/km 50). Red Cliff Bridge (mi 64/km 103). Battle Mountain (mi 65/km 105).

GRAND MESA
FLAT, ARE YOU SURE?

DIRT & GRAVEL

🌐 *High mountain, Advanced, 55% unpaved*　　　🌐 *Map strava.com/routes/2915366740144424674*

	Distance		E+		Difficulty		Appeal
⊦—⊦	**69 mi** (112 km)	⬆	**7,400 ft** (2,266 m)	📊	**4/5**	★	**5/5**

Grand Mesa, east of Grand Junction, is the largest flat-topped mountain in the world, stretching for over 40 mi (64 km). This extraordinary plateau, which sits above 10,000 ft (3,050 m), is all rocky escarpments, forests, and lakes (300 of them). Our route combining asphalt, dirt, and gravel starts from Grand Mesa Visitor Center and descends into the valley before reascending via Surface Creek Road (9 mi/14 km at 6%, the first third paved). Grand Mesa then unfurls its splendors on Crag Crest Trail all the way to Lands End Observatory, at the mesa's edge, offering views to the west that are simply magical.

DURANGO
END OF THE ROCKIES

🌐 *High mountain, Advanced, 70% unpaved*　　　🌐 *Map strava.com/routes/2913908250160240742*

	Distance		E+		Difficulty		Appeal
⊦—⊦	**68 mi** (110 km)	⬆	**5,400 ft** (1,647 m)	📊	**4/5**	★	**4/5**

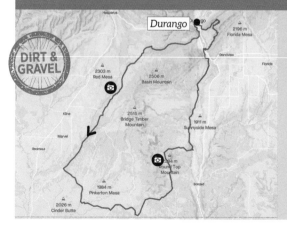

Durango (pop. 18,000) is a charming town that's closer to Albuquerque (200 mi/320 km) than it is to Denver (350 mi/565 km). Indeed, this region is known as the Four Corners, as Colorado, New Mexico, Arizona, and Utah meet nearby. We ride south (from Mountain Bike Specialists) to an area east of Mesa Verde National Park, between the La Plata and Animas Rivers, where the southern Rockies blend into the San Juan Mountains. We climb, mostly on dirt and gravel trails, through a landscape of dry prairie and imposing hills, to 7,500 ft (2,285 m). On the homeward leg, there's a final kick on the single tracks of Horse Gulch above Durango.

GRAND JUNCTION
VINES OR ROCKS? BOTH!

- ⊕ *High mountain, Intermediate, 0% unpaved*
- ⊕ *Map strava.com/routes/2913868897435883104*

- ⊕ *Test yourself mi 18 (km 29) strava.com/segments/10151939*
- ⊕ *Test yourself mi 40 (km 64) strava.com/segments/1144935*

👁 GREG'S EYE

Grand Junction is situated near the vineyards of Grand Valley and the fascinating canyons of Colorado National Monument. I invite you to combine the two. This is a must-ride, whether you're coming from Denver, Moab, or elsewhere.

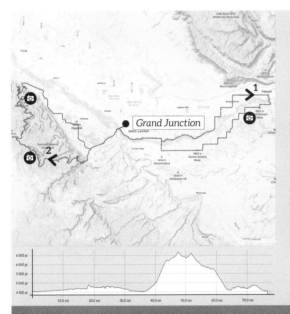

Grand Junction

In Grand Junction (pop. 65,000), the largest city in the west of the Centennial State, there is always a choice. For example, on the first day, take a tranquil 40-mi (64-km) ride through the Grand Valley vineyards to Palisade and back via both banks of the Colorado River. On the second, another 40 mi (64 km) of more energetic pedaling into the heart of extraordinary Colorado National Monument, with its canyons and five-star panoramas. Heading west, we reach scenic Rim Rock Drive (24 mi/39 km) via a stiff ramp to Cold Shivers Point (3.5 mi/5.6 km at 6.5%). You can, of course, do both in one day—if the 77-mi (124-km) distance doesn't put you off—for a double dose of biking and views. The other advantage of the all-in-one route is that you can return to Grand Valley the next day for a guilt-free tasting of its renowned merlot, syrah, and chardonnay.

Distance **77 mi** (124 km)	E+ **4,000 ft** (1,230 m)	Difficulty **3/5**	Appeal **5/5**

Air: Eagle County Regional Airport (2h by car), Denver International Airport (5h by car).
Car: 2h from Moab, 4h30 from Salt Lake City, 7h from Albuquerque, 7h30 from Las Vegas.

Bicycle Outfitters enjoys a fine reputation in Grand Junction, where it has been open since the 1990s. Strava Club. Retailer of Specialized, Scott, Santa Cruz, and Juliana.

**537 N. First Street
Grand Junction, CO 81501
gjbikes.com**

Colterris Winery (mi 21/km 34). Red Canyon (mi 46/km 74). Fallen Rocks and Upper Ute Canyon (mi 49/km 79). Coke Ovens (mi 54/km 87). Independence Monument (mi 57/km 92). Book Cliffs and Window Rock (mi 58/km 93).

MOAB
CINEMATIC SPLENDOR

⊕ *High mountain, Advanced, 0% unpaved*
⊕ *Map strava.com/routes/2912750401730798294*

⊕ *Test yourself mi 15 (km 24) strava.com/segments/613242*
⊕ *Test yourself mi 41 (km 66) strava.com/segments/4254801*

◉ GREG'S EYE

From *Rio Grande* to *Thelma and Louise*, Hollywood has popularized the majestic settings of the Canyonlands and Arches National Parks near Moab. Both are cult destinations for mountain bikers, but this asphalt route is equally thrilling.

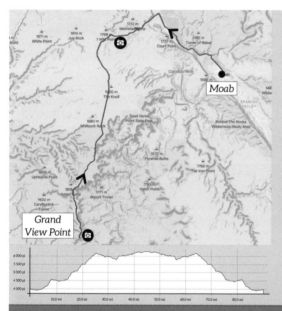

This 90-mi (145-km) route with a relief that's not too challenging is the one to cycle if you're only passing through Moab, or as the first in a series venturing onto trickier terrain: the sort of off-road treasures we glimpse at the entrance to Arches National Park (mi 4/km 6.5), toward Dead Horse Point (mi 26/km 42), and at the junction (mi 31/km 50) with White Rim Trail—a snaking 100-mi (161-km) gem. We're riding Island in the Sky Road, an asphalt ribbon across the eponymous high mesa with fascinating cliffs, colorful geological formations, and deep canyons plunging from 6,000 ft (1,830 m). The panoramas are exceptional all the way to Grand View Point Overlook, where we turn around to respool ourselves like an old-time movie reel, viewing it all again in reverse. Mesa Arch is worth stepping off the bike for, in both directions. Magical.

	Distance		E+		Difficulty		Appeal
⊢−⊣	**90 mi** (145 km)	⬆	**4,800 ft** (1,473 m)	📊	**4/5**	⭐	**5/5**

Air: Canyonlands Regional Airport (30 min by car), Salt Lake City International Airport (4h by car).
Car: 5h30 from Denver, 6h from Albuquerque, 7h from Las Vegas, 7h30 from Phoenix.

Rim Cyclery is the oldest bike shop in Moab, a pioneer on the emerging mountain bike market in the 1980s. Rentals. Retailer of Scott.

**94 W. 100 N.
Moab, UT 84532
rimcyclery.com**

Plateau Overlook (mi 20/km 32). Shafer Trail View Point (mi 34/km 55). Grand View Point Overlook (mi 45/km 72). Buck Canyon Overlook (mi 48/km 77). Mesa Arch (mi 51/km 82). Big Mesa View Point (mi 72/km 116). Monitor Butte (mi 76/km 122).

MANILA
NO THRILLA IN MANILA

- ⊕ High mountain, Advanced, 0% unpaved
- ⊕ Map strava.com/routes/2912737579860917974
- ⊙ Test yourself mi 13 (km 21) strava.com/segments/1895141
- ⊙ Test yourself mi 49 (km 79) strava.com/segments/7741722

◉ GREG'S EYE

The name Manila evokes a childhood memory for me: the Ali-Frazier boxing match, the famous Thrilla in Manila in the capital of the Philippines in 1975. This route in the other Manila, close to Wyoming, is an extraordinary ride above the Flaming Gorge Reservoir.

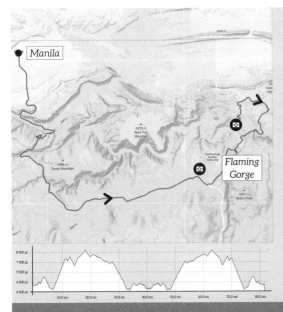

Manila

Flaming Gorge

The Salt Lake City area and Moab have their fair share of natural attractions, but the Flaming Gorge–Uintas National Scenic Byway, a remote road in northeast Utah, is one of the wonders of the Beehive State. We start from Browning's Café in Manila—gateway to Wyoming. The beautiful road snakes like a wavy V at 6,000 to 8,100 ft/1,830 to 2,470 m (take the altitude into account) south of the Green River and along the fabulous Flaming Gorge Reservoir as far as its 500-ft- (150-m-) high dam, and even a little farther if you want a dip halfway through the ride. The panoramas are superb—in both directions—and the climbing is suitably challenging: 4 mi (6.5 km) at 7%, then 0.7 mi (1 km) at 9%, and 3.6 mi (5.75 km) at 4% to reach Moose Ponds (mi 18/km 29); 5 mi (8 km) at 4.8% to climb back up from the US-191 Bridge (mi 49/km 79). Pure joy.

	Distance		E+		Difficulty		Appeal
	82 mi (132 km)	↑	**9,000 ft** (2,757 m)	📊	**5/5**	⭐	**5/5**

Air: Salt Lake City International Airport (3h by car).
Car: 4h from Pocatello, 5h from Moab, 5h from Cheyenne, 6h from Denver.

Altitude Cycle in Vernal, 60 mi (97 km) south of Manila, is the closest well-stocked bike shop to the route. Top-notch service. Retailer of Specialized.

**580 E. Main Street
Vernal, UT 84078**
altitudecycle.com

Lookout Sheep Creek (mi 8/km 13). Sheep Creek Overlook (mi 10/km 16). Greendale Overlook (mi 27/km 43). Firefighters Memorial (mi 30/km 48). Green River Dam (mi 34/km 55). Mustang Ridge Beach (mi 41/km 66).

OGDEN
THE WASATCH MONSTER

⊕ *High mountain, Expert, 0% unpaved*
⊕ *Map strava.com/routes/2913032057569407042*

⊕ *Test yourself mi 12 (km 19) strava.com/segments/18446960*
⊕ *Test yourself mi 37 (km 60) strava.com/segments/10777318*

◎ GREG'S EYE

Many skiers dream of visiting Powder Mountain, one of the largest ski resorts in the United States with slopes for all levels of ability. Pedaling up there is another matter: the scary 6-mi (9.75-km) climb to "Pow Mow" is one of the most ambitious cycling challenges around.

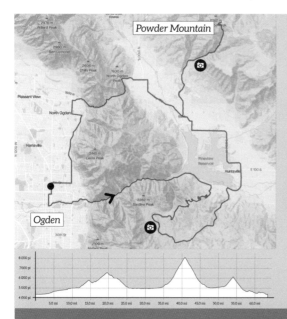

Powder Mountain

Ogden

You may scoff at a mere 6 mi (9.75 km), but if you manage to climb the wall to Powder Mountain—a ski resort in the Wasatch Range—without stepping off your bike, you'll find the distance sufficient. When Wolf Creek Golf Course comes into view (mi 35/km 56), ease up. Two-thirds of the climb are over 10%, with the toughest sections at 17% and a hellish 1 mi (1.5 km) in the middle at an average gradient of 14.4%! Connoisseurs compare Powder Mountain to the Angliru (Spain) and the Mortirolo (Italy)—bogeymen of the Vuelta and the Giro. Heading out from Ogden (pop. 90,000), 40 mi (64 km) north of Salt Lake City, the Wasatch Range rises magnificently before you. It's a thrill to climb historic Old Snowbasin (1.7 mi/2.75 km, then 4 mi/6.5 km, at gradients of 5% to 6%), followed by North Ogden Canyon (2 mi/3.25 km at 5%) on the homeward run.

	Distance		E+		Difficulty		Appeal
⊢–⊣	**64 mi** (103 km)	⬆	**7,700 ft** (2,355 m)	▊	**5/5**	★	**5/5**

Air: Salt Lake City International Airport (45 min by car). Car: 2h from Pocatello, 4h30 from Boise, 7h from Las Vegas, 8h from Denver.

Skyline Cycle, situated at the foot of the Wasatch Range, is a vibrant bike shop founded in 2006. Strava Club. Retailer of Giant, Salsa, and Raleigh.

834 Washington Boulevard Ogden, UT 84404 skylinecyclery.com

Pineview Reservoir (mi 10/km 16). Snowbasin Resort (mi 19/km 31). East Fork Overlook (mi 21/km 34). Ogden Valley (mi 54/km 87). North Ogden Lookout Point (mi 56/km 90).

SALT LAKE CITY
EMIGRATION VIBES

- ⊕ *High mountain, Advanced, 0% unpaved*
- ⊕ *Map strava.com/routes/2912734290408281154*
- ⊕ *Test yourself mi 14 (km 23) strava.com/segments/18548132*
- ⊕ *Test yourself mi 44 (km 71) strava.com/segments/12592078*

◉ GREG'S EYE

Salt Lake City is the perfect (big) city at the foot of the mountains. The proximity of the Wasatch Range, to the east, dazzles and beckons you up into its peaks. Start with Emigration Canyon and its thrilling natural extension, Big Mountain.

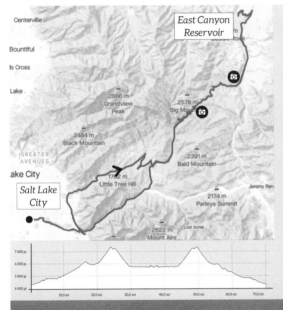

Salt Lake City's exceptional location is ripe for asphalt escapades via the sumptuous notches carved between the summits of the Wasatch Range. Emigration Canyon is the most popular and busiest, and riding it is an initiation rite in the city. Ward, City Creek, and Red Butte Canyons farther north and Millcreek, Big Cottonwood, and Little Cottonwood Canyons farther south can wait. Emigration Canyon Road ascends from between the vast University of Utah campus and Hogle Zoo, for 7.6 mi (12.25 km) of extraordinary scenery at an average gradient of 3.2%.

It resonates with history as the route Mormon emigrants took to complete their trek west in the mid-nineteenth century. The pleasure continues on Big Mountain (5.2 mi/8.3 km at 5.1%, with sections at 8%) and East Canyon Reservoir. The reverse climb up Big Mountain has several short ramps at 10%.

	Distance		E+		Difficulty		Appeal
⊢⊣	**70 mi** (113 km)	⬆	**6,800 ft** (2,076 m)	📊	**4/5**	⭐	**5/5**

Air: Salt Lake City International Airport (30 min by car). Car: 3h30 from Moab, 6h from Boise, 6h from Las Vegas, 7h30 from Reno, 8h from Denver.

Bicycle Center is a vast post-industrial space in south Salt Lake that's popular with locals. Strava Club. Retailer of Specialized.

2200 S. 700 E. Salt Lake City, UT 84106 bicyclecenter.com

This Is the Place Heritage Park (mi 8.5/km 14). Little Mountain Summit (mi 16/km 26). Affleck Park (mi 21/km 34). Big Mountain Summit (mi 24/km 39). East Canyon Reservoir (mi 31/km 50). Pony Express Trail Historical Marker (mi 44/km 71). Sugar House Park (mi 68/km 109).

SANDY
THE BRUTAL PASS

🌐 *High mountain, Expert, 0% unpaved*   🌐 *Map strava.com/routes/2913028499350795330*

	Distance		E+		Difficulty		Appeal
⊢–⊣	**80 mi** (129 km)	⬆	**9,700 ft** (2,948 m)	📊	**5/5**	⭐	**5/5**

The final section of road is now paved, but nothing comes easy on the cruel slopes of Guardsman Pass (9,717 ft/2,962 m), in the heart of the Wasatch Range. Like Powder Mountain farther north, the ascent via Midway, through aspen forest, is considered one of the most savage in the United States: 8.6 mi (13.8 km) at an average gradient of 8.7%, with the first third in double digits and one section at 18%! The Alpine Loop Scenic Byway (11 mi/18 km at 5%) provides an energetic warm-up on this high-mountain route (starting from Bingham Cyclery in Sandy). We descend Guardsman Pass via the stunning scenery of Big Cottonwood Canyon.

SALT LAKE CITY
A BREATH OF SALT AIR

🌐 *Fairly flat, Intermediate, 1% unpaved*   🌐 *Map strava.com/routes/2913038143849460106*

	Distance		E+		Difficulty		Appeal
⊢–⊣	**60 mi** (96 km)	⬆	**1,000 ft** (313 m)	📊	**2/5**	⭐	**4/5**

Turning your back on the Wasatch Range in no way diminishes the cycling experience in Salt Lake City. Heading west, the broad expanse of the Great Salt Lake offers a gripping contrast to the high mountains. This route (starting from Cranky's Bike Shop) is a massive breath of fresh air. Fill your lungs as you stand on the pier of Great Salt Lake State Park (mi 36/km 58), having explored downtown (Liberty Park, the unmissable Salt Lake Temple, and Capitol Hill—0.6 mi/1 km at 8%). Then turn for home through West Valley City and up the tranquil Jordan River Trail.

PANGUITCH
A MARVEL, FOR SURE

⊕ *High mountain, Expert, 0% unpaved*   ⊕ *Map strava.com/routes/2912730872923380802*

	Distance		E+		Difficulty		Appeal
⊢⊣	**133 mi** (214 km)	⬆	**10,538 ft** (3,212 m)	📊	**5/5**	⭐	**5/5**

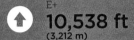

Cycling the 133 mi (214 km) of Scenic Byway 12 over one or several days requires excellent fitness and some logistics. You'll be richly rewarded. This point-to-point route from Panguitch (Quilt Walk Park), 250 mi (400 km) south of Salt Lake City, to Torrey (Rim Rock Inn) often tops the rankings of most beautiful road in the United States—and deservedly so. Bryce Canyon, Dixie National Forest, Escalante Natural Bridge, Grand Staircase–Escalante National Monument, Craft Creek Falls, and Capitol Reef National Park are highlights. The ascents of Red Canyon, Powell Point, the Hogback, and Homestead Overlook will satisfy the most ambitious riders.

WENDOVER
UNEXPECTED BORDER

⊕ *Fairly flat, Intermediate, 85% unpaved*   ⊕ *Map strava.com/routes/2912760473514263254*

	Distance		E+		Difficulty		Appeal
⊢⊣	**65 mi** (104 km)	⬆	**2,000 ft** (619 m)	📊	**3/5**	⭐	**4/5**

Wendover (pop. 1,500), 120 mi (195 km) west of Salt Lake City, is known for its proximity to Nevada (and the casinos in its twin city in that state, West Wendover, as gambling is prohibited in Utah). Yet the neighboring Silver Island Range (peaks above 7,000 ft/2,135 m) merits exploration. Most striking is Silver Island Loop Road—50 mi (80 km) of dirt and gravel from Bonneville Salt Flats to the edge of the Great Salt Lake Desert. The visual contrasts are stunning. On your left: mountains, scrubland, abandoned mines, and caves. On your right: salt flats that stretch to the horizon.

CARSON CITY
GREG'S SECRET

- 🌐 *High mountain, Expert, 0% unpaved*
- 🌐 *Map strava.com/routes/2911691405038991756*
- ⊙ *Test yourself mi 29 (km 47) strava.com/segments/4895190*
- ⊙ *Test yourself mi 57 (km 92) strava.com/segments/20921929*

👁 GREG'S EYE

Looking for a great Nevada ride? Let me take you back to the late 1970s, when I was still a future hope in what was a niche sport in this country. We lived in Carson City, and I knew these 85 mi (137 km) through the Sierra Nevada by heart: they were my training roads!

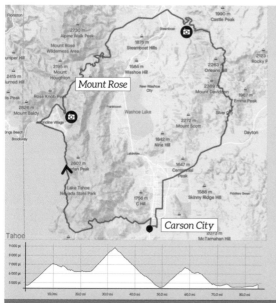

Mount Rose

Carson City

Thirty percent (25 mi/40 km) of this loop from Carson City (pop. 55,000)—the state capital—is climbing, with a total elevation gain close to 9,000 ft (2,745 m). This requires excellent fitness. Fortunately, you have the rocky, scraggy scenery of the Sierra Nevada to enjoy, as well as dazzling blue Lake Tahoe. First, we climb to Spooner Summit (9 mi/14 km at close to 5%, with sections at 8%), followed by 10 mi (16 km) beside Lake Tahoe. Before us rises the west slope of Mount Rose: 8.3 mi (13.4 km) with an average gradient of 6%. Beware of traffic on the descent—we're near Reno. Geiger Grade, the third obstacle on the menu, is quieter, but just as hard: 7.7 mi (12.4 km) at an average gradient of 5.2%. You'll have expended so many calories that a halt at Red's Old 395 Grill (mi 78/km 126), a BBQ staple in Carson City, is justly deserved.

Distance **85 mi** (136 km)	E+ **8,700 ft** (2,641 m)	Difficulty **5/5**	Appeal **5/5**

Air: Reno-Tahoe International Airport (30 min by car). Car: 2h30 from Sacramento, 4h30 from San Francisco, 6h from Medford, 7h from Las Vegas, 8h from Salt Lake City.

Bike Habitat is an excellent shop virtually at the foot of the Spooner Summit climb, south of Carson City. Retailer of Giant, Liv, and Salsa.

911 Topsy Lane Carson City, NV 89705 bikehabitat.com

Spooner Lake (mi 10/km 16). Secret Harbor Beach (mi 15/km 24). Ski Beach (mi 22/km 35). Lake Tahoe Scenic Overlook (mi 28/km 45). Mount Rose-Ski Tahoe (mi 35/km 56). Sunridge Overlook (mi 39/km 63). Geiger Lookout Wayside Park (mi 54/km 87).

RENO
UNFRIENDLY CLIMB

🌐 *High mountain, Expert, 70% unpaved*　　🌐 Map strava.com/routes/2912043890470256942

Distance	E+	Difficulty	Appeal
🚩 **44 mi** (71 km)	⬆ **5,600 ft** (1,701 m)	📊 **5/5**	⭐ **4/5**

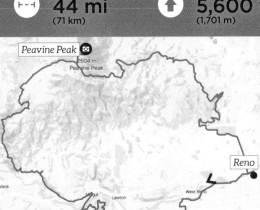

Peavine Peak

Reno

Pedaling west out of Reno, it doesn't take long to ride to the California state line, which lies less than 1 mi (1.5 km) from the halfway point on this route (starting from Dropout Bike Shop), at the beginning of the nearly 8.5 mi (13.75 km) climb on Hawk Meadow Trail to the radio towers of Peavine Peak (8,269 ft/2,520 m)—a silhouette familiar to all Reno inhabitants. The panoramic views are superb. The average gradient (7%) is less of a factor than the perilous state of the trail—rutted and loose in places—and several (long) sections as steep as 20%! Peavine Peak is a gravel challenge requiring excellent bike-handling skills.

CARSON CITY
BONANZA SPIRIT

🌐 *High mountain, Advanced, 85% unpaved*　　🌐 Map strava.com/routes/29123010017777655148

Distance	E+	Difficulty	Appeal
🚩 **65 mi** (105 km)	⬆ **5,600 ft** (1,720 m)	📊 **4/5**	⭐ **5/5**

Carson City

In the Pine Nut Mountains southeast of Carson City you'll find broad plains and valleys covered in bushy juniper and piñon pines. This was the setting of the classic Western series *Bonanza*. Heading out from the Nevada State Capitol, we're soon climbing at gradients of 5% to 6%, initially in Brunswick Canyon (from mi 8/km 13) and then northeast of Minden (from mi 41/km 66), much of it on Sunrise Pass, reaching 7,000 ft (2,135 m) close to Mineral Peak and 6,000 ft (1,830 m) below Rice Peak. Abandoned mines and natural springs dot the area. Beware of the sun: there's a reason the Cartwrights of *Bonanza* were never without their Stetsons.

WELLS
NOT AN ANGEL

⊕ *High mountain, Advanced, 0% unpaved*　　⊕ *Map strava.com/routes/2911690664896614930*

Distance	E+	Difficulty	Appeal
61 mi (99 km)	⬆ **4,700 ft** (1,420 m)	**3/5**	**4/5**

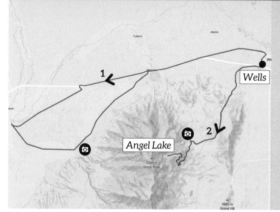

To reach Angel Lake in northeast Nevada, you ride through an arid landscape at an altitude of close to 6,000 ft (1,830 m). The modest lake sits at nearly 8,400 ft (2,560 m) in a superb cirque. The road is full of surprises: several barriers that you have to ride around, zero traffic, and a shallow 2-mi (3.25-km) descent between two ramps. The second, sinuous ramp to the summit is nastier (4.7 mi/7.5 km at close to 7%) than the first, which is straighter (3.6 mi/5.75 km at 5%). The scenery is wonderful. The route (from City Park in Wells) starts with a 38-mi (61-km) warm-up that takes the measure of the East Humboldt Range.

BOULDER CITY
THROUGH THE TUNNELS

⊕ *Low mountain, Intermediate, 15% unpaved*　　⊕ *Map strava.com/routes/2921027532525442760*

Distance	E+	Difficulty	Appeal
52 mi (84 km)	⬆ **3,820 ft** (1,164 m)	**2/5**	**4/5**

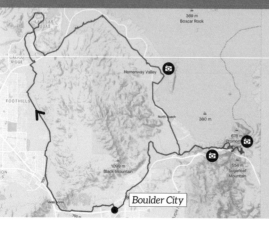

As tempting as it is to ride to Eldorado Canyon and the Colorado River (southwest of Las Vegas, barely 25 mi from the Strip), you have to contend with traffic and scores of motorbikes on US-95. But this route (starting from All Mountain Cyclery in Boulder City) is a more sedate and popular one, here in southern Nevada. It follows the delectable River Mountains Loop Trail and the Historic Railroad Trail with its extraordinary tunnels through the red rock. They lead (without any major challenges) to the Hoover Dam, an arch-gravity structure 1,244 ft (379 m) long and 726.4 ft (221.4 m) high, with fantastic panoramas along the way.

LAS VEGAS
FROM THE STRIP TO RED ROCK

- ⊕ Low mountain, Intermediate, 0% unpaved
- ⊕ Map strava.com/routes/2911657653675183500
- ⊕ Test yourself mi 10 (km 16) strava.com/segments/3286099
- ⊕ Test yourself mi 32 (km 51) strava.com/segments/11267601

👁 GREG'S EYE

Welcome to Las Vegas! This 60-mi (97-km) loop provides a different perspective on "Sin City" than the typical night spent roaming the casinos to play the slots. After a tour of the iconic Las Vegas Strip, we head west to extraordinary Red Rock Canyon. Mind the traffic.

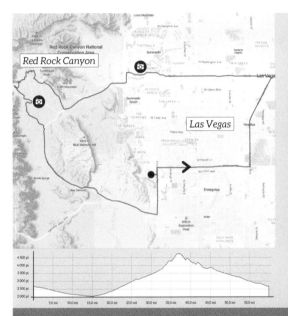

Las Vegas is known for wild nightlife, huge hotel-casinos, and its status as the Marriage Capital of the World. Cast those clichés aside and, after a good night's sleep, leave early to cycle the 5 mi (8 km) up Las Vegas Boulevard South—better known as the Strip—which is markedly less crowded at sunrise. From Mandalay Bay to the STRAT, we pass a good twenty temples to gambling, including the Excalibur, Caesars Palace, and the Mirage. West of the city, the 13 mi (21 km) of panoramic, wonderfully winding roads along Red Rock Canyon await you. In less than an hour, you'll have swapped architectural follies designed by man for the most sublime nature the Mojave Desert has to offer: breathtaking contrasts between gray and red cliffs, fossilized sand dunes, and other geological marvels. That's a true jackpot.

	Distance		E+		Difficulty		Appeal
	**60 mi** (97 km)		**3,300 ft** (997 m)		**3/5**		**5/5**

Air: Harry Reid International Airport, Las Vegas (20 min by car).
Car: 4h from Los Angeles, 4h30 from Phoenix, 6h from Salt Lake City, 7h from Carson City, 8h30 from San Francisco.

Pedal & Pour is a superb bike café on the western edge of town, close to the road to/from Red Rock Canyon, and as such makes an ideal base camp. Strava Club. Retailer of BMC.

9742 W. Maule Avenue Las Vegas, NV 89148 pedalpour.com

Welcome to Fabulous Las Vegas sign (mi 8.5/km 14). Caesars Palace and Eiffel Tower viewing deck (mi 11/km 18). STRAT (mi 13/km 21). Cottonwood Canyon (mi 25/km 40). Calico 1 (mi 33/km 53). High Point Overlook (mi 36.5/km 59). Red Rock RV Wash (mi 41/km 66).

A trail through the otherworldly scenery of Red Rock Canyon, Nevada.

CAPE ROYAL
GRAND CANYON RIM RIDE

⊕ *High mountain, Advanced, 10% unpaved*
⊕ *Map strava.com/routes/2898167718236956928*

⊕ *Test yourself mi 19 (km 31) strava.com/segments/1466756*
⊕ *Test yourself mi 27 (km 43) strava.com/segments/4053607*

◉ GREG'S EYE

If you come to Arizona, you'll want to experience the dizzying heights of the Grand Canyon. So you might as well do it by bike! This route along the North Rim requires some logistics, but what a reward if you start it in the afternoon, riding into the setting sun!

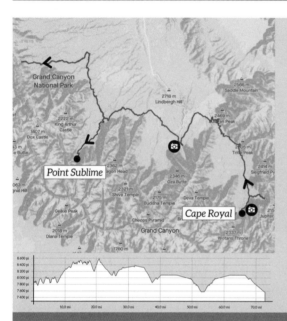

Two details: first, it's best to be properly organized unless you want to pedal well over 100 mi/161 km (even by the shortest route) and return to Cape Royal (where we start from the parking lot). For example, you could leave a vehicle at Point Sublime to jump into at adventure's end after sundown. Second, use a gravel bike so that you can reach all possible viewpoints (of which there are many on this route) overlooking one of the most fascinating sights in the world. You'll never tire of the Grand Canyon. It's dizzying in every way, both physically and geologically. Be aware, too, that we're at quite high altitude—over 8,000 ft (2,440 m) on Cape Royal Drive, Swamp Ridge Road, and Point Sublime Trail—the climate of north Arizona is arid, and resupply stops are nonexistent. So, plan well and you'll enjoy an extraordinary day.

	Distance		E+		Difficulty		Appeal
	76 mi (122 km)		**6,200 ft** (1,888 m)		**4/5**		**5/5**

Air: Flagstaff Pulliam Airport (4h by car).
Car: 6h from Phoenix, 6h30 from Salt Lake City, 7h from Las Vegas, 8h from Albuquerque.

Flagstaff Bike Revolution, just round the corner from the Amtrak station, is known for its efficient team, quality of service, and friendly welcome. Retailer of Giant, Liv, Salsa, and Kona.

3 S. Mikes Pike Street Flagstaff, AZ 86001 flagbikerev.com

Cape Royal (mi/km 0). Angels Window (mi 1/km 1.5). Walhalla Overlook (mi 2/km 3.5). Cape Final (mi 5/km 8). Vista Encantada (mi 15/km 24). Coconino Overlook (mi 26/km 42). Swamp Point (mi 53/km 85). Point Sublime (mi 75/km 121).

KAYENTA
FANTASTIC MONUMENT VALLEY

🌐 Hilly, Advanced, 40% unpaved   🌐 Map strava.com/routes/2898486121341277440

	Distance		E+		Difficulty		Appeal
⊢─┤	**84 mi** (136 km)	⬆	**3,400 ft** (1,048 m)	📊	**3/5**	★	**5/5**

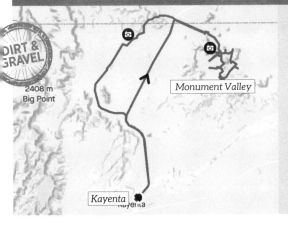

2408 m
Big Point

Monument Valley

Kayenta

Charge your smartphone before setting off on your adventure through Monument Valley, 150 mi (240 km) northeast of Flagstaff. The incredible series of vividly colored and strikingly shaped sandstone buttes, symbols of the American West, will give your camera a workout. At John Wayne's Point (mi 25/km 40), the start of the official 17-mi (27-km) loop that inspired this route, pose with your bike as your horse in imitation of the world-famous cowboy star in the film *Stagecoach*, which brought Monument Valley to the world. Three Sisters, Totem Pole, Spearhead Mesa, The Thumb, and East and West Mitten buttes will then be yours to explore.

COTTONWOOD
ABOVE THE VINEYARDS

🌐 High mountain, Advanced, 0% unpaved   🌐 Map strava.com/routes/2904372832362729044

	Distance		E+		Difficulty		Appeal
⊢─┤	**72 mi** (116 km)	⬆	**6,700 ft** (2,032 m)	📊	**4/5**	★	**4/5**

1841 m
First View

Cottonwood

1562 m
House Mountain

1069 m
Verde

1058 m
Sheepshead
Mountain

Mingus Mountain

Mingus Mountain

1073 m
Sugarloaf

Bignotti

1143 m
White Hills

2024 m
Goat Peak

Middle Verde

Cherry

Montezuma Castle
National Monument

Midd

Camp Verde

Mingus Mountain is a paragliding hot spot 100 mi (161 km) north of Phoenix and 50 mi (80 km) southwest of Flagstaff overlooking the vineyards of Verde Valley. Cottonwood (pop. 12,000) lies at the foot of the east slope. Switchbacks and superb panoramas carry you up the long climb (13.3 mi/21.4 km) to the sign reading, "Elevation 7,023 ft," which translates to 2,140 m. The average gradient is 5%, but it's irregular, with sections at more than 10% before and after former mining town Jerome. Starting at Verde Valley Bicycle Company, we do a 40-mi (64-km) warm-up past spectacular rock formations and the ancient cliff dwellings of Montezuma Castle.

SEDONA
AMONG RED ROCKS

DIRT & GRAVEL

- *High mountain, Advanced, 75% unpaved*
- *Map strava.com/routes/2904754423393772644*
- *Test yourself mi 7 (km 11.25) strava.com/segments/15145826*
- *Test yourself mi 72 (km 116) strava.com/segments/3115535*

👁 GREG'S EYE

If you're put off by the high temperatures in Phoenix and Tucson, head farther north in Arizona for a stop in Sedona before you reach Flagstaff. Here, at a height of 4,300 ft (1,310 m), the climate is mild, the cultural life vibrant, and the red rock landscape fascinating.

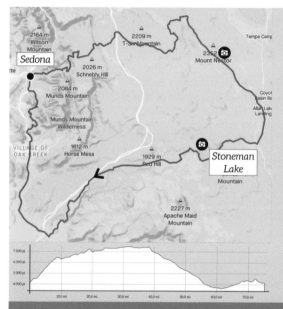

Sedona (pop. 10,000) is one of the most pleasant places in Arizona, known for its restaurants (our route starts from the Secret Garden Café; enjoy the terrace upon your return), its artistic community, and its magnificent natural surroundings. The sometimes surprising rock formations (such as those resembling Snoopy and Lucy from *Peanuts*) can glow red and orange depending on the position of the sun and its intensity. This mainly off-road route, 30 mi (48 km) of which run across the high plain of Coconino National Forest, has many surprises in store, from the ascent of Schnebly Hill (7 mi/11.25 km at 5%) all the way to Munds Mountain Wilderness on the way back into town. Riding between sandstone columns, sheer canyons, and forests of ponderosa pines, we even take the Arizona Trail for a few miles after Mount Nestor. A delight.

Distance **75 mi** (120 km)	E+ **5,900 ft** (1,808 m)	Difficulty **4/5**	Appeal **5/5**

Air: Flagstaff Pulliam Airport (30 min by car), Phoenix Sky Harbor International Airport (2h by car).
Car: 4h30 from Las Vegas, 5h30 from Albuquerque, 7h from Los Angeles.

Regroup Coffee + Bicycles, 130 mi (209 km) south of Sedona, is an accomplished iteration of the contemporary bike café. Strava Club. Rare bikes (3T, Bastion, Allied, and Spooky brands).

**1205 N. Scottsdale Road
Tempe, AZ 85281
regroupwithus.com**

Merry Go Round (mi 4/km 7). Schnebly Hill Vista (mi 7/km 12). Mount Nestor (mi 26/km 42). Stoneman Lake and Lake Mountain (mi 41/km 66). Bell Rock and Baby Bell Rock (mi 67/km 108). Cathedral Rock (mi 69/km 111). Chicken Point (mi 71/km 114).

PHOENIX
ABOVE THE VALLEY OF THE SUN

⊕ *Low mountain, Intermediate, 5% unpaved*
⊕ *Map strava.com/routes/2903702105026331244*

⊙ *Test yourself mi 38 (km 61) strava.com/segments/4917428*
⊙ *Test yourself mi 43 (km 69) strava.com/segments/741714*

👁 GREG'S EYE

South Mountain Park, which stretches over three low mountain massifs—Ma-Ha-Tauk, Gila, and Guadalupe—is a favored playground for Phoenix cyclists. We explore it on this paved route, although it's also well worth riding its 60 mi (97 km) of trails.

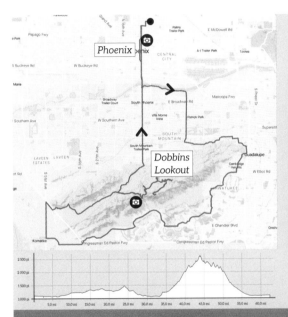

With peaks barely touching 2,500 ft (762 m), a scattering of giant cacti, scrubland, and pale rock, South Mountain Park, the largest municipal park in the country, is the preferred escape of the five million inhabitants of the sprawling urban area known as the "Valley of the Sun." The roads taken on our route link the most breathtaking viewpoints, whether over the expanse of the Sonoran Desert or the high-rises of downtown. Dobbins Lookout (mi 47/km 76) is a must. After a warm-up via the Salt River and the residential areas of Guadalupe and Ahwatukee, we begin gently to climb between the three massifs of South Mountain Park. Only the short ramps to the most stunning overlooks (between mi 43/km 69 and mi 49/km 79) exceed 6% average gradient in places. If you want to venture further afield—off-road—you'll need a gravel bike.

Distance	E+	Difficulty	Appeal
63 mi (101 km)	**3,300 ft** (993 m)	**3/5**	**4/5**

Air: Phoenix Sky Harbor International Airport (15 min by car).
Car: 2h from Tucson, 4h30 from Las Vegas, 6h from Los Angeles, 6h30 from Albuquerque.

The Velo, north of Midtown, is a friendly bike shop that's a favorite of the local cycling community. Weekly rides, Strava Club. Retailer of 3T, Giant, Cannondale, and Scott.

**2317 N. 7th Street
Phoenix, AZ 85006
thevelo.com**

National Trail (mi 40/km 64). Gila Valley (mi 44/km 71). Buena Vista (mi 46/km 74). Dobbins Lookout (mi 47/km 76). Holbert Lookout (mi 49/km 79). Japanese Friendship Garden and Phoenix Art Museum (mi 61/km 98).

CAVE CREEK
NORTHERN PHOENIX COLORS

⊕ Low mountain, Intermediate, 0% unpaved ⊕ Map strava.com/routes/2904330226031073380

Distance	E+	Difficulty	Appeal
61 mi (97 km)	**3,300 ft** (1,000 m)	**3/5**	**4/5**

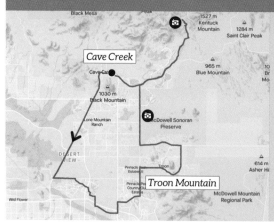

You'll never tire of the scenery of the Sonoran Desert around Phoenix. This route starts from Spur Cross Cycles in Cave Creek (pop. 5,000), on the edge of Tonto National Forest, between the north of the Arizonan capital and the west bank of the Verde River. It provides an array of contrasts and colors, from Black Mountain to the gentle slopes of Pinnacle Peak and Troon Mountain. The final (not too difficult) climb up to Seven Springs and Cave Creek, at the foot of Kentuck Mountain (5,013 ft/1,530 m), is framed by stunning rock formations and modest but refreshing waterfalls. Late-afternoon light lends a sublime touch to this ride.

TUCSON
A FOR ARIZONA

⊕ Very hilly, Intermediate, 0% unpaved ⊕ Map strava.com/routes/2904800881073701988

Distance	E+	Difficulty	Appeal
52 mi (84 km)	**2,200 ft** (672 m)	**3/5**	**4/5**

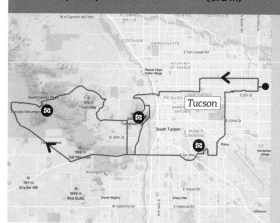

Here's an ideal route around Tucson (starting from Coasters bike café) for a warm-up/cooldown before/after tackling Mount Lemmon. We cruise downtown, then cross the University of Arizona campus and the Santa Cruz River to tease the hills of Sentinel Peak Park and Tucson Mountain Park as the sun sets over the Sonoran Desert. The slopes are short and perfectly toning: "A" Mountain—adorned with a giant letter (Arizona's initial, obviously) is 1.4 mi/2.25 km long at 5.5%, and 8% at the top; then Gates Pass (2 mi/3.25 km at 5%); before a final "wall" of 0.2 mile/0.3 km at 12%, between red rock columns and giant cacti. You won't be bored in Tucson.

TUCSON
SUMMIT OF THE SOUTH

- ⊕ *High mountain, Advanced, 0% unpaved*
- ⊕ *Map strava.com/routes/2902916771885892712*

- ⊕ *Test yourself mi 9 (km14) strava.com/segments/4737298*
- ⊕ *Test yourself mi 59 (km 95) strava.com/segments/8514838*

◉ GREG'S EYE

Mount Lemmon, the southernmost 9,000-footer (2,745 m) in the country, is an Arizonan must. I discovered it at age twenty thanks to a Tucson friend, Brian Smith. Coming to train here in late winter, before going back to Europe, was clearly a factor in my future successes.

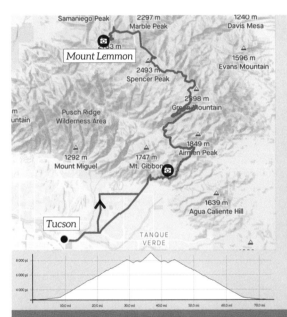

Riding the 21 mi (34 km) of Mount Lemmon Highway, northeast of Tucson, above the cacti and mesquite trees of the Sonoran Desert, is a rare experience. It combines physical exertion with visual delight; the panoramas on this perfectly asphalted road with wide shoulders are out of this world. The long effort (2h to 3h) requires peak fitness and preplanned provisions, even though the slope never exceeds 5% as it climbs between pale rocks and occasional firs. At the apex, just below Spencer Peak (mi 29/km 47), you can turn around or continue via Summerhaven and East Ski Run Road to the other side of Mount Lemmon Ski Valley and up to the summit of Mount Lemmon itself—the top of the Santa Catalina Mountains—with even more amazing views (additional 4.4 mi/7 km ascent and 1,400 ft/425 m of elevation gain). Debrief on the terrace of Viv's Cafe, mi 69 (km 111).

Distance	E+	Difficulty	Appeal
72 mi (116 km)	**8,100 ft** (2,482 m)	**4/5**	**5/5**

Air: Tucson International Airport (30 min by car). Car: 2h from Phoenix, 4h30 from El Paso, 6h from San Diego, 6h30 from Albuquerque.

Sabino Cycles, east of Tucson, has been operating for over a quarter of a century. Super atmosphere. Strava Club. Retailer of Specialized and Marin.

7045 E. Tanque Verde Road Tucson, AZ 85715 sabinocycles.com

Babad Do'ag Overlook (mi 11/km 18). Molino Canyon Vista (mi 13/km 21). Molino Basin (mi 14/km 23). Bug Spring Trailhead (mi 16/km 26). Thimble Peak (mi 17/km 27). Seven Cataracts (mi 18/km 29). Windy Point (mi 22/km 35).

PATAGONIA
WELCOME TO AZT

DIRT & GRAVEL

- ⊕ High mountain, Expert, 85% unpaved
- ⊕ Map strava.com/routes/2904432307430078564
- ⊕ Test yourself mi 10 (km 16) strava.com/segments/3643332
- ⊕ Test yourself mi 55 (km 89) strava.com/segments/3788119

👁 GREG'S EYE

Are you familiar with the Arizona Trail, or AZT, a legendary route that crosses the state from the Utah border in the north to the Mexican border south of Tucson? We discover it here on an amazing gravel day out through the wild landscape of Coronado National Forest.

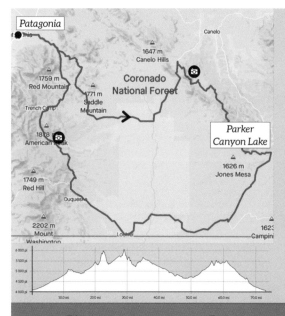

For 14 mi (23 km), from the east slope of Canelo Pass (mi 21/km 34) to the oasis of Parker Canyon Lake (mi 35/km 56), we pedal a legend of the West: the Arizona Trail—AZT for those in the know—the southern end of which is close to the Mexican border (which we brush at Lochiel, mi 50/km 80). The AZT—comprising 739 mi (1,190 km) of trails and single tracks from one end of the state to the other, by way of the Grand Canyon—accounts for only 20 percent of this route through Coronado National Forest, but it's simply thrilling. The Coronado Forest trails, which wind their way past mining ghost towns, can all be ridden on a gravel bike. Signs announce the presence of Gila monsters and mountain lions—both protected species. Start in the village of Patagonia, where you can refuel at the Wagon Wheel Saloon upon your return. Note that there are very few water points en route.

	Distance		E+		Difficulty		Appeal
⊢–⊣	**73 mi** (118 km)	⬆	**6,200 ft** (1,901 m)	📊	**4/5**	⭐	**4/5**

Air: Tucson International Airport (1h by car).
Car: 40 min from Nogales, Mexico, 3h from Phoenix, 5h from Las Cruces.

Peter, the founder of Shade Tree Cycling, adores bikes stuffed with electronics just as much as vintage models. His shop is situated 30 mi (48 km) west of Patagonia.

**2041 I-19 Frontage Road
Tumacacori-Carmen, AZ 85640
shadetreecycling.com**

San Rafael Valley (mi 12/km 19). Canelo Pass (mi 20/km 32). Lookout Knoll (mi 23/km 37). Collins Canyon (mi 29/km 47). Parker Canyon Lake (mi 35/km 56). Fray Marcos de Niza Historical Landmark (mi 51/km 82). American Peak (mi 61/km 98).

The rolling terrain of Skyline Drive in the heart of Shenandoah National Park, Virginia.

TAOS
THE ENCHANTED CIRCLE

- ⊕ High mountain, Advanced, 0% unpaved
- ⊕ Map strava.com/routes/2897809290020144328
- ⊕ Test yourself mi 37 (km 60) strava.com/segments/5419466
- ⊕ Test yourself mi 63 (km 101) strava.com/segments/4194634

👁 GREG'S EYE

New Mexico is called the "Land of Enchantment" because it contains some unexpected scenery, away from the desert and rock. The Enchanted Circle Scenic Byway, which starts and ends in Taos, is the finest example. And it has two little cols of more than 9,000 ft (2,750 m).

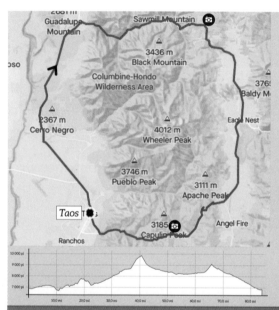

Taos (pop. 5,000), north of Santa Fe, owes its reputation to more than the memory of Kit Carson and its status as an artistic hub. The beautiful landscape around the Sangre de Cristo Mountains inspired the Enchanted Circle Scenic Byway, an 84-mi (135-km) loop to the northeast that is an absolute must-ride, as long as you feel up to the distance. The route explores Spanish colonial and mining history and a heritage of arts and crafts, as well as providing a breathtaking view of Wheeler Peak, the highest point in New Mexico (13,161 ft/4,010 m). There are two sublime "little" cols: Bobcat Pass (mi 40/km 64)—4 mi (6.5 km) at 5.5% after a long approach from Questa—and Palo Flechado Pass (mi 64/km 103)—2 mi (3.25 km) in ten switchbacks at an average gradient of 4.5%. The 15-mi (24-km) descent to Taos via the Rio Fernando de Taos canyon is sublime.

	Distance		E+		Difficulty		Appeal
	84 mi (135 km)		**6,000 ft** (1,834 m)		**4/5**		**5/5**

Air: Santa Fe Regional Airport (1h30 by car), Albuquerque International Sunport (2h15 by car).
Car: 3h from Pueblo, 4h30 from Denver, 8h30 from Oklahoma City.

Mellow Velo, close to the historic district, is a popular rendezvous for local cyclists. Gravel expertise. Excellent café. Retailer of BMC and Orbea.

132 E Marcy Street
Santa Fe, NM 87501
mellowvelo.com

Rio Grande Gorge Bridge (6 mi/10 km from mi 4/km 6.5). Houses of Red River (mi 36/km 58). Bobcat Pass (mi 40/km 64). Eagle Nest Lake (mi 56/km 90). La Jara Canyon (mi 67/km 108). Mascarenas Canyon (mi 72/km 116). Kit Carson Home (mi 84/km 135).

The sublime setting of the
Enchanted Circle, near Taos,
New Mexico.

SHIPROCK
THE NAVAJO TRAIL

⊕ *Very hilly, Intermediate, 60% unpaved*   ⊕ *Map strava.com/routes/2897759461665049800*

	Distance **61 mi** (99 km)		E+ **3,400 ft** (1,037 m)		Difficulty **3/5**		Appeal **4/5**

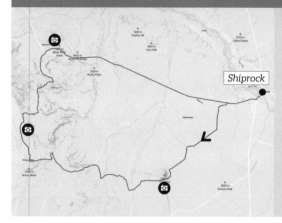

The trails of the Navajo Nation Reservation, in the Four Corners region of New Mexico, are inviting indeed. It's an amazing feeling to ride through the desert at altitudes of 5,000 to 6,000 ft (1,525 to 1,830 m), with nothing on the horizon but the geological curiosities of the Navajo Volcanic Field. Heading out from Shiprock (we start at Nizhóní Park), 200 mi (320 km) northwest of Santa Fe and Albuquerque, the striking Tse' Bit' A'i ("rock with wings" in the Navajo language) thrusting 1,800 ft (550 m) above the Colorado Plateau, is an iconic reference point. Don't worry about getting up there: climbing this Navajo religious site is forbidden.

ALAMOGORDO
EAST FROM GROUND ZERO

⊕ *High mountain, Advanced, 30% unpaved*   ⊕ *Map strava.com/routes/2896878537050575946*

	Distance **59 mi** (95 km)		E+ **6,800 ft** (2,088 m)		Difficulty **4/5**		Appeal **4/5**

Alamogordo, closer to El Paso (90 mi/145 km south) than Albuquerque (to the north), is famous as the base camp for the first nuclear test in history, which took place in the desert of White Sands, west of the town, in 1945. Heading in the opposite direction, we enter the less hostile but equally remote Lincoln National Forest and the superb Capitan Mountains. The irregular climb to Cloudcroft (17 mi/27 km at 4% via La Luz Canyon Road before US-82) is a New Mexico must. Our route (starting from Outdoor Adventures) then winds its way along wooded ridges up to 9,500 ft (2,895 m) on Cathey Peak, before taking a perfect gravel trail home.

ALBUQUERQUE
BREAKING GOOD

- ⊕ *High mountain, Expert, 12% unpaved*
- ⊕ *Map strava.com/routes/2896424250630250658*
- ⊙ *Test yourself mi 15 (km 24) strava.com/segments/21930359*
- ⊙ *Test yourself mi 51 (km 82) strava.com/segments/15713596*

◎ GREG'S EYE

I'm a diehard fan of the TV series *Breaking Bad*, set in Albuquerque, but "ABQ" deserves to be known equally well as a cyclist's town, not only because it's very spread out, but also because it has some amazing spots nearby, notably the Sandia Mountains.

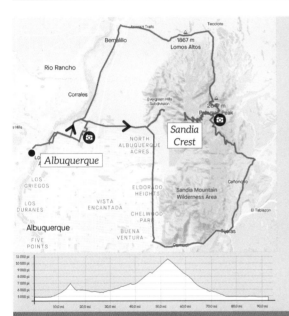

Sandia Crest

Albuquerque

There are many shorter routes to be ridden in and around Albuquerque (pop. 900,000 across its urban area), but this near century demonstrates how expansive "ABQ" is and shows off the beautiful Sandia Mountains. An aerial tramway (mi 17/km 27) goes up there; it takes longer on the popular paved bike lane of Tramway Boulevard, preceded by a vigorous warm-up on La Luz (mi 12/km 19): 2.5 mi (4 km) at 8%. At San Antonio (mi 39/km 63), we commence the ascent of Sandia Peak Ski Area: 5.7 mi (9.25 km) at 5.5% amid spruce, oak, white pine, and juniper, with an optional further 6.3 mi (10.25 km) at 6.2% up to Sandia Crest. It's a long sequence at an altitude of between 7,000 and 10,000 ft (2,135 and 3,050 m). The surface of the northern descent is quality gravel. For iconic shooting locations of *Breaking Bad,* head downtown, 10 mi (16 km) south of High Desert Bicycles.

Distance	E+	Difficulty	Appeal
93 mi (149 km)	**8,100 ft** (2,467 m)	**4/5**	**4/5**

Air: Albuquerque International Sunport (30 min by car). Car: 1h from Santa Fe, 4h from El Paso, 6h30 from Phoenix, 7h from Denver.

High Desert Bicycles is a quality establishment situated on the west bank of the Rio Grande Twenty years of experience and top-notch service. Retailer of Specialized, Salsa, and All-City.

6624 Caminito Coors NW Albuquerque, NM 87120 highdesertbicycles.com

Albuquerque from La Luz Summit (mi 14/km 23). Aerial Tramway (mi 17/km 27). Madera Canyon Overlook (mi 47/km 76). Sandia Crest (mi 53/km 85). Nine Mile Picnic Area (mi 57/km 92). Balloon Fiesta Park (mi 86/km 138).

SANTA FE
SANGRE DE CRISTO ASCENT

🌐 *High mountain, Advanced, 1% unpaved*   🌐 *Map strava.com/routes/2896682800505544804*

	Distance		E+		Difficulty		Appeal
⊢-⊣	**64 mi** (103 km)	⬆	**6,500 ft** (1,988 m)	📊	**4/5**	⭐	**4/5**

Perhaps surprisingly, skiers are a common sight in winter in Santa Fe (pop. 85,000), the city with the cleanest air in the United States. The ski runs of Ski Santa Fe start at close to 12,000 ft (3,660 m), below Tesuque Peak—the colossus of the Sangre de Cristo Mountains. In summer, cyclists climb the winding asphalt ribbon of Hyde Park Road (6.4 mi/10.3 km at 6.2%, then 1.2 mi/1.9 km at 4%), enjoying stunning views. Before that, having started from Bike N Sport, we make two 26-mi loops through this superb city of art and history, built in the adobe style, and home to the Santa Fe Margarita Trail—to be undertaken on foot, obviously!

JEMEZ SPRINGS
DOME IN SIGHT

DIRT & GRAVEL

🌐 *High mountain, Intermediate, 65% unpaved*   🌐 *Map strava.com/routes/2896679577263340644*

	Distance		E+		Difficulty		Appeal
⊢-⊣	**64 mi** (103 km)	⬆	**5,300 ft** (1,612 m)	📊	**3/5**	⭐	**5/5**

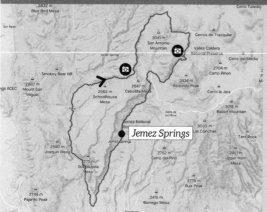

Leave behind the thermal waters and the ruins of religious retreats at Jemez Springs, 70 mi (113 km) west of Santa Fe, and explore the surrounding area—equipped with a gravel bike—on trails through the Jemez Mountains in the heart of the luxuriant Valles Caldera National Preserve. There are barely 20 mi (32 km) of paved road on this route (starting from Jemez Historic Site) that describes a loop northeast past Schoolhouse Mesa and Cebollita Mesa, before skirting San Antonio Mountain, then climbing on forest roads up to nearly 9,500 ft (2,895 m) below Redondo Peak, whose imposing volcanic dome is visible from Albuquerque, 50 mi (80 km) to the south.

MEXICO & CARIBBEAN

NUEVO LEÓN

TAMAULIPAS

QUERÉTARO

SAN LUIS POTOSÍ

VERACRUZ / OAXACA

YUCATÁN / QUINTANA ROO

CHIAPAS / BAJA CALIFORNIA SUR

JALISCO

MORELOS

PUEBLA

MEXICO CITY / GUANAJUATO

STATE OF MEXICO

AGUASCALIENTES

NAYARIT

SINAOLA / CHIHUAHUA

BAJA CALIFORNIA

BAHAMAS / VIRGIN ISLANDS

PUERTO RICO

MONTERREY
MONTERREY OVERLOOK

⊕ *Low mountain, Advanced, 4% unpaved*
⊕ *Map strava.com/routes/2870349997244130520*

⊕ *Test yourself mi 42 (km 67) strava.com/segments/13741303*
⊕ *Test yourself mi 48 (km 77) strava.com/segments/1446208*

◎ GREG'S EYE

Monterrey is the hometown of my friend Raúl Alcalá, "La Leyenda" ("the Legend") of Mexican cycling. Let me take you to los picos where he trained for the Tour de France. Raúl was a hell of an adversary! Tough the route may be, but the views over Monterrey are stunning.

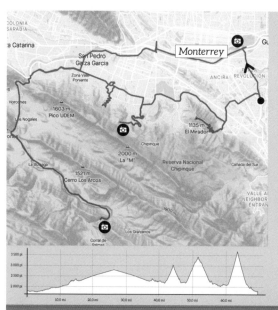

With gridlocked streets and tall buildings, bustling Monterrey, capital of Nuevo León State, might discourage would-be cyclists. Yet champion Raúl Alcalá grew up here, and the local cycling community attracts aficionados. The emblematic Cerro de la Silla looms over the city, but since there are no roads up it, budding climbers head to the foothills of Cumbres National Park, above the swanky San Pedro neighborhood. We follow the course of the Santa Catarina River through the city and beyond, to the Rompepicos dam (mi 26/km 42), before tackling three brutal ascents: Pedregal (mi 42/km 67)—2 mi (3.25 km) at 8%; Olinalá (mi 48/km 77)—3 mi (4.75 km) at 7%; and El Mirador, if you have the legs to handle thirteen switchbacks and 3 mi (4.75 km) at 10%— the last 2 mi (3.25 km) are on a dirt trail. From the top there is an extraordinary view of Monterrey.

	Distance		E+		Difficulty		Appeal
	70 mi (113 km)		**6,200 ft** (1,890 m)		**4/5**		**4/5**

Air: General Mariano Escobedo International Airport, Monterrey (40 min by car). Car: 5h from San Antonio, Texas, 6h from San Luis Potosí and 9h from Mexico City.

Ride My Bike has outlets in three Monterrey neighborhoods: Del Carmen, Cumbres, and Contry, where our ride starts. Retailer of Specialized.

**Avenida Revolución 3804
64850 Monterrey, Nuevo León
ridemybike.com.mx**

Macroplaza and its museums (mi 3/km 4.75). La Huasteca Bridge (mi 16/km 26). Pedregal (mi 42 / km 67). Olinala (mi 48/km 77). El Mirador (mi 63/km 101)

CIUDAD VICTORIA
BALCONIES OF THE EAST

⊕ *Low mountain, Advanced, 5% unpaved*   ⊕ *Map strava.com/routes/2916304068983698328*

	Distance		E+		Difficulty		Appeal
⊢⊣	**65 mi** (105 km)	⬆	**6,300 ft** (1,923 m)	📊	**4/5**	⭐	**4/5**

Ciudad Victoria (pop. 370,000), capital of the state of Tamaulipas, lies 180 mi (285 km) from Monterrey and 400 mi (645 km) from Mexico City. It's a gateway to the splendors of the Sierra Madre Oriental, which these two panoramic roads explore. Be prepared for two long ramps. The 126 has an 11.5-mi (18.5-km) climb at an average gradient of 3.5%, but it's irregular, with sections in the double digits. The 101 is gentler: 10 mi (16 km) at 5.3%. Pause for a selfie at Balcón del Chihue (mi 43/km 69) and Mirador Altas Cumbres (mi 49/km 79). Don't miss the Torre Bicentenario (mi 6/km 10) in Ciudad Victoria (where we start from MR Bike).

JALPAN DE SERRA
STUNNING SIERRA

⊕ *Low mountain, Expert, 80% unpaved*   ⊕ *Map strava.com/routes/2916320115090067980*

	Distance		E+		Difficulty		Appeal
⊢⊣	**49 mi** (79 km)	⬆	**7,300 ft** (2,240 m)	📊	**4/5**	⭐	**4/5**

The dirt and gravel trails of the Sierra Gorda, a stunning biosphere in the state of Querétaro, 135 mi (220 km) north of Mexico City, are deceptively tough. Our route, starting from the Franciscan mission church in charming Jalpan de Serra (pop. 26,000), climbs no higher than 6,200 ft (1,890 m). But it's a long climb: 1 mi (1.5 km) at 10% to start, then 10 mi (16 km) at 5.2%, and lastly 3.6 mi (5.75 km) at 7% after San Pedro Escanela and its El Salto del Agua waterfall. The final section along the glittering reservoir formed by the Jalpan dam is a delight. Stop at mi 11 (km 18) to admire the remarkable Tancama archaeological site.

AHUALULCO
THE ALTIPLANO POTOSINO

⊕ *Low mountain, Advanced, 78% unpaved*   ⊕ *Map strava.com/routes/2872953083529199798*

	Distance		E+		Difficulty		Appeal
	123 mi (198 km)	⬆	**3,700 ft** (1,140 m)		**4/5**		**5/5**

DIRT & GRAVEL

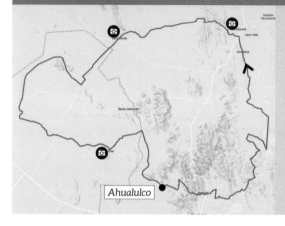

Ahualulco

San Luis Potosí (pop. 700,000) lies 5h north of Mexico City by car and is one of the country's most dynamic cities. So it's not surprising that gravel riding caught on very fast here. Northwest of San Luis, fast off-road trails stretch away across the high plain to the horizon. The relief is barely perceptible, and the vegetation is kept low by the strong winds. The Gravel México Altiplano Potosino (which inspired our route) was born here against a backdrop of remote villages and former haciendas. As scary as the distance might appear (a third of it runs through the neighboring state of Zacatecas), it nevertheless embodies gravel perfection.

BERNAL
WELCOME TO HELL!

⊕ *High mountain, Expert, 0% unpaved*   ⊕ *Map strava.com/routes/2872790034298084528*

	Distance		E+		Difficulty		Appeal
	132 mi (213 km)	⬆	**16,100 ft** (4,908 m)		**5/5**		**5/5**

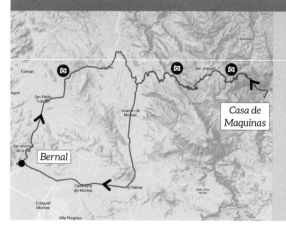

Casa de Maquinas

Bernal

This insane challenge in the Sierra Gorda, 140 mi (225 km) north of Mexico City, should never be attempted solo, and a support vehicle is recommended. At altitudes of 3,000 to 8,000 ft (915 to 2,440 m), this route has more than 16,000 ft (4,880 m) of elevation. It's a loop on the Fed 120 from the foot of Peña de Bernal—highest monolith (1,100 ft/335 m) on the continent—to Casa de Maquinas tunnel (mi 67/km 108). Your thighs will be burning even before you plunge to the tunnel, then begin a 5,000-ft (1,525-m) climb for nearly 10 mi (16 km)—average gradient 10% with sections at 12% to 15%! Escalera al Infierno (Stairway to Hell), as Mexican cyclists call it.

ORIZABA
MONSTER VILLAS PICO

⊕ *High mountain, Expert, 2% unpaved*
⊕ *Map strava.com/routes/2838585023153598344*

◎ *Test yourself mi 7 (km 11) strava.com/segments/26218385*
◎ *Test yourself mi 15 (km 24) strava.com/segments/25390538*

<◎ GREG'S EYE>

Villas Pico is one of the hardest climbs in the world: 18 mi (29 km) long, with more than 7,000 ft (2,135 m) of climbing up to 11,000 ft (3,355 m), with a fantastic view of Pico de Orizaba. Another challenge to bear in mind if you're passing through Mexico City.

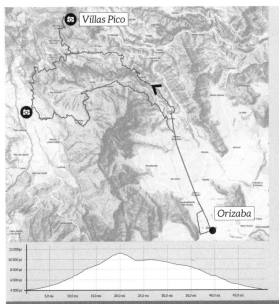
Villas Pico

Orizaba

Stunning Pico de Orizaba is the highest mountain in Mexico (18,491 ft/5,636 m) and the highest volcano in North America. The road up to Villas (11,000 ft/3,355 m)—a base for expeditions to the crater—is infamous as one of the hardest cycling ascents in the world. As you pedal out of Orizaba (pop. 120,000), you're already gently climbing, but it starts to kick up at La Perla (mi 7/km 11). The total ascent is 18 mi (29 km) at an average gradient of 7.6%, with a total of 5 mi (8 km) at 10% to 20%. Only a truly expert cyclist can hope to climb the Pico without stopping, particularly since you're already above 6,000 ft (1,830 m) by mi 9 (km 14). The final mile before Villas is unsurfaced, with a gradient of 7%. Villas Pico is a monster, yet the open road that approaches the volcano is enchanting. A rare entry on any cyclist's résumé.

	Distance		E+		Difficulty		Appeal
	50 mi (80 km)		**7,700 ft** (2,350 m)		**5/5**		**5/5**

Air: Puebla International Airport (2h10 by car), Tehuacán National Airport (1h30 by car). Car: 3h30 from Mexico City, 1h45 from Veracruz.

Transvision Bike, located close to the cable car, is forty years old. Retailer of Cannondale, Giant, and Liv.

**Avenida Oriente 2
94300 Orizaba, Veracruz
transvisionbike.com**

Xometla church (mi 14/km 22). Villas Pico (mi 20/km 32) is the closest you'll get to the volcano by bike. Texmola church (mi 30/km 48), with the volcano behind it. Back in Orizaba, take the cable car up to the viewpoint on Cerro del Borrego.

XALAPA
WINDING UP EL COFRE

⊕ *High mountain, Expert, 20% unpaved*   ⊕ *Map strava.com/routes/2870703334877266524*

	Distance		E+		Difficulty		Appeal
├─┤	**90 mi** (145 km)	⬆	**11,500 ft** (3,492 m)	▥	**5/5**	★	**5/5**

The smog over Xalapa (pop. 415,000) can be so thick that it obscures the primary landmark, Cofre de Perote—the country's eighth-highest peak. This mountain has a curious summit shaped like a cruise ship funnel. The road up to the TV Azteca transmission tower is extreme: more than 10,000 ft (3,050 m) of climbing in two stages totaling 40 mi (64 km). The first 15 mi (24 km) to Las Vigas de Ramírez are at 4% average gradient, and the 13 mi (21 km) from Perote are at 8%, with the last 6 mi (9.75 km) after El Conejo comprising a series of twenty-five switchbacks. You'll burst with pride as you look down at your route from 13,500 ft (4,115 m).

OAXACA DE JUÁREZ
CACTUS AND HOT CHOCOLATE

⊕ *Low mountain, Advanced, 75% unpaved*   ⊕ *Map strava.com/routes/2872507286338077872*

	Distance		E+		Difficulty		Appeal
├─┤	**57 mi** (92 km)	⬆	**4,700 ft** (1,435 m)	▥	**3/5**	★	**4/5**

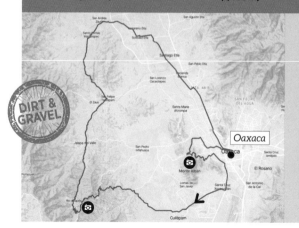

DIRT & GRAVEL

Oaxaca de Juárez is worth the 6h drive from Mexico City. Its colorful houses and cobbled streets make it an attractive destination. You can reach the foothills of the Sierra Madre del Sur by bike on quiet roads. Starting from Zona Bici Armenta, the gravel begins on the Monte Albán climb (2 mi/3.25 km at 7%) up to the Zapotec archaeological treasures. Further on, you'll be tested by beautiful dirt trails: 4.5 mi (7.25 km) at an irregular 7% average gradient toward Ranchería San Cristóbal, then a 1.1-mi (1.75-km) stretch at 10% on Cerro Mazaltepec, between cactus and agave. Enjoy a post-ride hot chocolate, reputedly to be the best in the world.

RÍO LAGARTOS
IN THE PINK

🌐 *Flat, Intermediate, 20% unpaved*　　　🌐 *Map strava.com/routes/2870767486255355484*

	Distance		E+		Difficulty		Appeal
⊢–⊣	**93 mi** (150 km)	⬆	**700 ft** (213 m)	📊	**2/5**	⭐	**4/5**

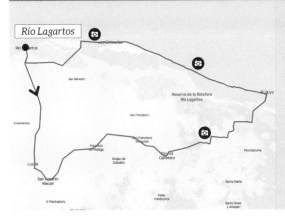

Río Lagartos

On the Yucatán Peninsula, turn your back to the beaches of the Riviera Maya and the ancient sites of Chichén Itzá and Uxmal and explore a unique natural world. From Río Lagartos, a little port that sits on a lagoon, our route sets off down a flat road into the protected biosphere of Ría Lagartos, passing wetlands and cenotes (natural pools). At El Cuyo, turn onto the dune belt separating the lagoon from the Gulf of Mexico for 25 mi (40 km), before hitting a dirt trail at Las Coloradas that runs alongside a natural reserve of pink flamingos with water tinted pink, too, by the vagaries of geological and chemical composition. Quite spectacular.

PLAYA DEL CARMEN
FOREST AND RIVIERA

DIRT & GRAVEL

🌐 *Flat, Intermediate, 40% unpaved*　　　🌐 *Map strava.com/routes/2870240454825695840*

	Distance		E+		Difficulty		Appeal
⊢–⊣	**76 mi** (122 km)	⬆	**400 ft** (115 m)	📊	**2/5**	⭐	**3/5**

Puerto Morelos

Playa del Carmen

Hotspot Playa del Carmen, on the east coast of the Yucatán Peninsula, is known more for its turquoise waters and white sand than for cycling. But you can enjoy some excellent moments in the saddle if you head inland from Wally B Bike Shop, leaving behind the tourist apartments to pedal through subtropical forest (suitable tires required) past natural pools, before a 20-mi (32-km) ride down the coast, between golf resorts and private beaches. The authentic fishing village of Puerto Morelos (mi 42/km 67) has a very different feel from Playa del Carmen—with its overrated Playacar district, sparse Mayan ruins, and ferry to the diving paradise of Cozumel.

Green water of the Gulf
of Mexico on one side, pink of
the lagoon on the other, with the
incredible Las Coloradas trail in
the middle, near Río Lagartos,
Yucatán.

TUXTLA GUTIÉRREZ
BREATHTAKING CANYON

Low mountain, Advanced, 92% unpaved   *Map strava.com/routes/2872538110713441456*

	Distance		E+		Difficulty		Appeal
	74 mi (119 km)	⬆	**7,000 ft** (2,125 m)		**4/5**	⭐	**5/5**

Sumidero Canyon

Tuxtla Gutiérrez

The Grijalva River rises from the Chiapas mountains, near the Guatemalan border, and empties into the Gulf of Mexico 300 mi (485 km) later. Near Tuxtla Gutiérrez (pop. 550,000), it passes through Sumidero Canyon, which was carved out of the mountain that looms above the river 35 million years ago. From Tuxtla, this exceptional promontory is reached by an 11-mi (18-km) trail at 5% average gradient. The views will take your breath away more than the preceding slopes. Our ride begins from F5 Store bike café and explores Berriozábal and the Ecoturistico Tzimbac park on an exclusively gravel route.

CABO SAN LUCAS
SIERRA AND CABOS

Low mountain, Advanced, 37% unpaved   *Map strava.com/routes/2870327165474015448*

	Distance		E+		Difficulty		Appeal
	59 mi (95 km)	⬆	**5,000 ft** (1,509 m)		**4/5**	⭐	**4/5**

San José del Cabo

Cabo San Lucas

Cabo San Lucas, the southernmost point in Baja California Sur, is a popular destination. San José del Cabo, 20 mi (32 km) northeast, is less well known. Los Cabos are linked by the final third of our route, heading straight into the sunset. It's nothing like the first two-thirds of the ride (starting from Thunder's Bikes Cabo) exploring the foothills of arid Sierra de la Laguna on dirt trails. This route threads through the little canyons of Río El Salto, between black oaks and strawberry trees, in an area so remote you can see coyotes and pumas. Do factor in the heat—a dip by the El Arco rock formation will be welcome at day's end.

GUADALAJARA
TEQUILA GRAVEL!

- ⊕ Low mountain, Advanced, 50% unpaved
- ⊕ Map strava.com/routes/2872457486057396406
- ⊙ Test yourself mi 50 (km 80) strava.com/segments/13800798
- ⊙ Test yourself mi 62 (km 100) strava.com/segments/3969301

👁 GREG'S EYE

Guadalajara may make you think of tequila and mariachis. But there is plenty of good cycling, too, and a gravel ride is a stunning way to leave Mexico's second metropolis behind, heading west into the little piece of heaven that's the Bosque de la Primavera.

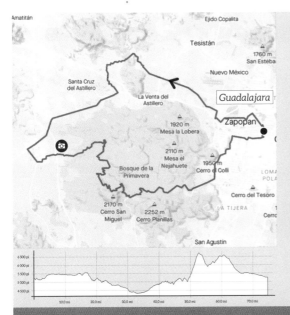

We'll visit Plaza de los Mariachis and Hospicio Cabañas—jewels of the capital of Jalisco State—later, and perhaps even make a pilgrimage to Tequila, an hour northwest. Guadalajara by bike awaits. In the absence of imposing mountains to explore, we break the monotony of the Atemajac Valley on trails less traveled. Gravel is queen: north of La Venta del Astillero, followed by nearly 30 mi (48 km) of dirt tracks through the hills of the Bosque de la Primavera. There are some tough ramps, such as the 2.5 mi (4 km) at more than 10% on the way up to Cerro San Miguel (mi 50/km 80). Although we never climb above 6,700 ft (2,045 m), the endless up and down results in a total elevation gain of nearly 6,000 ft (1,830 m) by the end of these 75 mi (120 km). Make sure you take full advantage of the many waterfalls and natural pools along the way.

	Distance		E+		Difficulty		Appeal
⊢–⊣	**75 mi** (120 km)	⬆	**5,900 ft** (1,812 m)	📊	**3/5**	⭐	**4/5**

Air: Miguel Hidalgo y Costilla International Airport, Guadalajara (30 min by car). Car: 2h30 from León, 5h from Puerto Vallarta, 6h from Mexico City.

Bike City has four outlets in Guadalajara, and an active community that holds weekly rides.

Eulogio Parra 3042 44670 Guadalajara, Jalisco bikecity.com.mx

Rancho El Roble (mi 19/ km 36). Mirador de Vias Verdes (mi 30/km 48). Cerro San Miguel (mi 52/km 84). Cerro Planillas (mi 60/km 97). On the way back, do make a 2-mile (3.25-km) detour to Guadalajara Cathedral (mi 75/km 120)

CUERNAVACA
EUROPEAN-STYLE

- ⊕ High mountain, Advanced, 18% unpaved
- ⊕ Map strava.com/routes/2871794309706997390
- ⊕ Test yourself mi 32 (km 51) strava.com/segments/8700960
- ⊕ Test yourself mi 40 (km 64) strava.com/segments/19064788

◉ GREG'S EYE

Hauling yourself up to San Juan Tlacotenco, at an altitude comparable to those of the great Alpine passes in Europe, might seem like an easy ride here in Mexico. Quite the contrary. This is a sublime challenge that's highly prized by the cycling community in Mexico City!

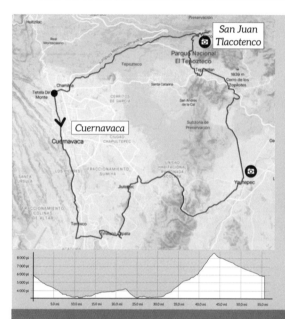

San Juan Tlacotenco

Cuernavaca

Dubbed "City of Eternal Spring," Cuernavaca (pop. 365,000) boasts preserved colonial architecture and is a popular weekend getaway for residents of Mexico City. The reason is simple: the capital of Morelos State lies at 5,800 ft (1,770 m)—lower than the nearest towns to Mexico City, Puebla and Toluca. Farther south, in the Apatlaco Valley, it gets as low as 4,000 ft (1,220 m). The nearly 12-mi (19.25-km) climb to the village of San Juan Tlacotenco (7,700 ft/ 2,350 m), above Tepoztlán and the El Tepozteco archaeological park, is a Mexican classic and a real challenge. If the 6 mi (9.75 km), average gradient of 4%, up to Tepoztlán don't entirely wear you out, the following 5 mi (8 km) to San Juan will: 8% average gradient, with sections as steep as 23%! You'll appreciate the pleasant pedal back down toward Cuernavaca on a 10-mi (16-km) dirt trail.

Distance **56 mi** (90 km)	E+ **5,300 ft** (1,608 m)
Difficulty **5/5**	Appeal **5/5**

Air: Benito Juárez International Airport, Mexico City (1h30 by car). Puebla International Airport (2h30 by car). Car: 1h30 from Taxco, 2h from Toluca.

Bike Track will celebrate its thirtieth birthday in 2023. It's quite MTB oriented, but stocks everything you need for road cycling. Retailer of Specialized and Scott, among others.

Francisco Villa, Buena Vista 62130 Cuernavaca, Morelos biketrack.mx

In front of the symbol of Cuernavaca, the former Cortés palace, now the Cuauhnahuac Museum (nr. mi 3/km 4.75). The former Apanquetzalco hacienda (nr. mi 29/km 47). San Juan Tlacotenco (mi 43/ km 69), in front of the Church of San Juan Bautista.

ATLIXCO
EL POPO XXL

- ⊕ High mountain, Expert, 10% unpaved
- ⊕ Map strava.com/routes/2838577676361547462

- ⊕ Test yourself mi 36 (km 58) strava.com/segments/9343146
- ⊕ Test yourself mi 60 (km 96) strava.com/segments/10728411

👁 GREG'S EYE

Climbing the Paso de Cortés, while continuously looking for the smoke from the crater of Popocatépetl to the right, is a challenging cycling experience that's one of the most exciting in the world! A must-ride, not too far from Mexico City.

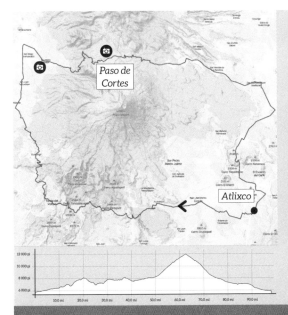

Paso de Cortes

Atlixco

Warning: very high altitude! Our route takes us up to 11,200 ft (3,415 m) on the Paso de Cortés—the highest surfaced pass in Mexico. Climbing from the west via Amecameca de Juárez (12 mi/19 km at an average gradient of 5.3%, with sections as steep as 9%) is tough from the first switchbacks due to lack of oxygen. It's a unique experience, with the country's third- and second-highest volcanoes nearby: Iztaccíhuatl (The White Lady) at 17,160 ft (5,230 m) and Popocatépetl (Smoking Mountain) at 17,802 ft (5,425 m). There's no better way to admire "El Popo" from every angle than this nearly 100-mi (160-km) circuit starting in Atlixco, southwest of Puebla. The climbing begins in the Atlixco valley, getting tougher as you pass Tochimilco and on to Ecatzingo de Hidalgo, before hitting the Paso. The 10-mi (16-km) descent, with grand views of El Popo, is spectacular.

	Distance		E+		Difficulty		Appeal
⊢–⊣	**98 mi** (158 km)	⬆	**11,017 ft** (3,358 m)	📊	**5/5**	⭐	**5/5**

Air: Benito Juárez International Airport, Mexico City (2h by car), Puebla International Airport, (1h by car). Car: 30 min from Puebla.

Planeta Ciclista on the Puebla-Matamoros road (190) is a popular rendezvous point. Retailer of Specialized, Orbea, and KHS.

Libramiento Puebla-Izúcar de Matamoros 3504 74290 Atlixco, Puebla Facebook @planetciclis

Cerro Xilotepelt (mi 18/km 29). From San Pedro Nexapa (mi 51/km 82) to Paso de Cortés (mi 62/km 100), on every bend you glimpse the smoke from El Popo. Santiago Xalitzintla (mi 73/km 117). Cerro de San Miguel (mi 94/km 151).

MEXICO CITY
"DESERT" ESCAPE

⊕ *High mountain, Advanced, 0% unpaved*
⊕ *Map strava.com/routes/2839153765939867308*

⊕ *Test yourself mi 11 (km 18) strava.com/segments/1011196*
⊕ *Test yourself mi 18 (km 29) strava.com/segments/763382*

👁 GREG'S EYE

Cycling has become very popular in Mexico City, a megalopolis that sprawls so much you'd think it impossible to pedal. Luckily, there are many bike lanes now, and luxuriant nature is never far away.

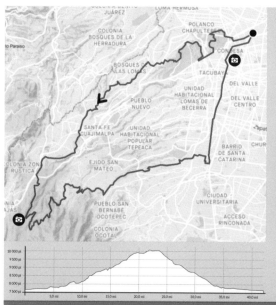

Vaster than New York City, and known for pollution and traffic, Mexico City (pop. 9.2 million/21 million for its metropolitan area) has become bike friendly. This popular route starts at the bike café Distrito Fijo and heads southwest. After a 7-mi (11.25-km) run through Chapultepec park, we pass the villas of Plan de Barrancas to reach the foot of the climb to the Desierto de los Leones National Park—Mexico's first national park, created a century ago and dubbed "desert" because of this mountain, covered in oyamel firs. Ahead lie 14 mi (22 km) of ascent with ramps as steep as 8%, and an average gradient of 4.5%, easing off by the abandoned monastery near the summit. Sitting above 10,000 ft (3,050 m), this has always been a place of contemplation for city residents. Return via Santa Rosa Xochiac, before Avenidas Revolución and Patriotismo.

Distance **42 mi** (68 km)	E+ **3,300 ft** (1,016 m)	Difficulty **4/5**	Appeal **5/5**

Air: Benito Juárez International Airport, Mexico City (to Distrito Fijo Club de Ciclismo, 1h by subway, 30-60 min by car).

Distrito Fijo Club de Ciclismo is one of the friendliest rallying points in Mexico City. Retailer of Bianchi, Masi, and Orbea.

**Calle Liverpool 61
06600 Ciudad de Mexico,
Federal District
dfcc.mx**

Estela de Luz tower and Chapultepec Castle (mi 1/km 1.5). Desierto de los Leones monastery (mi 20/km 32). Old streets of San Ángel (mi 35/km 56), around Plaza San Jacinto. Parque México (nr. mi 40/km 64).

MEXICO CITY
TO THE TOP OF THE CAPITAL

High mountain, Expert, 0% unpaved   Map strava.com/routes/2872580145473565872

Distance	E+	Difficulty	Appeal
82mi (132 km)	**5,500 ft** (1,664 m)	**5/5**	**5/5**

This long ride south from Galibier Cycling House gets 1,500 vertical feet (460 m) from the crater of Cerro Ajusco (12,894 ft/3930 m)—the highest point in Mexico City. The more than 20-mi (32-km) ascent in three segments starts with a pull toward the Oyameyo volcano, then around Xitle, before a loop through Cumbres del Ajusco National Park. The altitude requires acclimatizing, though these slopes are rarely steeper than 5%. In the city, we pass the 1968 Olympics stadium (mi 7/km 11), the Azteca stadium of the 1970 and 1986 World Cups (mi 11/km 18), and the velodrome where Eddy Merckx broke the hour record in 1972 (mi 75/km 120).

LEÓN
LANES AND TRAILS

DIRT & GRAVEL

High mountain, Intermediate, 64% unpaved   Map strava.com/routes/2872485050862230064

Distance	E+	Difficulty	Appeal
48 mi (77 km)	**4,900 ft** (1,502 m)	**3/5**	**4/5**

León (pop. 2 million), "La Perla del Bajío," right in the center of the country, is the most tranquil metropolis in Mexico, and cycling has something to do with it. León is one of the pioneering cities in Latin America in terms of cycling infrastructure. Setting out from Therapy Cycling Center, protected lanes take you swiftly and peacefully out of town to the dirt trails of the Sierra de Lobos—more than 20 mi (32 km) continuously off-road up to an altitude of 8,600 ft (2,625 m): so high that the scenery looks like desert. Ensure adequate hydration before Mirador del Gigante (2 mi/3.25 km at 9.5%) and then La Calera (1.5 mi/2.5 km at more than 10%).

TOLUCA
THE NEVADO TRAIL

DIRT & GRAVEL

- ⊕ *High mountain, Advanced, 60% unpaved*
- ⊕ *Map strava.com/routes/2870633182041784834*
- ⊙ *Test yourself mi 13 (km 21) strava.com/segments/5186045*
- ⊙ *Test yourself mi 24 (km 38) strava.com/segments/1308966*

👁 GREG'S EYE

All gravel lovers passing through Mexico City should bear in mind that less than an hour's drive west, there is one of the most fascinating experiences on the continent: the climb to Nevado de Toluca.

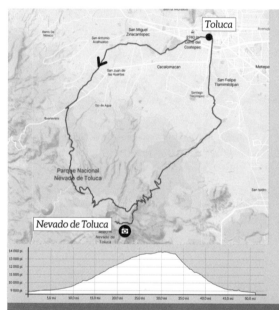

Gravel fans, here is one exceptional adventure! The permanently snowcapped peak of Nevado de Toluca (15,350 ft/4,680 m)—Mexico's fourth-highest summit—overlooks the town of the same name. Our route heads southwest from there to the climb. Toluca is an exhilarating conquest, but some care is required, since you're already at 8,750 ft (2,670 m) when you start the ascent. After an 18-mi (29-km) approach on asphalt as far as Parque de los Venados, at 12,000 ft (3,660 m), you hit a dirt trail that soon rises beyond all vegetation. Another 10 mi (16 km) at 4% average gradient takes you to a high-altitude paradise at the foot of the Nevado, between Lago de la Luna, Lago del Sol, and the crater of El Ombligo. Up there at 14,000 ft (4,270 m), it feels like you're on another planet. The descent is a pleasant 19 mi (30 km) of trail back to Toluca. Simply magical.

	Distance		E+		Difficulty		Appeal
	52 mi (83 km)		**5,600 ft** (1,714 m)		**4/5**		**5/5**

Air: Adolfo López Mateos International Airport, Toluca (30 min by car). Car: 1h from Mexico City, 1h15 from Valle de Bravo, 2h from Cuernavaca.

This route starts from *Friends México Performance* bike shop, close to Toluca's historic center. Retailer of Giant and Liv.

Venustiano Carranza, Ciprés 807 50120 Toluca, Mexico friendsmexico.com.mx

Puerta del Monte (mi 14/km 22). Between the two lakes ans beneath the summit of Nevado de Toluca (mi 30/km 48). Ejido Calimaya Park (mi 41/km 66). In Toluca, San Jose Cathedral and Lomas Altras (mi 52/km 83).

TLALNEPANTLA
THE "CERROS" OF GUADALUPE

⊕ *Low mountain, Advanced, 10% unpaved*
⊕ *Map strava.com/routes/2872388908417644726*

⊙ *Test yourself mi 12 (km 19) strava.com/segments/19217188*
⊙ *Test yourself mi 39 (km 63) strava.com/segments/16129691*

👁 GREG'S EYE

The Sierra de Guadalupe with its *cerros* (hills), regarded as relatively easy by local cyclists, has a number of intermediate challenges in its foothills, some slopes of which are fearsome indeed. An environment full of surprises to the north of Mexico City.

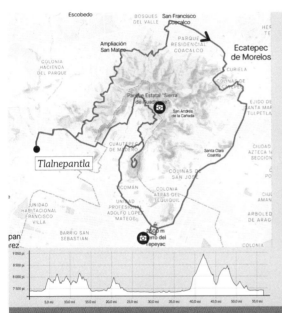

The rounded peaks of the Sierra de Guadalupe barely 1,500 ft (460 m) above the Valley of Mexico look so modest that they've been dubbed *cerros* (hills), despite topping out at close to 9,000 ft (2,745 m). Part of the Sierra Madre, the massif is compact, which makes for an unusual experience. This full circuit starting from industrialized Tlalnepantla takes you through eucalyptus forest above Buenavista, San Francisco Coacalco, and Ecatepec by way of five short but steep ramps (gradients in double digits) packed into barely 15 mi (24 km). Another 15-mi (24-km) stretch along the plain via Tepeyac (where the Virgin of Guadalupe supposedly appeared in the sixteenth century) leads to the Cerro del Chiquihuite: 3.2 mi (5.25 km) at a 9% average gradient. Amid wild landscape, picturesque neighborhoods, and cable bus lines, you don't notice the time pass.

	Distance		E+		Difficulty		Appeal
	57 mi (92 km)		**6,786 ft** (2,075 m)		**4/5**		**4/5**

Air: Benito Juárez International Airport, Mexico City (45 min by car).
Car: 30 min from Mexico City center, 1h from Toluca.

Transvision Bike close to Tlalnepantla station (west of the Sierra de Guadalupe). Retailer of Cannondale.

Avenida Gustavo Baz Prada 3315 54033 Tlalnepantla de Baz, Mexico transvisionbike.com

In front of Ehecatl (mi 20/ km 32). In front of Basilica de Guadalupe and the Monumento a los Indios Verdes (mi 33/km 53). At the top of Cerro del Chiquihuite (mi 42/ km 67). On the heights of Cuautepec (mi 47/km 75).

TEXCOCO DE MORA
TLALOC GRAN FONDO

⊕ *High mountain, Expert, 2% unpaved*   ⊕ *Map strava.com/routes/2870358087536835296*

Distance	E+	Difficulty	Appeal
⊢━┪ **91 mi** (146 km)	⬆ **7,700 ft** (2,340 m)	📊 **5/5**	★ **4/5**

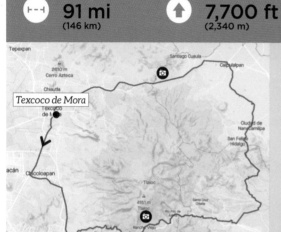

Iztaccíhuatl and El Popo are not the only iconic volcanoes close to Mexico City. To the north lies Mount Tlaloc (13,520 ft/4,120 m), named for the Aztec god of water. This full circuit of the peak by road—Gran Fondo style—starts from Sikkelhaus bike shop in Texcoco de Mora, ancient capital of the Acolhua. Don't be put off by the total E+: we never descend below 7,400 ft (2,255 m), with a maximum of 10,500 ft (3,200 m) at the summit of Llano Grande (mi 30/km 48)—a 13-mi (21-km) climb at an average gradient of 4.5%. The Sierra de Río Frío is verdant, with traces of multiple historical eras along the 91-mi (146-km) route. Plan for a full day out.

VALLE DE BRAVO
"TOUR DE FRANCE"

⊕ *High mountain, Advanced, 0% unpaved*   ⊕ *Map strava.com/routes/2839270560215675900*

Distance	E+	Difficulty	Appeal
⊢━┪ **76 mi** (122 km)	⬆ **8,000 ft** (2,422 m)	📊 **4/5**	★ **4/5**

Valle de Bravo (pop. 30,000), 100 mi (161 km) southwest of Mexico City, is known for its manmade lake, colonial architecture, and the Velo de Novia waterfall. Our ride is inspired by one of the Haute Route cycling events. The surrounding terrain is bumpy, ranging from 5,000 ft (1,525 m) to nearly 8,000 ft (2,440 m) at the top of the climb to Donato Guerra (6.5 mi/10.5 km at 5.3%, with two 2-mi/3.25-km sections at 8%).
It comes after the ascent of La Candelaria (superb hacienda Santa María Pipioltepec, mi 7/km 11) and precedes an exhilarating 15 mi (24 km) of winding road after Ixtapan del Oro. The locals have dubbed it "Tour de France."

AGUASCALIENTES
HOURS OF PLEASURE

- 🌐 Very hilly, Advanced, 45% unpaved
- 🌐 Map strava.com/routes/2870000212378911196
- ⊕ Test yourself mi 20 (km 32) strava.com/segments/8360551
- ⊕ Test yourself mi 40 (km 64) strava.com/segments/7498987

👁 GREG'S EYE

I stopped in Aguascalientes during the Vuelta a México back in 1988, but the town became a true cycling destination after Victor Campenaerts set the hour record here in 2019. The nearby Sierra Madre Occidental entices you out of town in search of adventure.

On April 16, 2019, Aguascalientes (300 miles/ 483 km northwest of Mexico City) made headlines when Belgian cyclist Victor Campenaerts broke the hour record here, covering 34.23 miles (55.089 km) in the magnificent Velodromo Bicentenario—the city's altitude of 6,200 ft (1,890 m) was certainly a contributing factor. The local community loves exploring the foothills of the Sierra Madre Occidental on mountain bikes and gravel frames. Our route west of Aguascalientes traverses two sections of mountain roads, across an arid landscape: 22 mi (35 km) through the Sierra Fría to the Abelardo L. Rodríguez dam, then 10 mi (16 km) from Sierra del Laurel to Cerro del Muerto. The latter's profile— said to resemble a person on a deathbed— was previously the sole local landmark for the 850,000 residents of Aguascalientes. It now has a rival: the Velodromo Bicentenario.

	Distance	E+	Difficulty	Appeal
	73 mi (117 km)	**4,100 ft** (1,259 m)	**3/5**	**4/5**

Air: Miguel Hidalgo y Costilla International Airport, Guadalajara (2h30 by car), Benito Juárez International Airport, Mexico City (6h by car). Car: 2h15 from San Luis Potosí.

República Número 1 in the Buenos Aires district (2 mi/3.25 km west of the Velodromo) is more than a bike shop: it's a perfect concept store dreamed up by the locals.

Avenida Fundición #2005 20010, Aguascalientes, Mexico republicanumero1.com

Close to Manga de los Limones (mi 32/km 51): panorama over Cerro del Muerto. Close to Puerto de Arriba (mi 48/km 77 to mi 51/km 82). In front of the Velodromo Bicentenario of course (mi 73/km 117).

BUCERÍAS
GRAVEL AT SUNSET

DIRT & GRAVEL

⊕ Low mountain, Advanced, 46% unpaved
⊕ Map strava.com/routes/2871056395987314178

⊕ Test yourself mi 38 (km 61) strava.com/segments/8427751
⊕ Test yourself mi 64 (km 103) strava.com/segments/6974982

◉ GREG'S EYE

The roads and trails that commence in Bucerías (where I had a house) and Puerto Vallarta are a must for cyclists on the Mexican Pacific. The rural backcountry is as spectacular as the coast. With the Sierra Madre Occidental not too far away, you're soon up in the hills.

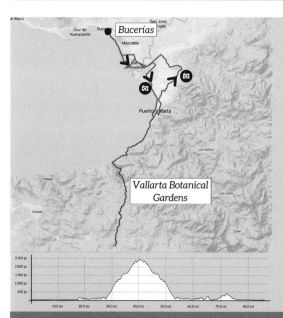

Bucerías

Vallarta Botanical Gardens

Bahía de Banderas neighbors discreet Bucerías (pop. 16,000) and opulent Puerto Vallarta (pop. 200,000) exude a passion for cycling, amplified by Canadian and American aficionados. This route (starting from Bici Bucerías) along the Pacific coast and into the foothills of the Sierra Madre Occidental has all the characteristics of the cycling practiced in the states of Nayarit and Jalisco. The asphalt is far from perfect, village streets are paved with large round cobbles, but the surface of the many dirt trails is smooth. In short, it's a joy if you take a gravel bike, which is essential here, despite being a tad heavier on the climb to the top of the Vallarta Botanical Gardens at 2,400 ft (730 m)—a 12-mi (19-km) pull at gradients of 3% to 5%—on the Fed 200. An early evening return is advisable to catch one of the remarkable Puerto Vallarta sunsets.

	Distance		E+		Difficulty		Appeal
	86 mi (138 km)		**5,700 ft** (1,739 m)		**3/5**		**4/5**

Air: Licenciado Gustavo Díaz Ordaz International Airport, Puerto Vallarta (10 min by car). Car: 5h30 from Guadalajara, 6h30 from Mazatlán, 11h from Mexico City.

Velo Bike in the village of Las Juntas, close to the airport (mi 9/km 14 or mi 71/km 115 on the way back) provides top-notch service. Retailer of Specialized.

Tepic 5757
48291 Las Juntas, Jalisco
velobikepv.com

Two options for sunset: return to the beaches north or south of Río Pitillal (mi 14/km 22), or the heights above Vista Vallarta golf course (mi 72/km 115). The ocean is also magnificent from the slopes of the Fed 200 before the botanical gardens.

MAZATLÁN
PACIFIC LIGHTHOUSE

🌐 *Hilly, Intermediate, 35% unpaved*   🌐 Map strava.com/routes/2872765688633733296

Distance	E+	Difficulty	Appeal
66 mi (106 km)	⬆ **2,700 ft** (818 m)	📊 **2/5**	⭐ **4/5**

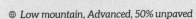

Mazatlán

Cabo San Lucas and the tip of Baja California lie nearly 300 miles (485 km) away, yet Mazatlán still enjoys unforgettable sunsets. The city is the country's largest port and the world shrimp capital, as well as a tourist destination. The final 10 mi (16 km) of this route (which starts at Kelly's Bicycle Shop) are an ode to this stretch of rocky coast, from the lighthouse on Crestón island (put your bike down to reach the Puente de Cristal mirador, 515 ft/157 m above the water) to the *malecón* (embankment) with surprising artworks. The hills, the Presidio River (mi 28/km 45, take a dip at the Siqueiros dam), and the Lomas de Monterrey wetlands also have charm.

CHIHUAHUA
A WHIFF OF ADVENTURE

🌐 *Low mountain, Advanced, 50% unpaved*   🌐 Map strava.com/routes/2872971925672403020

Distance	E+	Difficulty	Appeal
82 mi (131 km)	⬆ **6,300 ft** (1,920 m)	📊 **4/5**	⭐ **3/5**

Chihuahua

The vast state of Chihuahua, which abuts Texas and New Mexico to the north, sparks many fantasies, such as this XXL gravel adventure through the Sierra Madre Occidental—larger than the Grand Canyon and territory of the Indigenous Rarámuri. Good planning and logistics are required. Fortunately, Chihuahua City (pop. 800,000) is an ideal base camp. Our route alternates between roads and trails, through a landscape of ochre rock, overlooked by the low mountains surrounding the city. The initial eastern section takes us through the former mining area of Santa Eulalia, with splendid views west toward 6,000-ft (1,830-m) peaks.

ENSENADA
ALL SAINTS' VINES

⊕ Very hilly, Intermediate, 6% unpaved

⊕ Map strava.com/routes/2871328437459935202

⊕ Test yourself mi 13 (km 21) strava.com/segments/1051819

⊕ Test yourself mi 48 (km 77) strava.com/segments/1649647

◉ GREG'S EYE

Superb views over the Pacific Ocean and the most renowned vineyards in Mexico. What a ride! It reminds me of one of my dearest cycling memories: a road trip that I took with friends in Baja California, in 1990, to prepare for the Tour de France.

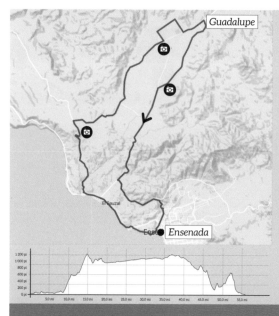

Ensenada (pop. 560,000) on the bay of Todos Santos, has retained the cachet of its Prohibition-era golden years. Its mild Mediterranean–type climate—exceptional in Baja California—helps maintain its status, as well as permitting cultivation of grapes and olives in the countryside. Indeed, 70% of Mexican grapes (chiefly chardonnay, cabernet sauvignon, and merlot) are grown in the areas south and north of Ensenada. Our route heads north for the most prestigious wine-growing estates of the Valle de Guadalupe (from mi 20/km 32) and the Valle de San Antonio de las Minas (mi 40/km 64), where grapevines stretch as far as the eye can see. We set off along the coast before tackling the ramps of Carmen and El Tigre in succession (each 2 mi/3.25 km long with an average gradient of 5%). Watch out for the "walls" of Puerto Veracruz and Las Peñitas on the way back.

	Distance		E+		Difficulty		Appeal
	56 mi (90 km)		**3,100 ft** (930 m)		**2/5**		**4/5**

Air: Tijuana International Airport (1h30 by car). Car: 2h from San Diego, California, 3h30 from Mexicali, 6h30 from Phoenix, Arizona.

We start from *Bajadventours Bike Shop and Lounge*, an establishment aimed more at mountain bikers, but wonderfully suited to our needs. Food and drink.

**Avenida Blancarte 154
22800 Ensenada, Baja California
Facebook @bajaventourstienda**

Summit of El Tigre (mi 14/km 22), with Salsipuedes Bay as a backdrop. And then wherever and how often you like in the abundant vineyards of Valle de Guadalupe.

NASSAU
JAWS, FOR REAL

⊕ Flat, Intermediate, 0% unpaved   ⊕ Map strava.com/routes/2837083616984384168

	Distance		E+		Difficulty		Appeal
⊢⊣	**62 mi** (100 km)	⬆	**1,200 ft** (350 m)	📊	**2/5**	★	**4/5**

Coral reefs, turquoise waters, white beaches: the Bahamas are heaven on earth. New Providence Island, 200 mi (320 km) east of Miami, is no exception. It's the most populous of the archipelago's 700 islands and the only one where sport cycling is possible. There's no climbing to speak of on this circuit, which starts at Cycles Unlimited in Nassau. Fort Fincastle and the colonial quarter precede the finest beaches on the north coast (Cable, Compass Point, Love) before hitting the most famous of all: Jaws (on the western tip), a shooting location for the eponymous film. We finish with a detour to the tourist playground of Atlantis Paradise Island.

SAINT THOMAS
PIRATE RAID

⊕ Very hilly, Advanced, 0% unpaved   ⊕ Map strava.com/routes/2839524614895030812

	Distance		E+		Difficulty		Appeal
⊢⊣	**41 mi** (66 km)	⬆	**6,300 ft** (1,935 m)	📊	**4/5**	★	**5/5**

Saint Thomas (80 mi/129 km) east of San Juan, Puerto Rico) is not the largest of the U.S. Virgin Islands, but despite covering an area one-tenth the size of New York City, it has a thousand things going for it, including terrain that lends itself to cycling. Its craggy relief (up to 1,555 ft/474 m at the top of Crown Mountain), jagged coastline, and dream beaches allow for a host of activities more respectable than the piracy of yore. Our circuit starts in Charlotte Amalie and requires some bravura. From Cabrita Point in the east to Botany Bay in the far west, via Magens Bay, the roads of "Rock City" are stunning, and sometimes surprising, with short ramps of 7% to 10%.

ARECIBO
CAVES AND TELESCOPE

⊕ *Low mountain, Advanced, 0% unpaved*   ⊕ *Map strava.com/routes/2868913108346382410*

	Distance		E+		Difficulty		Appeal
⊢–⊣	**58 mi** (93 km)	⬆	**6,300 ft** (1,933 m)	📊	**4/5**	⭐	**4/5**

This loop, barely 60 mi (96.5 km) inland from the Bike Shop in Arecibo ("El Diamante del Norte"), is 40 mi (64 km) west of San Juan on Puerto Rico's north coast. From the Ventana Cave and the Camuy River, you are guaranteed amazing views over Lago Dos Bocas and the Indigenous standing stones at Caguana. Once you make the switchback-packed Utuado climb (3 mi/4.75 km at 5%), you'll be on your way to the National Astronomy and Ionosphere Center (mi 46/km 74) and a breathtaking sight at the end of a bumpy road: what was once the largest radio telescope in the world—with a 1,000-ft (304.8-m) dish to track signals from space—which collapsed in 2020.

SAN JUAN
TROPICAL EL YUNQUE

⊕ *Low mountain, Advanced, 10% unpaved*   ⊕ *Map strava.com/routes/2869168691547152984*

	Distance		E+		Difficulty		Appeal
⊢–⊣	**91 mi** (146 km)	⬆	**6,400 ft** (1,947 m)	📊	**4/5**	⭐	**4/5**

Puerto Rico is known for its beaches. But the island's mountains are just as attractive. This route from Ciclo Pedal Bike Shop in San Juan combines the two with a strenuous climb to the near top of Pico El Yunque, the highest point in the eponymous national park: 3 mi (4.75 km) at an average gradient of 8%, then 6 mi (9.75 km) at 7%, up to 3,400 ft (1,040 m). More than the steepness, the humidity of the tropical forest is hard to take, as you ride past waterfalls and orchids, to the whistling of coquí frogs (symbol of Puerto Rico). The homeward leg along the Atlantic coast, from the white sands of Luquillo, will soothe any lingering pain.

PACIFIC COAST

CALIFORNIA
—
OREGON
—
WASHINGTON
—
HAWAII
—

ESCONDIDO
HIDDEN GIANT

- ⊕ High mountain, Expert, 0% unpaved
- ⊕ Map strava.com/routes/2920810101649424288
- ⊕ Test yourself mi 5 (km 8) strava.com/segments/273715
- ⊕ Test yourself mi 28 (km 45) strava.com/segments/12243844

👁 GREG'S EYE

I discovered these routes north of San Diego—one of the best training areas that exists—the year before I turned pro (I was barely twenty). You can't escape the Palomar Mountain climb, which equals the great Alpine cols in Europe in its difficulty (E+ of 4,500 ft/1,380 m).

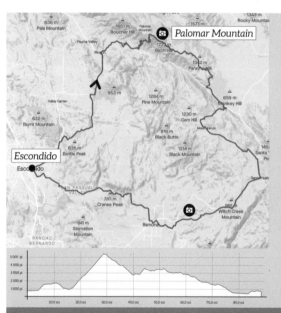

Palomar Mountain

Escondido

Urban Escondido, thirty minutes from downtown San Diego, is no longer a farming town, though we do pass avocado plantations and vineyards on our way to Palomar Mountain, pearl of the Peninsular Ranges, and back. The ascent is one of the toughest in California, with eighteen switchbacks that also attract motorcyclists, so take care. It has three parts: 5 mi (8 km) at an average gradient of 6.2%; barely 0.5 mi (1 km) of respite; then 7 mi (11 km), with 2 mi (3.2 km) in the middle at over 8%, and 0.5 mi (1 km) at 11% to wrap it up! At the summit of the route (mi 29/km 47, altitude of 5,300 ft/1,615 m), you can take South Grade Road up to the white dome of Palomar Observatory. This adds a further 4.5 mi (7.5 km) and 1,200 ft (365 m) of E+ but the view is superb. On the return leg, you can shave off 15 mi (24 km) by taking Pala Road west at Lake Henshaw (mi 40/km 64).

Distance **89 mi** (142 km)	E+ **8,700 ft** (2,652 m)	Difficulty **5/5**	Appeal **5/5**

Air: San Diego International Airport (30 min by car), Los Angeles International Airport (1h45 by car). Car: 2h30 from Ensenada, 5h30 from Phoenix, 8h from San Francisco.

BikeBling, a rallying point for the Escondido cycling community, organizes many rides. Strava Club. Retailer of Orbea, Pinarello, and Look.

333 E Grand Avenue Escondido, CA 92025 bikebling.com

Palomar Mountain Summit Circle (mi 29/km 47). Kica Mik Overlook (mi 30/km 48). Henshaw Scenic Vista (mi 38/km 61). Witch Creek Mountain (mi 60/km 97). Oasis Camel Dairy (mi 62/km 100). Poppaea and Grant James Vineyards (mi 66/km 106).

SAN MARCOS
HAVE A WAFFLE

⊕ Very hilly, Expert, 65% unpaved

⊕ Map strava.com/routes/2926442719619750854

⊕ Test yourself mi 27 (km 43) strava.com/segments/18488017

⊕ Test yourself mi 52 (km 84) strava.com/segments/1907001

👁 GREG'S EYE

The Belgian Waffle Ride is one of the most popular mass events in the United States. Created in San Marcos, north of San Diego, it was inspired by the relief of the Belgian Ardennes. This route is based on ten years of the BWR, which has offered new elements for each edition.

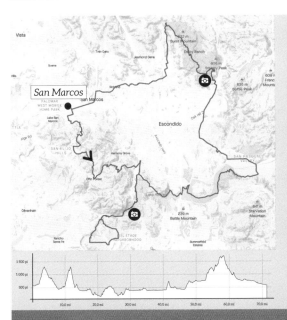

Only one letter differentiates Michael Marckx—a key figure in mass events on mixed surfaces—from legendary Eddy Merckx, and both are fans of the hilly Belgian Ardennes. In 2012, Marckx created an homage, the Belgian Waffle Ride, which went on to spawn similar events in North Carolina, Utah, and Kansas. San Marcos is not far from Escondido, the race's original base camp. Our route is inspired by ten years of the BWR, whose courses have been continually enhanced. It's a challenging ride, from both a physical and a technical point of view, such as on Way Up Trail (mi 10/km 16), the narrow Santa Fe Valley Trail (mi 20/km 32), San Pasqual Trail (mi 41/km 66), Sage Trail (mi 54/km 87), and Cougar Ridge Trail (mi 57/km 92), where it's better to ride as a small group than in a larger peloton. Superb scenery: Elfin Forest, Lake Hodges, San Pasqual Valley vineyards, Daley Ranch Preserve.

Distance	E+	Difficulty	Appeal
71 mi (114 km)	**6,900 ft** (2,105 m)	**4/5**	**5/5**

Air: San Diego International Airport (40 min by car), Los Angeles International Airport (1h30 by car). Car: 2h from Palm Springs, 2h30 from Ensenada, 6h from Phoenix.

Jim Rohn, founder of *Centre City Cycles*, knows the region by heart. Impeccable bike shop. Retailer of Marin and Kona. Also visit Lost Cyclery, 0.5 mi (1 km) to the north.

1145 Linda Vista Drive San Marcos, CA 92078 centrecitycycles.com

Double Peak (mi 3.5/km 5.5). Harmony Grove Overlook (mi 11/km 17.75). Escondido Overlook (mi 12/km 19). Lake Hodges (mi 29/km 47). San Pasqual Valley (mi 41/km 66). Hungry Hawk Vineyards (mi 47/km 76). Dixon Lake (mi 55/km 89). Burnt Mountain (mi 58/km 93).

PALM SPRINGS
ABOVE THE DESERT

🌐 *Low mountain, Advanced, 0% unpaved*   🌐 *Map strava.com/routes/2927626230533448918*

	Distance		E+		Difficulty		Appeal
⊢–⊣	**73 mi** (117 km)	⬆	**6,300 ft** (1,920 m)	📊	**4/5**	★	**4/5**

Palm Springs (pop. 50,000), the gateway to the Sonoran Desert, 110 mi (177 km) east of Los Angeles, is hot, so get your timing right. When the sun is low in the sky (early morning and evening) its light enhances the Coachella Valley and the San Jacinto Mountains surrounding the town. Two standout climbs: the 3 mi (4.75 km) at 9% of Tramway Road (mi 21/km 34) lead to the start of the Aerial Tramway—the largest rotating one in the world—with 360-degree views. The 13 mi (21 km) of the Pines to Palms Highway (mi 45/ km 72) climb at a regular 5% to Cahuilla Tewanet Vista Point with wonderful panoramas, especially from the seven switchbacks halfway up.

REDLANDS
OLDIES BUT GOODIES

🌐 *High mountain, Advanced, 0% unpaved*   🌐 *Map strava.com/routes/2920017607048902074*

	Distance		E+		Difficulty		Appeal
⊢–⊣	**65 mi** (105 km)	⬆	**7,900 ft** (2,410 m)	📊	**4/5**	★	**5/5**

Redlands, 60 mi (97 km) east of Los Angeles, boasts several historic buildings such as French château–style Kimberly Crest House. Beyond rises the enticing silhouette of the San Bernardino Mountains. We head out from Cyclery USA toward Old Waterman Canyon Road: 9 mi (14 km) at 7% (the last at 9%) up to Crestline, through a landscape of scrub and rock. After Lake Gregory, we attack a 3.2-mi (5-km) climb at 6.5% on the way to Lake Arrowhead. Kuffel Canyon Road (mi 36/km 58) doesn't disappoint (1.2 mi/2 km at 9%), before Rim of the World Highway—and a final effort up to 6,350 ft (1,935 m)—then a 20-mi (32-km) descent (watch out for traffic).

GLENDORA
THE LA BEAST

- ⊕ *High mountain, Expert, 0% unpaved*
- ⊕ *Map strava.com/routes/2925346116264870102*

- ✛ *Test yourself mi 13 (km 21) strava.com/segments/17860021*
- ✛ *Test yourself mi 20 (km 32) strava.com/routes/2925346116264870102*

👁 GREG'S EYE

Mount Baldy (4,700 ft/1435 m of elevation in less than 13 mi/21 km), popularized by the Tour of California, is one of the hardest climbs in the western United States. Incredibly, it starts at the edge of Los Angeles, rather as if Alpe d'Huez lay on the outskirts of Paris!

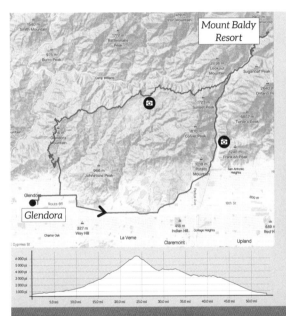

Mount Baldy Resort

Glendora

You have to have climbed Mount Baldy if you want any bragging rights at all in a Los Angeles peloton! It's the star route of the San Gabriel Mountains, northeast of LA. The champions of the Tour of California battled it out here in the 2010s. As you reach the last residential areas of Claremont, it can be a surprise to see the road rear up. The average gradient of the 12.7-mi (20.5-km) climb is 7%, but that's deceptive. From the 5-mi (8-km) mark, following two short tunnels, you're faced with 2 mi (3.25 km) at 9.2%. After that, don't feel bad about taking a break at Mount Baldy Lodge (mi 19/km 31), before the hardest part: 4.8 mi (7.75 km), including a 2-mi (3.25 km) segment at close to 10%, then 0.3 mi (0.5 km) at 14% to finish. It's a fearsome challenge, but the descent via Glendora Ridge Road, then Glendora Mountain Road, is long and easy, with very little traffic, and amazing views.

	Distance		E+		Difficulty		Appeal
⊢-⊣	**53 mi** (85 km)	⬆	**7,200 ft** (2,195 m)	📊	**5/5**	⭐	**5/5**

Air: Los Angeles International Airport (1h by car).
Car: 2h from Santa Barbara, 2h from San Diego, 2h15 from Bakersfield, 4h from Las Vegas, 6h from San Francisco.

Bicycle Central (open every day) is where the cycling community of Glendora (pop. 53,000) meets. Strava Club. Retailer of Trek and Masi.

**121 W Route 66
Glendora, CA 91740
thebicyclecentral.com**

San Antonio Canyon (mi 14/ km 23). Mount Baldy Summit (mi 24/km 39). Sunset Peak (mi 31/km 50). Peacock Saddle (mi 36/km 58). Glendora Mountain Road Lookouts (mi 43/km 69). Colby Trail (mi 45/km 72). Little Dalton Canyon (mi 49/km 79).

LOS ANGELES
HOLLYWOOD PARADE

⊕ *Low mountain, Advanced, 0% unpaved*   ⊕ *Map strava.com/routes/2928636814444306822*

	Distance		E+		Difficulty		Appeal
⊢⊣	**60 mi** (97 km)	⬆	**6,400 ft** (1,950 m)	◫	**4/5**	★	**5/5**

If it's a quiet ride you're after, look to the dirt trails of the Sonoran Desert or Death Valley. This is different, but how can you resist the call of the Hollywood Hills when you're staying in Los Angeles (as long as you can handle the traffic)? Starting from Bike Shop LA, there are no fewer than seven punchy ramps on our route: Franklin Canyon Drive above Beverly Hills; Wonderland Avenue; Laurel Canyon Boulevard; Outpost Drive; Mount Lee (final 1 mi/1.5 km at 10%); Mount Hollywood; and Mount Baby Bell. Make the obligatory selfie stop below the Hollywood Sign (mi 34/km 55). You'll almost merit your own star on the Walk of Fame (mi 56/km 90)!

WRIGHTWOOD
ANGELES EXCESS

DIRT & GRAVEL

⊕ *High mountain, Expert, 65% unpaved*   ⊕ *Map strava.com/routes/2929295123070436094*

	Distance		E+		Difficulty		Appeal
⊢⊣	**59 mi** (95 km)	⬆	**11,200 ft** (3,415 m)	◫	**5/5**	★	**5/5**

The area is full of summits, led by majestic Mount Baldy at 10,006 ft (3,050 m). This route, starting from Grizzly Café in Wrightwood, lies at 4,300 ft (1,310 m) to 8,500 ft (2,590 m). We're 70 mi (113 km) northeast of LA, on the trails, ridgelines, and valleys of the wonderful San Gabriel Mountains and Angeles National Forest. This over-the-top ride starts with a climb of close to 4 mi (6.5 km) at 11% and later one of 9.5 mi (15 km) at 6.2%, sprinkled with 12% ramps along the way, and it finishes with 4.6 mi (7.5 km) at 8%! You can cut short the route at several points. But how could you resist the colors and scenery of Inspiration Point, Jackson Lake, and Paradise Springs?

SANTA MONICA
TOPANGA FANCIES

🌐 *Low mountain, Advanced, 70% unpaved*　　　🌐 *Map strava.com/routes/2928366253533803500*

	Distance		E+		Difficulty		Appeal
⊢—⊣	**58 mi** (93 km)	⬆	**8,000 ft** (2,440 m)	📊	**4/5**	⭐	**5/5**

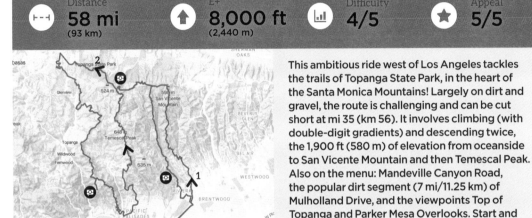

Santa Monica

This ambitious ride west of Los Angeles tackles the trails of Topanga State Park, in the heart of the Santa Monica Mountains! Largely on dirt and gravel, the route is challenging and can be cut short at mi 35 (km 56). It involves climbing (with double-digit gradients) and descending twice, the 1,900 ft (580 m) of elevation from oceanside to San Vicente Mountain and then Temescal Peak. Also on the menu: Mandeville Canyon Road, the popular dirt segment (7 mi/11.25 km) of Mulholland Drive, and the viewpoints Top of Topanga and Parker Mesa Overlooks. Start and finish at the Rapha Clubhouse Los Angeles, close to Santa Monica Pier.

CALABASAS
PAVED DREAMS

🌐 *Low mountain, Expert, 11% unpaved*　　　🌐 *Map strava.com/routes/2928417923214286454*

	Distance		E+		Difficulty		Appeal
⊢—⊣	**85 mi** (137 km)	⬆	**10,500 ft** (3,200 m)	📊	**5/5**	⭐	**5/5**

Calabasas

Calabasas, 30 mi (48 km) northwest of LA, is famous for its gated communities and celebrities. This ambitious route starts from the bike café Pedalers Fork, just off Mulholland Drive, with 9 mi (14.5 km) of dirt, before exploring the Santa Monica Mountains on paved roads. Topanga Canyon Boulevard then Saddle Peak Road (7.5 mi/12 km at an average gradient of 5% to 8%), Rambla Pacifico, and Piuma Road (4 mi/6.5 m at 8%) sap your energy. After Malibu, Latigo Canyon Road (5 mi/8 km at 5%, then 2 mi/3.25 km at 7%), with its perfect curves between terraced fields overlooking the ocean, is both agonizing and the embodiment of a cyclist's dream road.

SANTA BARBARA
PACIFIC CLIMB

- ⊕ Low mountain, Advanced, 0% unpaved
- ⊕ Map strava.com/routes/2919716711478331618
- ⊙ Test yourself mi 10 (km 16) strava.com/segments/8374574
- ⊙ Test yourself mi 16 (km 26) strava.com/segments/639737

◉ GREG'S EYE

I loved racing around here when I was a young cyclist. As soon as I discovered Santa Barbara, it became one of my favorite places in California. Gibraltar Road already had a reputation. Its asphalt is not in the best condition, but the views are stunning.

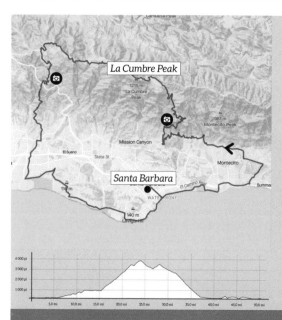

With its large white houses with red Mission-style tiled roofs, Santa Barbara (pop. 90,000), pearl of the American Riviera, has a certain cachet. The living is good here, between the ocean and the mountains 90 mi (145 km) northwest of Los Angeles. Santa Barbara is also the perfect base camp for one of the most beautiful (and toughest) climbs in California, offering amazing panoramas over the Pacific as far as the Channel Islands. Snaking through the Santa Ynez Mountains, Gibraltar Road is an irregular ascent. With an average gradient of 8% over the first 6 mi (9.75 km)—sections at 12%—before a final 1.2-mi (2-km) ramp (7.7%) up to La Cumbre Peak, it's no picnic! There are many views over the ocean as you round the bends, and the descent via Painted Cave Road is a joy. Celebrate this exceptional experience at Handlebar Coffee Roasters, three blocks from FasTrack Bicycles.

	Distance		E+		Difficulty		Appeal
	50 mi (80 km)		**5,800 ft** (1,770 m)		**4/5**		**5/5**

Air: Santa Barbara Airport (20 min by car), Los Angeles International Airport (2h by car).
Car: 2h30 from Bakersfield, 3h30 from San Diego, 5h from San Francisco, 5h30 from Las Vegas.

FasTrack Bicycles attracts cyclists from up and down the Central Coast and organizes several rides a week. Retailer of Pinarello, Orbea, Cervelo, and Trek.

118 W Canon Perdido Street Santa Barbara, CA 93101 fastrackbicycles.com

East Beach (mi 2/km 3.25). Fynx Avionics View (mi 17/km 27). La Cumbre Peak (mi 23/km 37). Camino Cielo Vista Point (mi 27/km 43). Lake Cachuma Vista Point (mi 30/km 48). Painted Cave Rocks (mi 32/km 51.5). Painted Cave Terrace View (mi 33/km 53). Stearns Wharf (mi 49/km 79).

SOLVANG
SUNNY SANTA YNEZ

- ⊕ Low mountain, Advanced, 1% unpaved
- ⊕ Map strava.com/routes/2925344626796529726
- ⊙ Test yourself mi 7 (km 11) strava.com/segments/1824427
- ⊙ Test yourself mi 23 (km 37) strava.com/segments/659335

👁 GREG'S EYE

Another little corner of cycling paradise in California! At the age of seventeen, I won the Solvang Criterium. I loved the unique atmosphere of this town founded by Danish emigrants, with its magnificent scenery. And Figueroa Mountain is a really beautiful climb.

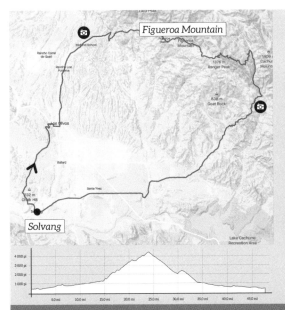

Figueroa Mountain

Solvang

Solvang (pop. 6,000), west of Santa Barbara, means "sunny field" in Danish. And sun was exactly what these Scandinavian emigrants came seeking in the early twentieth century, having found Midwest winters too harsh. The town has retained a number of windmills and colorful half-timbered houses. The Santa Ynez Valley beyond is sublime, with vineyards stretching to the horizon. You feel like you're in an extraordinary corridor as you ride through Ballard Canyon on the narrow, quiet, exposed climb of Figueroa Mountain (up to 4,400 ft/1,340 m)—every inch the equal of an Alpine col: an irregular 9.3 mi (15 km) at an average gradient of 6.3%, with the first 1 mi (1.5 km) at 11% and sections as steep as 15%. Chris Froome was long a regular here for his winter training.

	Distance		E+		Difficulty		Appeal
	48 mi (77 km)		**5,500 ft** (1,675 m)		**4/5**		**5/5**

Air: Santa Maria Airport (40 min by car), Santa Barbara Airport (40 min by car), Los Angeles International Airport (2h30 by car). Car: 3h from Bakersfield, 5h from San Francisco.

Dr J's, in Solvang, has been the go-to local specialist bike shop for nearly fifty years. Organized rides. Strava Club. Retailer of Specialized.

**1693 Mission Drive
Solvang, CA 93463**
drjsbikeshop.com

Ballard Canyon (mi 6/km 9.75) Figueroa Campground (mi 21/km 34). Ranger Peak (mi 24/km 39). Happy Canyon (mi 31/km 50). Old Mission Santa Inés Solvang Windmill, and Solvang Historic Village (mi 48/km 77).

CARMEL-BY-THE-SEA
BIG SUR FEAST

⊕ *Very hilly, Advanced, 0% unpaved*
⊕ *Map strava.com/routes/2919724997641404720*

⊕ *Test yourself mi 26 (km 42) strava.com/segments/2705744*
⊕ *Test yourself mi 71 (km 114) strava.com/segments/2171*

👁 GREG'S EYE

As long as you choose your day and leave early enough to avoid most of the traffic, there can be no finer meeting between road and ocean than Big Sur! I rode it with some friends on a road trip to train for the 1990 Tour de France and it was magical!

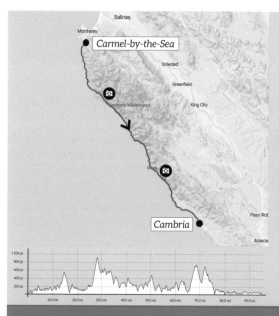

The most extraordinary road in North America might well be the one between San Francisco and Los Angeles: Highway 1, more specifically the section nicknamed Big Sur, which runs alongside the Pacific Ocean at the foot of the Santa Lucia Mountains. It's imperative to ride it from north to south in order to hug the edge of the impressive cliffs (up to 900 ft/m 275 high) and the many creeks. Starting from Carmel-by-the-Sea and finishing in Cambria (mi 95 /km 153) requires some logistics, as well as good physical fitness: not a single mile is flat, and there are several 1- to 2-mi (1.5- to 3.2-km) ramps as steep as 8%. You'll see surfers, elephant seals, and, with a bit of luck, whales. In Cambria, at the end of this fabulous near century that'll whiz past, take a seat on the terrace of the Canteen at Oceanpoint Ranch to reflect on all you've seen and experienced.

	Distance		E+		Difficulty		Appeal
	95 mi (153 km)		**7,500 ft** (2,285 m)		**3/5**		**5/5**

Air: San Jose International Airport (1h30 by car), San Francisco International Airport (2h by car). Car: 2h30 from Fresno, 4h from Bakersfield, 5h30 from Los Angeles, 8h from Las Vegas.

Carmel Bicycle, which has operated since 1988, is a sponsor of the Sea Otter Classic bicycling and outdoor festival. Strava Club: Velo Club Monterey. Retailer of Giant, Trek, and Cervelo.

26543 Carmel Rancho Boulevard Carmel-by-the-Sea, CA 93923 carmelbicycle.net

Kasler Point (mi 10/ km 16). Hurricane Viewpoint (mi 15/km 24). Pfeiffer Falls (mi 26/km 41). Partington Cove (mi 36/km 58). Kirk Creek (mi 54/km 87). Soda Springs (mi 68/km 109). Elephant Seals Viewing (mi 85/km 137). Hearst Castle (mi 89/km 143).

MARICOPA
FLOWER POWER

🌐 *Very hilly, Advanced, 70% unpaved*　　　🌐 *Map strava.com/routes/2928985569920764294*

	Distance		E+		Difficulty		Appeal
┝━┥	**86 mi** (138 km)	⬆	**4,500 ft** (1,370 m)	📊	**3/5**	⭐	**5/5**

Here's an unusual off-road experience, 110 mi (177 km) northwest of Los Angeles, not far from Bakersfield. Ride it in April or May, when Carrizo Plain National Monument blooms into life and the largest extant natural prairie in the Golden State is decked out in showy colors. Golden brush and tree lupin cover the ground in yellow and purple as far as the eye can see. Our route reaches it after a 6-mi (9.5-km) climb at 5.5% from Maricopa Unified School District. Up here, at 2,000 ft (610 m), we're well away from the oil fields of Midway-Sunset oil field. The 22 mi (35 km) of paved road to Soda Lake (mi 31/km 50) are highly recommended for the views.

FRESNO
FILL YOUR BOTTLE

🌐 *Low mountain, Intermediate, 0% unpaved*　　　🌐 *Map strava.com/routes/2927945067331834420*

	Distance		E+		Difficulty		Appeal
┝━┥	**74 mi** (119 km)	⬆	**3,900 ft** (1,190 m)	📊	**3/5**	⭐	**4/5**

If you find yourself riding in the rain one day near Fresno (pop. 500,000)—a 1h drive from Yosemite National Park—the locals will want to hear! Drought is a major topic of conversation in this farming community, and the land apparently one of the most fertile places in the world. Start from the Bike Shop in Woodward Park; here in the south of the San Joaquin Valley, fields of almonds, avocados, and grapes are everywhere. They thin out in the arid foothills of the Sierra Nevada. We climb to 2,000 ft (610 m) on Burrough Valley Road (4 mi/6.5 km at 5%, with sections as steep as 10%), and then tackle Watts Valley Road (2 mi/3 km at 4.5%).

KERNVILLE
FOOTSTEPS OF GIANTS

🌐 *High mountain, Advanced, 75% unpaved*
🌐 *Map strava.com/routes/2927561796963360982*

🔵 *Test yourself mi 17 (km 27) strava.com/segments/24012186*
🔵 *Test yourself mi 22 (km 35)strava.com/segments/5913380*

👁 **GREG'S EYE**

The giant trees of Sequoia National Park or here, in Sequoia National Forest further south, not far from Bakersfield (pop. 400,000), are a must-see. You catch a glimpse on this route, which climbs above 9,000 ft (2,745 m) on the Kern Plateau. The Trail of 100 Giants is nearby.

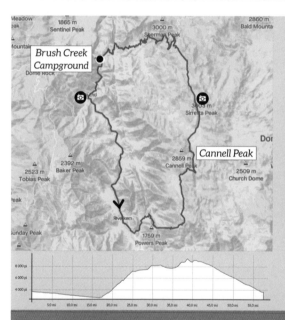

In this part of California, giant sequoias loom over the landscape. And 15 mi (24 km) west of our starting point (Brush Creek Campground, for a warm-up before tackling Cannell Meadow Trail) lies the Trail of 100 Giants, to be explored on foot. Encountering the enormous trees in person is like making your very first visit to New York City—you'll be dazzled. After cruising downhill beside the Kern River, almost to Lake Isabella, you'll spot other wonders too, though the effort will demand great concentration: 1.4 mi (2.25 km) at 10.5%, then 6 mi (9.5 km) at 11.8% (madness!) to reach the Kern Plateau at an altitude of over 7,000 ft (2,135 m). Cannell Trail is merciless. The forest track climbs again below Cannell Peak and then Sirretta Peak, between mi 29 (km 47) and mi 37 (km 60). The asphalt of Sherman Pass takes you back to the Kern River after 16 mi (26 km) of sweet euphoria.

	Distance		E+		Difficulty		Appeal
⊢⊣	**57 mi** (92 km)	⬆	**8,500 ft** (2,590 m)	📊	**4/5**	⭐	**5/5**

Air: Meadows Field Airport, Bakersfield (1h15 by car), Los Angeles International Airport (3h by car). Car: 2h30 from Fresno, 4h30 from Las Vegas, 5h from San Francisco.

Get A Bike, 50 mi (80 km) southwest of Kernville, is located close to the Bakersfield Museum of Art. Retailer of Orbea and BH.

213 E 18th Street
Bakersfield, CA 93305
getabikeusa.com

Packsaddle Cave (mi 4/km 6.5). Cannell Peak (mi 32/km 51). Sirretta Peak (mi 37/km 60). Sunset Point (mi 45/km 72). Johnsondale Bridge and South Creek Falls (mi 57/km 92).

FURNACE CREEK
DEATH VALLEY MADNESS

🌐 *High mountain, Expert, 0% unpaved*　　　🌐 *Map strava.com/routes/2921107693475549678*

	Distance		E+		Difficulty		Appeal
⊢–⊣	**117 mi** (189 km)	⬆	**14,600 ft** (4,459 m)	📊	**5/5**	★	**5/5**

Whitney Portal

Death Valley National Park

Furnace Creek

This insane route across an apocalyptic landscape, under blazing sun and in oppressive heat, is for super-trained ultra-cyclists. The aim: climb, in just one day, the 8,100 ft (2,470 m) that separate Furnace Creek—an oasis in the heart of Death Valley, at an altitude of -190 ft/-58 m (close to the lowest point in the country)—from Whitney Portal, opposite Mount Whitney, the highest summit in the contiguous United States (14,505 ft /4,521 m). Three big climbs: Towne Pass (16.6 mi/ 26.75 km at 5.6%); Father Crowley Summit (15 mi/24 km at 4%); and Whitney Portal (11 mi/ 17.75 km at 7.9%, with the final 3.5 mi/5.5 km at close to 10%). It's one crazy, bucket-list ride.

MAMMOTH LAKES
VOLCANIC CENTURY

DIRT & GRAVEL

🌐 *High mountain, Expert, 60% unpaved*　　　🌐 *Map strava.com/routes/2928269617675937772*

	Distance		E+		Difficulty		Appeal
⊢–⊣	**95 mi** (153 km)	⬆	**7,200 ft** (2,195 m)	📊	**4/5**	★	**5/5**

Mammoth Lakes

Casa Diablo Mountain

Picturesque Mammoth Lakes, situated between Yosemite and Death Valley National Park, has become a base camp for cyclists, owing to its peaceful surroundings and high-altitude trails. This century (starting from Footloose Sports) explores the Volcanic Tableland around Crowley Lake, Round Mountain, Casa Diablo Mountain, the climbing sites of Bishop and Owens River Gorge, and three ramps 2.5 mi (4 km) to 3.5 mi (5.5 km) long, with sections as steep as 9%. This rare adventure is punctuated by lava fields, scrubland, cliffs, and granite screes between the grandiose scenery of the White Mountains to the east and the Sierra Nevada to the west.

SAN JOSE
EARLY INNOVATOR

⊕ *Low mountain, Expert, 0% unpaved* ⊕ *Map strava.com/routes/2929047770035891966*

	Distance		E+		Difficulty		Appeal
⊢⊣	**56 mi** (90 km)	⬆	**7,500 ft** (2,285 m)	▥	**4/5**	★	**5/5**

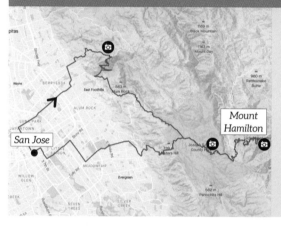

San Jose (pop. 1 million), capital of Silicon Valley, was already a seat of innovation in the late nineteenth century when James Lick funded the first high-altitude observatory, on Mount Hamilton (summit: 4,265 ft/1,300 m) in the Diablo Range. The climb (we start from Bicycle Express) is a prized local challenge: four stages of 1.5 mi (2.5 km) to 6.3 mi (10 km) each, with average gradients of between 4.7% and 6%. Sierra Road on the way out and Quimby Road on the way back are the toughest: 3.6 mi (5.75 km) and 1.2 mi (2 km), each at 9%! Descending from Lick Observatory (open to visitors), enjoy a great view from Jupiter's Bluff (mi 36/km 58).

OAKLAND
MOUNT DIABLO WARM UP

⊕ *Low mountain, Advanced, 0% unpaved* ⊕ *Map strava.com/routes/2928945524496451864*

	Distance		E+		Difficulty		Appeal
⊢⊣	**85 mi** (137 km)	⬆	**6,500 ft** (1,980 m)	▥	**4/5**	★	**5/5**

Mount Diablo, the terror of East Bay cyclists (summit at 3,700 ft (1,130 m), 10-mi/16-km climb at 6%, with sections at 17%), and the promise of its panoramas will beckon as you ride out of Oakland (pop. 450,000). No need to attempt the feat on your first day, though. Instead, ride this route from Luckyduck Bicycle Café to explore the lush Oakland-Berkeley Hills. There's some challenge on Claremont Avenue (2.2 mi/3.5 km at 8%) not long after the start, and Redwood Road on the way back. Ballinger Canyon Road (mi 37.5/km 60) and Cull Canyon Road (mi 53.5/km 86) are optional, but why miss such scenery?

PALO ALTO
SILICON VALLEY ESCAPE

- 🌐 Low mountain, Advanced, 0% unpaved
- 🌐 Map strava.com/routes/2920835679385367860
- ⊕ Test yourself mi 8 (km 13) strava.com/segments/8109834
- ⊕ Test yourself mi 32 (km 51) strava.com/segments/628189

👁 GREG'S EYE

Palo Alto Bicycles was my first sponsor ($15,000 a year was huge for an eighteen-year-old). Its founders had invented the Avocet: the first cycle computer on the market. It was also cycling enthusiast Steve Jobs's regular bike shop! Tunitas Creek Road is the real jewel of this ride.

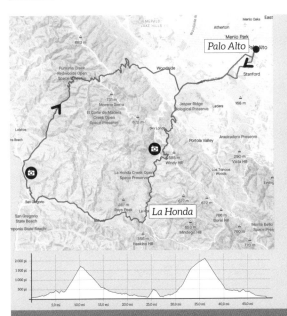

Hewlett Packard, Stanford University, and Facebook are just some of the names that put Palo Alto (pop. 70,000) on the map. There's nothing like the neighboring Santa Cruz Mountains to soothe the Silicon Valley stress. We start from (and end at) Stanford's superb campus before twisting, cantankerous Old La Honda Road (3 mi /4.75 km at a merciless 8%), whose scenery evokes the Alps. Its descent leads—after Stage Road (1 mi/1.5 km at 7%)—to the cliffs overlooking the magnificent Pacific Ocean. After Tunitas Beach (mi 27/km 43), we turn our backs on the waves for the long (9 mi/14 km), narrow, winding delight of Tunitas Creek Road, lost in the sequoia forest. Its average gradient of 4% seems reasonable, but the 3 mi (4.75 km) following the junction with Lobitos Creek Road (mi 31/km 50) are at a harsh 8% average gradient, with sections at 11%. Refuel at the Bike Hut (mi 29/km 47).

Distance	E+	Difficulty	Appeal
49 mi (79 km)	**4,800 ft** (1,465 m)	**3/5**	**5/5**

 Air: San Francisco International Airport (20 min by car). Car: 20 min from San Jose, 40 min to Oakland, 2h from Sacramento, 6h from Los Angeles.

 Palo Alto Bicycles, just outside the Stanford campus, will soon celebrate its centenary! A must-visit. Strava Club. Retailer of Trek, Look, Surly, and Kona.

171 University Avenue
Palo Alto, CA 94301
paloaltobicycles.com

 Stanford University campus (mi 1/km 1.5 to mi 3/km 4.75). Searsville Lake (mi 7/km 11). Windy Hill Summit (near mi 11/km 17.75). Ocean Overlook (mi 26/km 42). Skyline Boulevard (mi 36/km 58). Stanford University Arboretum (mi 49/km 79).

SAN FRANCISCO
TO MTB BIRTHPLACE

- ⊕ Low mountain, Advanced, 0 % unpaved
- ⊕ Map strava.com/routes/2919743468629186164
- ⊕ Test yourself mi 9 (km 14) strava.com/segments/4783121
- ⊕ Test yourself mi 28 (km 45) strava.com/segments/632391

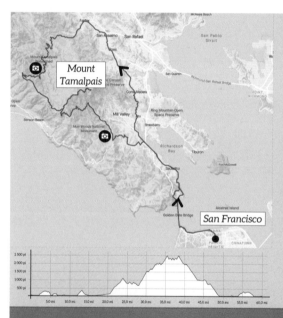

Mount Tamalpais

San Francisco

Leaving San Francisco via the bike lane on the ocean side of the Golden Gate Bridge is an unforgettable cycling experience, particularly when combined with a 60-mi (97-km) loop via Mount Tamalpais in Marin County.

The low-mountain landscape (highest point: 2,500 ft/760 m) is gorgeous, with pine forests and views over the Pacific and San Francisco Bay. Head through Sausalito (glance over at Alcatraz Island), then Fairfax (Marin Museum of Bicycling, mi 17/km 27), and Azalea Hill, before passing Alpine Dam and onto the roller coaster of Seven Sisters, taking you up toward Ridgecrest Boulevard and the three peaks (West, Middle, and East) of Mount Tamalpais. It was on the fire roads of these slopes that four pioneers (Gary Fisher, Joe Breeze, Charlie Kelly, and Tom Ritchey) invented the mountain bike in the 1970s by customizing Schwinn cruisers.

Distance	E+	Difficulty	Appeal
60 mi (97 km)	**5,500 ft** (1,686 m)	**4/5**	**5/5**

Air: San Francisco International Airport (40 min by car). Car: 1h from San Jose, 2h30 from Sacramento, 6h30 from Los Angeles, 9h from Las Vegas, 10h30 from Portland.

The elegant *Rapha CC* Clubhouse San Francisco, in the hip northern Cow Hollow neighborhood, is worth a visit (café, coworking) even if you're not riding.

2198 Filbert Street San Francisco, CA 94123 rapha.cc

Fort Point Historic Site and Golden Gate Bridge (mi 3/km 4.75). Alcatraz Island (mi 6/km 9.75). Alpine Dam and Cataract Falls (mi 28/km 45). Mount Tamalpais East Peak (mi 37/km 60). Mount Tamalpais West Peak (mi 38/km 61). San Francisco Vista (mi 41/km 66).

SAN FRANCISCO
TREASURE HUNT

⊕ Very hilly, Advanced, 0% unpaved   ⊕ Map strava.com/routes/2929073163857140478

Distance	E+	Difficulty	Appeal
⊢⊣ **59 mi** (95 km)	⬆ **5,800 ft** (1,780 m)	⬛ **3/5**	★ **5/5**

It takes days to begin to really know San Francisco (pop. 900,000), stuffed as it is with treasures and surprises. This route (starting from American Cyclery) provides a taste. And what a feast, in less than 60 mi (97 km)! To start: the ocean and San Bruno Mountain (2.9 mi/4.7 km at 7%). The relief that follows around Twin Peaks opens the way to the steepest streets, as well as the greenest (Harry Street, mi 30/km 48). Next, the Embarcadero with its legendary piers, and challenging Lombard Street (mi 40/km 64): short, tight switchbacks and a gradient of up to 30%! Return via the Presidio, Golden Gate Bridge Vista Point, Lincoln Park, and Golden Gate Park.

FOLSOM
NO BLUES CIRCUIT

⊕ Very hilly, Intermediate, 0% unpaved   ⊕ Map strava.com/routes/2927333344007905484

Distance	E+	Difficulty	Appeal
⊢⊣ **47 mi** (76 km)	⬆ **4,200 ft** (1,273 m)	⬛ **2/5**	★ **4/5**

Johnny Cash sang the "Folsom Prison Blues." This route's starting point (Folsom Bikes) is situated less than 0.5 mi (0.75 km) from the famous state prison that opened in 1880. This historic Gold Rush city (pop. 80,000) also sits on an idyllic 18-sq-mi reservoir. Sultry summers expose sandbanks prized by the residents of Sacramento, which is just a 30-min drive away. This clockwise circuit of Folsom Lake, on pretty rolling roads through the green, wooded foothills of the Sierra Nevada, is as easy as it is lovely. As you leave Auburn, the climb up the confluence of the North and Middle Fork American Rivers is a bracing 1.8 mi (3 km) at 8%.

HEALDSBURG
PRO SENSATIONS

⊕ Low mountain, Expert, 4% unpaved
⊕ Map strava.com/routes/2921117119246287342

⊕ Test yourself mi 14 (km 23) strava.com/segments/4553260
⊕ Test yourself mi 58 (km 93) strava.com/segments/3515

👁 GREG'S EYE

I felt much emotion when I rediscovered this route through vineyards and the Sonoma Mountains, and along the Pacific Ocean. It was my favorite during a winter training camp before I went professional in 1981. Come on and experience the sensations of a future pro!

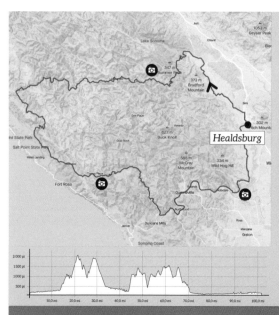

Healdsburg

Healdsburg (pop. 11,000), very close to Santa Rosa, north of San Francisco, is an idyllic spot set between gently rolling hills, where three famous wine-making areas meet: the Alexander, Dry Creek, and Russian River Valleys. Setting out for these 102 mi (164 km) and more than 10,000 ft (3,050 m) of elevation gain (with no hope of cutting things short beyond mi 40/km 64) is clearly a test of mental strength. The gorgeous scenery does relieve the suffering amid the thick forest of Skaggs Hills (five ramps of 1 mi/1.5 km to 3 mi/4.75 km in length, at gradients of 7% to 13%), the wonderful tundra of Seaview Road 1,500 ft (455 m) above the ocean (slopes as steep as 16%), and on the Little Black Mountain climb (1 mi/1.5 km at 8%). Greg LeMond managed it at the age of nineteen. Refuel at Cazadero General Store (mi 70/km 113) and Coffee Bazaar (mi 84/km 135).

	Distance **102 mi** (164 km)	⬆	E+ **10,500 ft** (3,200 m)	📊	Difficulty **5/5**	⭐	Appeal **5/5**

Air: Charles M. Schulz–Sonoma County Airport, Santa Rosa (20 min by car), San Francisco International Airport (1h30 by car), Sacramento International Airport (2h by car).
Car: 3h30 from Redding, 4h30 from Reno, 7h from Los Angeles.

Spoke Folk Cyclery in Healdsburg is the place to seek tips on the best routes. Strava Club. Retailer of Specialized and Bianchi.

**201 Center Street
Healdsburg, CA 95448**
spokefolk.com

Lake Sonoma (mi 15/km 24 and mi 20/km 32). Skyview (mi 22/km 35). Centennial Mountain (mi 28/km 45). Odiyan Retreat Center (mi 48/km 77). Haupt Creek Vineyards (mi 50/km 80). Seaview Road (mi 59/km 95 to mi 63/km 101). Pole Mountain (mi 65/km 105). Rocky Beach (mi 79/km 127).

ST. HELENA
ENCHANTED NAPA VALLEY

- ⊕ Very hilly, Intermediate, 0% unpaved
- ⊕ Map strava.com/routes/2921080417512230382
- ⊛ Test yourself mi 9 (km 14) strava.com/segments/11947360
- ⊛ Test yourself mi 44 (km 71) strava.com/segments/7210208

◉ GREG'S EYE

I remember a tough Mount Veeder/Oakville Grade Road sequence during the Coors Classic in the 1980s, and a superfast descent (take care) to St. Helena. This route explores the heights of the Napa Valley—a paradise for winemakers and cyclists alike.

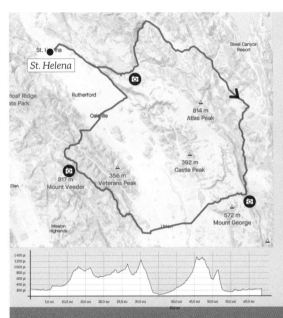

The splendor of the extensive vineyards, the Mediterranean climate, the relatively quiet roads, and the beauty of the surrounding hills make the Napa Valley one of the loveliest places for recreational, contemplative cycling in the United States! From its charming heart—St. Helena (pop. 6,000)—we ride up into the Vaca Mountains, heading east on Chiles Pope Valley Road (4 mi/6.5 km, at 3.5%) and later George Climb (2 mi/3.2 km, at 5.5%). When you cross to the west side of the valley, the Mayacamas Mountains are even more demanding, as you climb tricky Mount Veeder between cypresses and scrubland (4.8 mi/7.75 km at 4.5%, with the last mile at between 8% and 11%) then Oakville Westside (1.3 mi/2 km at 5%). When you finish, hold fire on a tasting of the Napa Valley's finest vintages and stop in at Caffe della Valle (mi 64/km 102) for an espresso and a gelato.

	Distance		E+		Difficulty		Appeal
	64 mi (102 km)		**4,800 ft** (1,465 m)		**3/5**		**5/5**

Air: Charles M. Schulz–Sonoma County Airport (40 min by car), San Francisco International Airport (1h20 by car), Sacramento International Airport (1h30 by car). Car: 30 min from Napa, 3h30 from Reno, 7h from Los Angeles.

St. Helena Cyclery is the oldest specialized bike shop in the valley. Precious advice on routes. Rentals. Strava Club. Retailer of BMC and Trek.

1156 Main Street St. Helena, CA 94574 sthelenacyclery.com

Gandona Winery and Lake Hennessey (mi 7/km 11). Mount George and Napa Valley (mi 30/km 48). Progeny Winery (mi 41/km 66). Mount Veeder and Enchanted Hills (mi 47/km 76). Oakville Grade View (mi 52/km 84).

ALPINE VILLAGE
EUROPEAN LOOK-ALIKE

- ⊕ *High mountain, Expert, 0% unpaved*
- ⊕ *Map strava.com/routes/2920844614402785184*
- ⊙ *Test yourself mi 41 (km 66) strava.com/segments/1051772*
- ⊙ *Test yourself mi 60 (km 96) strava.com/segments/22319525*

◎ GREG'S EYE

At 91 mi (146 km), with more than 9,000 ft (2,745 m) of elevation gain, this outsized route (which I rode when I lived in Reno) is the best way to explore the Californian Alps south of Lake Tahoe. Sharp, snowy peaks, crystal-clear lakes, pine forests: you'd think you were in the European Alps.

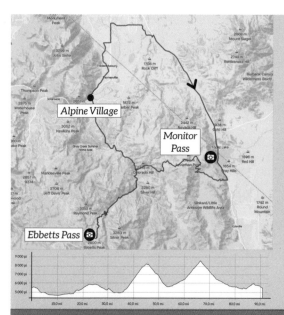

The two cols on this route are formidable indeed! The east slope of Monitor Pass (8,314 ft/2,534 m at its peak) climbs for 9.3 mi (15 km) from Topaz Lake, at an average gradient of 6.5% (mostly at 7% and 8% except for the final third). Ebbetts Pass (8,730 ft/2,660 m) is shorter (7.4 mi/12 km) and gentler (5.1% average gradient) but fearsome (3 mi/4.75 km at 8%) once you reach 7,000 ft (2,135 m). So much for the data. The setting is the Californian Alps, a high-altitude region of the Sierra Nevada that looks very much like Switzerland or Austria in places. Alpine Village, where we start from Mad Dog Café, seems to have been teleported directly from the Tyrol! The foot of Monitor Pass is a more arid environment, approached via a 25-mi (40-km) segment through neighboring Nevada. If you left out the Ebbetts Pass climb, this loop would be 66 mi (106 km) long for 6,200 ft (1,890 m) of elevation gain.

Distance	**E+**	**Difficulty**	**Appeal**
⊢–⊣ **91 mi** (146 km)	⬆ **9,200 ft** (2,805 m)	◧ **5/5**	★ **5/5**

Air: Reno-Tahoe International Airport (1h by car).
Car: 40 min from Carson City, 2h30 from Sacramento, 4h from San Francisco, 7h from Los Angeles, 7h from Las Vegas.

Tahoe Sports Ltd is an outdoors store that's one of the many specialized emporiums in South Lake Tahoe, 30 mi (48 km) north of Alpine Village. Retailer of Specialized.

**4000 Lake Tahoe Boulevard
South Lake Tahoe, CA 96150
tahoesportsltd.com**

Mesa Vista (mi 3/km 5). Carter Canyon (mi 23/km 37). Topaz Lake (mi 33/km 53). Big Springs View (mi 42/km 68). Ebbetts Peak and Kinney Reservoir (mi 66/km 106). Diamond Valley (mi 87/km 140).

TAHOE CITY
DONNER MEMORY

- ⊕ *High mountain, Advanced, 0% unpaved*
- ⊕ *Map strava.com/routes/2919708705381613794*

- ⊕ *Test yourself mi 11 (km 17.75), strava.com/segments/1584992*
- ⊕ *Test yourself mi 27 (km 43), strava.com/segments/705976*

👁 GREG'S EYE

Don't leave Tahoe City without having pedaled the tranquil 50 mi (80 km) of the Tahoe-Pyramid Trail to Reno, Nevada, along the Truckee River. But the route described here, through the Donner Pass (with its stunning views) is also a Northern California must-ride.

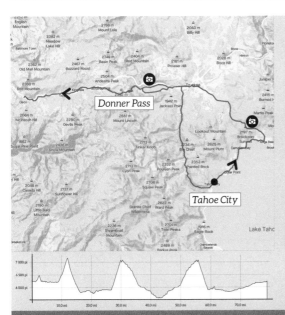

This was the favorite route of Peter Sagan, (megastar of the Tour of California in the 2010s) when he stayed by the shores of Lake Tahoe, the largest high-altitude lake (6,200 ft/1,890 m) in North America. It also evokes the Donner Party, one of the grisliest episodes in the conquest of the West. Yet unlike members of that expedition in the winter of 1846-47, you'll find enough places to refuel along the way and won't need to resort to cannibalism. There are three climbs: Brockway Summit (3.2 mi/5 km at 5.6%); then both sides of the Donner Pass (3.3 mi/5.3 km at 7% from the east, 5 mi/8 km at a gentler gradient from the west)—turn around at Cisco Grove. The views over Lake Tahoe, Donner Lake, and the snowy peaks of the Sierra Nevada are magical. You can cut the ride to 54 mi (87 km) and 3,700 ft (1,130 m) of elevation if you turn around at the Donner Pass.

Distance	E+	Difficulty	Appeal
79 mi (127 km)	**5,200 ft** (1,585 m)	**4/5**	**5/5**

Air: Reno-Tahoe International Airport (1h by car), Sacramento International Airport (2h).
Car: 45 min from Reno, 3h30 from San Francisco, 4h from Redding, 8h from Los Angeles.

Olympic Bike Shop extends a warm welcome beside the lake, close to charming Rosie's Café in Tahoe City. Strava Club. Retailer of Cannondale.

620 N Lake Boulevard Tahoe City, CA 96145 olympicbikeshop.com

Tahoe Vista (mi 7/km 11). Brockway Summit (mi 12/km 19). Donner Memorial State Park (mi 23/km 37). Donner Lake (mi 26/km 42). Donner Pass (mi 30/km 48 and mi 55/km 89). McGlashan Point (mi 56/km 90).

REDDING
SHASTA SURPRISES

- ⊕ *Very hilly, Intermediate, 55% unpaved*
- ⊕ *Map strava.com/routes/2919797770672483356*
- ⊕ *Test yourself mi 17 (km 27) strava.com/segments/923334*
- ⊕ *Test yourself mi 53 (km 85) strava.com/segments/783121*

👁 GREG'S EYE

If you're coming from Oregon and are not sure where to put your wheels down in California (an embarassment of riches), try Redding up north with its trails, river, and lakes at the foot of the Cascade Mountains.

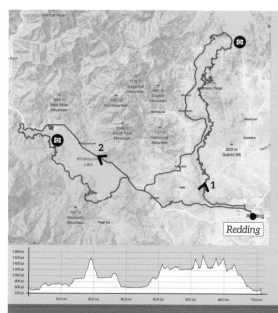

Redding

This route starting in Redding (pop. 95,000), in western Shasta County, is exciting from the first pedal strokes. We cross the Sacramento River on the elegant Sundial Bridge with its 710-ft-(215-m)- long glass surface. The tone is set. There are many wonderful moments on this mixed-surface ride to Shasta and Whiskeytown Lakes—emblematic reservoirs of Northern California. We reach the first on 24 mi (39 km) of single tracks—delicate bike handling required—including an extraordinary panorama from Chamise Peak (2 mi/3.25 km at 6%). After Shasta Dam, it's a tranquil cruise down the (paved) Sacramento River Trail, before the ramp of Eureka Way up to the shore of Whiskeytown Lake. Views are guaranteed from the south bank on the hilly gravel trail of South Shore Drive. Back in Redding, Chain Gang recommends (among others) Final Draft Brewing.

Distance **71 mi** (114 km)	E+ **5,600 ft** (1,705 m)	Difficulty **3/5**	Appeal **4/5**

 Air: Redding Municipal Airport (20 min by car), Sacramento International Airport (2h30 by car). Car: 3h30 from San Francisco, 3h30 from Reno, 5h from Bend, 7h from Portland.

 Chain Gang is a family shop that's been operating in Redding for nearly half a century, with staff who have expert knowledge of the local trails. Retailer of Giant, Liv, and Santa Cruz.

1540 Division Street Redding, CA 96001 chaingangbikeshop.com

 Sundial Bridge (mi 1/km 1.5). Sacramento River (mi 8/km 13). Chamise Peak (mi 19/km 31). Shasta Dam (mi 26/km 42). Whiskeytown Lake Visitors Center Viewpoint (mi 41/km 66). Whiskeytown Lake from South Shore Drive (mi 51/km 82, mi 53/km 85, mi 57/km 92, and mi 59/km 95).

TAHOE CITY
A TOUR OF THE LAKE

🌐 *High mountain, Intermediate, 0% unpaved*   🌐 *Map strava.com/routes/2920740566365861576*

Distance	E+	Difficulty	Appeal
⊢–⊣ **71 mi** (114 km)	⬆ **4,200 ft** (1,280 m)	📊 **3/5**	⭐ **5/5**

The California/Nevada state line bisects Lake Tahoe, the second-deepest body of water (1,650 ft/503 m) in the United States. As a result, 40% of this route (starting from Olympic Bike Shop) runs through Nevada. No matter, the lake is magical from every side. Ride it clockwise, of course, to be as close as possible to the turquoise, translucent waters—in the nineteenth century, Mark Twain wrote that it was possible to count a trout's scales at a depth of 180 ft (55 m)! That is less true today, but the experience, spiced up with a few ramps at up to 6%, is still fantastic. Make a halt at Zephyr Cove or South Lake Tahoe, opposite Tahoe City, for a refuel.

CHESTER
VOLCANIC PROMISE

🌐 *High mountain, Advanced, 0% unpaved*   🌐 *Map strava.com/routes/2928336297285578118*

Distance	E+	Difficulty	Appeal
⊢–⊣ **104 mi** (167 km)	⬆ **7,100 ft** (2,165 m)	📊 **4/5**	⭐ **5/5**

An imposing volcano, with a crater at 10,450 ft (3,185 m) that erupted a century ago, pale rocks, ochre dunes, valleys dotted with flowers, and lakes like mirrors. Such is the strange landscape of Lassen Volcanic National Park, which we approach from the south, starting at Bodfish Bicycles in Chester. First up is Volcanic Legacy Scenic Byway around Lake Almanor, before this long day's prime objective, Lassen Peak: 15 mi (24 km) of climbing on the wide SR-89, at an average gradient of 4.5%, but never more than 7%. The col lies at 8,450 ft (2,575 m), from where you can make the 2-mi (3.25-km) walk to the crater's edge on the Lassen Peak Trail.

ASHLAND
SIKIYOU SURPRISES

DIRT & GRAVEL

- ⊕ High mountain, Expert, 70% unpaved
- ⊕ Map strava.com/routes/2910514891357198818
- ⊕ Test yourself mi 16 (km 26) strava.com/segments/4437681
- ⊕ Test yourself mi 32 (km 51) strava.com/segments/702945

◉ GREG'S EYE

Mount Ashland, the highest summit in the Siskiyou Mountains, and the focus of this route, is only 5 mi (8 km) from the California state line. The surrounding area is one of the best cycling spots in Oregon, whether on asphalt or gravel.

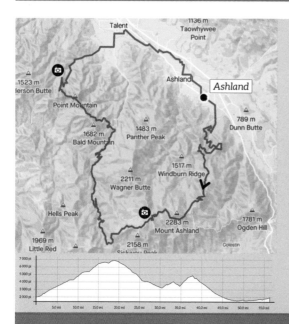

California may be close by, but Ashland (pop. 22,000) is proud of its own status as a center of culture (its Oregon Shakespeare Festival is famous), wine growing, and cycling—with a vast playground in nearby Rogue River-Siskiyou National Forest, between the Cascades and the Siskiyou Mountains. This mainly off-road route plunges into the heart of the latter. Mount Ashland and its ski area (mi 15/km 24) boast an ascent of 18 mi (29 km) through alpine pastures, clearings, red fir, mountain hemlock, and scrubland, at an average gradient of 5%, but with a few ramps in double digits toward the summit. As you pass McDonald Peak, you're at 7,000 ft (2,135 m). Keep something in the tank for the steep cliffs on the way back (2 mi/3.25 km at 11%, mi 34/km 55). The thought of a glass of pinot noir or chardonnay in Ashland will sweeten any suffering.

Distance	**E+**	**Difficulty**	**Appeal**
56 mi (91 km)	**8,300 ft** (2,525 m)	**5/5**	**5/5**

Air: Rogue Valley International–Medford Airport, (30 min by car), Mahlon Sweet Field, Eugene (3h30 by car).
Car: 3h from Eugene, 3h30 from Bend, 4h30 from Portland, 6h from San Francisco.

Siskiyou Cyclery also offers rental service near Southern Oregon University. Retailer of Specialized and Surly.

1729 Siskiyou Boulevard Ashland, OR 97520 siskiyoucyclery.com

Mount Ashland Ski Area (mi 15/km 24). McDonald Peak (mi 19/km 31). Bald Mountain (mi 37/km 60). Point Mountain (mi 39/km 63). Anderson Butte (mi 41/km 66). Upper Five Vineyard (mi 46/km 74).

CRATER LAKE
MAKE MINE A DOUBLE!

- ⊕ *High mountain, Advanced, 0% unpaved*
- ⊕ *Map strava.com/routes/2909761488416338350*

- ✚ *Test yourself mi 7 (km 11.25), strava.com/segments/29010254*
- ✚ *Test yourself mi 32 (km 51) strava.com/segments/1809188*

⊙ GREG'S EYE

Crater Lake is one of the most surprising and spectacular sights in North America. Its panoramic road is an Oregon must-ride, with magical views over deep-blue water so clear you can make out shapes at depths of more than 120 ft (37 m)!

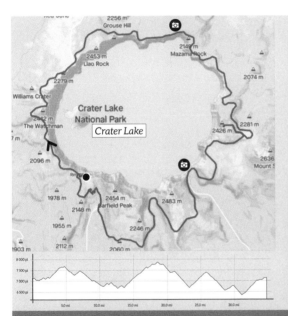

Does a mere 35 mi (56 km) sound too short to bother? Once you've completed this extraordinary loop around Crater Lake, in southern Oregon, you'll want to do it all again! The water-filled caldera of Mount Mazama in the Cascades range and its landscape of sheer cliffs and conifer forests provide one of the most beautiful cycling experiences you can have. The high-altitude (6,400 to 7,800 ft/1,950 to 2,375 m) panoramic road around this geological marvel, a 6-mi- (9.75-km)-wide lake that is the deepest (1,950 ft/595 m) in the United States, is not an easy ride. But its five ramps, 1 to 3 mi (1.5 to 4.75 km) long at average gradients of 4.5% to 6%, offer breathtaking views. As you climb each of them, you'll marvel at how lucky you are to be here. No tour of the Far West would be complete without this loop, which starts from the Rim Village Visitor Center at Crater Lake.

Distance	E+	Difficulty	Appeal
35 mi (56 km)	**4,100 ft** (1,256 m)	**3/5**	**5/5**

Air: Mahlon Sweet Field, Eugene (2h30 by car), Portland International Airport (4h by car). Car: 2h from Bend, 5h from Reno, 6h30 from San Francisco.

Bicycle Jones (delicious snacks), close to the Amtrak station in Klamath Falls, is among a cluster of shops that are the closest to Crater Lake (60 mi/97 km to the north).

**808 Klamath Avenue
Klamath Falls, OR 97601
bicycle-jones.business.site**

Discovery Point (mi 1.5/km 2.5). Watchman Overlook (mi 4/km 6.5). Merriam Point (mi 6/km 10). Mazama Rock (mi 11/km 18). Skell Head (mi 15/km 24). Cloudcap Overlook (mi 18/km 29). Phantom Ship Overlook (mi 23/km 37). Vidae Falls (mi 25/km 40).

Wizard Island in Oregon's Crater Lake is a marvel.

JACKSONVILLE
FIRST DANCE

⊕ *Low mountain, Intermediate, 0% unpaved*   ⊕ *Map strava.com/routes/2910617134217721744*

⊢⊣ Distance	⬆ E+	📊 Difficulty	⭐ Appeal
75 mi (120 km)	**4,200 ft** (1,277 m)	**3/5**	**4/5**

The city of Medford (pop. 85,000), where Ginger Rogers, unparalleled dancer of Hollywood's golden age, lived, is a significant point of interest in southern Oregon, as is its neighbor, Ashland. This long route, heading west from Cycle Analysis in Jacksonville, is an ideal warm-up before embarking on one of the more ambitious challenges on the harsh slopes of the Siskiyou Mountains. We tackle three bracing ramps: Jacksonville Hill (sections at 8%), Munger Creek Road (2.2 mi/3.5 km, finishing at 5%), and Sterling Creek Road (5.7 mi/9 km at 4%, with sections up to 10% toward the top). You'll feel far from the rumbling traffic of nearby I-5.

CORVALLIS
FLORAL PARADISE

⊕ *Low mountain, Advanced, 70% unpaved*   ⊕ *Map strava.com/routes/2910450669118056336*

⊢⊣ Distance	⬆ E+	📊 Difficulty	⭐ Appeal
61 mi (98 km)	**7,200 ft** (2,210 m)	**4/5**	**5/5**

Marys Peak, the highest point (4,097 ft/1,250 m) in the Oregon Coast Range, is a blessed summit. On a clear day you can enjoy unbeatable views west toward the Pacific Ocean and east toward the peaks of the Cascades, all in an exceptional botanical setting of rare wildflowers and noble firs. Our route departs Bike N Hike in Corvallis (pop. 60,000), known as the heart of the Willamette Valley, on perfect trails overlooking the Marys River. Conserve some energy for the final ramps of the climb on East Ridge Trail, which are tough indeed: 2 mi (3.25 km) at 10%, with a section at 17%. Paradise must be earned.

SISTERS
ALONGSIDE VOLCANOES

- ⊕ High mountain, Expert, 1% unpaved
- ⊕ Map strava.com/routes/2910579007470330768
- ⊕ Test yourself mi 8 (km 13) strava.com/segments/23902463
- ⊕ Test yourself mi 44 (km 71) strava.com/segments/9926005

◉ GREG'S EYE

Demanding, spectacular cycling! The west slope of McKenzie Pass is one of the most attractive panoramic routes in the country, and Three Creek Lake Road leads almost to the foot of the majestic Three Sisters. Fear not: none are likely to erupt!

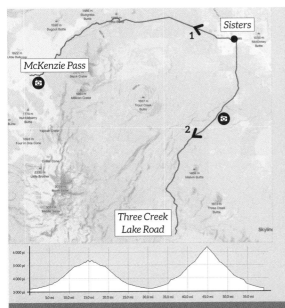

McKenzie Pass

Sisters

Three Creek
Lake Road

The small town of Sisters, near Bend, in central Oregon, provides swift access to the sublime paved roads up to the Cascade Volcanic Arc, where nothing has erupted in a very long time. This audacious route takes in McKenzie Pass and Three Creek Lake Road, involving two ascents (14 mi/23 km, then 10 mi/16 km). We start with the west slope of McKenzie Pass, at an average gradient of barely 4%, with a few ramps up to 8%. It's an enchanting climb, due not only to the winding road, but also to the contrast between the thick forest at the bottom and the open lava fields of Black Crater toward the top. Three Creek Lake Road is straighter, but the average gradient is nearer to 6%, with several ramps close to double digits. The views of Broken Top and its glaciers straight ahead and the Three Sisters (Faith, Hope, and Charity) to the right are a thrilling motivation.

	Distance		E+		Difficulty		Appeal
⊢⊣	**59 mi** (95 km)	⬆	**5,500 ft** (1,674 m)	📊	**4/5**	★	**5/5**

Air: Mahlon Sweet Field, Eugene (2h30 by car), Portland International Airport (3h by car). Car: 30 min from Bend, 2h from Eugene, 6h from Seattle, 8h30 from San Francisco.

Blazin Saddles (founded 2010) keeps its promise of "Cycle N Style." Rentals. Strava Club. Retailer of BMC, Giant, and Liv.

**413 W. Hood Avenue
Sisters, OR 97759**
blazinsaddleshub.com

Little Butte (mi 7/km 11). Windy Point (mi 14/km 23). Lava Camp Lake (mi 16/km 26). Three Sisters (mi 32/km 51 and mi 41/km 66). Trout Creek Butte (mi 36/km 58). Three Creeks Meadow and Broken Top (mi 44/km 71).

SANDY
MOUNT HOOD VIEW

⊕ *High mountain, Advanced, 0% unpaved*   ⊕ *Map strava.com/routes/2907257477247776998*

	Distance		E+		Difficulty		Appeal
⊢–⊣	**73 mi** (118 km)	⬆	**7,100 ft** (2,179 m)	📊	**4/5**	★	**5/5**

In Portland, you'll hear of the ascent of Mount Hood, a stratovolcano with a recognizable cone 60 mi (97 km) east of the city. This typically involves climbing the road up to Timberline Lodge (5,800 ft/1,770 m), a ski resort and historic monument that offers the most spectacular view of the highest peak in Oregon (11,249 ft/3,429 m). From Rhododendron, it's 15 mi (24 km) at an average gradient of 5.6% on busy US-26 (four lanes), then on Timberline Highway (mi 33/km 53), with a section at 11% before the summit. Our route starts from Sandy Bicycle in Sandy, taking Marmot Road (away from US-26) for 20 mi (32 km). The descent is via West Leg Road.

THE DALLES
GRINDER SERIES SPIRIT

DIRT & GRAVEL

⊕ *High mountain, Advanced, 60% unpaved*   ⊕ *Map strava.com/routes/2907210923732958924*

	Distance		E+		Difficulty		Appeal
⊢–⊣	**73 mi** (118 km)	⬆	**7,800 ft** (2,372 m)	📊	**4/5**	★	**5/5**

The Beaver State has caught the gravel bug, as evidenced by the success of the Oregon Gravel Grinder Series. Those events inspired this route that starts from SPR Bicycle in The Dalles (pop. 16,000) on the Columbia River, 80 mi (129 km) east of Portland. We approach the fascinating silhouette of Mount Hood from the east, as far as Fivemile Butte (climb to the top of the lookout tower—without your bike) and Perry Point: more than 20 mi (32 km) of ascent on farm roads and forest trails far from traffic. The slope is hardest over the final 3 mi (4.75 km) of Eight Mile Trail (gradient at 7% to 11%), but worth it for the view of Mount Hood.

You'll see the instantly recognizable cone of Mount Hood, Oregon, approaching on trails from The Dalles.

PORTLAND
ISLAND AND WEST HILLS

- Very hilly, Intermediate, 0% unpaved
- Map strava.com/routes/2910222294178171314
- Test yourself mi 26 (km 42) strava.com/segments/2519371
- Test yourself mi 47 (km 76) strava.com/segments/668798

◉ GREG'S EYE

Ah, Portland! Its parks, its bridges, its "green" buildings, its microbreweries, its cafés, and its bike paths. All of these things make the largest city in Oregon extremely pleasant to experience by bike. This escapade to the northwest is a local classic.

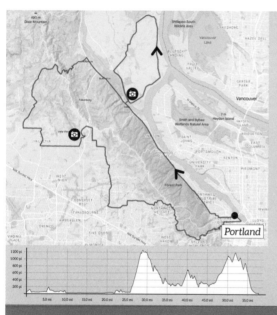

Portland

Durable, innovative, accessible: Portland's residents often use these three adjectives to describe their vision of the future. And you can bet the bicycle plays a leading role! Portland and its wider urban area (pop. 2.4 million) are not only bike friendly, but also easy to pedal out from, as on this two-part route to the northwest.

The first section is flat and fluvial, along the Willamette River and lush green Sauvie Island. The second part is steep and dynamic, tackling several lovely ramps in the West Hills: Logie Trail Road (2.5 mi/4 km at 8.4%), Old Cornelius Pass (1.6 mi/2.6 km at 5%), Bonny Slope (3 mi/4.75 km at 4.5%), and Cornell Mountain (1 mi/1.5 km at 7%). Revel in superb scenery—dotted with farms, vineyards, and forests—before careening down Pittock Drive to reach the city again in just a few minutes.

Distance **58 mi** (93 km)	**E+** **4,700 ft** (1,431 m)	**Difficulty** **3/5**	**Appeal** **4/5**

Air: Portland International Airport (30 min by car). Car: 2h from Eugene, 3h from Bend, 3h from Seattle, 6h30 from Boise, 10h from San Francisco.

Cycle Town Coffee Roasters, in trendy Slabtown, north of downtown, is one of the main rendezvous points for Portland's pedaling community.

1626 NW Thurman Street Portland, OR 97209
cycletowncoffeeroasters.com

Sauvie Island Bridge (mi 22/km 35). Mason Hill Park (mi 31/km 50). Plumper Pumpkin Patch and Tree Farm (mi 39/km 63). Valley View Park (mi 49/km 79). Cornell Mountain (mi 52/km 84). Pittock Acres Park (mi 54/km 87).

WENATCHEE
HERE COMES THE BADGER!

- 🌐 *Low mountain, Expert, 2% unpaved*
- 🌐 *Map strava.com/routes/2905529604224583114*
- ➕ *Test yourself mi 11 (km 18) strava.com/segments/20722478*
- ➕ *Test yourself mi 65 (km 105) strava.com/segments/680666*

👁 GREG'S EYE

This route is a nod to my friend Bernard "The Badger" Hinault, the champion and teammate who left the biggest mark on my racing career. Badger Mountain, above the Columbia River, 150 mi (240 km) east of Seattle, is one of the most popular climbs in Washington State.

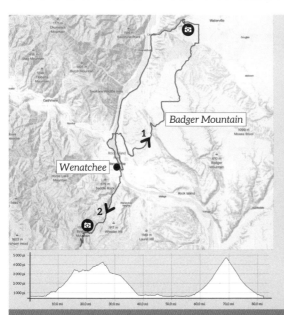

Badger Mountain

Wenatchee

"The Badger" is not only the nickname of cycling legend Bernard Hinault—it's also the name of this formidable climb above Wenatchee (pop. 35,000) and the Columbia River Gorge: 9 mi (14 km) long, at an average gradient of 6.5%, hitting double digits as you ride out of town. The slopes offer superb panoramas, but you'll find yourself having to fight like, well, a badger. They continue on the arid Columbia Plateau with a 5-mi (8-km) stretch at 3%. Feel free to ride this route over two days in order best to tackle the ascent of Mission Ridge on the west bank: 10 mi (16 km) at an average gradient of 6.8%, up to 8% over the last 4 mi (6.5 km). On the way back, sample a cider at Union Hill Cider Company (near the airport). It's the best in the Pacific Northwest, just as the best cider in France is also found in the west: in Brittany, Hinault's birthplace and home.

Distance	E+	Difficulty	Appeal
82 mi (132 km)	**9,100 ft** (2,778 m)	**5/5**	**4/5**

Air: Seattle-Tacoma International Airport (2h30 by car), Tri-Cities Airport, Pasco (2h30 by car). Car: 3h from Spokane, 4h30 from Vancouver, 5h from Portland.

Full Circle Cycle enjoys a superb location close to the Wenatchee Amtrak station. Retailer of Pinarello, GT, and Jamis.

318 S. Chelan Avenue Wenatchee, WA 98801 fullcirclecyclewa.com

Badger Mountain Hairpin (mi 14/km 23). Badger Mountain Summit (mi 16/km 26). Badger Mountain Ski Area (mi 27/km 43). Tyee View (mi 32/km 51). Corbaley Canyon (mi 36/km 58). Squilchuck Creek (mi 65/km 105). Mission Ridge Ski Resort (mi 69/km 111).

OLYMPIA
INLETS AND CAPITOL

⊕ Very hilly, Advanced, 0% unpaved   ⊕ Map strava.com/routes/2906257550567870378

	Distance		E+		Difficulty		Appeal
⊢-⊣	**74 mi** (119 km)	⬆	**3,900 ft** (1,191 m)	⬗	**3/5**	★	**4/5**

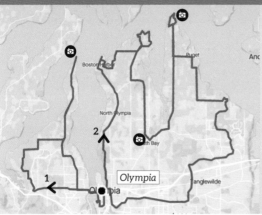

Olympia (pop. 52,000), 60 mi (97 km) southwest of Seattle, is the relaxed capital of Washington State. Life here, at the bottom end of Puget Sound, is heavily influenced by water. Before heading off to defy the Olympic Mountains—which rise to the northwest like a scenic backdrop—try this route (starting from Deschutes River Cyclery) that features inlets with oyster farms, secluded beaches, and, sometimes, visiting whales, as it winds its way through tranquil rolling countryside, past golf courses and vineyards. Eld, Budd, and Henderson Inlets are explored from tip to toe, after the impressive State Capitol and magnificent Priest Point Park.

SEQUIM
OLYMPIC CHALLENGE

⊕ Low mountain, Expert, 75% unpaved   ⊕ Map strava.com/routes/2906847985958936174

	Distance		E+		Difficulty		Appeal
⊢-⊣	**78 mi** (126 km)	⬆	**9,100 ft** (2,767 m)	⬗	**5/5**	★	**5/5**

From Sequim (pop. 7,000) in the north of the Olympic Peninsula, you can undertake a tranquil summertime exploration of the superb lavender farms of Dungeness Valley, by the Salish Sea across from Victoria, British Columbia. Or pedal south on a gravel bike into the Olympic Mountains. This challenging route (starting from Ben's Bikes) is a whole day's exhilarating adventure on quiet forest trails tackling some proper slopes (with gradients up to 10%)—Mount Zion, Little River Summit, and Mount Townsend—reaching an altitude of 3,600 ft (1,095 m). The homeward leg via Lord's Lake and Blyn is somewhat easier.

SPOKANE
ACCENTUATE THE POSITIVE

🌐 *High mountain, Advanced, 0% unpaved*   🌐 *Map strava.com/routes/2906545676246578370*

	Distance		E+		Difficulty		Appeal
⊢⊣	**77 mi** (124 km)	⬆	**6,200 ft** (1,902 m)	📊	**4/5**	⭐	**4/5**

Mount Spokane

Spokane

Bing Crosby, the unforgettable singer of timeless hits like holiday favorite "White Christmas," grew up in Spokane (pop. 230,000 today) in the early twentieth century. This major hub of eastern Washington State boasts an exciting peak, Mount Spokane, which stands at 5,850 ft (1,785 m) and has a most delicious ascent: 13 mi (21 km) at an average gradient of 5.5%, with sections as steep as 11% in places. A meaty challenge, and do take care on the descent. The refreshing charm of Riverfront Park and the Spokane Falls awaits (mi 74/km 119). And why not stop for a tasting at the renowned Arbor Crest Wine Cellars (mi 65/km 105)?

WINTHROP
UP OLD BALDY!

DIRT & GRAVEL

🌐 *High mountain, Expert, 60 % unpaved*   🌐 *Map strava.com/routes/2906943948001435874*

	Distance		E+		Difficulty		Appeal
⊢⊣	**69 mi** (111 km)	⬆	**8,600 ft** (2,631 m)	📊	**5/5**	⭐	**5/5**

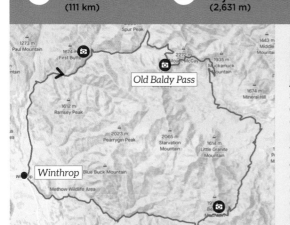

Old Baldy Pass

Winthrop

Expect some incredible views at the top of this long (21 mi/34 km), irregular ascent of Old Baldy Pass! Reaching an altitude of 6,375 ft (1,945 m), just 1,500 ft (455 m) below the eponymous summit, the narrow trail overlooks the immensity of the North Cascades and the twisted pines of Okanogan-Wenatchee National Forest. The only places to refuel on this exceptional route (starting from the Old Schoolhouse Brewery in Winthrop) are two saloons on the same block in Conconully (turn off at mi 39/km 63). West Fork Road (on the way out—8 mi/13 km) and Lester Road (on the way back—2 mi/3.25 km) are very unevenly paved and will require some effort.

SEATTLE
JEWEL OF THE NORTHWEST

- Hilly, Advanced, 0% unpaved
- Map strava.com/routes/2905821009579710922

- Test yourself mi 16 (km 26) strava.com/segments/14867931
- Test yourself mi 58 (km 93) strava.com/segments/629503

◉ GREG'S EYE

Seattle, the city of Starbucks, Amazon, Bill Gates, and Jimi Hendrix, is also one of the greenest in the United States. Bicycles rule here, and this classic route east via Lakes Washington and Sammamish and Mercer Island is a perfect introduction to Seattle by bike.

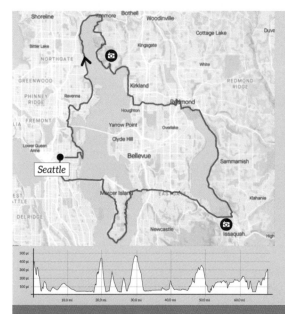

In Seattle, pearl of the Northwest, turn your back on the ocean and Puget Sound, on downtown and its emblematic Space Needle, and go east. From the hip Pike/Pine neighborhood, with its converted warehouses and repurposed garages, head to Lake Washington, Lake Sammamish, and Mercer Island: natural destinations for a cycling escapade in this metropolis of 3.5 million. The bike lanes are many and the drivers considerate. By keeping a little inland, this route throws up several challenging ramps (none longer than 2 mi/ 3.25 km) toward Saint Edward State Park, Rose Hill, Bellevue, and on mischievous Mercer Way. It's a joy that offers numerous viewpoints over the Seattle skyline, without getting too close to it. If you're cycling the Emerald City, these roads are a must-ride.

Distance **68 mi** (109 km)		E+ **3,500 ft** (1,080 m)		Difficulty **3/5**		Appeal **5/5**	

Air: Seattle-Tacoma International Airport (30 min by car). Car: 1h from Olympia, 2h30 from Vancouver, 3h from Portland, 4h30 from Spokane.

Good Weather, in the heart of Pike/Pine, is one of the most spacious and pleasant bike-cafés in North America. Retailer of Orbea, Surly, Ritchey, Rodeo Labs, and Otso.

1424 11th Avenue (in the alley) Seattle, WA 98122
goodweatherinseattle.com

Holmes Point Drive (mi 20/ km 32). Juanita Woodlands Park (mi 23/km 37). South Rose Hill Park (mi 29/km 47). Lake Sammamish State Park and Sunset Beach (mi 44/ km 71). West Mercer Way (mi 60/km 97). Faben Point (mi 63/km 101).

EASTON
CASCADE MOUNTAINS SHOW

🌐 Low mountain, Advanced, 90% unpaved   🌐 Map strava.com/routes/2906891545987161804

	Distance		E+		Difficulty		Appeal
⊢–⊣	**67 mi** (108 km)	⬆	**6,600 ft** (2,000 m)	📊	**4/5**	★	**5/5**

There can't be another route offering equally sumptuous views of the Cascade Range landscape. From the Hitching Post café/grocery in the village of Easton, 70 mi (113 km) southeast of Seattle, we explore both sides of the Yakima River valley, almost entirely on trails, away from busy I-90. The relief is impressive. To the southwest: energy-sapping Tacoma Pass (very irregular, 8 mi/13 km at 3%) and Stampede Pass (5 mi/8 km at 6%). To the northeast: between Lakes Keechelus and Kachess, the battery-draining ascent of National Forest Road 4934 (5 mi/8 km at 7% including 2 mi/3.25 km at 9% and 10%). But what stunning views!

SAN JUAN ISLANDS
SLOWPEZ BLISS

🌐 Very hilly, Intermediate, 0% unpaved   🌐 Map strava.com/routes/2906479221896244468

	Distance		E+		Difficulty		Appeal
⊢–⊣	**50 mi** (80 km)	⬆	**3,400 ft** (1,032 m)	📊	**2/5**	★	**5/5**

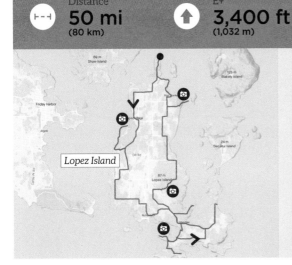

Slowpez, Friendly Isle, Bicyclist's Island: there's no shortage of nicknames for Lopez Island, the most welcoming of the 700 islands and islets in the San Juan archipelago in the Salish Sea. Bikes are everywhere here, rolling along between cedars and fields of pink tulips. Less hilly than its neighbor Orcas (sort of) and less busy than its neighbor San Juan, Lopez Island is a perfectly peaceful place of fishing villages, bays, beaches, and hills rising to 350 ft (105 m) above the sea (Lopez Hill, mi 38/km 61). Our route starts at Lopez Ferry Landing, a 1hr crossing from Anacortes (2h30 from Seattle) and 45 min from Friday Harbor.

Cascade Range is near Stampede Pass in the heart of Okanogan Wenatchee National Forest, Washington.

SEATTLE
ELLIOT BAY CIRCUIT

🌐 Hilly, Intermediate, 0% unpaved

🌐 Map strava.com/routes/2906235836674206914

	Distance		E+		Difficulty		Appeal
⊢–⊣	**47 mi** (75 km)	⬆	**2,100 ft** (648 m)	▥	**2/5**	★	**4/5**

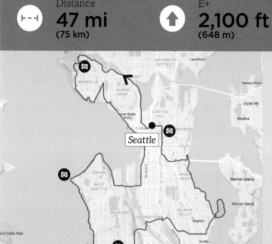

Riding out from the Rapha Club House in Pike/ Pine, we explore Seattle from Elliot Bay to the high-rises of downtown, finishing in the east with Seward Park, Lake Washington Boulevard, the I-90 Trail, and Little Saigon. There is no shortage of bike paths in the north around Magnolia and Queen Anne, including Discovery Park with its 1-mi/1.5-km ramp at 9%, nor in the west: Elliot Bay Trail, Alaskan Way, West Seattle Bridge, and Alki Trail. Take care around the Fauntleroy Ferry Terminal (mi 27/km 43) and King County International Airport (mi 32/km 51). Between the two, a climb to Westcrest Park: 1 mi (1.5 km) at 10%, another at 5%.

SEATTLE
HI, MICROSOFT!

🌐 Hilly, Intermediate, 0% unpaved

🌐 Map strava.com/routes/2906194730146482090

	Distance		E+		Difficulty		Appeal
⊢–⊣	**53 mi** (85 km)	⬆	**2,900 ft** (887 m)	▥	**2/5**	★	**4/5**

This route (starting from Métier Racing and Coffee in Pike/Pine) explores the wider Seattle area westward, taking the I-90 Trail across Lake Washington to Lake Sammamish. We ride counterclockwise, through May Valley at the foot of Cougar Mountain, returning via Redmond and Evergreen Point Floating Bridge. "McDonalds" Hill (mi 13/km 21) will get you up on your pedals, as will Bel-Red Road (mi 38/km 61), which leads to the headquarters of Microsoft (founders Bill Gates and Paul Allen were both born in Seattle), and Capitol Hill (mi 50/km 80). The final miles are a delight as you approach the Space Needle and the downtown towers.

HILO
UNIQUE MAUNA KEA

🌐 *High mountain, Expert, 11% unpaved*   🌐 *Map strava.com/routes/2905426575221933634*

	Distance		E+		Difficulty		Appeal
⊢⊣	**88 mi** (142 km)	⬆	**13,800 ft** (4,215 m)	📊	**5/5**	⭐	**5/5**

Mauna Kea

Hilo

Climbing the sacred mountain of Mauna Kea, on the island of Hawaii, is an adventure. The ascent starts right at the Pacific Ocean and carries on up to 13,750 ft (4,190 m), on the edge of this dormant volcano, skirting one of the world's best astronomy sites. The climb is 40 mi (64 km) long and four times the elevation gain of the legendary Alpe d'Huez in France, with fierce gradients (1 mi/1.5 km at 13% at 8,500 ft/2,590 m) similar to those of the Zoncolan in Italy, and 7 mi (11.25 km) of dirt track at 11.4% to finish—like the Finestre Pass in Italy! Hilo far below (where we start from Mid Pacific Wheels) and the surrounding scenery look divine.

MAKAWAO
THE GORGEOUS HIGHWAY

🌐 *Very hilly, Advanced, 0% unpaved*   🌐 *Map strava.com/routes/2905437665364479434*

	Distance		E+		Difficulty		Appeal
⊢⊣	**84 mi** (135 km)	⬆	**7,536 ft** (2,297 m)	📊	**3/5**	⭐	**5/5**

Makawao

Hana

Maui, the second-largest island in the Hawaii archipelago by surface area, with 150 mi (240 km) of coastline, is a cyclist's paradise. This 120-mi (193-km) route (starting from Krank Cycles in Makawao) along the northern coast of Valley Isle on the HI-360, or Hana Highway, is extraordinary. You'll encounter over 600 switchbacks above the turquoise ocean, cross 59 (mostly narrow) bridges, ride through tropical forest, and pass impressive cliffs and sublime waterfalls. The Big Climb at mi 26/km 42 (4.5 mi/7.25 km at 5%) is the only challenge, and you'll find food trucks along the way where you can refuel with barbecue ahi tuna and banana bread.

INDEX

ACKNOWLEDGEMENTS

DEEP THANKS TO ALL OF THE AMERICAN, CANADIAN,
AND MEXICAN CYCLISTS OF THE STRAVA COMMUNITY,
WITHOUT WHOM THIS CYCLING ATLAS WOULD HAVE NEVER APPEARED.
IN PARTICULAR: SHANE TROTTER, AMIT BHATTACHARYYA, STEFAN EBERLE,
BONGZILLA, ALEX RENNY, SHANE COOPER, ANDREW DEEK, PETE D.,
PAUL WILLERTON, FRANCISCO GUTIERREZ, PASCAL HERVÉ,
JEAN-YVES COUPUT, ANNE-MARIE LEFEBVRE.

PICTURE CREDITS